Public Sociolo

Series editor: **John Brewer**,
Northern Ireland and **Neil M**
University, Canada

Public Sociology series addresses not only what sociologists do, but what sociology is for, and focuses on the commitment to materially improving people's lives through understanding of the social condition. It showcases the wide diversity of sociological research that addresses the many global challenges that threaten the future of humankind.

Forthcoming in the series:

The Public and Their Platforms
Public Sociology in an Era of Social Media
Mark Carrigan and **Fatsis Lambros**, January 2021

The Public Sociology of Waste
Myra J. Hird, December 2021

Find out more at
bristoluniversitypress.co.uk/public-sociology

PUBLIC SOCIOLOGY AS EDUCATIONAL PRACTICE

Challenges, Dialogues and Counterpublics

Edited by
Eurig Scandrett

First published in Great Britain in 2022 by

Bristol University Press
University of Bristol
1-9 Old Park Hill
Bristol
BS2 8BB
UK
t: +44 (0)117 954 5940
e: bup-info@bristol.ac.uk

Details of international sales and distribution partners are available at bristoluniversitypress.co.uk

© Bristol University Press 2022

British Library Cataloguing in Publication Data
A catalogue record for this book is available from the British Library

ISBN 978-1-5292-0142-0 paperback
ISBN 978-1-5292-0140-6 hardcover
ISBN 978-1-5292-0143-7 ePub
ISBN 978-1-5292-0141-3 ePdf

The right of Eurig Scandrett to be identified as editor of this work has been asserted by him in accordance with the Copyright, Designs and Patents Act 1988.

All rights reserved: no part of this publication may be reproduced, stored in a retrieval system, or transmitted in any form or by any means, electronic, mechanical, photocopying, recording, or otherwise without the prior permission of Bristol University Press.

Every reasonable effort has been made to obtain permission to reproduce copyrighted material. If, however, anyone knows of an oversight, please contact the publisher.

The statements and opinions contained within this publication are solely those of the editor and contributors and not of the University of Bristol or Bristol University Press. The University of Bristol and Bristol University Press disclaim responsibility for any injury to persons or property resulting from any material published in this publication.

Bristol University Press works to counter discrimination on grounds of gender, race, disability, age and sexuality.

Cover design: Andrew Corbett

Bristol University Press uses environmentally responsible print partners.

Printed in Great Britain by CPI Group (UK) Croydon, CR0 4YY

Contents

List of Illustrations viii
Notes on Contributors ix
Acknowledgement xvi
Series Editors' Preface xvii

    Introduction 1
    Eurig Scandrett

Section I: Publics

I.0   Provocation I: Class, Gender and Identity: Axes of 13
      Structure and Difference in Subaltern Counterpublics
      Eurig Scandrett

I.1   Mad People's History and Identity: A Mad Studies 25
      Critical Pedagogy Project
      Elaine Ballantyne, Kirsten Maclean, Shirley-anne Collie,
      Liz Deeming and Esther Fraser

I.2   'Seeing Things Differently': Gender Justice and 37
      Counter-Hegemony in Higher Education
      Lesley Orr and Nel Whiting

I.3   Domestic Abuse Survivors: Public Sociology and the 53
      Risks of Speaking Out
      Julie Young

I.4   A Public Sociology for Post-industrial Fife 65
      Paul Gilfillan

I.5   Public Sociology and the Invisibility of Class 79
      Eurig Scandrett

| I.6 | Dialogue I: Subaltern Counterpublics
Eurig Scandrett and Paul Gilfillan | 93 |

Section II: Knowledges

II.0	Provocation II: 'Really Useful' Public Sociology Knowledge *Eurig Scandrett*	111
II.1	Crossing the Quadrant: Policy Research and Public Sociology *Jan Law*	121
II.2	Recreating Knowledge for Social Change: Convergences between Public Sociology, Feminist Theory and Praxis of Refugee and Asylum-Seeking Women's Integration in Scotland *C. Laura Lovin*	135
II.3	Young People, Alcohol, Dialogical Methods *Emma Wood*	153
II.4	Young Children and Participative Research Enquiry: A Case for Active Citizenship *Maria Giatsi Clausen*	171
II.5	English Last: Displaced Publics and Communicating Multilingually as Social Act and Art *Alison Phipps, Tawona Sitholé, Naa Densua Tordzro and Gameli Tordzro*	183
II.6	The Construction of 'Public Knowledge' within Community Planning Partnerships: Reducing Structurally Embedded Inequalities at Local Level? *Marion Ellison*	199
II.7	Dialogue II: 'Really Useful' Public Sociology Knowledge *Eurig Scandrett, Marion Ellison and C. Laura Lovin*	217

Section III: Practices

III.0	Provocation III: Public Sociology Practices, Privatising Universities *Eurig Scandrett*	227
III.1	Precarity as an Existential Phenomenon within a Post-industrial Labour Market *Philip Mignot and Ricky Gee*	239
III.2	Student–Public–Sociologist: On Dialogue with our First Public, and in Widening Access to Higher Education *Karl Johnson*	253
III.3	Experts by Experience: Art, Identity and the Sociological Imagination *John R. Docherty-Hughes, Elaine Addington, David Bradley, Linda Brookhouse, Jenny Bunting, Lorna Cosh, John Dane, Robert Lindsay and Christine Raffaelli*	267
III.4	Community Engagement: Cultivating Critical Awareness *Jim Crowther and Mae Shaw*	287
III.5	Reflections on our Critical Service Learning Provision: Is it Critical or Are We Social Justice Dreamers? *Sharon Hutchings and Andrea Lyons Lewis*	299
III.6	Trade Unionism as Collective Education *Lena Wånggren*	315
III.7	Dialogue III: Public Sociology Practices, Privatising Universities *Eurig Scandrett, Jim Crowther, Sharon Hutchings, Karl Johnson, Mae Shaw and Lena Wånggren*	331
	Conclusion *Eurig Scandrett*	343
Index		357

List of Illustrations

Figures

I.1.1	Mad People's History and Identity course flyer	28
II.3.1	Model of critical dialogue for youth solidarity	166
III.3.1	*No* by Stephen Sutcliffe	272
III.3.2	*The Blind Leading the Blind* by Laila Shawa	275
III.3.3	*Exiled* by Jo Spence	276
III.3.4	*Bute Mansions, Gibson Street, Glasgow* by Andrew Hay	279
III.3.5	*Madame X* by Alexander Guy	281

Tables

II.1.1	Burawoy's ideal-type of public sociology and policy sociology	125

Notes on Contributors

Elaine Addington is Open Museum Curator at Glasgow Museums Resource Centre.

Elaine Ballantyne is Senior Lecturer in Occupational Therapy at Queen Margaret University. A qualified occupational therapist, she has worked as a clinician and manager in a variety of contexts including mental health, social work and acute medicine. She is the course leader for the 'Mad People's History and Identity' course and completed her doctorate exploring the student experiences and impacts of being on the course and the links to activism.

David Bradley is a graduate of and co-producer of knowledge in the Glasgow Museums Public Sociology project.

Linda Brookhouse is a graduate of and co-producer of knowledge in the Glasgow Museums Public Sociology project.

Jenny Bunting is Community Participation Coordinator at Glasgow Association for Mental Health.

Shirley-anne Collie was a student on the 'Mad People's History and Identity' (MPHI) course in the year 2015. She went on to be active in many projects in mental health and activism. She is currently a Public Sociology student at Queen Margaret University. She has been part of a participatory action research project evaluating the experiences and impacts of being a student of the MPHI course.

Lorna Cosh is a graduate of and co-producer of knowledge in the Glasgow Museums Public Sociology project.

Jim Crowther is Honorary Fellow at the University of Edinburgh and has published widely on the themes of popular education, critical literacy and the politics of lifelong learning. He was the editor of *Studies in the Education of Adults* between 2010 and 2015 and a founder member of the International Popular Education Network.

John Dane is a graduate of and co-producer of knowledge in the Glasgow Museums Public Sociology project.

Liz Deeming was a student on the MPHI course in 2014. She is currently a Public Sociology student at Queen Margaret University. She has been part of a participatory action research project evaluating the experiences and impacts of being a student of the MPHI course.

John R. Docherty-Hughes is Senior Lecturer in Sociology and Social Policy at Queen Margaret University, with an interest in pedagogical innovation and widening participation in higher education, which enable adult learners to experience higher education, and sociology in particular, in their own communities.

Marion Ellison is Reader in European Public Sociology and Policy. Her specialisms include comparative social policy and welfare in Europe, work and employment in Europe, multilevel governance in Europe, comparative child care law, policy and practice in Europe, comparative professional social work and comparative public management and governance. She is Visiting Professor at Ca'Foscari University, Venice.

Esther Fraser was a student on the 'Mad People's History and Identity' (MPHI) course in 2015. She went on to be active in many projects in mental health and activism. She is currently a Public Sociology student at Queen Margaret University. She has been part of a participatory action research project evaluating the experiences and impacts of being a student of the MPHI course.

Ricky Gee is Senior Lecturer in Sociology at Nottingham Trent University and is the course leader for the BA Sociology degree. The current focus of his research is on career articulations of recent graduates from university and the influence of the neoliberal imperative of employability.

Maria Giatsi Clausen studied Occupational Therapy in Athens, and continued her studies in Scotland, where she completed her PhD. She is Senior Lecturer in the Division of Occupational Therapy and Arts

Therapies at Queen Margaret University. Her research interests lie in the areas of children's rights and agency. She has expertise in qualitative research methodologies, particularly in participative research enquiry. She is also a trade union activist and, currently, co-president of the local UCU trade union branch.

Paul Gilfillan is Senior Lecturer in Sociology at Queen Margaret University. He is an organic intellectual and liberation sociologist whose work emerges from a working-class milieu and local public for whom the notion of 'integral liberation' is largely meaningless. His *A Sociological Phenomenology of Christian Redemption* (2014) is the first transcendental account of working class subject-formation and integral liberation based upon a socially determined subjectivity 'all the way down' simultaneously capable of cognitional agency; putting the much-heralded 'anthropocentric shift' upon a proper experimental footing within a non-secularist sociological horizon (in line with the tradition of Scottish personalist thought) that is 'fit for purpose' in the late-modern context.

Sharon Hutchings is Senior Lecturer in Sociology teaching on BA and MA sociology courses and co-leads service learning with Andrea Lyons Lewis. She is a member of the Work Futures Research Group and currently evaluating the Nottingham Together initiative. Having worked extensively in adult and community education she endeavours to bring those values and practices to her work in higher education.

Karl Johnson is a former student of Queen Margaret University, where he now lectures in Public Sociology. He works on widening access/participation in higher education, gender equality activism in Shetland, and using fiction/pop culture in Sociology. Follow him on Twitter at @karlpjohnson.

Jan Law is Teaching Fellow at Abertay Sociology department. She has a background in social policy research and education in sociology, criminology and social policy.

Robert Lindsay is a graduate of and co-producer of knowledge in the Glasgow Museums Public Sociology project.

C. Laura Lovin is Senior Researcher in the School of Education at Strathclyde University. Funded by the Leverhulme Foundation, her current research focuses on the educational experiences of youth from eastern Europe and Syria as they arrive in Glasgow at a geopolitical juncture defined by Brexit negotiations, refugee humanitarianism and the politics of securitisation.

Andrea Lyons Lewis is Senior Lecturer in Sociology and teaches modules on BA Criminology and BA Sociology. She is the Department of Sociology's co-lead (with Sharon Hutchings) for service learning. This involves working with a wide range of local not-for-private profit organisations on social justice action and research projects with second year students. She is currently a member of the Work Futures Research Group.

Kirsten Maclean is an advocacy worker with CAPS Independent Advocacy and has worked with the Oor Mad History project for ten years. She is also a PhD candidate looking at the links between popular education, citizenship and activism for people with experience of mental health issues. Her research is based at Strathclyde University, in partnership with the Program for Recovery and Community Health, Yale University. Kirsten trained in Community Education at Edinburgh University.

Philip Mignot is Senior Lecturer in Sociology at Nottingham Trent University and is a former director of the Career Studies Unit at the University of Reading. The current focus of his research is on higher education and the competing discourses of employability to be found in the marketised university.

Lesley Orr is a fellow of New College, University of Edinburgh, and has previously held appointments at the Universities of Edinburgh and Glasgow. She is a historian of gender, feminism, religion and social movements in twentieth-century Scotland. Recent research projects and publications include work on Scottish war resistance and the Women's Peace Crusade 1914–1919; churches, gender and sexuality in late twentieth-century Scotland; and Speaking Out: Recalling 40 years of Women's Aid in Scotland. She is a member of the teaching team for the innovative Gender Justice and Violence course at Queen Margaret University. Lesley has a long-standing commitment to challenging gender injustice, abuse and violence against women – in Scotland and internationally. She has extensive research, training and consultancy experience, working with the Scottish Government and the women's sector including Zero Tolerance, Rape Crisis and Scottish Women's Aid. Lesley is involved in non-party progressive politics and active citizenship initiatives with Common Weal, Women for Independence National Committee, and as a long-standing member of the Iona Community.

Alison Phipps is UNESCO Chair in Refugee Integration through Languages and the Arts at the University of Glasgow and Professor of Languages and Intercultural Studies. She is De Carle Distinguished Professorship at University of Otago, and was Distinguished Visiting Professor at Waikato University, Aotearoa New Zealand 2013–2016, Thinker-in-Residence at the EU Hawke Centre, University of South Australia in 2016, and Visiting Professor at Auckland University of Technology. She was Principal Investigator (PI) for the £2 million AHRC Large Grant 'Researching Multilingually at the Borders of Language, the body, law and the state'; co-director of the £20 million Global Challenge Research Fund project on South–South Migration and Inequality, the world's largest migration research centre; and PI on a recent Arts and Humanities award for £2 million for cultural work in the Global South.

Christine Raffaelli is Senior Lecturer in Drama and Performance at Queen Margaret University.

Eurig Scandrett is Senior Lecturer in Sociology at Queen Margaret University and programme leader for BSc and MSc programmes in Public Sociology. After an initial career as a research scientist, he spent 15 years in community education including as Head of Community Action at Friends of the Earth Scotland. He is a trade union, environmental and solidarity activist and works on popular education and informal learning in environmental justice movements.

Mae Shaw is an honorary fellow of the School of Education at the University of Edinburgh. She has worked as a community development practitioner in a variety of settings and published extensively on the politics and practice of community development. She is a founding member of the editorial board of *Concept* (the free online practice/theory journal: concept.lib.ed.ac.uk) and the international *Community Development Journal*. She is co-editor of the international book series Rethinking Community Development. Her publications include *Politics, Power and Community Development* (2016) *Community Engagement: A Critical Guide* (2017), and *Arts, Culture and Community Development* (forthcoming).

Tawona Sitholé is a poet, playwright, mbira musician, educator and facilitator. His ancestral family name, Ganyamatope, is a reminder of his heritage, which inspires him to make connections with other people through creativity, and the natural outlook to learn. As co-founder of Seeds of Thought arts group, Tawona's work involves supporting and facilitating access to the creative arts. Tawona is Poet-in-Residence for GRAMNet and works in a variety of settings and institutions. As he continues to write, teach and perform, mostly he appreciates his work for the many inspiring people it allows him to meet.

Naa Densua Tordzro is a fashion and textile artist, singer and storyteller working as an affiliate artist and research assistant with the Unesco Chair for Refugee Integration through Language and the arts. Originally from Ghana she lives and works in Glasgow and has presented her work worldwide as speaker and keynote accompanier, including in the European Parliament. In 2017 she partnered with BBC Singer–Songwriter of the Year, Karine Polwart, in a musical collaboration at the Edinburgh Festival. She is undertaking research on decolonizing fashion at the University of Glasgow.

Gameli Tordzro is a Ghanaian multiple arts professional and a Creative Arts researcher consultant in Glasgow. He is the Artistic Director of Pan African Arts Scotland and was a researcher and PhD student within the Creative Arts and Translating Cultures Hub of the Researching Multilingually at Borders project at the University of Glasgow. His research interests include arts, culture, language, migration and global peace and global education. His current focus is on arts as language for research. Gameli is the Musician-in-Residence with GRAMNet. He began his work with the UNESCO Chair in September 2017, and successfully defended his PhD thesis in 2018.

Lena Wånggren is a teacher and researcher working at the University of Edinburgh, where she is also a local trade union representative, adding to her role as Vice President of University College Union Scotland. She works on literature, feminism and social justice, pedagogy, and the medical humanities.

Nel Whiting is a long-standing activist in the women's movement and equality campaigns. She is currently Equality Charters Programme Adviser (Scotland) for Advance HE and a tutor in History and Art History at the University of Dundee, before which she was Learning and Development Coordinator at Scottish Women's Aid for 15 years.

She has published in the fields of gender-based violence and feminist analysis of portraits.

Emma Wood is Senior Lecturer in Communication at Queen Margaret University and Course Leader of its MSc Digital Campaigning and Content Creation. Her research and practice focusses on ways in which dialogue can be used to enable marginalised groups to understand their lived experience as expertise, organise to communicate their views and take action to challenge oppressive social norms. She is chair of the charity STEKAskills, a Scottish charity aimed at connecting Scottish communities with their contemporaries in Malawi to bring about social change and works in close partnership with the grassroots Malawian NGO, STEKA, which creates sustainable futures for young survivors.

Julie Young is an independent sociology researcher, whose interests include all aspects of gender-based violence, specialising in domestic abuse. She is also interested in gendered attitudes and discourses relating to women and alcohol. Funding for her PhD research featured in this case study was provided by Queen Margaret University.

Acknowledgement

Much of the concept, the content of the introduction and the provocations, and the editing of contributors' chapters, were the result of a joint effort between me and Maddie Breeze of Strathclyde University. During the production of the book, differences of opinion led Maddie to withdraw, and to remove her name as co-editor. It is a source of deep regret to me that Maddie made this decision, particularly as I continue to believe that public sociology provides an important space in which deeply held and principled differences between academics and activists committed to achieving social justice can be aired and negotiated, even when disagreements continue. However, it is perhaps because of the passionate commitment and ethical integrity which public sociologists bring to their praxis, that makes this project particularly difficult. I respect Maddie's decision and we remain colleagues engaged in struggles that we share, respectful arguments where we disagree, and friends.

It is important to acknowledge that a considerable amount of this book has emerged from her insight and intelligence, and through the valuable debates, both serious and convivial, which we have shared. I do not believe that this book would exist without that contribution.

Eurig Scandrett

Series Editors' Preface

Sociology is a highly reflexive subject. All scholarly disciplines examine themselves reflexively in terms of theory and practice as they apply what the sociologist of science Robert Merton once called 'organised scepticism'. Sociology adds to this constant internal academic debate also a vigorous, almost obsessive, concern about its very purpose and rationale. This attentiveness to founding principles shows itself in significant intellectual interest in the 'canon' of great thinkers and its history as a discipline, in vigorous debate about the boundaries of the discipline, and in considerable inventiveness in developing new areas and subfields of sociology. This fascination with the purpose and social organisation of the discipline also reflects in the debate about sociology's civic engagements and commitments, its level of activism, and its moral and political purposes.

This echoes the contemporary discussion about the idea of public sociology. 'Public sociology' is a new phrase for a long-standing debate about the purpose of sociology that began with the discipline's origins. It is therefore no coincidence that students in the twenty-first century, when being introduced to sociology for the first time, wrestle with ideas formulated centuries before, for while social change has rendered some of these ideas redundant, particularly the Social Darwinism of the nineteenth century and functionalism in the 1950s, familiarity with these earlier debates and frameworks is the lens into understanding the purpose, value and prospect of sociology as key thinkers conceived it in the past. The ideas may have changed but the moral purpose has not.

A contentious discipline is destined to argue continually about its past. Some see the roots of sociology grounded in medieval scholasticism, in eighteenth-century Scotland, with the Scottish Enlightenment's engagement with the social changes wrought by commercialism, in conservative reactions to the Enlightenment or in nineteenth-century encounters with the negative effects of industrialisation and modernisation. Contentious disciplines, however, are condemned to always live in their past if they do not also develop a vision for their future; a sense of purpose and a rationale that takes the discipline forward. Sociology has always been forward looking, offering an analysis and diagnosis of what C. Wright Mills liked to call the human condition. Interest in the social condition, and in its improvement and betterment for the majority of ordinary men and women, has always been sociology's ultimate objective.

At the end of the second millennium, when public sociology was named by Michael Burawoy, there was a strong feeling in the discipline that the professionalisation of the subject during the twentieth century had come at the cost of its public engagement, its commitment to social justice, and its reputation for activism. The vitality and creativity of the public sociology debate was largely fuelled by what Aldon Morris called 'liberation capitalism', created in social movements of political engagement outside of the universities in the years after the social turmoil and changes of the 1960s.

The discipline has mostly reacted positively to Burawoy's call for public sociology, although there has been spirited dissent from those concerned with sociology's scientific status. Public sociology represents a practical realignment of the discipline by encouraging a focus on substantive and theoretical topics that are important to the many publics with whom the discipline engages. Public sociology, however, is also a normative realignment of the discipline through its commitment to enhance understanding of the social condition so that the lives of people are materially improved. Public sociology not only changes what sociologists do, it redefines what sociology is for.

Sociology's concern with founding principles is both a strength and a weakness of the discipline. Nothing seems settled in sociology; the discipline does not obliterate past ideas by their absorption into new ones, as Robert Merton once put it, as the natural sciences insist on doing. The past remains a learning tool in sociology and the history of sociology is contemporaneous as we stand on the shoulders of giants to learn from earlier generations of sociologists. We therefore revisit debates about the boundaries between sociology and its cognate disciplines, or debates about the relationship between individuals and society, or about the analytical categories of individuals, groups, communities and societies, or of the primacy of material conditions over symbolic ones, or of the place of politics, identity, culture, economics and the everyday in structuring and determining social life. The boundaries of sociology are porous and, as many sociologists have asserted, the discipline is a hybrid, drawing ideas eclectically from those subjects closely aligned to it.

This hybridity is also sociology's great strength. Sociology's openness facilitates inter-disciplinarity, it encourages innovation in the fields to which the sociological imagination is applied, and opens up new topics about which sociological questions can be asked. Sociology thus exposes the hidden and the neglected to scrutiny. There is very little that cannot have sociological questions asked of it. The boundaries of sociology are thus ever expanding and widening; it is limitless in applying the sociological imagination. The tension between continuity and change – something evident in society generally – reflects thus also in the discipline itself. This gives sociology a frisson that is both fertile and fruitful as new ideas rub up against old ones and as the conceptual apparatus of sociology is simultaneously revisited and renewed. This tends to work against faddism in sociology, since nothing is entirely new and the latest fashions have their pasts.

Public sociology is thus not itself new and it has its own history. Burawoy rightly emphasised the role of C. Wright Mills and broader frameworks allow us to highlight the contribution of the radical W.E.B. DuBois, the early feminist and peace campaigner Jane Addams, and scores of feminist, socialist and anti-racist scholars from the Global South, such as Fernando Henrique Cardosa in Brazil and Fatima Meer in South Africa. Going back further into the history of public sociology, the Scots in the eighteenth century were public sociologists in their way, allowing us to see that Burawoy's refocusing of sociology's research agenda and its normative realignment is the latest expression of a long-standing concern. The signal achievement of Burawoy's injunction was to mobilise the profession to reflect again on its founding principles and to take the discipline forward to engage with the relevance of sociology to the social and human condition in the twenty-first century.

Despite the popularity of the idea of public sociology, and the widespread use of such discourse, no book series is singularly dedicated to it. The purpose of this series is to draw together some of the best sociological research that carries the imprimatur of 'public sociology', done inside the academy by senior figures and early career researchers, as well as outside it by practitioners, policy analysts and independent researchers seeking to apply sociological research in real-world settings.

The reflexivity of professional sociologists as they ponder the usefulness of sociology under neoliberalism and late modern cosmopolitanism, will be addressed in this series, as the series publishes works that engage from a sociological perspective with the fundamental global challenges that threaten the very future of human kind. The relevance of sociology will be highlighted in works that address these challenges as they feature in global social changes but also as they are mediated in local and regional communities and settings. The series will thus feature titles that work at a global level of abstraction as well as studies that are micro ethnographic depictions of global processes as they affect local communities. The focus of the series is thus on what Michael Ignatieff refers to as 'the ordinary virtues' of everyday life, social justice, equality of opportunity, fairness, tolerance, respect, trust and respect, and how the organisation and structure of society – at a general level or in local neighbourhoods – inhibits or promotes these virtues and practices. The series will expose, through detailed sociological analysis, the dynamics of social suffering and celebrate the hopes of social emancipation.

The discourse of public sociology has permeated outside the discipline of sociology, as other subjects take up its challenge and reorientate themselves, such as public anthropology, public political science and public international relations. In pioneering the engagement with its different publics, sociology has therefore once again led the way, and this series is designed to take the debate about public sociology and its practices in new directions. In being the first of its kind, this book series will showcase how the discipline of sociology has utilised the language and ideas of public sociology to change what it does and what it is for. This series will address not only what sociologists do, but also sociology's focus on the commitment to enhance understanding of the social condition so that the lives of ordinary people are materially improved. It will showcase the wide diversity of sociological research that addresses the many global challenges that threaten the future of humankind in the twenty-first century.

These qualities are admirably represented in the volume *Public Sociology as Educational Practice* that inaugurates this series, edited by Eurig Scandrett. Eurig has drawn together a set of authors who challenge the very boundaries and practices of public sociology. Coming as they do from critical and radical education studies, the volume applies the practices and normative principles of public sociology to address educational practice in schools, in neoliberal universities and in the community. In so doing, it explores the boundaries between radical education studies and public sociology by addressing the publics, knowledges and practices that shape educational practice in these spheres.

Public Sociology as Educational Practice is as much a critique of public sociology as of educational practices in the way it advocates an emphasis on subaltern counterpublics and explores the interface between theory and practice in the public sociology of educational practices in the classroom and in the community. Contributors reflect this interface, with some being university researchers and others community practitioners. While they are nearly all Scottish-based, the arguments advanced about educational practices when understood through the lens of public sociology, are global in their significance and impact. They add to our knowledge of educational practices as well as to our practice of public sociology.

The volume chiefly argues that public sociology should be conceived as a form of dialogue occurring in critical social spaces. In this volume, the dialogue is between teachers and pupils, researchers and publics, and practitioners and theoreticians, which occur, in this case, in social spaces that confront and challenge the binary divide between the parochial and the universal, the local and the global, and the neoliberal university and subaltern counter-spaces. The critique of neoliberal university practices in favour of advocacy for subaltern counter-practices shines through in the volume. The contributors look to public sociology praxis, in the form of such diverse activities as dialogical pedagogy, informal learning, participatory action research, community development, service learning, policy work, art, and multilingual practices, to re-envision educational practices in the university, as well as in schools and community learning settings.

This is public sociology put to use. It is public sociology as a normative realignment. By using the lens of public sociology, the volume seeks to radically change what purpose educational practices serve, giving public sociology itself a purpose in promoting social change. As editors, we therefore very warmly welcome this volume to the series.

John D. Brewer and Neil McLaughlin
Belfast and Toronto
February 2020

Introduction

Eurig Scandrett

Public sociology, the contributors to this volume demonstrate, shares affinities with radical education practice, and this book furthers debates in the dialogue between public sociology and radical education inside, outside, and at the edges of academia. The book as a whole echoes a methodology developed and popularised by public sociologist Michael Burawoy, the extended case methodology (Burawoy, 1998) to facilitate critical dialogue between practitioners of public sociology and education in contested relation to the constitution of 'publics', the production of sociological knowledge, and different contexts of pedagogical practice.

Radical education practice includes such forms as popular education (Crowther, Galloway and Martin, 2005); democratic education (hooks, 2003); community education (for example Tett, 2010); critical pedagogy (Giroux, 1988); pedagogy of the oppressed (Freire, 1972). These forms resonate with public sociology in the sense that it is committed to dialogue between 'public' knowledges and sociological theory. *Public Sociology as Educational Practice* therefore starts from Burawoy's (2005: 9) propositions that 'as teachers we are all potentially public sociologists', and that 'between the organic public sociologist and a public is a dialogue, a process of mutual education' (2005: 8) as a point of departure, to claim that the curriculum of that mutual education requires dual accountability. Public sociology knowledge should not be validated exclusively by the institutions and epistemologies of professional sociology, but rather the validity – and usefulness – of public sociology is established in and through dialogue with publics and, in particular, with subaltern counterpublics. This proposition raises a number of problematics, and critical questions about the relationships between 'sociologists' and 'publics' in different educational contexts.

Dialogue is central to the practices of public sociology education explored in this book, and the dialogical pedagogy of Paulo Freire, whose influence is fundamental to diverse forms of radical education, is cited repeatedly by the contributors to this book, who are working in public sociology in a range of disciplines and professional contexts. Initially outlined in his *Pedagogy of the Oppressed* (Freire, 1972; first published in English in 1970 and in Portuguese in 1968), Freire's methodology frames education as a dialogue between the knowledge of the educator and the knowledge of the learner. Drawing on Marxism, phenomenology, Christian humanism and liberation theology, Freire developed these methods whilst working in literacy education with poor workers and peasants in his native Brazil. He emphasised the value of the knowledge that the poor bring to the educational context, as well as challenging the oppression that kept them in poverty. Thus, for Freire, education is a praxis, a dialogue between reflection and action, in which 'to speak a true word is to transform the world' (Freire 1972: 60). Moreover, his educational method is aimed, not merely at literacy in its narrow sense, but at conscientisation (*conscientização*), the development of critical consciousness, through a process of dialogue between everyday concrete and particular knowledge, and the abstract and theoretical knowledge through which the everyday context can be critiqued, analysed and challenged. In this process, 'generative themes' emerge which enable the production of new, critical knowledge. Freire's educational work in Brazil came to an end with the military coup d'état in 1964. Following a period in prison, Freire went into exile, promoting his educational philosophy globally, until he was able to resume his work in Brazil in 1979.

The centrality of dialogue in Freire's method can be seen throughout this book – between educator and learner; researcher and participant; concrete and abstract knowledge; reflection and action; and between sociologies and publics.

The book therefore articulates a distinctive and innovative approach to understanding public sociology education, in both form and content, and presents a collection of pedagogical case studies in critical and reflexive conversation with each other, framed and facilitated by an on-going and cumulative argument that situates the cases in social and political context. The dynamic of the book's chapters is shaped by three *Provocations*, in each case followed by several *Cases* which respond to the provocation. Following the case chapters, *Dialogue* sections give an opportunity for the contributors and editor to engage in critical discussion and extend theoretical arguments based on the case material. In this way we 'locate the everyday life' of public sociology education 'in its extralocal and historical context', which is consistent with extended case methodology (Burawoy, 1998: 4).

Michael Burawoy is one of the most significant figures in the development of public sociology, and his 2004 presidential address to the American Sociological Association 'For Public Sociology' has generated considerable debate within the discipline (Burawoy, 2005 and, for example, Clawson et al, 2007). Burawoy's argument for public sociology in 2004 to his North American professional sociology audience, moreover, is based on a considerable experience of engaging sociologically in a wide range of public contexts. Drawing on extensive ethnographic research in the Zambian copper industry, and subsequently through working in factories in the USA, Hungary and Russia, Burawoy challenged the positivism dominant within sociology at the time, and developed and advocated a research methodology – the extended case – in which the emersion of the ethnographic researcher in their specific social context can contribute to a rigorous analysis of sociopolitical processes and thus interrogate sociological theory (Burawoy, 1998, 2009). As with Freire, the methodological principle deployed is dialogue. What Burawoy calls 'reflective science'

> deploys multiple dialogues to reach explanations of empirical phenomena. Reflexive science starts out from dialogue, virtual or real, between observer and participants, then embeds such dialogue within a second dialogue between local processes and extralocal forces that in turn can be comprehended only through a third, expanding dialogue of theory with itself. (Burawoy, 1998: 5)

Public Sociology as Educational Practice does not deploy the same level of rigour of Burawoy's method, but does follow the same principles, by interrogating and extending the theoretical development of public sociology itself through the reflective analysis of contributors who, in various ways, are participants and observers of their own praxis in public sociology education in and around the universities of Scotland and England in an increasingly divergent neoliberal political context.

This book therefore integrates elements of both an edited collection and a multiauthored monograph to argue that doing public sociology education poses a series of productive challenges to how public sociologists understand the constitution of publics, the production of sociological knowledge, and the dialectics of practice both in and outwith institutions of higher education (HE).

Public Sociology as Educational Practice comprises three substantive sections, addressing I Publics, II Knowledges, and III Practices. Each section begins with theoretical–analytical provocations, which raise a series of overarching questions to which the case studies, and the dialogues between them, respond:

1. **Publics:** Who are the 'publics' of public sociology education? Drawing on Nancy Fraser's formulation of the subaltern counter-public, the section explores who constitutes a 'subaltern counter-public'? Who produces curricula in public sociology education, and how? Who is included and excluded by the practice of public sociology education?
2. **Knowledges:** What special knowledges can public sociology pedagogies generate? The theoretical point of departure here is 'really useful knowledge', the nineteenth century working class demand for control of educational curricula. How can public sociology knowledge be validated as 'really useful' by the participants in public sociology education, both practitioners and publics?
3. **Practices:** How is public sociology education practised in diverse contexts? Where do public sociology educators locate their practice with respect to communities and movements of publics? What institutions and forms of educational organisation allow for public sociology education? How can public sociologists work in, with, despite, and against institutions of HE – indeed, is it possible to do public sociology education in increasingly neoliberal universities?

Asking these questions in dialogue with case studies is not intended to showcase 'best practice', but rather to develop practitioners' reflexive ethnographic observations of their own work as situated participant-observers, following the extended case method (Burawoy, 1998). In this way the book argues not only that the practice of public sociology education necessitates asking critical questions about the relationship between publics, sociological knowledge, and the practices of sociologists in various institutional and social contexts, but that responding to these questions is a continuous process of excavating, negotiating and resisting structures of oppression, exclusion, and exploitation. This raises further questions about who legitimises public sociology knowledge – and how. Furthermore, the process of discerning and interrogating tentative answers to these problematics is essentially dialogical and derives from key forms of educational praxis.

Contributors make use of visual images and variations in prose style and authorial voice in order to present and discuss their cases, and the perspectives of publics, including students and research participants, are included throughout the book. *Public Sociology as Educational Practice* is structured so that authors have the opportunity to 'talk back' to each other, responding, questioning, developing and challenging each others' analysis of what it means to do public sociology education.

Public Sociology as Educational Practice therefore aims to:

1. Frame, and further, emergent debates on the practice of public sociology education through reflexive discussion of, and critical dialogues between, a collection of pedagogical, research and practice orientated case studies.
2. Provide a timely, essential, and provocative resource for students, educators and practitioners working in public sociology education and related fields.
3. Generate fresh responses to vexing disciplinary questions, including what – and who – sociological knowledge is for, and the relationship between publics, sociology and institutions of HE.

This collection seeks to go beyond Burawoy's (2005: 7–8) advocacy of 'organic public sociology in which the sociologist works in close connection with a visible, thick, active, local and often counterpublic ... to validate these organic connections as part of our sociological life', to claim that working with subaltern counterpublics is central to public sociology, and that this work should be validated through dialogue with such counterpublics, as much as (or perhaps rather than) by a body of professional sociologists. To make such a claim is not designed as a form of quality control for the practice of public sociology, but rather to raise a problematic about the role of public sociologists and their publics, in interrogating the nature of subalternity through analysis of structures of oppression, exclusion and exploitation and the forms of resistance to these structures. This explores questions about who legitimises public sociology knowledge and the extent to which it is 'really useful' (Johnson, 1976; Scandrett et al, 2010) to the interests of emancipatory projects of subaltern counterpublics. Furthermore, the process of discerning and interrogating tentative answers to these problematics is essentially dialogical and derives from key forms of educational praxis – in the sense that Antonio Gramsci asserted that 'every relationship of 'hegemony' is necessarily an educational relationship' (Hoare and Smith, 1971: 350).

Gramsci's insight is significant. A trade union organiser and founder of the Communist Party of Italy in the 1930s, Gramsci was imprisoned by Mussolini's fascist government and, whilst in prison, sought to analyse how power relations were maintained in different historical periods. He utilised the concept of hegemony to describe how the working class and other oppressed groups buy into sets of assumptions, or 'common sense', which serve to reproduce their own exploitation and the interests of dominant groups. He argued that hegemony in advanced capitalist societies reduces the requirement for coercion by the state, the ruling class or alliances of powerful groups, and is negotiated in civil society through the reproduction of sets of assumptions, meanings and practices. Hegemony can also be challenged, and alternative meanings and practices built from working class and subaltern groups based on consent and 'good sense', that is 'counter-hegemony', This can be understood as a pedagogical process.

Since most of the contributors, and indeed most public sociologists, are or have been located in universities, we look to opportunities for this praxis primarily in or at the fringes of HE, even whilst the pressure and disciplinary practices of neoliberal economics is driving HE in directions which are anathema to such public sociology education. At the same time the practices of public sociology education are explored in contexts beyond universities.

Public Sociology as Educational Practice arises from the aggregate experiences of a group of public sociologists doing educational work across institutional boundaries. Collectively the authors have a wealth of experience teaching sociology and public sociology, including university-based (undergraduate, postgraduate, and 'outreach') sociology teaching, curriculum development (including the development of BSc and MSc public sociology programmes), and experiences in adult and popular education, lifelong learning, and social movement learning. This educational work has overlapped with research and knowledge exchange collaborations with community based and social movement organisations, community education and advocacy projects.

The editor and most contributors are based in Scotland. To some extent this is because the idea for this book emerged from the experience of developing new undergraduate and postgraduate programmes in public sociology at Queen Margaret University, a small and rather marginal new university on the outskirts of Edinburgh, and drew on the networks to which the contributors are connected in Scotland. However, there is also a distinctive role for public sociology (education) to be grounded in a particular concrete social situation. In his 'Thesis IX: Provincialising American Sociology', Burawoy (2005: 20) argues that public sociology has a 'national specificity', a statement that is only necessary when speaking from the hegemon of the American Sociological Association and the University of California, Berkley. At Queen Margaret University and, moreover, in Scotland, one of the junior nations in the UK, the provincial and peripheral context of our public sociology practice is evident (and the two contributions from England's Nottingham Trent University experience their own provincialism). Connell has suggested that, in the context of post-colonial neoliberalism, sociologies of resistance from the periphery take on a particular significance:

> 'public sociology' ... is not an option within the metropole ... Rather it is a necessity on a world scale. Neoliberal globalisation itself pushes sociology into an oppositional position, since the very act of naming social structures is an obstacle to the triumph of market ideology. (Connell, 2011: 118)

Scotland is somewhat peripheral within Europe but with a history both of partnership in British colonial exploitation and in intellectual leadership.

Scotland provides a valuable position for an extended case study in public sociology education, in terms of publics, knowledges and practices and, in particular, in the context of contested statehood. Throughout its 300-year union with England, Scottish publics have been structured by its civil society, which has retained a distinctive autonomy through its legal establishment, media, church, education, trades unions etc. As a birthplace of the Enlightenment, Scotland has also been an outward looking producer of knowledge, at times closer to developments in mainland Europe than in its neighbour, England and, more recently, a focus for cultural renaissance. Its institutions of HE, at least until the end of the nineteenth century, retained a distinctive curricular identity (Davie, 1961) and an academic home for more working class students (Cooke, 2006), whilst political devolution in 1999 has generated increasing policy divergence from HE in the rest of the UK.

The book comprises seventeen substantive chapters – cases – which are organised into three sections: Publics, Knowledge and Practices. Each section begins with a theoretical-analytical provocation by the editor and ends with a dialogue. The provocations introduce each section, develop a substantive argument concerning public sociology education, and raise a series of overarching questions to which the case chapters respond, some of which with their own provocations. In preparing their cases, all contributors (many of whom are not professional sociologists) were provided by email with an early version of the provocation around public sociology education, in order to encourage reflection on their experiences, and to influence the argument that they wanted to develop in their chapters. For the dialogues, case contributors were provided with a revised provocation, late drafts of all the chapters in their section, and some emergent, generative themes identified by the editor. They were invited to engage with one another and with the editor with a view to challenging, interrogating and developing further the argument about the section's theme in the context of wider political and historical processes. Most of this communication occurred by email, by choice of the contributors. The level of engagement with dialogue varied considerably from section to section, and only around half of the case contributors ultimately participated in developing the dialogues. The three sections are framed by the editor's introduction and conclusion, which, together, it is hoped, provide an overall coherence to the argument on public sociology education.

References
Burawoy, M. (1998) 'The extended case method', *Sociological Theory*, 16(1): 4–33.
Burawoy, M. (2005) 'For public sociology', *American Sociological Review*, 70: 4–28.
Burawoy, M. (2009) *The Extended Case Method: Four Countries, Four Decades, Four Great Transformations, and One Theoretical Tradition*, Berkley: University of California Press.
Clawson, D., Zussman, R., Misra, J., Gerstel, N., Stokes, R. and Anderton, D. (eds) (2007) *Public Sociology: Fifteen Eminent Sociologists Debate Politics and the Profession in the Twenty-first Century*, Berkeley and London: University of California Press.
Connell, R. (2011) *Confronting Equality: Gender, Knowledge and Global Change*, Cambridge: Polity Press.
Cooke, A. (2006) *From Popular Enlightenment to Lifelong Learning: A History of Adult Education in Scotland 1707–2005*, Leicester: NIACE.
Crowther, J., Galloway, V. and Martin, I. (eds) (2005) *Popular Education: Engaging the Academy, International Perspectives*, Leicester: NIACE.
Davie, G. (1961) *The Democratic Intellect: Scotland and her Universities in the Nineteenth Century*, Edinburgh: Edinburgh University Press.
Freire, P. (1972) *Pedagogy of the Oppressed*, London: Penguin.
Giroux, H.A. (1988) *Teachers as Intellectuals: Toward a Critical Pedagogy of Learning*, Massachusetts: Bergin & Garvey Publishers.
Hoare, Q. and Smith, G.N. (1971) *Antonio Gramsci: Selections from Prison Notebooks*, London: Lawrence and Wishart.
hooks, b. (2003) *Teaching Community: A Pedagogy of Hope*, New York: Routledge.

Johnson, R. (1976) "Really useful knowledge': radical education and working-class culture 1790–1848', in Clarke, J., Critcher, C. and Johnson, R. (eds) *Working Class Culture: Studies in History and Theory*, London: Hutchinson, pp 7-28.

Scandrett, E., Crowther, J., Hemmi, A., Mukherjee, S., Shah, D. and Sen, T. (2010) 'Theorising education and learning in social movements: environmental justice campaigns in Scotland and India', *Studies in the Education of Adults*, 42(2): 124–140.

Tett, L. (2010) *Community Education, Learning and Development* (3rd edn), Edinburgh: Dunedin Academic Press.

SECTION I

Publics

PROVOCATION I

Class, Gender and Identity: Axes of Structure and Difference in Subaltern Counterpublics

Eurig Scandrett

The section raises questions about the 'who' of public sociology education, and the inclusions, exclusions, and power relationships that inhere in definitions of 'the public'. This provocation makes the case that public sociology primarily engages with subaltern counterpublics (Fraser, 1990) – those engaged in resistance, resilience, or building alternatives to some form of oppression, exploitation, or injustice.

In a key section of his address to the American Sociological Association, 'Burawoy (2005: 7–8) argues that there is a distinctive *'organic public sociology'*

> in which the sociologist works in close connection with a visible, thick, active, local and often counterpublic. The bulk of public sociology is indeed of an organic kind – sociologists working with a labor movement, neighborhood associations, communities of faith, immigrant rights groups, human rights organizations. *Between the organic public sociologist and a public is a dialogue, a process of mutual education.* The recognition of public sociology must extend to the organic kind which often remains invisible, private, and is often considered to be apart from our professional lives. The project of such public sociologies is to make visible the invisible, to make the private public, to validate these organic connections as part of our sociological life. (Burawoy, 2005: 7–8) (my emphasis)

This provocation attempts to take this argument further by claiming that public sociology primarily engages in this project of mutual education with subaltern counterpublics. Thus, the question of who and what constitutes a public, and with which publics sociologists engage, involves sociologically informed questions of power, structure, oppression and justice, and about the dynamics of resistance and emancipation.

Further questions arise as to what and who constitutes 'the subaltern' and what and how publics 'counter'. Understandings of the subaltern emerge both from sociological analysis of structures of oppression, exploitation, and exclusion (whether or not such sociological analysis is done by 'sociologists') and also from collective self-expression and political demands for justice that emerge from subaltern groups. At the same time, what constitutes a 'counterpublic' (and in what ways they are 'counter') emerges, for the public sociologist, from dialogue with the praxis of those engaged in struggle against structures and representations that oppress, exploit and exclude. Discerning the subaltern nature and the structures of countering by publics in dialogue with sociological knowledge is primarily a hegemonic task, involving critical interrogation of interests embedded in claims, practices and knowledge in order to expose and confront passive consent to a common sense that is reproducing oppressive and exploitative power relations: in Gramsci's terms 'every relationship of 'hegemony' is necessarily an educational relationship' (Hoare and Smith, 1971 p.350). Thus, public sociologists engage in projects that are both political and pedagogical.

There is a parallel argument in the field of popular education, concerning what constitutes the 'popular'. In this context, the term popular education is a translation from Portuguese *educação popular* and Spanish *educación popular*. As Kane (2001: 8) explains:

> In Spanish or Portuguese, 'popular' means 'of the people', 'the people' being the working class, the unemployed, 'peasants', the 'poor' and sometimes even the lower middle-class: it excludes and stands in contradistinction to the well-off middle class and the rich.

Popular in this context therefore requires some form of sociological analysis, however rudimentary: an understanding of how power is sociologically situated. Popular education therefore differs from 'public education', in which the public is undifferentiated by class or power relations. 'A class analysis, then, is at the heart of "*educación/educação popular*", the task of which, essentially, is to pursue an educational practice that will best serve the interests of the "popular classes".' (Kane 2001: 9). Moreover, popular education has also been taken up in a range of emancipatory educational projects, for instance in gender politics, anti-colonial struggle, around communities of place and interest and in the politics of identity. The 'popular classes' have therefore extended to mean any group which claims a subaltern status which it seeks to challenge.

A tension between class-based and other structural analyses of power and oppression versus a more diffuse understanding of diversity and exclusion, has been significant in sociology and wider social theory since the latter part of the twentieth century (Fraser and Honneth, 2003). It is in this sociologically informed critique, as it is expressed in the practices of groups seeking emancipation, that public sociology has an important role. Sociologists are not united in their interpretations of axes of power and oppression and, therefore, where to locate subalternity, but this is the arena of public sociology where such informed debate with, and in, communities making claims on social justice must take place.

Analysis of the subaltern inevitably draws on Gramsci, whose innovative use of the term has enabled such nuanced interpretation. Crehan (2016) summarises the different ways in which scholars have interpreted Gramsci's use of subaltern, and in particular in relation to class. We draw on three insights from Crehan's analysis that are particularly useful here.

The first is that she argues that Gramsci used subaltern classes or social groups to be broader than proletariat or working class, but not infinitely broad, and always the development of the proletariat is central under capitalism. This is linked to Gramsci's insistence on a more fluid and dynamic understanding of the relationship between the economic base and the social superstructure than some of his Marxist comrades. Gramsci argued that the productive conditions were the ultimate determining factors of social life 'in the last analysis', but not the only determining factor, nor a direct causality (Crehan, 2016: 20).

The second insight is that subaltern social groups need to be understood dialectically as both an abstraction and a specific group at any particular time.

> As a totality, the condition of subalternity is broadly inclusive, encompassing all those who are oppressed rather than oppressing, ruled rather than ruling ... Once, however, we are talking about a specific time and place, subalterns, for Gramsci, are always particular kinds of subaltern ... The point is that if we want to define subalternity precisely, then we need to know which particular subalterns, at which particular historical moment, we are talking about. What defines their specific form of subalternity? (Crehan, 2016: 15–16)

This is a particularly useful analytical point when we are looking for subaltern subjects of public sociology. Publics are subaltern at particular times and in particular contexts, which are the result of historical processes, which involves a social complexity, behind which, in the last analysis, are the productive and reproductive conditions of life.

Finally, Crehan argues that subalternity is essentially an epistemological as well as an ontological category. Subaltern social groups produce knowledge, albeit, initially, in the fragmented and incoherent form of 'common sense', and eventually, as the group generates its own intellectuals, in the form of a coherent totalising knowledge that incorporates rational critique and emotional passion. First, as Crehan points out, in Italian

> *senso comune* (common sense), the term Gramsci uses for all those heterogeneous beliefs people arrive at not through critical reflection, but encounter as already existing, self-evident truths … is a far more neutral term than the English common sense … [and emphasises] the held-in-common (*comune*) nature of the beliefs. (Crehan, 2016: x)

Second, the intellectuals that Gramsci refers to are not traditional intellectuals but rather organic to the group, that is they are a subcategory of the subaltern group whose function is to make coherent and articulate the good sense behind the common sense. As Crehan summarises it:

> Together, subaltern experience and the intellectuals that are born of it give rise to a new culture and a new common sense, a common sense with deep roots in subaltern experience that carries the emotional charge of traditional beliefs while reflecting a coherent, rational philosophy. (Crehan, 2016: 58)

Discernment of subalternity is, however, inadequate for public sociology, which requires a moment of agency, of normative choice, of solidarity. The claims of subaltern groups for social justice constitutes action, for change, for a redistribution and recognition: 'to speak a true word is to transform the world' (Freire, 2005: 87). Moreover, the sociological analysis of subalternity is forged in the struggle for emancipation. As Juliet Mitchell noted about the historical conditions of the women's movement in 1966, the action against oppression and the critical analysis of the causes of that oppression, go hand in hand.

> The Women's Liberation Movement is at the stage of organizing our 'instinct' of our oppression as women, into a consciousness of its meaning. This will become a rational consciousness as we come to understand the objective conditions which determine this oppression. At the moment, the essential 'instinct' coexists with the possibilities for transforming it into rational consciousness. (Mitchell, 1971: 98)

The understanding of public sociology analysis of subalternity presented here demands a refusal to accept the structures of oppression and exploitation being analysed. It requires the public sociologist to 'take sides', to engage in social struggle. Sociology is the 'second moment' – it supports the development of analytical tools which can be of value to the subaltern in their / our struggles against oppression, exploitation and injustice. Our publics must be counterpublics.

Nancy Fraser first used the phrase 'subaltern counterpublic' in her analysis of the public sphere in Habermas' writing (Fraser, 1990). She points out that the public sphere gives the impression of being public and open to engagement in communicative rationality by all participants, yet is in reality dominated by those sections of the public with preferential access to power, to shape and set the terms of the public sphere. Thus, those sections of the public that are disempowered in the public sphere require alternative counterpublic spheres in order to address the power imbalance and insist on challenging those power differentials that exclude them. In the same way, we understand public sociology as being committed to these struggles against exclusion, oppression and exploitation by privileging those subaltern publics who are engaged in struggles for justice, equality, liberation, and also to become part of these struggles through the practice of our public sociology.

Such struggles moreover must be understood historically, and as embodying socially produced contradictions. Categories of oppression and exploitation can intersect and be contradictory, and drive social change in unpredictable ways. Many emancipatory struggles have found accommodation with (or even embraced) neoliberal capitalism, from feminism (Fraser, 2016) to environmental justice (Carter, 2016). A class analysis borne of industrial class struggles of previous eras needs to be employed critically, interrogated and tested in the context of a particular post-industrial working class whose appetite for struggle appears (as Gilfillan points out in case I.4) to have waned, whilst recognising the struggle within the totality of the global working class.

The nature of subalternity, of oppression and exploitation is connected with current debates on the nature of social justice claims by social movements. The selection of case studies in this collection foregrounds some of these tensions, drawing on the conceptual power but also the problematisation of categorisations of injustices and justice claims. Class remains a central analytical category in sociology, especially in the European traditions of Durkheim, Marx and Weber, as well as in the practices of Burawoy's organic public sociology and Latin American popular education. Unequal access to economic power and exploitation of, or exclusion from, the labour process has been an important mobilising force in the construction of counterpublics. Nonetheless, as Gilfillan argues in case I.4, in a post-industrial context, even in working class areas most clearly at the mercy of economic processes, class no longer operates straightforwardly as a mobilising structure and the institutions of class emancipation, both liberal and radical, do not have the same purchase as in previous industrial and social democratic eras.

Martin (2005) has argued the value for educators of conceptualising two 'paradigms' of justice: a *structural* paradigm, which gives ontological precedence to particular structures of exploitation or oppression – usually class, although also structural feminist understandings of gender or critical anti-colonial understandings of 'race' – and a *difference* paradigm in which there is no ontological privilege in any claims of injustice, but rather power and oppression occurs amongst multiple, intersectional identities. There is of course a fertile debate within social theory between structure and difference; intersectional and super-structural analyses; the relative independence or co-constitution of forms of oppression and the extent to which some (and how many) axes of exploitation are more fundamental than others (Crenshaw, 1989; Butler, 1990; Fraser and Honneth, 2003; Olson, 2008; Bhattacharya, 2017; McNally, 2017). In the Marxist, materialist tradition, class as a structural relationship to production and central locus of exploitation is analytically privileged in relation to social and cultural forms of oppression. The deterministic and reductionist tendency within Marxism and other structural theories have been critiqued from the perspective of social movements resisting oppression on the grounds of identity, culture, and symbolic forms of exclusion, who have often found the post-structural analysis of Foucault more fruitful than Marx. Fraser (2008; Fraser and Honneth, 2003) has framed the analysis of social justice around axes of redistribution and recognition, without privileging either but rather identifying the contradictions in addressing both simultaneously. McNally and Ferguson (2015) have sought to locate multiple co-constitutive oppressions within the exploitation of capitalist totality. These models of understanding exploitation, oppression and injustice – and therefore the relations of subalternity and resistance – have been fruitfully employed in sociological theory. It is useful here to draw on the heuristics of 'structure and difference' and of 'redistribution and recognition' and their employment in sociological theory, in our assessment of the subaltern counterpublics of public sociology education.

It is important to rehearse, and to defend, a public sociology for which class is central. The Marxist tradition has of course been of fundamental importance in understanding the macroscopic processes through which social change has occurred. The undisputed dominance of capitalist means of production throughout the world: the regularity of its crises; the tendency of capital to move into ever more areas of social life as it accumulates; the commodification of social forms; the incorporation of people into class relations; the tendency for the rate of profit to decline and the subsequent demand for increased productivity, increasing intensity and mechanisms of exploitation; substitution of labour for technology; fetishism of the commodity and the ubiquitous role of ideology; all require the claims of Marx and sociologists who draw on his analysis to be taken seriously. And so must the central driving force for social change in this analysis, class struggle. As many Marxist scholars have argued, class struggle does not necessarily always take traditional forms at the point of labour exploitation. Harvey (1996), for example, argues that the dynamics of capitalism demand that class struggle, whilst central, be understood in its totality, including struggles over ideology, non-capitalist social relations, contestations over environmental resources etc, while Gilfillan (2014) argues in the Scottish context the successful rise of nationalism is largely the result of those working class generations born from the 1960s having integrated questions of culture and (national) identity with more established forms of class struggle.

Public sociology must engage with these contested forms of class struggle, but that is not to say that there is a working class that must constitute the central public with which praxis occurs. On the one hand, the creative dynamics of capitalism have ensured that new phases and innovations have emerged – industrialism, financialisation, colonialism, globalisation, social democracy, neoliberalism, accumulation by dispossession, the 'knowledge economy', the 'gig economy' – all producing different pressures on class formation, class struggle and hegemonic alliance building. And, on the other hand, theorists of intersectionality have pointed out the relative autonomy of multiple axes of oppression that include social locations across a spectrum of maldistribution and misrecognition (or structure and identity) that all need to be addressed at both an abstract level and in the experiences of collective struggles of publics (Crenshaw, 1989; Hill Collins and Bilge, 2016). Interpreting the subaltern in public sociology requires an understanding of capitalism as a central organising principle and source of exploitation, whilst also incorporating an analysis of other forms of oppression that are 'structurally relational to' (Bhattacharya, 2017: 3), but not reducible to capitalist relations of production.

The relationship of class exploitation to forms of oppression around gender, 'race', disability, sexuality, mad identity etc is an important area where sociologies interact with subaltern counterpublics in potentially fruitful ways. The insights of intersectionality theory have recognised the relative autonomy of diverse, non-reducible forms of oppression, although as McNally writes, this has, at times, led to a form of atomism and individualisation.

> The great accomplishment of intersectionality theory was to expand the framework of discussion – initially to race, gender, and class, and more recently to other relations of oppression, such as those of sexuality and ability ... Rarely, however, have attempts been made to think all of these relations as co-constituting parts of the differentiated unity that comprises a concrete social totality. (McNally, 2017: 108–109)

Meanwhile, social reproduction theorists have recently sought to integrate these oppressions, each with their own 'relational autonomy' (McNally, 2017: 105) systematically into a class-based analysis of capitalism (Battacharya, 2017; and see Yuval-Davis, 2007).

Whilst recognising therefore that class remains a central analytical category within public sociology in interpreting categories such as subaltern counterpublics, where does that leave the practice of public sociology with the central collective agent of history in Marxist theory, the working class, and in particular in the context of post-industrial, post-welfare state, neoliberal Europe? The cases in this section explore a range of categories of subalternity.

Ballantyne et al's Case I.1 on mad studies foregrounds the experiences of mad-identifying people. With its roots in the anti-psychiatry and disabled people's movements, mad studies explores the processes of disciplinary governmentality that serves to oppress through the categorisation of difference. Mad is an identification selected by people whose experience of the social implications of mental distress (mediated through psychiatric services, social attitudes, pharmaceutical industries etc) are oppressive but who are reclaiming that category in their collective resistance to that oppression. Mad identify, therefore, becomes an expression of subaltern counterpublic, and the pedagogical practice of mad people's history and identity becomes a public sociology dialogue.

Gender politics is thoroughly bivalent, with clear elements of both materialist-redistributive and symbolic-recognition dimensions, and different forms of feminism constitute a clear example of public sociology knowledge generated through a subaltern counterpublic. The analysis of gender in public sociology education, therefore, provides an opportunity to explore some of the public contestations, between multiple feminisms and their relation to materialist, post-structural, critical race, and queer theories. Cases I.2 and I.3 explore these contestations, through Young's case of feminist participatory action research with women with experience of domestic abuse, whilst Orr and Whiting explore of the counter-hegemonic praxis of feminist activists and public sociology students in an educational programme on gender justice.

The changing nature of class is problematised in the final two cases in this section, which form a contrasting pair. In Case I.4 Gilfillan reflects on his work with the Workers Educational Association, an organisation founded on class as a central organising relation of injustice and historically the home for Marxist and non-Marxist explorations of the role of class in relation to other forms of oppression – and at times as a sparring partner with other Marxist educators. Gilfillan questions the extent to which class retains a role for educational practice in post-industrial society, but also the public sociology analyses that are founded on class, that he caricatures as the 'Old Left project'. Scandrett, in Case I.5, picks up this theme, pointing out that the changing, complex and diverse nature of class has often led sociologists – including public sociologists – to neglect or even deny its significance. This 'invisibility of class' in both theoretical sociology and education practice has implications for public sociologists where class analysis risks becoming abstract from the reality of class exploitation.

References

Bhattacharya, T. (2017) 'Introduction', in Bhattacharya, T. (ed) *Social Reproduction Theory: Remapping Class, Recentring Oppression*, London: Pluto Press, pp 1–20.

Burawoy, M. (2005) 'For public sociology', *American Sociological Review*, 70: 4–28.
Butler, J. (1990) *Gender Trouble: Feminism and the Subversion of Identity*, New York: Routledge.
Carter, E.D. (2016) 'Environmental Justice 2.0: New Latino environmentalism in Los Angeles', *Local Environment*, 21(1): 3–23.
Crehan, K. (2016) *Gramsci's Common Sense: Inequality and its Narratives*, Durham, NC and London: Duke University Press.
Crenshaw, K. (1989) 'Demarginalizing the intersection of race and sex: a black feminist critique of antidiscrimination doctrine, feminist theory and antiracist politics', *University of Chicago Legal Forum*, Article 8.
Fraser, N. (1990) 'Rethinking the public sphere: a contribution to the critique of actually existing democracy', *Social Text*, 25/26: 56–80.
Fraser, N. (2008) *Scales of Justice: Reimagining Political Space in a Globalizing World*, Cambridge: Polity Press.
Fraser, N. (2016) *Fortunes of Feminism: From State-Managed Capitalism to Neoliberal Crisis*, London: Verso.
Fraser, N. and Honneth, A. (2003) *Redistribution or Recognition?: A Political-Philosophical Exchange*, London: Verso.
Freire, P. (2005) *Pedagogy of the Oppressed* (30th anniversary edition), London: Continuum.
Gilfillan, P. (2014) *A Sociological Phenomenology of Christian Redemption*, Guildford: Grosvenor House Publishing Ltd.
Harvey, D. (1996) *Justice, Nature and the Geography of Difference*, Oxford: Blackwell.
Hill Collins, P., and Bilge, S. (2016) *Intersectionality*, Malden: Polity Press.
Hoare, Q. and Smith, G.N. (1971) *Antonio Gramsci: Selections from Prison Notebooks*, London: Lawrence and Wishart.
Kane, L. (2001) *Popular Education and Social Change in Latin America*, London: Latin American Bureau.
Martin, I. (2005) 'Reflections on the diversions of diversity', *Paper presented at the 35th Annual SCUTREA Conference 3 July–7 July 2005, University of Sussex, England, UK*, www.leeds.ac.uk/educol/documents/141980.htm
McNally, D. (2017) 'Intersections and dialectics: critical reconstructions in social reproduction theory', in Bhattacharya, T. (ed) *Social Reproduction Theory: Remapping Class, Recentring Oppression*, London: Pluto Press, pp 94–111.
McNally, D. and Ferguson, S. (2015) 'Social reproduction beyond intersectionality: an interview', *Viewpoint*, 31 October. www.viewpointmag.com

Mitchell, J. (1971) *Women: The Longest Revolution, Women's Estate*, London: Penguin, pp 75–122.
Olsen, K. (ed) (2008) *Adding Insult to Injury: Nancy Fraser Debates her Critics*, London: Verso.
Yuval-Davis, N. (2007) 'Intersectionality, citizenship and contemporary politics of belonging', *Critical Review of International Social and Political Philosophy*, 10: 561–574.

CASE I.1

Mad People's History and Identity: A Mad Studies Critical Pedagogy Project

*Elaine Ballantyne, Kirsten Maclean, Shirley-anne Collie,
Liz Deeming and Esther Fraser*

Introduction

Mad People's History and Identity (MPHI) is a Mad Studies course delivered at Queen Margaret University (QMU), Edinburgh, Scotland. It aims to build a community of learners, activists and engaged academics in an educational space to analyse their lived experiences and critique the dominant 'psy' discourses. The course privileges the student's experiential knowledge of mental distress, psychiatrisation and oppression and the perspectives of Mad Studies activists and scholars. Beresford (2016) asserts that the experiential knowledge of madness has been historically marginalised and devalued by the dominant positivist 'expert', whose analysis reduces the credibility and legitimacy of survivor knowledge within research, policy, practice and learning. Mad people continue to challenge the subjugation and dismissal of their experiences, knowledge, perspectives and histories. This course aims to address the power and epistemic imbalance of the overwhelming majority of material about mental distress written by those who study and label them (Crepaz-Keay and Kalathil, 2013). This case study will provide an overview of the MPHI course, reflect on its history and development, explore its philosophical underpinnings, include the student voice and critique the opportunities and challenges of working with this public within a neoliberal university.

Mad people's history and identity

Dominant discourses of mental health are frequently depoliticised and mental illness is constructed as an individual problem, an individual medical issue to be dealt with privately. LeBlanc and Kinsella (2016) argue that alternative perspectives to the bio-medical model are excluded from the mainstream, in particular the narratives of those who identify as mad or having mental health issues. This results in testimonial and hermeneutic injustice. MPHI aims to subvert epistemic injustices and centralise counter-hegemonic views of madness, purposefully placing lived experience at the centre of the curriculum and locating this in a social movement history and context.

MPHI is a Mad Studies critical pedagogy project. The task of critical pedagogy is defined by a process in which individuals develop a deep awareness of the social structures that oppress them individually and collectively and result in resistance and counter-hegemony (Giroux, 1983: 111). MPHI aims to deploy counter-knowledge and subjugated knowledge as a strategy for contesting regimes of truth. Menzies et al (2013) assert: 'Mad Studies is an exercise in critical pedagogy – in the radical co-production, circulation, and consumption of knowledge' (14). MPHI also aims to increase the credibility of Mad knowledge by addressing the epistemic injustice experienced by the Mad community. MPHI is part of a wider project, 'Mad Studies'. Mad Studies is an emerging discipline within the UK (Beresford, 2014). With origins in Canada, it has been discussed and promoted by a number of scholars. LeFrançois et al (2013) provide a comprehensive definition:

> Mad Studies: an umbrella term that is used to embrace the body of knowledge that has emerged from psychiatric survivors, Mad-identified people, anti-psychiatry academics and activists, critical psychiatrists and radical therapists. This body of knowledge is wide-ranging and includes scholarship that is critical of the mental health system as well as radical and Mad activist scholarship. (337)

The reappropriation of the term 'mad' within the movement is an activist interruption in the discourse of mental illness (Church, 2013). In the context of this work, the subaltern counterpublic involved are people with lived experience of mental health issues. As a 'public', people with mental health issues are constructed as many things, mainly users of services, victims of stigma, a statistic, perpetrators of violence, poor souls, and welfare fraudsters. Mental health is understood through a myriad of lenses the dominant one of which is the hegemonic lens of psychiatric bio-medical expertise, history and knowledge. This dominant discourse argues that 'mentally ill' people are sick/ill and in need of treatment and management by those who know better. People's madness and distress is understood as unruly, over-emotional, manipulative and irrational (O'Donnell, 2007).

The MPHI course was launched in 2014 at QMU. MPHI was designed, delivered and evaluated in partnership with academics at QMU, CAPS Independent Advocacy and people with lived experience of mental health issues. The course is funded by NHS Lothian's Mental Health and Wellbeing programme. As a widening participation module, applicants require only the lived experience of mental health issues to attend. It aims to make the university a more accessible space for the students, who may have faced barriers to accessing formal education. It also attracts activists that are already involved with activism around mental health or the 'Mad movement'. The partnership has delivered courses in 2014, 2015, 2016 and 2018 with academic accreditation validated by the university. The flyer below was distributed throughout Scotland:

The curriculum covers the following weekly topics:

What is Mad People's History and Mad Studies?
Philosophy of the course
What is madness?
The history of confinement and treatment
Madness and intersectionality
Madness and activism

The students have an option to complete an assignment. Photovoice is used as the assignment to facilitate visual representations of individual and collective experiences of madness. Students are encouraged to take a photograph, analyse the image in relation their experiences and embed this critique within a theoretical framework. Photovoice is a qualitative methodology designed to engender greater engagement and participation by 'researched' communities (Wang et al, 1996). The course is reviewed annually in response to student evaluations. More recently a more in-depth exploration was carried out using participatory action research. The research explored the experiences and impacts of being part of the MPHI course and critiqued the

PUBLIC SOCIOLOGY AS EDUCATIONAL PRACTICE

Figure I.1.1: Mad People's History and Identity course flyer

MAD PEOPLE'S HISTORY & IDENTITY

A FREE course by, about and for people who have lived experience of mental health issues.

For more information please contact
Elaine Ballantyne
Telephone: 0131 474 0000
E Mail: EBallantyne@qmu.ac.uk

6 April – 11 May 2016

What is 'Mad People's History and Identity'?

Mad People's History & Identity is an exciting new 5 week course starting soon at Queen Margaret University and open to anyone who has lived experience of mental health issues.

We'll cover topics including:

What Is Mad People's History?
A History of Confinement and Treatments
What is Madness?
Madness, Gender and Sexuality
Activism

This course will give you the chance to:

- Learn more about mad people's history and identity in a relaxed and supportive setting
- See yourself and others as "experts by experience"
- Connect with advocacy and activist organisations, locally, nationally and internationally
- Develop confidence and skills to prepare you for further or higher education
- Complete an optional piece of writing to achieve 20 credits nationally recognised university credits (20 credits at SCQF level 7)
- Discuss entry into college and university

WHERE? Queen Margaret University

WHEN? Wednesdays from 10.15am to 3.15pm, 6 April – 11 May 2016.

HOW MUCH? FREE

HOW DO I FIND OUT MORE AND APPLY? Contact module coordinator Elaine Ballantyne:

EBallantyne@qmu.ac.uk
0131 474 0000 (ask for Elaine Ballantyne when prompted)

This project is a partnership between Queen Margaret University, CAPS Independent Advocacy and NHS Lothian Mental Health and Wellbeing Programme.

Source: authors' own

relationship between critical education, activism and emancipation. The research was co-produced by former students and the partners of the course.

The student perspectives of the course highlighted the importance of: gaining knowledge, building social connections and activism.

> The course had a very positive impact on me and has boosted my confidence and I have regained my thirst for knowledge. I found doing the essay cathartic, and liberating. I found that I was beginning to choose my identity for myself. I now believe that madness is not just a psychological or psychiatric issue but a sociological issue as well. I made new friends and came to realise that I wasn't alone in my suffering. I have reclaimed the word mad and see myself as a mad person and student. I came to realise that the narratives of mad people are important to the study of madness. (Liz)

> On the flyer for the MPHI was that we are 'experts by experience'. This for me was the first and most positive thing I'd heard/felt about my own mental health. Learning the true history of Madness from the perspective of the mad person rather than the medical folk was and is truly liberating. Also the kudos of being at university was good even although a bit daunting. I made new friends from class and attended the course the following year as a supportive friend. I have gone on to attend Mad Studies conferences, a PAR research course in Durham then was part of the Mad Studies PAR research team. I feel I've become a low key activist of sorts. (Esther)

> I went on the mad studies course in 2015 at QMU, and it's changed my life. I was very nervous on my first day, but I was soon at ease, and very passionate about the work. It is open for people with lived experience and it was free. I felt proud I was at university helping myself learn more knowledge and contributing with other students. I've gone on to do public sociology and have just finished my exam. I've been involved with various projects on mental health awareness. I feel stronger within myself. (Shirley-anne)

MPHI course was inspired by a project that grew out of the mental health service user movement in Lothian, Oor Mad History

(OMH) (CAPS, 2010), a community history project based at CAPS Independent Advocacy. OMH was set up to record and promote the history of collective advocacy or activism by people with mental health issues. People involved in collective advocacy in Lothian had begun to feel disheartened in the early 2000s. Rather than developing their own campaigns or agendas, they found they were continually responding to NHS or local authority consultations and what mattered to them as a collective was slipping off the end of the page. There was a sense that key people were losing touch with the movement or passing away. There was a need to do something about recording this collective history before it was lost. Another inspiration for OMH was the work of David Reville and Kathryn Church at Ryerson University in Toronto, Canada where they had developed a course called 'Mad People's History' within the Disability Studies department. Mad People's History (MPH) is defined by Church: 'The discourse of MPH challenges the dominant psychiatric paradigm by placing the experience of people with mental health issues or who have been labelled Mad at the centre of the curriculum and knowledge formation' (Church, 2015: 265)

Initially the aim of OMH was to gather together a paper-based archive and to establish an oral history project. Oral history has the power to revitalise mental health activism, and a way for marginalised groups to reclaim and tell their own stories and, in so doing, situate themselves as active agents of change rather than simply passive receivers of services (O'Donnell, 2007). OMH held an event and exhibition at QMU and it was there that links with academics within the university were made and plans to develop a MPH course there began.

Mad Studies

Costa (2014) reinforces the centrality of mad people within Mad Studies:

> Mad Studies is an area of education, scholarship, and analysis about the experiences, history, culture, political organising, narratives, writings and most importantly, of the PEOPLE who identify as: mad; psychiatric survivors; consumers; service users; mentally ill; patients, neuro-diverse; inmates; disabled. (Costa, 2014: 4)

Beresford (2015) frames Mad Studies as a hopeful alternative, as a chance to build a body of knowledge that challenges the dominant medical model: 'Mad Studies offers us a rallying cry and a rallying point to inspire and energise' (259). Menzies et al (2013) introduce Mad Studies as a movement, an identity, a stance, an act of resistance, a theoretical approach and a burgeoning field of study. Mad Studies and MPH aim for a liberatory and emancipatory pedagogy, theory and praxis (Freire, 1972). Praxis is defined by Freire (1972: 99) as: 'reflection and action upon the world in order to transform it'. Freire asserts that praxis is not only cerebral but it involves action and reflection. The philosophy of this educational Mad Studies project is underpinned by Freire's critical pedagogy with an emphasis on praxis. Mad Studies is relevant to a range of differing yet interconnected social movements and a range of academic disciplines, stressing the importance of an intersectional analysis and resistance to shared experiences of oppressions. Mad Studies has a role to play in building alliances with other social movements including the women's, disability, civil rights and LGBT movements.

Mad Studies is one discourse challenging the exclusion of mad people's experiences and voices and creating an ongoing, living history from a lived experience perspective. MPHI offers a space to develop the expert and experiential knowledge of people with experience of mental health issues or mad identified people, through a process of designing and participating in education that generates and centres survivor knowledge, promotes survivor voices and creates both a visual and written history of the experiences and impacts of being involved in MPHI.

Mad people's history and identity within the university

The processes and outcomes of engaged scholarship have a duty to move beyond and outside academic discourse, to work in solidarity with communities or groups that are treated unfairly in the social world (Angrosino and Rosenberg, 2011; Lincoln, Lynham and Guba, 2011).

However, the university setting is not unproblematic and Mad scholars and activists have recently critiqued the relationship of Mad Studies within academia. Russo and Beresford (2014: 154) acknowledge valuable accomplishments of non-survivor academics and stress the difference between those: 'who work with us – and not on us – is rooted in very different premises and motive'. Mad scholars also explore new complexities for the Mad knowledge and narratives within academia. Having initially struggled for inclusion and recognition, there is concern to protect such narratives from colonisation and control taken from their authors by academics. Russo and Beresford

(2014) assert that the problems of exclusion and colonisation of mad people's knowledge must be raised and the question is 'How can academia be opened up to the contribution of 'outsider' perspectives and ensure that the work towards epistemic justice is undertaken in equal partnership?'(156)

This raises questions about the role and motivations of academics working with social movements and their publics. Cresswell and Spandler (2012: 15) focus on the role of academic allies in the psychiatric survivor movement and debate the definition of the engaged academic. The debates within the literature raise key concerns of whether Mad Studies can be protected from being undermined, invalidated and subverted within academia and the role of the engaged academic in supporting and being an ally to the movement. Kleidman (2006) asserts that this requires the creation of relationships and cultures that support agitational conversations between scholars and activists necessary to future directed collective partnerships.

However, Scandrett and Ballantyne (2019) assert that this is not insurmountable to effectively value, include and promote experiential knowledge to undermine a neoliberal academic context. Nevertheless, they also acknowledge this is associated with risk. In relation to the MPHI course, they assert:

> It has raised some important questions about what constitutes a mad positive university, one which honours and legitimates hitherto silenced voices and privileges criteria of inclusion and recognition over selection and competition. In its small way MPHI provides seeds of what might undermine the neoliberal university, especially through the public health recognition in the receipt of NHS funding. As such, however, it is also vulnerable to the progressive attack of neoliberalism in both universities and the health service, subject to severe austerity cuts and increasing marketisation. (Scandrett and Ballantyne, 2019: 11)

Conclusion

Public sociology creates a space where practices (of scholars and activists) and publics (subaltern counter publics) can draw on sociological resources critically and dialogically. Mad people's history is an exercise in critical pedagogy to promote mad peoples' counter-narratives. It shares the aims of public sociology to work with activists and publics to engage in resistance, resilience, and building alternatives to the oppression, exploitation and injustices experienced by marginalised communities, including mad people.

Within a neoliberal climate, collectivism and resistance have never been more critical and, at the same time, never so difficult to achieve. What role can academia play in supporting social movement learning, facilitating counter-hegemonic narratives of madness and distress within the university? A space where publics can come together, engage with alternative views, begin to ask questions of the dominant discourse? And what role can this work play in individual and collective identity making and the developing of critical and political agency? People who have experience of madness and distress can create their own discourses, their own stories and promote their own alternatives. Social movements have historically used counter-hegemonic narratives as an integral part of their organising, so creating new narratives and disrupting the dominant one can bolster individual and collective power and potentially lead to political and social change.

If MPHI is to stay relevant it must relate to the everyday practicalities of human life and struggle. To practise Mad Studies means

> engaging our current world of suffering and injustice and seeking to change it, while simultaneously ... dreaming of a society brave and moral enough to eschew the whole paradigm of mental health and illness, replacing it with the creation of real community and real help. (Menzies et al, 2013: 18)

Ultimately Mad Studies is not just about the world of psychiatry or mental health; the stakes are higher, 'for to study madness is to probe at the very foundations of our claims to be human' (Menzies et al, 2013: 21). MPHI offers a space where people can come together in challenging times to find human connection, solidarity, possibility, hope and emancipation.

References

Angrosino, M. and Rosenberg, J. (2011) 'Observations on observation: continuities and challenges', in Denzin, N.K. and Lincoln, Y.S. (eds) *The Sage Handbook of Qualitative Research*, Thousand Oaks, CA: Sage, pp 467–478.

Beresford, P. (2013) 'Foreword', in Lefrançois, B.A., Menzies, R., and Reaume, J. (eds) *Mad Matters: A Critical Reader in Canadian Mad Studies*, Toronto: Canadian Scholars' Press Inc, pp ix–xii.

Beresford, P. (2014) 'Mad Studies is an idea that is new to the UK, but one that offers fresh hope of improving the lives of people experiencing distress, argues Professor Peter Beresford', *Mental Health Today*, Nov/Dec: 7.

Beresford, P. (2015) 'Distress and disability: not you, not me, but us?', in Spandler, H., Anderson, J. and Sapey, B. (eds) *Madness, Distress and the Politics of Disablement*, University of Bristol: Policy Press, pp 245–259.

Beresford, P. (2016) 'The role of survivor knowledge in creating alternatives to psychiatry', in Russo, J. and Sweeney, A. (eds) *Searching for a Rose Garden: Challenging Psychiatry, Fostering Mad Studies*, Monmouth: PCCS Books, pp 25–35.

Beresford, P. and Russo, J. (2016) 'Supporting the sustainability of Mad Studies and preventing its co-option', *Disability & Society*, 31(2): 270–274.

Church, K. (2013) *Four Burning Questions with Kathryn Church, Director of the School of Disability Studies at Ryerson University. McGill Reporter*, https://reporter.mcgill.ca/four-burning-questions-with-kathryn-church-director-of-the-school-of-disability-studies-at-ryerson-university/

Church, K. (2015) "It's complicated': Blending disability and Mad Studies in the corporatizing university', in Spandler, H., Anderson, J. and Sapey, B. (eds) *Madness, Distress and the Politics of Disablement*, University of Bristol: Policy Press, pp 261–270.

Costa, L. (2014) 'Mad Studies: what is it, and why you should care?', *Bulletin*, 518: 1–15.

Crepaz-Keay, D. and Kalathil, J. (2013) *Personal Narratives of Madness: Introduction* (companion website for Fulford et al [2013] *The Oxford Handbook of Philosophy and Psychiatry*), http://global.oup.com/booksites/content/9780199579563/narratives

Cresswell, M. and Spandler, H. (2012) 'The engaged academic: academic intellectuals and the psychiatric survivors movement', *Social Movement Studies: Journal of Social, Cultural and Political Protest*, 1(17): 1–17.

Freire, P. (1972) *Education for Critical Consciousness*, New York: Seabury Press.

Giroux, H. (1983) *Theory and Resistance in Education*, Westport, CT: Bergin and Garvey Press.

Kleidman, R. (2006) 'Public sociology, engaged scholarship, and community organizing', *Journal of Applied Sociology*, 23(1), Special Joint Issue with *Sociological Practice* (Spring 2006): 68–82.

Leblanc, S., and Kinsella, E.A. (2016) 'Toward epistemic justice: a critically reflexive examination of 'sanism' and implications for knowledge generation', *Studies in Social Justice*, 10(1): 59–78.

Le François, B.A., Menzies, R. and Reaume, G. (2013) *Mad Matters: A Critical Reader in Canadian Mad Studies*, Toronto: Canadian Scholars' Press.

Lincoln, Y.S., Lynham, S.A. and Guba, E.G. (2011) 'Paradigmatic controversies, contradictions, and emerging confluences', in Denzin, N.K. and Lincoln, Y.S. (eds) *The Sage Handbook of Qualitative Research* (4th edn), Thousand Oaks, CA: Sage, pp 97–128.

O'Donnell, A. (2007) *Mad People's History: The Potential Use of Oral History by a Collective Advocacy Group*, Edinburgh University (unpublished MSc thesis).

Menzies, R., LeFrançois, B.A. and Reume, G. (2013) 'Introducing Mad Studies', in LeFrançois, B.A., Menzies, R. and Reaume, G. (eds) *Mad Matters: A Critical Reader in Canadian Mad Studies*, Toronto: Canadian Scholars' Press, pp 1–22.

Russo, J. and Beresford, P. (2014) 'Between exclusion and colonisation: seeking a place for mad people's knowledge in academia', *Disability & Society*, 30(1): 153–157.

Scandrett, E. and Ballantyne, E. (2019) 'Public sociology and social movements: incorporation or a war of position?', in Breeze, M., Costa, C. and Taylor, Y. (eds) *Time and Space in the Neoliberal University*, Basingstoke: Palgrave Macmillan, pp 169–190.

Wang, C., Burris, M. and Xiang, Y. (1996) 'Chinese village women as visual anthropologists: a participatory approach to reaching policymakers', *Social Science and Medicine*, 42, 1391–1400.

CASE I.2

'Seeing Things Differently': Gender Justice and Counter-Hegemony in Higher Education

Lesley Orr and Nel Whiting

Introduction

This chapter is rooted in the reflexive experience of feminists in Scotland struggling for gender justice – particularly the movement to resist and end men's violence against women (VAW). Our case study focuses on a course 'Gender Justice and Violence: Feminist Approaches' (GJV), the fruit of an ongoing partnership between Scottish Women's Aid (SWA) and Queen Margaret University (QMU). Offered every year since 2007, the course engages with debates concerning public policy, professional practice and political activism – particularly in relation to gender-based violence and abuse. The module teaching sessions bring together practitioners and activists (who register as associate students at QMU) alongside full-time sociology students. This enables a challenging process of mutual learning which highlights both the tensions and the transformative potential of grounding social theory in the sometimes divergent standpoints of these overlapping groups. The course is delivered by, and open to, both women and men. The curriculum draws on the struggles of the women's movement and of pro-feminist men, and utilises the work of engaged feminist scholars across a range of academic disciplines, including history, philosophy, criminology and gender studies, as well as sociology. Its presence demands that the practice of activists and the movements which have driven social change are taken seriously within this higher education institution, and that the rigorous analysis of feminist scholars and their methodological approaches becomes a resource for those working in the field. As such, the provision of this course and its impact is, we argue, a counter-hegemonic contribution to gender justice in neoliberal higher education.

The significance of the QMU/SWA collaborative partnership is here located in the wider social and political context of feminist struggles since the 1970s, and now in post-devolution Scotland – the context in which the co-authors have engaged in education, training and activism. The women's liberation movement of the 1970s was the catalyst for naming domestic abuse as a social problem and developing a structural analysis of gender inequality as both cause and consequence of men's violence against women (Browne, 2014; Scottish Women's Aid, 2018) Women's Aid (WA) emerged as the cutting edge of that movement, not only developing practical support services, but also at the forefront of struggles for justice and rights, contesting prevailing theories (and 'common sense') which purported to 'explain' domestic abuse, and insisting on analysis grounded in understanding the gendered structure of patriarchy. For over 40 years, SWA (and the wider anti-VAW movement) has developed 'really useful knowledge' (Johnson, 1976; Scandrett et al, 2010) and educational practices: drawing upon, provoking and participating as partners with scholar-activists oriented towards social change. This feminist movement, a subaltern counter-public (Fraser, 1990), has created parallel space for generating a public sociology of alternative voices, theories and analyses, feeding directly into policy and legislation.

Challenging violence against women: the Scottish context

The centrality of education and public sociology to the movement against VAW in Scotland is best understood in the historical context of the feminist movement. A classic feminist issue, the naming, analysis and elimination of VAW was a central pillar of the (so-called) second wave women's liberation movement in Britain. Women subjected by their husbands/partners to threats, intimidation, humiliation and violence had mostly been expected to put up and shut up. 'You've made your bed ... don't wash dirty linen in public ... what goes on behind your front door is nobody else's business.' Excessive violence was put down to men who were drunk or feckless (and invariably working class) brutes, the women they lived with were habitually blamed for 'making them do it': characterised as bad, mad or both. Such tropes were deeply embedded as 'everyday knowledge' about marriage: difficult to challenge, not least because the power interests it serves were masked behind what was regarded as 'normal'. But the consciousness-raising work of women's liberation groups in the early 1970s generated a radically different understanding, rooted in women's own experiences and standpoints. The personal became political as they broke the silence of centuries (Dobash and Dobash, 1992). The origins of SWA lie in this movement for women's liberation. The desire among some feminists for practical engagement that would contribute to personal and social change found a focus in activities to address wife battering (later referred to as domestic violence and/or abuse), a pervasive reality largely hidden from public attention, legitimised and normalised by prevailing legal, religious and cultural frameworks.

The movement developed an analysis of domestic violence as a heavily gendered pattern of coercive controlling behaviour – a constellation of abuse (Dobash and Dobash, 2004) which both reflected and served to consolidate male privilege and power: socially structured in the private realm of intimacy, marriage and family, and also in public institutions. This contested the prevailing explanations which pathologised or excused individual men, blamed women, or located the problem in family systems, generational cycles of violence, or subcultures of violence, class and alcohol. And it located domestic abuse on a complex continuum of gendered violations experienced by girls and women in all domains and across the life course as cause and consequence of inequality. Since the 1970s SWA has contributed in significant ways to the shaping of social policy and to changes in the wider political and cultural environment of Scotland (Mackay, 2010; Lombard and Whiting, 2016).

The development of WA as a pioneering network of local service providers – offering refuge, advocacy and support to women, children and young people – was inseparable from its distinctive feminist ethos, collective organisational structure and governance. It began as an oppositional movement with an explicit commitment to radical social change and, as such, local groups often encountered hostility and suspicion. Interviewed for the 40th anniversary oral history project Speaking Out: Recalling Women's Aid in Scotland, an early activist recalled that aggressive reactions were common when she went out to give talks: 'because what we were saying was rocking the status quo and there were a lot of people who had a lot to gain by pretending that it didn't happen or blaming the women themselves for what was going on' (Scottish Women's Aid, 2018). Refuges and

WA collectives were laboratories for women living in ways that were certainly regarded as 'rocking the status quo'. Personal experience and observation of women's lives transformed by the feminist ethos of resistance and autonomy gave strategic and campaigning purchase to struggles with the Establishment – the local state and its agencies; the legal framework; academic and 'expert' consensus; media, community and cultural institutions. Although some WA activists adopted a radical separatist, anti-state position, others were socialist feminists who did not simply reject state institutions, but wanted to infuse and transform them into effective agents for gender and social justice. In practice, each WA group had no choice but to negotiate with councillors, social workers, housing officials, the police, the media and local communities – and, importantly, with Scots law and its legislators. In the process they informed, educated and began to change the narrative around domestic violence. They were engaging in a war of position.

SWA (established in 1976 to undertake national coordinating, campaigning, policy and educational work) was from the outset committed to challenging both the ideological and structural bases of patriarchy, as these were manifested in dominant discourses and everyday practices (Dobash and Dobash, 1992). Because these emerging feminist ideas, campaigns and services were so innovative, the shared process of learning was intense. Education and training have always been central to the organisation's values, orientation and strategy. SWA pedagogy and practice is grounded in the 'really useful knowledge' generated by thousands of women claiming their voices and rights – not least to become authors and interpreters of their own lives. Their experiences, and the movement's engagement in dialogical interrogation of meanings and patterns as revealed through gender lenses, have been central to the intellectual task of reframing and theorising domestic abuse. Collaboration with academics has been vital: in the 1970s, a team of young sociologists at Stirling University conducted groundbreaking work, based on a historical overview of marriage as social institution, extended interviews with women in refuges, and police records. Published as 'Violence against wives: a case against the patriarchy' (Dobash and Dobash, 1979), it was the first major piece of research on domestic abuse undertaken in the UK and confronted the myths about 'wife battering' head on. Rebecca and Russell Dobash argued that elimination of domestic abuse required a fundamental transformation in societal and economic structures of oppression: 'The problem lies in the domination of women. The answer lies in the struggle against it' (Dobash and Dobash, 1979: 243).

The involvement of politically engaged feminist action-researchers, including the Dobashes, Liz Kelly (who developed the influential concept of a continuum of sexual violence) (1988), Evan Stark (2007) and more recently a new generation of productive Scotland-based academics (some of whom are course alumnae) has been profoundly important in that struggle (for example Lombard and McMillan, 2013; Scottish GBV Research Network, 2018). Their pioneering research but also the practice of alliance building and nurturing of scholar-activists have been formative in shaping the purpose and content of the GJV module. Initially those who were directly involved in WA were not academics and, likewise, the Dobashes did not undertake their research with a feminist hypothesis – but many activists were engaging with literature and developing the analysis in situ, and some moved from WA into academia (Fran Wasoff, Esther Breitenbach etc) while the Stirling research team became overtly feminist and engaged. There has been much toing and froing and mutual influence between activism and academia over the years, which has become more systematised in the early twenty-first century.

It is important also to note the changing political context. During the bleak Thatcher years, women in Scotland suffered a double dose of democratic deficit. The so-called doomsday scenario meant that from 1979 to 1997, under the UK's 'first past the post' voting system, Scotland (which throughout the period, and increasingly at each general election, returned a Labour majority) was repeatedly subjected to a Westminster Conservative government throughout the UK that it did not elect. But it was also true that the majority of Scots – women – were almost entirely invisible in parliamentary representative politics. In 1987, the 72 Scottish constituencies returned ten Conservative MPs, but only three women. This had a galvanising impact on the Scottish women's movement at a time when its English equivalent was fragmenting (Breitenbach and Mackay, 1996). Feminists increasingly got involved in trade unionism, civil society organisations and party politics, arguably adopting a more 'realistic' and less 'revolutionary' orientation. From the 1980s, municipal feminist political space was being carved out in local authority women's committees and units. The 1992 Edinburgh Council Zero Tolerance (ZT) Campaign was a strikingly effective Gramscian mobilisation of organic intellectuals and women's 'good sense' for a high-profile feminist public campaign to name and tackle men's violence against women. Rooted in Kelly's (1988) analysis of the continuum of violence as structural power, it set out to 'build a new set of truths': to challenge the dominant discourse and government policy that it was women who had to alter their behaviour in response to fear, threat and harm caused by men; to develop strategic responses of provision, protection and prevention (the three Ps of ZT); and to tackle root causes and the wider social context of VAW and gender inequality. ZT had a high immediate impact, but was both enabled by, and also consolidated, women's networks and alliances during the pre-devolution constitutional debate. The convergence of feminists working inside and outwith the state coalesced around the demand for equal representation, but lobbied hard for a Scottish parliament to embody a new, more democratic and participatory style of politics. Seizing the opportunity to 'get in on the ground floor', feminists gained leverage for the effective intervention of theorising, analysis and activism in the 'new politics' of Scotland (Mackay 1996).

This was most salient in getting a gendered analysis of domestic abuse and violence against women embedded in the work of the Scottish Executive Government from 2007. SWA, given due recognition as the leading source of knowledge and practice-based expertise, played a key role in this process. Since the advent of the Scottish Parliament, there has been marked divergence from Westminster policy, which has taken a supposedly 'gender-neutral' approach to domestic abuse.

In 2000 the Scottish Executive published 'The National Strategy to Address Domestic Abuse in Scotland', recognising 'a need to challenge and change attitudes which perpetuate domestic abuse, which cannot be tackled effectively without education and training' (Scottish Executive, 2000: 13). This was followed in 2004 by the National Training Strategy (NTS), which aimed to ensure 'that all workers who come into contact with women, children and young people who have experienced domestic abuse, and men who have used violence, have the knowledge, understanding and skills required' (Scottish Executive, 2004: 4). In 2009 the strategic focus broadened to incorporate all forms of VAW (underpinned by acknowledgement that these are both cause and consequence of gender inequality) and, through its various iterations, has continued to have a strong educational component. As part of the commitment to NTS, funds were allocated to create multi-agency training consortia in each health board area to ensure that staff could access training. One of two staff appointed by the Scottish Government to coordinate the NTS (Lesley Orr) was based at SWA 2005–2009 in acknowledgement of the organisation's lead role in addressing domestic abuse.

Scottish Women's Aid and Education for Gender Justice

SWA's training work (led and undertaken for 16 years by Nel Whiting) has various focuses: to provide frontline staff with an understanding of the dynamics of domestic abuse to enable them to provide a more effective service to those experiencing it; to provide policy makers and practitioners with in-depth understanding of the gendered legacy and present-day constructs that have led to and maintain women's inequality to enable them to make strategic or practice decisions that sets domestic abuse within a gendered context; to act as a bridge between theory and academic research and practice. Prior to the development of the GJV course this work was delivered in two main ways: (1) a nationally advertised training programme focusing on various manifestations of domestic abuse, delivered in training, seminar or study day formats. The training programme sought to make connections between current theory and research and practice responses; (2) by responding to local or sector-specific needs by developing tailored training in consultation with service providers. This work includes providing regular lectures at the Scottish Police College, the Scottish Prosecution College and at the Judicial Institute for Scotland.

The NTS placement at SWA, allied with the organisation's ongoing commitment to provide high quality training on domestic abuse and to support the implementation of the training strategy, led to the development by the authors of a series of 'study days' offered to workers addressing gendered violence in different statutory and voluntary organisations. They were aimed particularly at those (usually busy practitioners themselves but champions of the issue) who were engaged in delivering VAW training through the local training consortia. We recognised the wealth of practical experience in addressing issues of violence against women, but workers told us what they felt would be needed to develop their skills and understanding. They wanted to learn about theories and academic approaches to framing the issues; they looked for evidence-based knowledge to support their recognition of the gendered nature of the problems they were addressing, and therefore the work they were doing. They wanted to be equipped to challenge those people, sectors and agencies, including project funders, who disputed that VAW is gendered. They knew the importance of making connections across the continuum of VAW (Kelly, 1988; Boyle, 2019), when operating in a policy environment that placed different forms and domains of VAW (for example domestic abuse, sexual violence, commercial sexual exploitation) in separate silos, and funded responses accordingly. They needed conceptual tools to explain how this was underpinned by a patriarchal system that provided a conducive context for multiple forms of VAW, interlinked in complex ways in women's lives.

The guiding principle of the study days (and indeed of SWA training in general) was that practitioners needed skills for safe practice and often desired a robust theoretical knowledge of issues but did not have the time to undertake the research and reading as they were too busy providing direct support services. Our role was therefore to act as a bridge between theory and practice, to undertake and assess relevant research, and to create learning opportunities that provided both input and reflective space to engage with theoretical concepts. We devised a series of study days on topics requested by colleagues in the sector: gender and the gendered analysis of VAW; 'what about the men?'; the continuum of VAW; intersectionality and VAW; LGBT people and domestic abuse; understanding commercial sexual exploitation as VAW. The study days proved to be enormously popular – in take up but also for building self-efficacy in relation to training provision, campaigning and lobbying work, and enabling practitioners to develop the arguments and confidence they needed to defend services. The study days were the cradle in which the GJV course was nurtured.

Gender Justice and Violence: Feminist Approaches

Rooted in the challenges training consortia across Scotland faced in facilitating greater understanding and commitment to addressing VAW in diverse situations, and stimulated particularly by the study days, we identified a widespread desire for innovative research-based learning opportunities at tertiary level, to encourage the integration of feminist social theory, reflective practice and action for change. A validated course would also offer relevant accreditation for workers and activists with a wealth of practical experience, many of whom had not previously accessed higher education.

In seeking an academic partner for the initiative, QMU seemed an obvious choice for many reasons. Originally established as the Edinburgh School of Cookery in 1875, its founders were prominent in the nineteenth century women's movement as campaigners for female vocational education and career opportunities. As a new university, QMU's declared mission was to foster innovation, participation and lifelong learning, and sociology lecturer Eurig Scandrett (already known to us as an environmental activist and committed pro-feminist) was developing the university's programme in social justice and public sociology, building on work in collaboration with community-based and campaigning non-governmental organisations. This context was important, because our intention was to conceptualise and frame VAW as a gendered justice issue requiring radical societal structural change, not (as other nevertheless useful higher education courses have done) as a women's safety, public health or criminal justice matter:

A module that takes women's struggles against men's violence as its central problematic illuminates the wider aspects of gender justice in its historical and political context. It therefore provides an effective mechanism for introducing analyses of gender justice in the context of claims for social justice. Intellectually and pedagogically, SWA's standpoint as an expressly feminist movement is a welcome contribution to an engaged academic programme in social justice (Orr, Scandrett and Whiting, 2013).

The course was developed and validated in 2007, with teaching reflecting the principles of active, collaborative and experiential learning. The aims are:

- to introduce an overview of gender-based violence as global and social injustice;
- to explore and critically examine explanatory frameworks for understanding male VAW;
- to explore and critically examine the links between theory and practice in tackling male VAW;
- to provide a foundation for critical reflection and engaged action in commitment to gender justice.

Course content is structured around interrogation of central themes: gender, violence, inequality, masculinity, justice, power, resistance and change. The issues are contextualised historically, but also connected directly to the experiences and struggles of particular oppressed 'publics' in relation to domestic abuse, rape, prostitution, pornography, trafficking and commercial sexual exploitation, honour-based violence and female genital mutilation (FGM). Key conceptual frameworks and theorists include hegemony, masculinity, intersectionality (Gramsci, Connell, Crenshaw); feminist analyses of coercive control and the constellation of abuse (Stark, Johnson, Dobashes et al); discourse (Butler, Foucault et al); continuum of violence (Kelly et al); social movements, and socialist feminist politics of justice (Fraser). Locating the curriculum in feminist analyses can encounter challenges from students with divergent perspectives from within or outwith feminism. Several 'contested issues' are addressed directly – in particular prostitution and pornography – in which a feminist analysis is emphasised and students encouraged to engage with these arguments in forming their views.

Core teaching is by the three main tutors, with contributions over the years from others including FGM survivors and activists (former/current QMU masters students) and two postgraduate students who have themselves been course participants. Importantly, students are encouraged to share their own knowledge and experiences; to listen and work with one another in discussions and small group presentations. But also, respectfully, to challenge and wrestle with conflicting views and tensions. The full-time students are on average younger and embark on the module in the final year of their degree programme, so they are at home with one another, with academic study and with the institution. But the associate and full-time students do not constitute clearly defined blocs. There are different dynamics of power and relationship in each module cohort. Many, but not all associate students are graduates, often already familiar with and utilising relevant research in their work contexts. Some of the full-time students have worked or are volunteering in community projects, or are activists in their own right. The everyday circumstances and lived realities of both full-time and associate students are likewise not clearly differentiated – they are often dealing simultaneously with studies, employment (whether part-time or full-time), negotiating the complex demands of parenthood, relationships and financial precarity in the current austerity environment. They represent a range of subject positions and identities, shaped by the intersections of gender, sexuality, class, ethnicity, ability and so on, which largely constitute the subject matter under consideration. Some, inevitably, have personal experience of gender-based violence (GBV). The classroom becomes a dynamic space for highlighting and interrogating the gendered dimensions of their experiences – within and beyond the university. Central to our pedagogy has been critical and reflexive mutual learning and encouraging students to use theoretical and conceptual tools for challenging the 'common sense' of dominant individualist neoliberal discourses (for example on pornography and prostitution) with structural and intersectional feminist analyses. Inevitably flashpoints and heated emotions may come to the surface, but student evaluations and our own observations over the years indicate that the module is experienced as largely productive, enlightening and often transformative for participants.

'Seeing things differently': Students reflect on the course as catalyst for learning and change

> I would say this course launched a life time of passion and activism in gender equality and justice. (Former student)

Burawoy argues that 'students are our first public for they carry sociology into all walks of life' (Burawoy, 2005). The truth of that observation has been evident in the GJV course, especially since our students, conversely, carry all walks of life into the sociology classroom. Over the years, hundreds of women and men have taken the module. The students, as activists and engaged scholars, constitute a subaltern counterpublic that generates its own intellectuals in coherent form, which incorporates rational critique and emotional passion (see provocation). Evaluations, anecdotal evidence and ongoing contact – particularly with those who work in the Scottish VAW sector – bear witness to the significant impact the course has made to lives as activists, workers, academics.

One former full-time student, for example, now works for a WA group providing support to children and young people affected by domestic abuse. She was involved in a participation project with young survivors coordinated by SWA and the office of the Children and Young People's Commissioner Scotland, and spoke at the SWA annual conference.

A midwife of 22 years stated 'the course gave me a voice to tackle subject matter that is not easy to discuss. It gave me the confidence to go to my manager and say "this isn't good enough, it needs to change".' The session described by the student as 'a real light bulb moment' was about FGM. After the course she approached her clinical manager as she was angry that 'the system' was letting down women who had undergone FGM. She worked with her manager to find a way to improve the situation. She is now the specialist midwife – gender based violence and female genital mutilation lead midwife for her health authority (a position that previously did not exist). She has spoken at conferences and seminars both locally and nationally, been a member of the Scottish Government group that has formulated the national action plan on FGM, and was part of the working group that formulated the interagency guidelines on FGM.

For another participant who worked at a local rape crisis centre, the course was the impetus for a shift in direction:

> Although I took part in the QMU/SWA gender justice course in 2007 the impact of its content has stayed with

me to this day. I still have my course notes and reader which I refer to regularly. Without wanting to sound overly dramatic I feel the course had a life changing impact on me personally and professionally. The course transformed my understanding of the dynamics involved in gender-based violence (GBV) and helped me recognise GBV as an international phenomenon. Having this new perspective opened my eyes dramatically, it improved my understanding of the context in which women experience intimate violence and thereby had an immediate and positive effect on my support work. It contextualised the many experiences of GBV I have had personally throughout my life and transformed my standpoint from one of acceptance and inevitability that such things would happen to me and other women, to one of empowerment and understanding that GBV is not acceptable and can and should be challenged. Although I had been working in the field for several years, I would say this course launched a lifetime of passion and activism in gender equality and justice. It has enabled me to transform my own life and pursue a career in academia researching GBV. In turn I hope my research will contribute to transforming the lives of other women for many years to come, a legacy which can be credited directly to the course. In short, this course has been inspirational.

Other students attest to the impact in their personal and working lives:

> It increased my confidence around framing the issues theoretically – linked feminist passion with theoretical analysis. The course has reinforced my feminism and revealed a strong radical pulse!

> It has been crucial, and an understanding of these issues has ramifications for every other struggle – class, race etc. Concepts such as hegemony and models for analysis open up so much.

> Gender analysis of social norms, arrangements and roles will help in my work with perpetrators.

> Within my work as a practitioner nurse in HMP [Her Majesty's Prison] Edinburgh the course has given me

confidence and understanding to open up the subject of gender justice, gender inequality and the impact of domestic violence with colleagues and managers. Working in a male dominated workplace the course has highlighted the need to correct colleagues who display misogyny (not only through sexism but also homophobia and transphobia). It has given me even more confidence to open up the subject of sexual and domestic abuse with female prisoners and because of a wider understanding of the sometimes complex issues within relationships overshadowed by domestic abuse, I feel my patients feel safe discussing these issues with me, and understood.

New confidence to challenge managers and others with authority and privilege, to open up contentious subjects, to articulate alternative analyses, to demand changes in practice and attitudes: these are important ways that course participants talk about taking control of knowledge and using it to shift power relations in favour of those who experience exploitation or oppression in given contexts. While these accounts reflect primarily on gendered dynamics operational at mundane and intermediate levels of institutions (see Hearn and Parkin, 2001), the module has also helped facilitate naming, resisting and collective action to tackle structural violations – not least by consolidating feminist understanding and solidarity in the Scottish anti-VAW movement, and at key sites of struggle.

References

Boyle, K. (2019) 'What's in a name? Theorising the inter-relationships of gender and violence', *Feminist Theory*, 20: 1.

Breitenbach, E. and Mackay, F. (2010) 'Feminist politics in scotland from the 1970s to 2000s: engaging with the changing state', in Breitenbach, E. and Thane, P. (eds) *Women and Citizenship in Britain and Ireland in the 20th Century: What Difference did the Vote Make?*, London: Continuum, pp 153–169.

Browne, S. (2014) *The Women's Liberation Movement in Scotland*, Manchester: Manchester University Press.

Buroway, M. (2005) '2004 Presidential Address: For public sociology', *American Sociological Review*, 70/1: 4-28.

Dobash, R.E. and Dobash, R. (1979) *Violence Against Wives: A Case Against the Patriarchy*, New York: Free Press.

Dobash, R.E. and Dobash, R. (1992) *Women, Violence and Social Change*, London: Routledge.

Dobash, R.E. and Dobash, R. (2004) 'Women's violence to men in intimate relationships: working on a puzzle', *British Journal of Criminology*, 44/3: 324–349.

Fraser, N. (1990) 'Rethinking the public sphere: a contribution to the critique of actually existing democracy', *Social Text*, 25/26: 56–80.

Hearn, J. and Parkin, W. (2001) *Gender, Sexuality and Violence in Organisations*, London: Sage.

Johnson, R. (1976) '"Really Useful Knowledge": Radical education and working-class culture 1790–1848', in Clarke, J., Critcher, C. and Johnson, R. (eds) *Working Class Culture: Studies in History and Theory*, London: Hutchinson, pp 7-28.

Kelly, L. (1988) *Surviving Sexual Violence*, Cambridge: Polity Press.

Lombard, N. and McMillan, L. (eds) (2013) *Violence Against Women: Current Theory and Practice in Domestic Abuse, Sexual Violence and Exploitation*, London: Jessica Kingsley.

Lombard, N. and Whiting, N. (2015) 'Domestic abuse: feminism, the government and the unique case of Scotland', in Goel, R. and Goodmark, L. (eds) *Comparative Perspectives on Gender Violence: Lessons from Efforts Worldwide*, Oxford: Oxford University Press, pp 155–168.

Mackay, F. (1996) *Getting there, being there, making a difference?: gendered discourses of access and action in local politics*, University of Edinburgh (unpublished PhD thesis).

Mackay, F. (2010) 'Gendering constitutional change and policy outcomes: substantive representation and domestic violence policy in Scotland', *Policy & Politics*, 38(3): 369–388(20).

Orr, L. Scandrett, E. and Whiting, N. (2013) 'An educational approach to gender justice', *Concept*, 4/1: 1–4.

Scottish Executive (2000) *National Strategy to Address Domestic Abuse*, https://www2.gov.scot/Resource/Doc/158940/0043185.pdf

Scottish Executive (2004) *Domestic Abuse: A National Training Strategy*, www.womenssupportproject.co.uk/userfiles/nat%20training%20strategy(1).pdf

Scottish Government (2009) *Safer Lives, Changed Lives: A Shared Approach to Tackling Violence Against Women in Scotland*, www.womenssupportproject.co.uk/userfiles/file/Safer%20Lives_Changed%20Lives.pdf

Scottish Government (2018) *Equally Safe: Scotland's Strategy for Preventing and Eradicating Violence Against Women and Girls*, www.gov.scot/publications/equally-safe-scotlands-strategy-prevent-eradicate-violence-against-women-girls/

Scottish Women's Aid (2017) *Speaking Out: 40 Years of Women's Aid in Scotland*, https://womenslibrary.org.uk/gwl_wp/wp-content/uploads/2017/12/Speaking-Out-40-years-of-Womens-Aid-1.pdf

Stark, E. (2007) *Coercive Control: How Men Entrap Women in Personal Life*, Oxford: Oxford University Press.

CASE I.3

Domestic Abuse Survivors: Public Sociology and the Risks of Speaking Out

Julie Young

Introduction

Decades of feminist research and advocacy have given voice to a recognition of domestic abuse as a social problem, driven by structural factors in society, underpinned by and perpetuating gender inequality. Yet, at an individual level, women experiencing domestic abuse may be left feeling they have lost their voice both literally and metaphorically. The hidden nature of coercion and control means their lived reality has no public audience (Stark, 2007). In a society where victim blaming and sexism is pervasive, women anticipate how they will be judged, and this fear of disclosure generates a form of gendered shame that continues to operate to silence women (Enander, 2010). The 'Same Hell, Different Devils' study used a feminist participatory action research (FPAR) approach and deployed the visual method of photovoice, with women survivors of domestic abuse in Scotland, to enable them to make sense of their experiences of domestic abuse and their own alcohol use, in a group setting (Young, 2016). The research offered an opportunity for participants to have their voices heard and to explore the wider societal power structures that impact on their experiences.

In this case study, exploring the concept of 'voice', I consider the benefits, challenges and risks faced by the women survivors of domestic abuse who participated in this research, that I consider an example of organic public sociology: a form of sociology where the researcher works with an engaged public to generate knowledge for the purpose of social change (Burawoy, 2005). I pose the following questions: What risks did survivors face as 'silenced' marginalised public attempting to speak out in a society underpinned by gender inequality?; Does such generated knowledge have an educational life beyond the research setting? I also explore the idea of survivors as a constituted subaltern counterpublic in their own right (Fraser, 1990). Nancy Fraser's (1990) notion of the subaltern as discursive spaces occupied by generally subordinated social groups, such as women under patriarchy, is useful when considering feminist activist work in the field of domestic abuse. Fraser calls such spaces subaltern counterpublics, as they represent parallel discursive entities 'where members of subordinated social groups invent and circulate counter discourses, which in turn permit them to formulate oppositional interpretations of their identities, interests, and needs' (Fraser, 1990: 67). Viewed within the context of public sociology, the women survivors in this case study may be considered a subaltern counterpublic who, given the opportunity, were able to recognise and challenge gendered, oppressive, silencing regimes both within their intimate relationships and in the public domain, despite the risks inherent in doing so.

Background

Societal recognition of domestic violence as a public problem has been revolutionised since the last decades of the twentieth century in the UK and the USA (Dobash and Dobash, 1998; Stark, 2007). The political activism of the women's movement, where the personal became political, resulted in a proliferation of refuge shelters, policy changes, advocacy services and international recognition of domestic abuse as a human rights issue (Dobash and Dobash, 1998; Stark, 2007). Scotland has an impressive history of feminist activism in this field, contributing to the development of an advanced devolved policy, recognising coercive control and adopting the term 'domestic abuse', shifting the focus away from physical violence. The Scottish Government has also adopted a gendered analysis of all forms of violence against women, conceptualising gender-based violence as a function of gender inequality, and an abuse of male power and privilege (Scottish Government, 2009). This ongoing body of change has been possible through activists operating as a subaltern counterpublic, working to challenge dominant discourses and deliver alternative understandings and practices. It was this context combined with contemporary feminist frameworks (Stark, 2007; Johnson, 2008; Connell, 2012) that motivated me to make sense of this phenomenon through the lived experience of survivors with the hope of raising more public awareness of its complexity. Having previously interviewed women survivors of domestic abuse, I knew I wanted to adopt a more participatory approach in order for the women's voices to be heard, but also for them to have more control and involvement in the production of knowledge. This led me to favour a collaborative methodology and specifically the photovoice method.

The research

I used a FPAR approach that blends participatory action research and critical feminist epistemology by advocating that women must be actively involved in all stages of the research process (Letherby, 2003; Reid et al, 2006). Photovoice (Wang and Burris, 1997) involves participants creating photographs that represent the reality of their lives; these were then critically analysed in a group setting with other survivors. The theoretical underpinnings of photovoice are provided by Paulo Freire's (1996) approach to education for critical consciousness, combined with critical feminist theory and a community approach to documentary photography (Wang and Burris, 1997). Wang and Burris (1997) argue that this opens up the possibility of counter-narratives that challenge hegemonic views. It was this raising of critical consciousness – conscientisation: a process of developing a critical awareness of one's social reality (Freire, 1996) – that opened up the potential for the education part of this project. Using his form of problem-posing education, Freire (1996) recognised that one means of enabling this critical discussion and conscientisation was through the visual image. This approach of using visual images as objects to be decoded, objects that represented situations that others could relate to (Freire, 1996), was of fundamental value to allowing the critical dialogue to take place in the group sessions. Through the photovoice group process, the eight women survivors of domestic abuse, recruited in collaboration with a local Women's Aid group, were encouraged to find confidence in their own voices. Engagement with feminist sociological theory and a process of reflection enabled them to move from their personal experiences to an understanding of social forces that impacted those experiences. Yet, as an often-silenced subjugated group, survivors of abuse, speaking out is not without risk.

What risks do survivors take in speaking out?

It was clear from the outset of the study that the concept of voice or 'having a voice' was extremely important to the women participants. Yet I was aware that, as researchers, even in our privileged positions, we do not 'give voice' to those in less powerful positions, but we do need to be part of the process of breaking down the barriers for speakers and listeners (Maguire, 2000). While storytelling can be a transformative tool for oppressed groups it may also be risk-laden. Assumptions may be made by people in positions of power that marginalised individuals would grasp any opportunity to tell their stories. Yet, what Holtby et al (2015: 319) call 'this disclosure imperative' may carry an element of risk where their stories are laid open to inspection, judgement and potential appropriation. Story-tellers, while challenging dominant narratives, may also face pressure to make their story more socially acceptable in the face of the power of the audience, who decide what stories are taken up or not (Charania, 2005, cited in Holtby et al, 2015: 319). It was therefore important to create a safe space for their stories to be shared, in a familiar setting, involving Women's Aid support worker at each session.

It became clear through the women's narratives that they were in an ongoing process of trying to make sense of their experiences. They had engaged with explanations of domestic abuse through the Freedom Programme (Freedom Programme, 2016) and support sessions within Women's Aid. Participation in the photovoice sessions provided a further step in providing a better understanding of their experiences relating to wider social issues that impacted their lives both then and now. But this process was not without its challenges as some women clearly struggled to accept these new explanations. Occasionally I observed the women deferring to the support worker, or looking to her for guidance. I had concerns when the support worker would intervene with the 'company line' sometimes, almost to correct them or remind them of how they should understand their experiences. This tended to happen when they were reflecting upon issues of blame and responsibility, with women still tending towards a self-blame narrative or excusing their partner's behaviour. I argue that the survivors' ambiguous relationships with these alternative discourses are indicative of the power of the 'wallpaper' of overlapping dominant societal discourses on domestic abuse and alcohol to which all women are exposed (Young, 2016). But survivors' narratives showed they had faced the additional challenge of having these reinforced by the compelling voice of their abusive partners. The support workers' input reflected a more 'informed' commentary, an institutional discourse based on feminist understandings of domestic abuse and alcohol use, versus a personal one, despite them being survivors themselves. There seemed to be a power imbalance here, working against the egalitarian principles of FPAR, suggesting our ability to eliminate power dynamics in the research setting are always limited. The positive benefits of including support workers' involvement may have been offset against the minimal risk of participants feeling constrained in telling authentic stories that did not conform to an acceptable narrative. Such observations also led me to consider if I was engaging with multiple, yet overlapping, publics: professionals and survivors, who may share the ultimate goal of social justice but may have different agendas in the immediate research space.

However, as stories of coercion and control emerged through the group sessions, it became clear that the women welcomed the opportunity to express their views, having been silenced within their intimate relationship and sometimes wider social settings. Within their relationships, silencing was often expressed in terms of not being allowed to have a voice, or to express an opinion, for fear of retribution. This was regularly articulated in terms of expressions such as 'it always had to be his way or the highway' and 'I felt worthless and just felt ... empty ... and I had nae voice' or 'that was me I had to watch what I said or no' speak at all'. A powerful representation of this notion was captured in an image created by a participant where she poses in a chair with her mouth taped up and is captioned: 'I could not have an opinion of my own. Always had to watch what I said. When I did speak I had to make sure it was what he wanted to hear.' The women's narratives align with contemporary feminist frameworks that highlight the importance of power and control within the abusive relationship (Stark, 2007). The power held by the abuser makes his authoritative voice a compelling force as it regularly reintroduces fear and doubt, defining his version of reality, leaving the woman in a state of doublethink: a conflicted state holding contradictory thoughts and beliefs in her head at one time (Herman, 1992; Pain, 2012). This was commonly experienced as constant criticism in how they performed as wives, women and mothers, often framed, and experienced, as a failure in femininity. Above all else, the risks faced in speaking out, or talking back, were well understood by the participants. Negotiating this risk had been part of their daily life, yet their narratives were interwoven with acts of resistance.

Beyond the intimate relationship, 'silencing' consisted of a reluctance to speak out for fear of being judged or not being believed. Women felt judged on multiple levels by different sectors of society – family, colleagues, service providers, the general public – and the power and impact inherent in those judgments. They reflected a strong sense of being pathologised and therefore judged and marginalised because of something that had happened to them. This victim-blaming discourse is commonly found in media reports (Berns, 2009) and is reflected in the ubiquitous question of 'why doesn't she just leave?' thus framing women as responsible for ending the abuse. However, during the discussions the women did recognise these double standards that must be negotiated and located them clearly within the context of gender inequality.

Women talked of the reaction of others as they tried to rebuild their lives, some describing being treated 'like a leper' or 'having two heads' if they disclosed having been victims of abuse. Demonstrating an awareness of such attitudes, women reported a level of internalised shame that they carried forward in interactions with others. Talk of the need to hide from the gaze of others for fear of judgement had been present since our introductory session where several women engaged in a discussion about looking down all the time: having difficulty in holding their heads up. This internalised fear of being judged may be considered a form of gendered shame (Enander, 2010). Bartky (1991) argues that shame for women is attunement to the social environment. In a society where victim-blaming and sexism is pervasive, women anticipate how they will be judged. Parallels can be seen here in the broader social context with the discourse around the #MeToo movement, where a simple reading frames survivors of sexual violence speaking publicly as transformative and empowering. Yet, in a culture of continued victim-blaming, women speaking out risk a backlash from those whose power and privilege are threatened (White and McDonald, 2018).

Yet the women in this research were not only willing to tell their stories but also to challenge assumptions made by academia. Traditionally, decisions made by research ethics boards are based upon an assumption that those in the academy are able to protect participants better than they are able to do themselves (Ponic and Jategaonkar, 2012). Eikeland (2006: 42) refers to this as 'condescending ethics' that can result in a form of 'othering' that reinforces participant powerlessness and marginalises them further in the process of knowledge production. For example, insistence on anonymity should not necessarily be assumed, as women who have been chronically silenced may wish to claim their experiences as their own. This transpired to be highly relevant to some participants in this project. What became a significant part of the images as a collection was the decision by three of the women to place themselves, in a recognisable way, within their own photographs. The risks of doing so in relation to publications and public dissemination of the research had been discussed at the start of the project and were revisited at multiple points. Yet this became an important aspect of involvement for those women who felt it was time that they were not only heard, but also seen, to be speaking out. It was clear from the discussions that the women were well experienced in assessing risk and it was respectful to enable them to make an informed decision. Combined with the power to define what was significant within their stories, each of these can be considered important acts of autonomy within the research experience The women in this project can be considered a subaltern counterpublic in their own right as they not only generated knowledge that challenged public discourses around domestic abuse but also challenged the power of the academy in how they created and presented that knowledge. Engaging with such a counterpublic enables a dialogue, a process of mutual education (Burawoy, 2005). In doing public sociology we must listen to participants as not only experts in their own lives but as individuals capable of truly informed consent regarding risk assessment and capable of exercising control over the research content.

Does such generated knowledge have an educational life beyond the research setting?

The aim of creating a photographic exhibition had been agreed since the onset of the project as a specific participatory goal. While the women embraced the idea that their photographs might contribute on some level to raising awareness of the issues surrounding domestic abuse and alcohol use, they appeared sceptical that it would have any impact with regards to major social change. They were probably correct, but this should not allow us to undervalue the achievements of this collaborative enterprise. What was important was the process of collating the knowledge generated on the subject through their photographs and texts, and taking that opportunity to have the women's voices heard. We had an opportunity to exhibit our work at a local funding launch event attended by local politicians, police, non-governmental organisations (NGOs) and the general public. Here was a chance for their voices to be heard and their efforts to be viewed by a range of different publics. The day of the event was the first chance they had to view their work in its final form. It was clear when we met that day that they were really proud of their work, seeing it on display with others taking an interest in viewing it, provoked feelings of pride, with one woman articulating this as being the best part of the project. The visual aspect of this project provided not only an alternative means of dissemination with participant involvement but also an opportunity to engage with, and potentially influence, different publics. For a silenced, often marginalised group of women, participating in organic public sociology presented an opportunity to individually, and collectively, have their voices heard.

This project represented an example of doing public sociology as a means of education, yet more opportunities arose to engage with further publics within, and beyond, the university. One of the key desired social changes articulated by the women survivors was a better understanding of domestic abuse, particularly through education at all levels. A unique opportunity arose for me to work with a group of final year undergraduate drama students who planned to produce a performance piece on the subject of domestic abuse, for academic assessment. However, they had little knowledge of the subject. Initially, through a group seminar, I shared the current sociological understandings of domestic abuse, supported by examples from the survivors' testimony. Here were drama students engaging with public sociology and feminist theory. I could see, even at this stage, the emotional impact this was having on the students to hear the harsh reality of the women's lived experiences. I managed the risk of trauma by having access to emotional support throughout the project. With minimal intervention from me, the students took copies of the transcripts of the group sessions, cutting them up and reworking them into a new story of domestic abuse, performed as a 30-minute on-stage drama. A critical remit in the assessment was to demonstrate authenticity, and this was creatively achieved through the use of the survivors' words voiced on stage. As an audience member, I experienced the performance as powerful and highly emotional as I recognised the voices of the women interwoven through this new story. This impact was evident across the rest of the audience who consisted of academics, students and members of NGOs.

A significant aspect of the project was the impact upon the students themselves. All the students found the work very emotionally challenging but ultimately spoke about the personal growth they experienced in respect of the new knowledge gained in understanding this social issue. Some talked of having become advocates involved in educating their family and friends on the topic, which again reflected the Freirian consciousness-raising experience. For one student the process led to personal disclosure of her own experiences of abuse to our limited working group. But, more positively, she reflected upon how her new understanding had really helped her make sense of those experiences. Additionally, the only male student in this drama group articulated his difficulty in performing the voice of the male perpetrator, which was recorded and played as a background track to reflect the internal voice in the woman's head. He found it very challenging to use the menacing language. As a result of this additional collaboration within the university, not only were the survivors' voices being heard but they were providing the education they had called for, through the conduit of organic public sociology utilising artistic means. Equally, knowledge generated by survivors has the potential to impact different publics in a multitude of ways, sometimes allowing a development of new advocates ready to challenge dominant discourses. Such an opportunity was only possible by the courage of women survivors willing to risk speaking out.

As a public sociologist I have witnessed, through dissemination of this research using photos and women's narratives, the power of their work. At exhibitions, in teaching situations and at conferences I have seen a range of reactions, particularly to the photographs; shock, horror, pity, respect for their courage and outrage at the persistence of such abuse of women. Sadly, I have heard occasional disrespectful comments from men at the exhibitions. I have also experienced both challenges to my integrity for using the images in teaching and, at the other end of the spectrum, appreciation for exposing the issues. Engaging with this research has provoked personal disclosures of abuse and provided opportunities for consciousness–raising. All these reactions reinforce the power of organic public sociology, in particular, combined with creative methods.

Conclusion

It can be risky for marginalised and silenced groups to speak out or attempt to take action in the public sphere where they are disempowered by inequality. The women participants took risks. By participating in general they risked misrepresentation and exploitation. In the group sessions they risked judgement, retraumatisation as they recounted their experiences. As they made conscious decisions about including themselves in the photographs some of them rejected the cloak of anonymity wishing not only to be heard but to be seen to be speaking out. This meant they risked exposure in public, despite knowing the risks of judgement and victim-blaming. But the opportunity to take these risks was made possible historically by the actions of subaltern publics, of feminists as both activists and practitioners engaged in the ongoing struggle for justice and gender equality. They have created alternative counterpublic spheres where survivors can be supported by practitioners and researchers in reframing their experiences through engagement with sociological ideas. Survivors, in this project, found their collective voice in challenging gendered, oppressive, silencing regimes both within their intimate relationships and in the public domain. By doing public sociology we, as researchers, can engage in conversation with these counterpublics by designing research that offers opportunities for creativity, education, empowerment and personal growth. Equally we must recognise potential risks and design to mitigate against these.

This project also highlighted how valuable knowledge generated by survivors can have a powerful impact well beyond the original research setting by engagement with multiple different publics. Such opportunities are perpetuated by the use of creative methods, indicating the value of arts-based approaches in public sociology, enabling marginalised groups to have their voices heard by a broader audience.

References

Bartky, S.L. (1991) *Femininity and Domination: Studies in the Phenomenology of Oppression (Thinking Gender)*, London: Routledge.

Berns, N. (2009) *Framing the Victim: Domestic Violence, Media, and Social Problems*, New Jersey: Transaction.

Burawoy, M. (2005) '2004 presidential address: for public sociology', *American Sociological Review*, 70: 4–28.

Connell, R.W. (2012) 'Gender, health and theory: conceptualizing the issue, in local and world perspective', *Social Science & Medicine*, 74(11): 1675–1683.

Dobash, R.E. and Dobash, R.P. (1998) *Rethinking Violence Against Women*, London: Sage.

Eikeland, O. (2006) 'Condescending ethics and action research', *Action Research*, 4(1): 37–47.

Enander, V. (2010) 'A fool to keep staying: battered women labeling themselves stupid as an expression of gendered shame', *Violence Against Women*, 16(5): 5–31.

Freedom Programme (2016) *The Freedom Programme*, www.freedomprogramme.co.uk/

Fraser, N. (1990) 'Rethinking the public sphere: a contribution to the critique of actually existing democracy', *Social Text*, 25/26: 56–80.

Freire, P. (1996) *Pedagogy of the Oppressed*, London: Penguin.

Herman, J.L. (1992) *Trauma and Recovery: From Domestic Abuse to Political Terror*, London: Pandora.

Holtby, A., Klein, K., Cook, K. and Travers, R. (2015) 'To be seen or not to be seen, photovoice, queer and trans youth, and the dilemma of representation', *Action Research*, 13(4): 317–335.

Johnson, M.P. (2008) *A Typology of Domestic Violence*, New Hampshire: Northeastern University Press.

Letherby, G. (2003) *Feminist Research in Theory and Practice*, Buckingham: Open University.

Maguire, P. (2000) *Doing Participatory Action Research: A Feminist Approach*, Amherst: University of Massachusetts.

Pain, R. (2012) *Everyday Terrorism: How Fear Works in Domestic Abuse*, https://womensaid.scot/wp-content/uploads/2017/07/EverydayTerrorismReport.pdf

Ponic, P. and Jategaonkar, J. (2012) 'Balancing safety and action: ethical protocols for photovoice research with women who have experienced violence', *Arts & Health: An International Journal for Research*, 4(3): 189–202.

Reid, C., Tom, A. and Frisby, W. (2006) 'Finding the 'action' in feminist participatory action research', *Action Research*, 4(3): 315–332.

Scottish Government (2009) *Safer Lives: Changed Lives. A Shared Approach to Tackling Violence Against Women in Scotland*, https://www2.gov.scot/Resource/Doc/274212/0082013.pdf

Stark, E. (2007) *Coercive Control: How Men Entrap Women in Personal Life*, Oxford: Oxford University Press.

Wang, C. and Burris, M.A. (1997) 'Photovoice: concept, methodology, and use for participatory needs assessment', *Health Education & Behavior*, 24(3): 369–387.

White, D. and McDonald, P. (2018) 'As the Kavanaugh backlash shows #MeToo hasn't gone far enough', *The Guardian*, www.theguardian.com/commentisfree/2018/oct/05/people-worry-metoo-has-gone-too-far-it-has-not-gone-far-enough

Young, J. (2016) 'Women's experiences of domestic abuse and alcohol: same hell different devils', Queen Margaret University (PhD thesis).

CASE I.4

A Public Sociology for Post-industrial Fife

Paul Gilfillan

Introduction

Having been an associate member of the Workers' Educational Association (WEA) from attending WEA courses when conducting research into the politicisation of Scottish national identity (Gilfillan, 2014), the WEA seemed an ideal public to partner with in light of Burawoy's (2005) call for sociologists to engage with the likes of church groups, the labour movement and the working class. When going to meet with the WEA education development manager for Fife ('Maesie') at her Lumphinnans office in March 2017, it seemed appropriate to park in Gagarin Way opposite the WEA office as this street name indicated the previous industrial era when this former 'pit village' had earned the local nickname 'Little Moscow' thanks to a Communist tradition strong enough to have streets named after heroes of the Soviet Union. However, in light of 1980s deindustrialisation and the flight of private capital from the central Fife corridor from Buckhaven and Methil in the east to Ballingry and Lochore in the west, Burawoy's question 'are there any publics out there?' (in Tamdgidi, 2008: 140) was a topic I wanted to explore with Maesie.

Paul: Does the WEA struggle for local publics?
Maesie: One of the biggest challenges for the WEA is the fact that we are still a very, very traditional organisation; still trying to work to fairly traditional values and aspirations. An yet society is movin on all the time. And so the

	models and the approaches that we used even 20 years ago are no really relevant any more. So one of the things that we're having to do, and we absolutely sit doon an talk about this regularly, is how do we make ourselves more relevant to people in the way that people live and work and move around now, because we believe that the content of the education that we offer is still relevant.

Paul: What are the values of the WEA? Is it empowerment via education?

Maesie: Absolutely! We talk about 'social purpose' education; which means that anything we are delivering is about enabling people to think very, very critically about their situations. About the things that impact on their lives. So it's no just a case of comin an doing a creative writin class because that's something yer interested in. We'll actually use that as the tool, or the enabler, to get people to start to think aboot some of the issues that impact on their lives; whether that's poverty, or whether that's drugs and alcohol.

Paul: How do you get people through the door of the WEA?

Maesie: A lot of what Ah've been doin in Fife is engagin wi community workers who are on the ground and actually people who work with community and voluntary organisations. So ma job is persuading them that the education we've got to offer is relevant to the people they're workin with. An actually that's harder than ye would think. Because community work has changed so much over the years as well. And one of the biggest challenges we've got noo is that the majority of community work is aboot gettin people into employment. It's not about education! It's about getting them into work! An something that Ah discovered the other day there, you know I wrangle with this all of the time, I get really frustrated at times, but community workers no longer see the work the WEA does as bein relevant. When Ah went into community work and people before me, the majority of the people were community activists, they were political activists, they were trade union activists, and they've got this degree, this professional qualification that enabled them to take on paid work; that allowed them to do even more with the passion and the enthusiasm that they have. I feel now,

	and Ah'm sure there's people that would argue this, it has become very much a professional career.
Paul:	As opposed to a vocation for social and political change?
Maesie:	Yes.
Paul:	Can you give me an example of where you have sat in front of a community education worker and you've thought 'Man, we are totally on different pages.'
Maesie:	Oh! Too many examples! Ah mean for a start, the majority of them they'd never heard e the WEA before. Ah mean at one time that would have been unheard of. You know community workers would just know who this organisation was, and what it done and what it stood for. That's why I was talking about educating them aboot who we are, and how our education is different from the mainstream adult education that a lot of them are being asked to deliver which is all about employability skills. An a lot e them jist dinnae seem to get the whole thing about democracy an active citizenship. They jist don't see it at all.

Maesie (born 1968, from Ballingry, graduated in 1999) embodies what might be described as the Old Left's 'longing for total revolution' (Boltanski, 2002) and in the interview extract above we see her struggling to reconcile herself to the 1980s/1990s, which *inter alia* saw the radical decline among a new generation of community workers of the credibility of the once-mainstream goal of reorganising society and economy along the lines of socialism or some form of collectivism. Maesie clearly wants a model of emancipation that is about much more than employability, but not only community workers but the main funders of WEA Fife (Fife Council) and the leadership of WEA Scotland have adapted to the new post-industrial era, which has seen the triumph of neoliberalism and the failure of the Old Left project. Attending WEA Scotland's annual general meeting in December 2017 and leafing through the glossy WEA Scotland 2015 annual report, an emphasis upon employability is clearly highlighted, with the director of WEA Scotland citing 'education focused on employability' as the *primary* goal of how the WEA makes an impact in people's lives through its educational activities; and how:

> This year, we formed an excellent relationship and benefitted greatly from sponsorship and partnership with Scottish Widows–Lloyds Banking Group. The impact

for students of Scottish Widows volunteers giving them additional support whilst engaged in WEA employability programmes has been outstanding. (WEA Scotland, 2015: 1)

While courses that involve 'working towards qualifications in Employability and Wellbeing at SCQF level 3' are a good thing in so far as becoming literate and numerate is indeed empowering, and while one can wholeheartedly agree with the director that the WEA's work has 'achieved transformational outcomes', it seems the WEA's model of empowerment – in light of no other paths to liberation being spelled out – sits comfortably alongside a neoliberal model insofar as the education that delivers transformational outcomes is one that integrates its students into the market. The leadership of the WEA, then, has pragmatically recognised that an earlier rhetoric of social revolution via education is more distant and utopian than ever, and this development is clearly at odds with Maesie's conviction that 'one of the biggest challenges we've got noo is that the majority of community work is ... not about education! It's about getting them into work.'

Education for what and for whom (after the 'social question' has been solved)?

On 5 July 2017 a roundtable discussion among WEA Fife members and stakeholders was held at the Benarty Centre with the remit of the day spelled out in a handout given to attendees:

> As a partner / supporter / advocate / contributor to the WEA in Fife currently or in the past, we would like to invite you to take part in a roundtable to enable you to contribute to discussion about the WEA's continuing role in the provision of adult education in Fife.

Maesie's opening words to the gathered audience were: 'I believe the WEA is as relevant today as ever as the largest national provider of adult education', and she proceeded to detail WEA Fife literacy programmes, the range of SQA qualifications available, how and where the WEA in Fife is delivering IT skills to pensioners and others, outlined WEA courses aimed at developing 'skills for reminiscence', 'mindfulness', 'human rights' and 'all kinds of invisible disabilities' before concluding with a run-through of aims and goals such as 'addressing inequality', 'combatting health inequalities', 'combatting social exclusion' and 'promoting active citizenship'. After this opening presentation a members-only discussion followed, so the Fife Council representatives (ie funders) and WEA staff left the room so members and tutors could talk freely. As a newly active member I quickly learned this event was the first of its kind, with one female member telling the group:

> 'The members [of the WEA] never meet. I don't know what's going on in the WEA. I've no idea what the range of provision is. I've never received a list of classes or whatnot from the WEA in Fife. I wasn't asked what I'm interested in; if I'd like to be a tutor.'

At this, one of the tutors present told the group: 'This is the first time we tutors have met'; followed by one of the Fife committee members telling the group: 'The Fife WEA committee isn't allowed to know who its members are. So no wonder we can't communicate with them!'

In light of Maesie's misgivings highlighted earlier in the interview extract, the question uppermost in my mind at the roundtable as a professional sociologist was, if adult education is not only for employability, then what else is it for and for whom is it aimed, as my own view is that in so far as the arrival of material affluence to West European working classes during the period 1950–1973 (Toniolo, 1998) means the nineteenth-century 'social problem' has largely been solved, the WEA, to remain mainstream in its appeal, must align itself with the post-material *cultural issues* that impact the lives of their local publics; must follow its target audience and perform a *turn to culture* if it is to provide a post-material 'liberation through culture' paradigm in its adult education programmes. It seems clear that, if democratic election results are a guide to how content (or otherwise) 'the people' are, little remains of the Old Left's longing for total revolution, and so the New Left has shifted its focus to the realm of culture, with the 'social carrier' of this New Left being largely middle class activists appealing to largely middle class publics and causes (identity politics, environmental movements). A task for the WEA, then, in areas of deindustrialisation that have very high SIMD (Scottish Index of Multiple Deprivation) rankings is to make the same shift of focus to culture but identify a *different* cultural project. However, while Maesie wants to make the WEA relevant again and affirms this issue is endlessly discussed as a priority, the following exchange reveals there has been little engagement by Fife WEA with the transformative politicisation of culture and nationality that has been on-going in Scotland for a generation and more.

Paul: I wanted to ask how the never-ending constitutional question that defines Scotland today impacts the WEA. I mean would there be somebody sitting there saying 'Look, we're gonna have to harness this whole thing at some level, because whether you agree with it or not, this nationalism is driving us someplace,' you know? I mean the whole energy generated by the 2014 referendum, has the WEA said to itself, 'Right. We're gonnae have to respond'?

Maesie: No. No. If I'm being honest. There hasn't been that conversation at all. No.

Paul: That surprises me.

Maesie: I know.

Paul: I'd have thought you'd've been all ready to jump on it and say we'll use this as …

Maesie: We've got quite an unusual set up and it's actually something that our new director when he came into post last summer picked up on immediately, was that we've got these six regional offices across Scotland, an there's very little commonality in terms of what they do and what they focus on.

Paul: So, there's political education but there's no constitutional question, which is the big political thing?

Maesie: Well, the thing for me is it's there on the table wi me driving it. But as I said when we started this conversation, the big challenge for me is gettin the community workers out there in the community to understand that these things are important and that we are in a position to deliver them. And that's the thing I was saying to you, a lot of the community workers are not interested in having that conversation.

Paul: Can you by-pass them? As the WEA can you say clearly there's a space or an appetite to discuss these things?

Maesie: For me, going back to what Ah've said about community workers, a lot e them are gatekeepers in their communities that they work in as well, and that's why I've wanted to get them on side.

Paul: Do you sometimes think in the middle of the night 'Oh God! I'm just no getting anywhere wi this social worker', who just doesn't get it?

Maesie: Yeah! It's incredibly, incredibly frustrating. I spend probably every day thinking there must an easier way to crack this.

But I think there isnae! There's so many things that have changed and continues to change.

I propose that the extraordinary situation of avoiding the constitutional question referred to by Maisie above is a 'blood relative' of a deeper ambivalence vis-à-vis *Scottish culture*; something that was highlighted again when interviewing the chairman of the Fife WEA area committee in January 2018 when he informed me: 'The WEA the noo nationally is a melting pot. We no longer have a Scottish identification although we are tryin to keep a Scottish identification.' While Maesie alludes to standing frustrations such as relying on gatekeepers to access local publics, I would speculate in light of the failure to anticipate and ally with the New Scotland discourse whether Maesie (and the WEA) is stuck in an obsolete model of liberation-via-education; in a pre-devolution, industrial-era universalist (and Scottish-less) model of adult empowerment that has failed to deconstruct and reinvent itself and align with post-1980s/1990s political, economic and cultural conditions; and so offers a model of liberation that will only appeal to that fraction of the working class that failed to make the transition to affluence, privatism, consumerism and culture, and so offers little to most of the local working class population/public.

Shortly after meeting with Maesie I interviewed an Edinburgh-based WEA office-bearer where we discussed the possibility of collaborating in the development and delivery of a WEA course in Fife. At this meeting in August 2018 I learned that Fife WEA had secured a service agreement with Fife Council which meant funding for another three years to deliver courses for isolated learners and the unemployed, with a focus on mental health, creative writing and building confidence and self-esteem. When turning to the topic of WEA Fife delivering political literacy workshops, I began by asking:

Paul: What is your working model of liberation? And how is that reflected in the courses? At the Benarty round table [July 2017] I got no sense whatsoever of what the model for empowerment via education of the WEA is; I mean this whole thing about empowerment via political education. At the Benarty meeting I just couldn't see it. Didn't hear it being articulated.

Alan: You're absolutely right to pinpoint the fact that we're a bit kind of nebulous at the moment. We're a bit, we don't have a clear enough vision on all that in my opinion you know; that's absolutely the case. But what we can't be seen to be

	doing is to be favouring a political party or a political stance because we are a non-political, non-religious organisation.
Paul:	Tell me how that works, being a non-political organisation if your speciality is workers' education and delivering political literacy? Surely you are [politically] Left?
Alan:	Most of the staff are certainly. But we're reliant on public funding as well, so we need to be careful about what we're saying in case all of a sudden it gets stopped because maybe somebody doesn't like our views on things. So you have to be to a large extent apolitical.
Paul:	My analysis as a sociologist would be that once upon a time the WEA had a tremendous social and class function; providing adult education. But now that the State heavily invests in adult education it seems to have stolen your function and audience. I mean now there's no mention of class. No mention of workers. So there seems to be confusion as to what the purpose, function and audience of the WEA is. When I've interviewed WEA staff, they voice frustration that community education workers in Fife just don't get the WEA *raison d'être*. But my analysis wonders if it's the WEA that doesn't get it; if it's the WEA that doesn't have a theory of empowerment of a largely affluent working class anymore. I mean does the WEA have a product to offer the ordinary working class person?
Alan:	What I'd say is funding is such an issue that to stay running we need to make sure that we have money coming in. So that might mean some of the time we're doing courses to people who are not our target audience, but we're using that money to deliver other types of stuff as well.

Despite the administrative burdens of WEA managers such as the continual need to apply for funding and 'never-ending' report-writing for funders, Alan clearly wants to respond to his 'target audience' and so the fundamental issues of social class remains central not only to the good work of the WEA, but remains a key analytical category for sociology. The task of thinking the post-industrial working class in terms of their relation to the economy where they experience subordination to other social actors who enjoy different and better-rewarded positions remains key, then, to both the sociological imagination and the WEA. However, the post-industrial working class in so far as it is a potential public for the WEA is unlike their industrial forefathers as they no longer live a vital and visceral relationship to economic production because they no longer directly produce commodities sold for profit to enrich a capitalist owner, and so no longer see themselves principally through the 'mirror of production' (Baudrillard, 1975). If we look at this potential working class public through the mirror of (Scottish) culture, however, a new post-industrial terrain for class analysis and adult education opens up in so far as this class lives a subordinate relationship to the production and consumption of culture, so that to *not* be 'a bit kind of nebulous' the WEA might explore and develop an adult education that asks whether their local publics occupy a position of subordination in the realm of representations and the symbolic realm, and whether there is a specifically Scottish/Fife component to this relationship to culture and representation that can be explored and brought to consciousness via adult education as a basis for (cultural) agency and action.

Education for cultural struggle/inclusion

The topic of how the *relationship to culture* is integral to understanding the post-industrial class condition emerged after reflecting on Maesie's description of a WEA project that involved working with poor women.

> A piece of work we did in Inverkeithing was very interesting. There is a community worker down in the south-west Fife area, the West Fife villages right up tae Dalgety Bay. Applied theatre's one of her passions. So she done a piece of work wi a group e women from Fraser Avenue in Inverkeithing. Now that area is kind e notorious. It's got a reputation an it's bein pulled doon at the moment. That whole area. Jist like they did wi Rosewell Drive in Lochore. An it's bein rebuilt by a housin association. So both the Council and the housin association both claim to have been consultin wi the community. An of course the community are caught in the middle e that. 'We've nae idea whit's gaune oan. Naebdy's tellin us.' Ah mean they're real Fifers. They're really broad. So Theresa as their community worker wanted tae explore that wi them. An it's very much on a simple level; the language that's bein used was way beyond anything these women understood. Single parents wi kids in the flats doon there. So Theresa used applied theatre as an approach to start to get them to think about some of the issues that impact on them. They done a few performances but they done a really interesting

one on housin. It was brilliant. But the WEA was asked to go in on the back of these performances an do some work wi them around democracy and active citizenship. And a couple of our tutors went in an we briefed them. 'This will be very, very basic level. These people have not been engaged in anything political.' But even they were amazed at how little these people were engaged, and how little they understood. An it was very much back to basics. Explaining a lot e the words that we take for granted an use all the time in daily life. They jist didnae understand them. They knew *nothing* about politics. Not one of them had ever voted in their life before. But one of the other things that came out of doing that piece of work wi them was also that they understood *nothin* about Scottish *culture*. And they understood *nothing* about Scottish history either. So that all came out in the weeks that we worked with them. I don't know how it came aboot. There was some question about Scottish history and they could identify wi William Wallace because of the *Braveheart* film, and they were able to identify wi Mary Queen of Scots because she was held locally, and that was the level of their knowledge aboot Scottish history. And when there was a bit e exploring aboot Scottish culture they didn't even know what they were bein asked. So we were astounded. An that's only one small group e women in one street in one community in Fife. Ah'm sure you could take that same conversation tae many, many other groups in other streets and other communities in Fife and ye'd find exactly the same thing. An Ah think that's the crux e where we are as a people.

Discussion

Reflecting on Maesie's testimony, I propose that a route to renewing the relevance of WEA Fife might can be built on an analysis of there being two different publics: firstly, there is a public characterised by the level of estrangement from culture alluded to by Maesie above, whereby this condition of *cultural poverty* is submerged and invisible to those living this condition, and brings to mind Noble's (1982: 90) description of the challenge of cultural revival faced by Muir and MacDiarmid in the 1920s as 'akin with that faced by Christ with Lazarus'. Secondly, in light of the rise of nationalism at the ballot box and the widespread discourse of Scots suffering a *representational deficit* in terms of the State's public broadcasting service, for example, there is a public that *is* angry and *is* conscious of suffering the *cultural injustice* of insufficient cultural representation as a result of others exercising more control and having greater access to the British and Scottish public realms of representation than they do.

Furthermore, if there is within the WEA a reticence to engage with the constitutional debate, this is likely to surface in a similar reticence to engage with the meaning of place and locality not only in relation to the new *post-industrial* context, but also in the sense of exploring the meaning of being local, provincial and national in the new post-industrial context. Significantly, this questioning is being carried out by Fife-based writers of fiction as well as sociologists and ethnographers such as Marc Augé (2009) who has addressed the question of modernity's *non-places* while Bauman (2002) has written about 'the lonely nowherevilles of liquid modernity', and local playwright and screenwriter Gregory Burke (2001) has addressed the issue of post-industrial *anomie* in Fife and playwright David Greig (in Billingham, 2007: 77) has indicated what might be described as a 'public literature' based on his experience of:

> Travelling through Fife and the old Scottish mining villages there and realizing that the trains didn't stop there anymore – they just went whizzing by. I suddenly thought: the really violent places aren't the inner cities but these deserted towns. I then tried to imagine myself living in them: I thought it would be intolerable. Why did these places exist, why did people still stay there?

I propose that a narrative or model for WEA Fife to frame its regional public's cultural predicament or 'the crux e where we are as a people' (Maesie), so as to raise awareness of the past and present as well as current choices for the future, is the Muir–MacDiarmid frame (see Bicket, 2017: 5), according to which Scottish culture has 'disintegrated' and declined as a result of lacking its own centre of gravity. For Edwin Muir (1887–1959), in the opinion of Hugh MacDiarmid, Andrew Noble and Allen Tate the most brilliant twentieth-century critic of Scottish literature, until the sixteenth century the Scots thought, wrote, spoke and felt in one language, but at the English-backed Protestant Reformation of 1560 and subsequent dynastic Union of Crowns in 1603 which saw the Scottish court leave for London, there occurred a split between the language in which Scottish people feel (Scots) and the language in which they write (English). For Muir, this 'split' condition (reminiscent of Pierre Bourdieu's notion of *habitus clivé*) has had calamitous cultural consequences and has remained in place ever since, still describing the predicament of the Scottish writer today.

The rival frame to the Muir–MacDiarmid thesis is the 'North British Whig' frame, which enthusiastically reconciled itself to the end of Scotland's distinctive and autonomous culture in so far as assimilation to English power and culture enriched Scotland economically and culturally beyond its native powers and resources. The social carrier of this cultural frame of Whiggery was the upper and middle classes, and it found a powerful ally not only in Scotland's educational system but in the sociological imagination of the Scottish Enlightenment's account of modernisation, which saw liberation and progress in weak, backward local cultures being assimilated to vigorous modernising capitalist cultures. In the Scottish context, then, the extinction of the Scots language was justified in so far as speaking Scots in public discourse, for example, into the modern Anglophone era was 'psychologically immediate but socially isolating' (Geertz, 1993: 243). According to critics of this cultural frame such as Muir, Enlightenment figures such as Adam Smith, David Hume and Lord MacAulay were propagandists for a *Scottish-less* modernity and after the (apparently) final defeat of Jacobitism in 1745 as its great historical rival for imagining Scotland, this frame controlled how Scotland was imagined by most Scots.

Muir's account of post-sixteenth century Scottish culture borrows from Gregory Smith the idea of the *Caledonian antisyzygy* which viewed Scottish culture as 'split' between two contrasting muses: one celebrating the material and empirically existing reality, and another muse at home exploring the realm of fantasy. However, if by writing 'that Scottish life is split in two is certain ... But that it has always been split in two is false' (Noble, 1982: 62) Muir identified a creative recuperation of Scotland's pre-Calvinist past as the way to Scotland's cultural healing, he was sceptical as to whether the Scots language could be the linguistic medium through which that cultural resurrection could take place.

As an organic sociologist living in one of Greig's 'deserted towns' and someone who instantiates Muir's predicament in so far as I speak and feel in Scots in my domestic and local contexts, but speak and write in English in my professional public contexts, a task open to me as a public sociologist is to help develop WEA Fife course material that recognises that not only is politics in Scotland divided between Left and Right and on the question of the politicisation of national identity, but there is a deeper *long durée* division regarding the very existence and place of *Scottish culture* in modernity, to the extent that each side of this division has its own theorists with dialectically opposed theories of culture and history. However, in so far as today working class Scots still speak a version of Scots and experience the symbolic violence and cultural exclusion from the English-speaking public sphere (see *The Herald*, 1993), the predicament of a 'split condition' does *not* occur among many working class Scots, and so WEA Fife can draw upon this 'living relic' or pre-Calvinist 'wholeness' as a point of anchorage and departure in so far as these local publics incarnate a condition of social marginality and cultural integrity that can be mobilised educationally; so that the aim of empowerment via education can be renewed and the condition of *modernity-as-antisyzygy* can be overcome without need of the elitist path of going back to the 'great Catholic poets using the Vernacular' (MacDiarmid, in Noble, 1982: 90) as such an educational path simply starts with the remnants of spoken Scots and builds on this foundation. However, it seems likely that identifying with and mobilising this level of subalternality will come at the price of accusations of promoting archaism and 'anti-employability' (as per Geertz 1993: 243).

Interestingly, while Muir was directly involved in delivering adult education to a male working class public when teaching at Newbattle College in the 1950s, he had concluded that it would seem 'Scotland's historical destiny is to eliminate itself in reality, as it has already wellnigh eliminated itself from history and literature' (Noble, 1982: 37). Muir, then, did not foresee the present-day basis upon which the *long durée* project of resuscitating Scots culture is being built, ie the restoration of the Scottish Parliament after a hiatus of 292 years. Because Scotland's centre of gravity has been (partially) restored, the WEA can find a new lease of life in so far as it responds to the challenge of providing education for cultural inclusion in this new context. Moreover, being mindful of Alan's concerns regarding impartiality, WEA Fife, of course, need not officially adopt the Muir–MacDiarmid thesis or require it from its tutors, far less impose it upon its publics. Instead, it is perfectly feasible to have WEA classes in affluent north-east Fife, for example, adopt the North British Whig theory of culture should this suit its tutors or middle class public, while tutors in post-industrial central Fife working with a different public can adopt variations of the Muir–MacDiarmid thesis. This pluralist position vis-à-vis culture echoes the pluralist position of public sociology vis-à-vis politics in so far as it can just 'as well support Christian Fundamentalism as it can Liberation Sociology or Communitarianism' (Burawoy, 2005: 8–9).

References

Augé, M. (2009) *Non-places: Introduction to an Anthropology of Supermodernity*, London: Verso Books.

Baudrillard, J. (1975) *The Mirror of Production*, St. Louis: Telos Press.

Bauman, Z. (2002) 'In the lowly nowherevilles of liquid modernity: comments on and around Agier', *Ethnography*, 3: 342–349.

Bicket, L. (2017) *George Mackay Brown and the Scottish Catholic Imagination*, Edinburgh: Edinburgh University Press.

Billingham, P. (2007) *At the Sharp End: Uncovering the Work of Five Contemporary Dramatists*, London: Methuen.

Boltanski, L. (2002) 'The Left after May 1968 and the longing for total revolution', *Thesis Eleven*, 69: 1–20.

Burawoy, M. (2005) 'For public sociology', *American Sociological Review*, 70: 4–28.

Burke, G. (2001) *Gagarin Way*, London: Faber and Faber.

Geertz, C. (1993) *The Interpretation of Cultures*, London: Fontana Press.

Gilfillan, P. (2014) *A Sociological Phenomenology of Christian Redemption*, Guildford: Grosvenor House Publishing.

The Herald (1993) 'Sheriff judges aye-aye a contemptible no-no', www.heraldscotland.com/news/12706321.sheriff-judges-aye-aye-a-contemptible-no-no/

Muir, E. (1936) *Scott and Scotland: The Predicament of the Scottish Writer*, London: Routledge.

Noble, A. (1982) *Edwin Muir: Uncollected Scottish Criticism*, London: Vision Press Ltd.

Tamdgidi, M.H. (2008) 'Public sociology and the sociological imagination: revisiting burawoy's sociology types', *Humanity and Society*, 32: 131–143.

Toniolo, G. (1998) 'Europe's Golden Age, 1950–1973: speculations from a long-run perspective', *Economic History Review*, LI(2): 252–267.

Workers' Educational Association (2015) *Annual Report 2014–15*, Edinburgh.

CASE I.5

Public Sociology and the Invisibility of Class

Eurig Scandrett

Problems with class

The rationale for this chapter is different from the others in this collection. Firstly, as editor, I was struck by the paucity of explicit references to class – whether in terms of identity, structure or as a category of analysis – in the various cases in this collection. The authors of the various cases are practising public sociology focused on gender, ethnicity, refugee status, mental health, age, and issues ranging from alcohol to migration, environmental pollution to violence – and even around trade union organising – without explicit reference to class. Many of the people with whom our authors are practising public sociology are working class, yet class was not being explicitly referred to as a category of public. This struck me as surprising, especially since class is a major (and for some sociologists, *the* major) systemic cause of injustice and exploitation, and increasingly so under the austerity regime of neoliberalism, as well as a significant (or *the* significant) collective agent for transformation. I therefore decided to include a chapter specifically addressing this issue.

Secondly, Paul Gilfillan's work (Case I.4), which does focus on class explicitly, raised some interesting and difficult questions. Whilst his chapter analyses the issues faced by the Workers Education Association, his ethnographic research in a working class community in Fife also generated some narratives from white working class men which were highly resentful of what is perceived as the imposition of 'diversity' by a cultural elite, onto an established, Scottish working class culture.

Paul illustrated this with a particular quotation from an interview with 'Alec', which drew on narratives of misogyny, racism and homophobia. Such narratives are certainly not unique to working class white men in Fife, nor are they representative of working class communities, but 'Alec' may be taken as symbolising someone who occupies a relatively subaltern class position, and simultaneously a relatively dominant position in relations of gender, race, and sexuality. However, what is significant for public sociology is how the invisibility of class in public narratives *facilitates* 'Alec' in misinterpreting the source of his grievances, transferring them onto the symbolic representation of the resistance of other subaltern groups. This is particularly pertinent when class has such a significant explanatory role in understanding exploitation at a time when class exploitation is growing.

Elsewhere, Paul describes a subjectivity (or 'politics of being') in which working class identity is associated with conservative values of family, religion and locality as *integralism*, the 'systematic or integral de-differentiation of lifespheres; characterised as nationalist, post-secular, regionalist, sustainable, pluralist' (Gilfillan, 2011: 2). This raises questions for public sociology, and for the purposes of this collection, of the apparent invisibility of class in the practices of public sociologists.

I would wish to reassert the centrality of class in analysis and agency, relatively invisible though it may have become in post-industrial societies. This centrality is not deterministic, but rather seen within a totality with forms of oppression such as gender, race, sexuality, in 'relational autonomy' (McNally, 2017: 105) to each other. In this totality it may be necessary to 'revisualise' the working class, to ask, with Bhattacharya (2017a): 'who constitutes the global working class today in all its chaotic, multi-ethnic, multigendered, differently abled subjectivity?' (p. 3)

In light of these issues I decided that a chapter specifically looking at the role of class in public sociology would be valuable. Thus, in the autumn of 2018 I emailed ten people who I know of through professional and political networks, who work, or have worked, in working class education, sociology research, community work and/or political organisation, to invite them to comment on this issue. In particular, contacts were asked

1. To what extent is *class* explicitly referred to by you or others in your work?
2. To what extent have you or others made use of sociological ideas in your work?

Responses were received from five people, all male educators in sociology or related fields, who provided their reflections by email, telephone and face-to-face conversations. No claim is made here about sociological method or reliability: their reflections, along with other, informal discussions with others, constitute 'soundings' from those working in the field who have an interest in class and public sociology, which helped me to explore my own thinking on these issues.

Some years ago, Joyce Canaan and colleagues raised similar questions in relation to working class university students. Jenkins et al (2011) discuss their 'failure' to enable students to recognise the impact of class on their life chances, in contrast with other sociological locations such as gender and race, which these same students found easier to identify. The authors' use of autobiographical pedagogies to facilitate students' sociological imagination – to identify those social structures that have impacted on students' personal experiences – proved highly effective at exploring gendering and racialising social processes, but not 'classifying' processes. Jenkins et al (2011) explain this phenomenon with reference to aggressive individualising and marketising processes and the disenfranchising and dismantling of working class institutions since the introduction, in the 1980s, by Margaret Thatcher's Conservative Government, of neoliberal economic policy in the UK. Whilst class has been excluded from public discourse, over the same period it has also been eschewed in much sociological literature, despite some notable exceptions (see below).

In other publications on the same theme, Canaan (2013) drew on the dynamic, contested and constructed nature of identity of which sociology encourages exploration, and problematises fixed or essentialist understandings. She identified a dominant narrative of 'moral Darwinism', in which the success of the wealthy is contrasted with the moral culpability of the poor. In such a cultural context there are strong incentives for working class students not to identify with the stigmatised 'working class', but rather the aspirant middle class. Thus, at the same time as the capitalist class was strengthening its hegemony and privilege through attacks on working class institutions and fiscal policies of redistribution in favour of the rich, class identity was being distorted and, as it became more meaningless, erased from public narrative. The working class were the failed or feckless poor: who would wish to own this subjectivity? However, the working class student participants in Canaan's research and pedagogy demonstrated a competent academic appreciation of class, its material position and cultural value, albeit one in which their subjectivities were silent. Class was an attribute of others, to be demonised or aspired to, as a descriptor of comfort zones and shame. The link between subjective and analytical understandings of class – between Mills' 'private troubles' and 'public issues' – had broken down, even for these sociologically literate students. However, Canaan argued that this trend was starting to reverse following the economic crash of 2008, with an increase in class consciousness, the evaporation of aspiration and the descent into financial hardships of many of the working and 'middle' class: 'classification is becoming easier to cognise and therefore recognise as governments here and elsewhere are producing greater class polarisation now than previously' (Canaan, 2013: 29). Some years on from the crash and Canaan's paper, the question may be asked whether class consciousness has returned. Arguably, although there is an increased public narrative of class as an 'effect' of structural inequality (for example through the 'we are the 99%' slogans of the Occupy movement), class has not entirely re-established itself as its explanation.

Soundings

The distinction between class identity and class analysis was identified as significant by the people whose soundings contributed to this chapter, albeit acknowledging some of the contradictions that this generates. Although not participants in sociological research, nonetheless their comments are helpful in assessing the state of class in public sociology and selective quotations are included here (contributors referred to as S1–S5). Whilst emphasising that class identity is important to him ('Class is part of my identity. I'm a white working class man, trade union member, communist party member'), one interviewee, a former community worker stated:

> Class is usually implicit in community work, occasionally explicit. It is always implicit, the class analysis is behind what I do. If class comes up it is a great opportunity. It doesn't often. That's how hegemony works – it isn't mentioned, it is assumed not to be an issue whereas it is very much an issue. (S3)

The implicit nature of class analysis was raised in a number of contributions:

> All of my work has been driven by a class analysis even though I may be guilty in simply having that speak for itself and not being made explicit enough … For me class

analysis is very different from simply mentioning class ... But it is also very much as class as agency — as a driving force of everything in society. (S2)

The emphasis on analysis, on the Marxist, or at least Marxian, understanding of class, and of the use of class analysis to understand the dynamics of society, was a major theme: 'For me class is not a 'state of rich or poor', it's a relationship between those who provide labour power and those who own it. And is continually changing' (S5). For one person this is explicitly linked to public sociology: 'Groups of public sociologists are working with a "naturalistic" understanding of class, from experience, but without an analysis' (S1). The role of Left parties, especially Marxist parties, was highlighted by a number of contributors. S3 commented explicitly 'The role of the left parties is important, delivering a class analysis.' S2 described himself as 'an unreconstructed Marxist of the SWP tradition and keep to that without necessarily referring to Marxist literature in all of my writing', although in recognition of the value of being more explicit about class, S1 cautioned about the risk of over-emphasis and that 'we shouldn't talk about class all the time in an SWP manner'.

If Left parties, especially Marxist parties, play an important role in ensuring a narrative of class and class analysis is retained in public discourse, then the problem of the disappearance of class is certainly correlated with the declining influence of Left parties. At its peak in the 1940s, the Communist Party of Great Britain (CPGB) had around 60,000 members (Davies, 1996) but declined sharply following the Soviet invasion of Hungary in 1956. The party split in 1988 with the formation of the Communist Party of Britain (CPB), and the CPGB was wound up in 1991. Membership of the CPB has not exceeded 1,000 for 20 years. The Socialist Workers Party (SWP) at its peak in the 1970s probably had 5,000 members but has declined in recent years. Edward Platt (2014) claimed that the SWP membership at that time was around 2,000 but falling.

Gilfillan's ethnographic research took place in an area where the influence of Marxist parties might be expected to be felt more strongly than most places — West Fife, which includes the last ward in Britain to be represented by a Communist councillor up until 2016. Nonetheless, as he outlines in his chapter in this volume, despite electing a representative of a working class institution, such institutions do not necessarily resonate with many of the post-industrial residents.

Moreover, another issue raised in soundings was the lack of attention to class by professional sociologists.

> You are absolutely right to flag the relative absence of class in much of the relevant literature that you have in mind. Where or when it does get mentioned, it tends to be one of a long list of 'isms' or is covered by proxy or is referred to implicitly as one of a list of social and economic inequalities. And that's before we even get to occupational and other limited measures or definitions of class. (S2)

> I think it is part of the wider flight from class in the postmodernism of sociology in the 1980s. Groups of Public Sociologists are working with a 'naturalistic' understanding of class, from experience, but without an analysis. People have an experience of being patronised by being on the receiving end of a kind of left wing pedagogy of class. The narrative is that 'working class communities of the 1970s and 1980s were oppressive for women and people of colour and people with diverse sexualities, and that the breakdown of working class communities that came from Thatcherism was in some ways 'liberating', that it was a good experience for women and gays being away from these working class communities'. This is simplistic and in many ways retrograde. I find that people who talk about intersectionality have a tendency to leave class out. (S1)

This complaint has often been made in the sociological literature (Canaan, 2013; Wright, 2015b; McNally, 2017; Bhattacharya, 2017b). However, there are sociologists who continue to insist on class as an important category of current social experience, for example Mike Savage, Erik Olin Wright and David Harvey. (Whilst not, strictly speaking, a sociologist, David Harvey's work has been so influential on sociology that it is relevant to include him in this.)

Sociological approaches to class

One theme raised by a number of commentators relates to the complexities of class as understood by sociologists. Within classical Western sociology, the two distinct analytical approaches to class – Weber's linear analysis of life chances, and Marx's relational analysis of relations of production – have provided very fertile material for social analysis. In late capitalism these have been interrogated, adapted and amended as new social and economic conditions have generated the opportunity for new class positions or class fragments, in particular Bourdieu's contribution of the interaction between class and culture.

As a partnership between the British Broadcasting Corporation (BBC) and academic sociologists, the 'Great British Class Survey' (GBCS) would constitute a classical case of Burawoy's 'traditional public sociology'. Starting with the assumption that 'Traditional British social divisions of upper, middle and working class seem out of date in the twenty-first century, no longer reflecting modern occupations or lifestyles', the authors developed a class analysis based on three forms of capital accumulation: economic, cultural and social (Savage et al, 2013; Savage, 2015). Referencing Bourdieu as a key inspiration for their approach, they analysed data gathered through the GBCS and identified patterns in the possession, and accumulation, of these forms of capital.

As a result, they propose a 'new model of social class' that comprises seven groups: elite; established middle class; technical middle class; new affluent workers; traditional working class; emergent service workers; and (drawing on Standing's (2011) proposal to recognise the emergence of a new class) the precariat (see also Wright, 2015c). Individuals in Britain can be allocated to one or other of these groups through the BBC's 'class calculator' (I am classed as an emergent service worker – economically insecure but with a cultured social life – despite being considerably older than the average age of this class). The authors propose that this analysis helps to undermine the enduring – and constantly reproduced – moral stigmatisation that has been associated with class and, in particular, lower classes, which renders the elite invisible.

Savage's approach recognises that there is a dynamic and historical aspect of class, in particular in relation to the ways in which social and cultural (as well as economic) capital accumulates and thence inequalities in capital are (re)produced. However, each of the forms of capital are treated as linear and hierarchical, so although the seven classes are not neatly hierarchical (since the 'homology' between economic, social and cultural capitals is not exact), nonetheless the class categorisation is essentially linear rather than relational and the interpretation is largely descriptive rather than analytical.

Erik Olin Wright was a leading theoretical sociologist working on class. His conception of 'contradictory locations in class relations' (Wright, 1985) has been particularly influential and useful for interpreting what appears to be a diminution in the role of class in late capitalism. Recently, Wright (2015a, 2015b, 2015c) has attempted to integrate Marxist class analysis with non-Marxist understandings of class, including Weberian and the kind of empirical approach of Savage (2015)'s GBCS (what Wright has called stratification sociology). He interprets

> different ways of talking about class as each identifying different clusters of causal processes at work in shaping the micro and macro aspects of economically rooted inequality in capitalist societies. For some questions and problems, one or another of these clusters of mechanisms may be more important, but all are relevant to a full sociological understanding of economic inequality and its consequences. (Wright, 2015a: 2–3)

Wright argues that stratification theory focuses on class as individual attributes; Weberian theory focuses on class as opportunity-hoarding; and Marxist theory focuses on class as domination/exploitation. Three sociological approaches focusing on different aspects of class, identifying different clusters of causal processes and therefore addressing different problems. In a more dynamic version of this categorisation, he proposes the metaphor of a game, in which the lowest, 'situational' level of analysis (what he calls micro-classes) relate to conflicts in which actors, both collective and individual, promote their interests within the rules of the game (surviving capitalism); Weberian meso-analysis addresses the institutional level in which conflicts arise about the rules of the game and how these might be changed (managing capitalism in different ways); whilst Marxist macro-analysis addresses the game itself, and the conflicts over playing an alternative game (socialism).

A significant contribution of David Harvey (2005, 2006, 2010) to the analysis of class comes from his conception of neoliberalism as the restoration of class power and the rise of a new phase of primitive accumulation in capitalist political economy, which he refers to as 'accumulation by dispossession'. Harvey argues that, whilst the classical Marxist extraction of surplus value through the labour process continues to be fundamental to understanding capitalism and its contradictions, and in particular he notes the increasingly precarious existence of workers or 'precariat', this is often obfuscated by the 'second grand category of the dispossessed, which is much more complicated in its composition and in its class character' (Harvey, 2010: 243) and is formed through accumulation by dispossession. This latter category is highly fragmented. Whilst Harvey stops short of arguing that the victims of accumulation by dispossession constitutes a 'new class', he does propose that these diverse and fragmented exploited and oppressed groups need to play a role in resisting the power grab of the capitalist class:

> The political unification of diverse struggles within the labour movement and among those whose cultural as well as political-economic assets have been dispossessed appears to be crucial for any movement to change the course of human history. The dream would be a grand alliance of all the deprived and the dispossessed everywhere. The aim would be to control the organisation, production and distribution of the surplus product for the long-term benefit of all. (Harvey, 2010: 247)

It is thus feasible to extrapolate from Harvey's analysis a proposal that accumulation by dispossession provides the economic driving force for class formation of disparate and fragmented groups, much as early capitalism generated the working class from the diverse peasant, dispossessed and artisanal groups forced to sell their labour power to the owners of capital.

Subaltern counterpublics of class

What are the implications of these sociological analyses of class for public sociology praxis? Below I outline six reflections:

1. Applying the logic of our approach to public sociology, we should ask: who or what is a subaltern class, and how are they becoming a counterpublic? In identifying a public, sociologists are largely working at a situational level, in which Savage (2015) and his colleagues identify the precariat and perhaps the traditional working class and emergent service workers as subaltern, whereas Harvey (2010) identifies the range of exploited and dispossessed groups as having potential for class formation following accumulation by dispossession, and certainly the opportunity to have common cause with both secure and precarious working class against capitalist class ascendency. It is likely to be a task of the public sociologist to engage with these diverse class formations in their attempts to defend or improve their life chances through the different levels of conflict: protection of basic human rights and dignity at a situational level; redistribution of resources from those classes with privileged access; and to analyse their collective position in class relations, in the recognition that this is likely to be contradictory.

Engaging as a public sociologist with a subaltern counterpublic in class relations requires a class self-identification (stratification), recognition of class inequality (opportunity hoarding) and analysis of exploitation (Marxist).

2. Our soundings suggest that implicit class analysis is possible even when explicit class reference (or self-identify) is not. Indeed, the degree of class visibility, and the opportunities for explicit class representation, is in constant flux – as the conflicts of interest between classes are made more or less exposed by economic factors and the actions of class actors – from above and from below.

3. Conflicting and contradictory class locations, which can serve to obscure class relations, can also be used to expose them (see Wånggren, Case III.6 in this volume). Industrial action in recent years by workers generally understood in Weberian linear class terms as privileged or middle class – junior doctors and university lecturers – demonstrates the proletarianising tendency of capitalism and (with Harvey 2010) that class is a social position in relation to productive forces and commodification. Class analysis allows me to see my organisation of industrial action through my trade union at my university in opposition to job cuts and redundancies as 'class struggle', even though the jobs that are at risk would be categorised as a 'professional occupation' (Socio-Economic Classification class 2) and the individuals whose jobs are at risk might come from a wide range of class backgrounds and identities. However, the systemic analysis of the causes of the job losses from cuts in public services and privatisation provides the analytical tools to understand academic workers as increasingly proletarianised (selling labour power in a market) or precariatised (fragmented and casualised work in a deregulated market). To name the industrial action as class struggle, beyond the confines of fellow union activists, is, however, unlikely to resonate, since the academics and related colleagues are unlikely to identify themselves as working class, proletariat or precariat – indeed, in some cases even as workers. Their contradictory location means that academic workers engage in local industrial action (militant particularism) through which they might recognise their position as a proletariat exploited through relations of (knowledge) production.

4. Wright encourages the integration of what appears to be conflicting forms of analysis. It is possible to act at a micro-level to defend the interests of a group within the rules determined by the ruling group, and even work at a meso level to attempt to influence the practice and implementation of these rules, whilst understanding

macro class relations. Students as worker in the precarious economy (as explored by Mignot and Gee, Case III.1 in this collection); widening access to students from working class and deprived backgrounds (Johnson's Case III.2); and the interests of capital and proletarianisation of academic staff, can be held together as part of an integrated but contested analysis.

5. There are opportunities for addressing this through Cox and Nilsen's (2014) social movement process approach in which recognition of class, inequality and exploitation occurs through step changes in the process through which collectively organised subaltern groups (movements from below) make demands on social structures, defended by movements from above, in the interests of improving life chances and then, reaching the limitations of concessions within these social structures, make demands at a higher level of social organisation. By realising the limits of situational action (playing by the rules) to challenging opportunity hoarding (gaming or bending the rules) and then through the limits at this level it is possible to move towards an analysis that questions the game itself.

6. Sociological questions of class formation, class distinction, class emergence, class fragmentation are best examined with, through and by subaltern counter public action, and engaging with the difficult questions of who such subaltern classes are, and how they might counter their subalternity.

A public sociology masters student was wearing a t-shirt with a phrase written in Slovak. I asked her what it meant – it was an old Slovak Communist Party slogan along the lines of 'Intellectuals: get out of the coffee shops and into the factories'. We agreed that today one would be more likely to find the proletariat working in the coffee shops than in the factories, and that the public sociologist might be as likely to be working amongst the precarious workers in the service sector as with the traditional industrial working class. The student also had a precarious job in retail alongside her studies.

It may be that the decline of class means that explicit engagement in counterpublic sociology with subaltern classes is unlikely to be common, but class analysis – and being promiscuous and fleet of foot in recognising class exploitation – whether through labour process, precariatisation, accumulation by dispossession or opportunity hoarding – and deepening the class analysis through the social movement process – is where the contribution of organic public sociology resides.

References

Bhattacharya, T. (2017a) 'Introduction', in Bhattacharya, T. (ed) *Social Reproduction Theory: Remapping Class, Recentring Oppression*, London: Pluto Press, pp 1–20.

Bhattacharya, T. (2017b) 'How not to skip class: social reproduction of labor and the global working class', in Bhattacharya, T. (ed) *Social Reproduction Theory: Remapping Class, Recentring Oppression*. London: Pluto Press, pp 68–93.

Canaan, J.E. (2013) 'Where did class go, why may it be returning?: a view from sociology students', *Journal for Critical Education Policy Studies*, 11(1): 27–48.

Cox, L. and Nilsen, A.G. (2014) *We Make Our Own History: Marxism, Social Movements and the Crisis of Neoliberalism*, London: Pluto Press.

Davies, A.J. (1996) *To Build A New Jerusalem*, London: Abacus.

Gilfillan, P. (2011) 'Scottish Nationalism', *Concept*, 2(1), http://concept.lib.ed.ac.uk/article/view/2309

Harvey, D. (2005) *A Brief History of Neoliberalism*, London: Verso.

Harvey, D. (2006) 'Neoliberalism and the restoration of class power', in Harvey, D. *Spaces of Global Capitalism: Towards a Theory of Uneven Geographical Development*, London: Verso, pp 7–68.

Harvey, D. (2010) *The Enigma of Capital and the Crises of Capitalism*, Oxford: Oxford University Press.

Jenkins, C., Canaan, J., Filippakou, O. and Strudwick, K. (2011) 'The troubling concept of class: reflecting on our 'failure' to encourage sociology students to recognise their classed locations using autobiographical methods', *Enhancing Learning in the Social Sciences*, 3(3).

McNally, D. (2017) 'Intersections and dialectics: critical reconstructions in social reproduction theory', in Bhattacharya, T. (ed) *Social Reproduction Theory: Remapping Class, Recentring Oppression*. London: Pluto Press, pp 94–111.

Platt, E. (2014) 'Comrades at war: the decline and fall of the Socialist Workers Party', *New Statesman*, May, www.newstatesman.com/politics/2014/05/comrades-war-decline-and-fall-socialist-workers-party

Savage, M. (2015) (in collaboration with N. Cunningham, F. Devine, S. Friedman, D. Laurison, L. McKenzie, A. Miles, H. Snee and P. Wakeling) *Social Class in the 21st Century*, London: Pelican.

Savage, M., Devine, F., Cunningham, N., Taylor, M., Li, Y., Hjellbrekke, J., Le Roux, B., Friedman, S., and Miles, A. (2013) 'A new model of social class? Findings from the BBC's Great British Class Survey experiment', *Sociology*, 47(2): 219–250.

Standing, G. (2011) *The Precariat: The New Dangerous Class*, London: Bloomsbury.
Wright, E.O. (1985) *Classes*, London: Verso.
Wright, E.O. (2015a) 'From grand paradigm battles to pragmatist realism: towards an integrated class analysis', in Wright, E.O. *Understanding Class*. London: Verso, pp 1–18.
Wright, E.O. (2015b) 'The death of class debate', in Wright, E.O. *Understanding Class*. London: Verso, pp 139–156.
Wright, E.O. (2015c) 'Is the precariat a class?', in Wright, E.O. *Understanding Class*. London: Verso, pp 157–174.

DIALOGUE I

Subaltern Counterpublics

Eurig Scandrett and Paul Gilfillan

The dialogue around publics took the form of an invitation to the contributors to respond to a narrative around generative themes emerging from the cases in this section, and the extent to which the problematics posed in the provocation were responded to. Whilst all contributors were invited to participate, this dialogue took the form of an extended email correspondence between Paul Gilfillan, author of Case I.4, and Eurig Scandrett, editor and author of Case I.5, which is itself a response to an earlier version of Paul's case study. Whilst this inevitably puts a restriction on the diversity of voices in the section (not least because the only voices are those of the two male contributors), the correspondence between Paul and Eurig has provided the opportunity to examine, test and interrogate in some depth, the proposition of public sociology engagement with subaltern counterpublics.

In the provocation for this section, it is proposed that the publics with whom public sociologists should be engaging are best understood through Nancy Fraser's (1990) formulation of the subaltern counterpublic. The public sociologist therefore has a role in contributing to the analysis of subalternity in terms of understanding social axes of oppression, exploitation and injustice, and contributing to the strategies of countering these. The means of analysis and strategy development is through dialogue between the resources of sociology (and other academic disciplines) and the praxis of publics engaged in struggle, and this dialogue is a pedagogical task. This argument builds on Burawoy's 'Between the organic public sociologist and a public is a dialogue, a process of mutual education' (Burawoy, 2005: 7) and, more politically, Gramsci's 'every relationship of "hegemony" is necessarily an educational relationship' (Hoare and Smith, 1971: 350). How useful is this proposition?

The choice of cases from which to develop our dialogue have been drawn from selected forms of public sociology practice. In the newly emergent field of Mad Studies, the knowledge of mad-identifying people who have experience of psychiatric diagnosis or mental distress is validated and valued through a dialogical education programme *Mad People's History and Identity*. The feminist movement has constructed an analysis of violence from the collective experience of women, and demonstrates the ongoing engagement with this analysis through dialogue between practice and theory in pedagogy and in participatory research. The central but problematic nature of class as a locus for public sociology is illustrated through the tension between class analysis and working class identity in workers' and community education.

Arguably, framing public sociology as dialogue with subaltern counterpublics prompts the question of legitimacy in public sociology, and the requirement for public sociologists to justify our work in terms of subalternity and countering, both to our academic peers and to our publics – a dual accountability. In this context a theme regularly emerging is the constant risk of the sociologist 'colonising' the subaltern, and exploiting their struggles for the purposes of an academic political economy that values such engagement in narrow terms of market share, institutional reputation and impact. This is an important consideration, of which our contributors are keenly aware (although the risks associated with the metaphor of colonisation has also been highlighted). The contributors take a range of approaches in addressing this through the case studies: through multiple co-authorship and reporting of co-authored photovoice, to extensive quoting from participants and taking soundings from key informants. The focus of the cases has been the subaltern counterpublics with whom an educational engagement is occurring.

However, what of publics that are found not to meet the criteria of subalternity or counter public? What, for example, of subalterns that are not 'countering'. Gilfillan's working class in Fife are portrayed as affluent and show little interest in either engagement in 'empowerment through education' or engaging in any other form of class struggle against the owners of industrial capital that have abandoned their communities. By contrast, the axis of empowerment that has more purchase is cultural, and in particular in relation to a 'New Scotland discourse' and the unstable constitutional settlement within the UK. At the same time as class is undermined as a category of subaltern counter-public, forms of class exploitation are becoming more pronounced and varied. With the impact of austerity eroding any experience of affluence of the working class, it is not clear that this will lead to a revival in class analysis.

The category of subaltern counterpublic remains a point of departure in unexpected ways. University academics (which describes most public sociologists at least some of the time), whilst enjoying some relative privileges compared with other groups, nonetheless constitute subaltern counterpublics when we collectively resist the causes of our exploitation as workers – an issue that Lena Wånggren returns to in section III of this collection. And there are many public sociologists engaging not with subaltern groups directly, but with those who act in solidarity with, for example, colonised and persecuted people internationally, with the environment, or with those for whom countering may carry high risk (asylum seekers). For these diverse forms of public sociology, how useful is the heuristic of the subaltern counterpublic?

In Fraser's concept of subaltern counterpublic, 'public' refers to a public sphere in which subaltern groups express and advocate their interests. To what extent is the practice of public sociology concerned with the creation of new spaces of public sphere – often in or connected to the university – which can be enriched through the dialogues between struggle and knowledge?

The provocation identified a tension between a structural analyses of subalternity, and subaltern identity. Mad is an identity – it is a term with which some people with experience of psychiatric labelling have identified, based on symbolic, cultural and epistemic exclusion. The response to exclusion is to reclaim that categorisation and subvert its social construction in order to value mad experience. In this project, mad-identified people draw on whatever resources can provide the analytical power that is 'really useful' to their struggle – which includes, but is not limited to, sociology. A question that a sociologist might raise is, what is the next step beyond valuing 'ignored voices'? As Sapouna and O'Donnell (2017) challenge: anti-psychiatry is not enough, mad-friendly spaces is not enough, nor even how madness intersects with gender, 'race', sexuality, disability etc. Is there a need for a structural analysis of madness from the perspective of the mad people's movement? What is the function of madness in totalising social structures such as capitalism or patriarchy? What is the source of oppression around which madness can mobilise? To what extent is Mad Studies 'counter hegemonic'?

Feminism is Fraser's classic subaltern counterpublic, constructed by women who are excluded from the public sphere, who organise their own space in order to re-enter the public sphere from a position of strength and an analysis of their oppression. Gender is structural and also cultural – Fraser's bivalent category (Fraser, 1995). As Orr and Whiting (Chapter I.2), and Young (Chapter I.3) explore, the resources deployed in the practice of challenging gender-based violence through education and research include, but are not limited to, the sociological.

Class is structural and retains robust analytical power but, as Gilfillan and others recognised, there is a decline in identification with subaltern classes. Is this a role that public sociologists play (as Scandrett's 'soundings' suggest, Chapter I.5), to introduce class analysis opportunistically in contexts where it is necessary but not obvious? This is the sociological imagination – and sometimes it requires quite a leap of imagination – which is the task of the public sociologist. Erik Olin Wright (2015)'s assessment of the different levels of analysis that class requires: micro, meso and macro; to which, he suggests, sociology based on empirical, Weberian and Marxian sources correlate. To this end, a challenge for public sociologists might be to engage simultaneously with the totality of the micro-level of experience, the meso level of policy and the macro level of exploitation. Freire's pedagogy, in which the concrete and the abstract are constantly brought together for mutual interrogation to generate new knowledge is key here, as a number of contributors allude. But such practice clearly remains problematic in the institutions of education, from community work and the Workers Education Association to the university, each of which is pressed to perform non-dialogical functions of 'employability'.

On the contrary, in some cases the invisibility of class results in a misidentification of structures of oppression to be countered and deflected onto other subaltern groups. The experience of exclusion from the public sphere amongst some subaltern groups can lead to resisting the efforts of others to counter their own sources of oppression. This is not a new phenomenon, but a revival in racism, xenophobia, misogyny and homophobia and the populist far Right movements of identitarianism and ethnic nationalism makes this an urgent challenge, not least to public sociologists. What role can public sociologists play with publics whose subalternity is exploited and counterpublic spaces directed against a liberal cosmopolitanism that is associated with celebrating diversity and challenging multiple sources of oppression? This is perhaps a departure from Burawoy's ambivalence, strongly criticised by others (for example Arribas Lozano, 2018) that 'public sociology has no intrinsic normative valence, other than the commitment to dialogue around issues raised in and by sociology. It can as well support Christian Fundamentalism as it can Liberation Sociology or Communitarianism' (Burawoy, 2005: 8–9). Can public sociology really support racist populism? Does public sociology have anything to say to those drawn towards it?

There are occasions where the interests of different subaltern groups appear to conflict and here it seems that there is a need to identify shared sources of oppression around which counterpublic activity can be mobilised – without thereby reinforcing other forms of oppression. Examples of this include conflicts between workers and the environment, regularly played out in local environmental justice struggles (for example Scandrett et al, 2012) and in Scotland at the time of writing through the tensions in the trade union movement over Just Transition. Other areas of apparent conflicts of interest are within and on the edges of feminism, such as those emerging in Orr and Whiting's *Gender Justice and Violence* programme, conflicts over prostitution/sex work; pornography and trans rights, issues which have become highly charged at the time of writing, in some cases, leading to the silencing of committed activist-academics. Whilst public sociology might be an ideal place for negotiating these interfaces within a totality, in practice these sociological analyses also come with identity. Categories such as radical feminist, Marxist, mad-positive, trans-inclusive etc are not merely committed sociological critiques, but also become identities that can also exclude. There is an emotional as well as intellectual engagement with counterpublics that makes the work of public sociology affective as well as analytical. How can public sociology negotiate these milieu in order to make its distinctive contribution?

Turning to the cultural, to what extent, as Gilfillan suggests, is a 'New Scotland discourse' a counterpublic sphere in which public sociology needs to take its place? As Burawoy (2005: 20) has indicated, public sociology needs to be 'provincialised', in his case as 'American' (the USA) and elsewhere (Burawoy, 2008) 'for California'. In the case of all contributors to this section, our 'province' is Scotland, and a Scotland with a changing sense of itself. To what extent do these discussions in fact contribute to a public sociology for, or of, Scotland?

The inclusion of Eurig's chapter (I.5) as a rejoinder to Paul's analysis (Chapter I.4) has continued as a dialogue on the importance of class for public sociology, and some of this is quoted in this dialogue. For Paul, the battle between Fraser's (and Scandrett's) and Burawoy's definition seems to be fundamental. But, he wonders if it is resolved? Why is Fraser's notion of the subaltern counterpublic especially privileged? If public sociology is defined as Fraser does (and not as Burawoy does) then we sociologists have to engage with a subaltern group that is also counterpublic.

Paul argues that sociology faces the kind of irrelevance to the working class that has befallen for example the Labour Party in Scotland, unless it maintains the connection to the working class. English sociologists Evans and Tilley (2017) argue there has occurred a sharp decline in the perceived relevance of the Left-wing political parties since the 1990s; in the UK there is evidence the Labour Party has become more of a home for middle class professionals than the manual workers it was founded to represent (Evans and Tilley, 2017: 151). In addition, although public sociologists can be accused of colonising the subaltern (an issue not faced by Paul with decades of ethnographic study of his own working class community), he notes that there is a price to be paid by the public sociologist. We have to suffer their stigma too if we study them. Contagion! We pay a price. It is not sexy or something of prestige in middle class academia. And working class people do not thank you for it either! So there are reasons imminent to the university that invisiblise class.

Gilfillan and Scandrett in dialogue

During the production of the book, much debate was triggered by an interview quoted by Paul from his ethnographic research in Fife. In order to reflect some of this debate, and as a contribution to dialogue on public sociology, this quotation is reproduced here along with excerpts from the dialogue that has followed.

Paul (ethnographer):
In May 2018 I interviewed 'Alec,' a forty-eight year-old plumber with Fife Council (and Associate WEA member thanks to attending one of the local history group classes) who was at my house to do some repairs. As we chatted he asked what line of work I was in that meant I was able to work from home. I told him I was a sociologist; which provoked the query, 'What's that, then'? I replied it meant studying contemporary society and social change; which led Alec to voice his opinions on a range of topics:

Alec: Honestly, they're tryin tae brek up the family. Family values. They're wantin tae turn them oan ther heid. What's good: bad. And what's bad: good. An it's only happened in the last six months tae a year. They're tryin tae; it wis a couple years ago, two or three years ago. Ah used tae say tae Mary [wife]: 'Ken this, ken what fuckin annoys me, they're makin the man oot tae be a complete clown, eh? It doesnae matter if it's a soap pooder advert or ken like buyin a loaf e breid; he comes back wi ... ken what Ah mean? Makin the man oot tae be a complete an utter muppet. An yer thinkin every fuckin advert's like that! If it wis the ither wiy aroond they'd be hivin kittens. 'How dare ye portray women as ...' ken? It slowly creeps in. Wee things creepin in. Ah cannae sit an watch the telly wi Mary these days because Ah jist; like she wis watchin a crime thing the other night an two black guys and, Bulletproof or somethin it's called, and, it's like a modern day The Sweeney eh? An ah wis like, 'Ah'll tell ye what's gonnae happen here. The boss Regan is gonnae be a woman, right? There'll be like fuckin, two eh Islamic women runnin aboot there whose like senior detectives. There'll be two guys, eh, white guys, who are the guys that are makin the mistakes, an who're talkin like clowns, bein absolute muppets, and the two black guys'll be the heroes. Am ah right or am ah wrang?' 'Oh jist shut yer pus an dinnae watch it if ye dinnae want tae watch it!' [wife] An ah was 'Am Ah right or am Ah wrang? Am seen it right here the noo!'

Paul: Me and the wife watch aa' these Scandinavian crime dramas, an Ah'll say before it starts: 'Ah'll tell ye what will happen. The hero is a woman. And the people who are commitin aa' the crimes are Christian fundamentalists or anti-liberals.'

Alec: Aye! Yer wane e the extreme sort e views that are just conflicting wi everybody else in the programme. They make them oot tae be a bit e an oddball. Aye. It's slowly but surely jist brainwashin people. An Ah'd say that wi the race thing tae. In the last six months ye cannae fuckin watch an advert oan the telly where the man an wife are no fuckin mixed race. It's like somebody has tell't them. Like there's a quota or a target tae be met. Ah've said that tae Mary. An aa' Ah get is 'Since when did ye turn intae a racist?' Ah says 'Ah'm no bein racist, am jist pointin oot tae ye; d'ye no think that's a bit odd?' 'No it's no. It's racist' she says. 'Yer on YouTube too much.' As says 'Ah'm no on YouTube too much. Ah read quite a lot an aw.' Ah says Ah can see what's happenin. So Ah've got tae sit an shut ma pus a lot. They're just pushin an agenda. An it's the same with the gay thing. An every time Ah point this oot it's like 'So are ye some sort e homophobic racist?' Ah says 'Ah'm no. Ah'm jist pointin oot tae ye it's odd that aa e a sudden.' Bit the guid thing is because ah work wi a lot e boys fae years ago talkin aboot, they're noo catchin oan tae things like that. An they're sayin 'Aye, it's fuckin shockin, eh?' Yer run e the mill boys on a building site are beginning tae notice things. Whoever's daen this, has got everybody's really checkin their sels oot wi things like that. Everybody's feart tae speak oot. Where nowadays Ah'm jist, tell it as ah see it, ken? People are censoring themsels. They're feart tae speak oot. Ah'm pretty confident folk'll jist, there'll be some sort e [inaudible at this point] comes doon; as Ah say Ah work wi boys who they've nae political persuasion whatever; who'll jist sit an read the sports pages an they're gone, 'How is this; this is fuckin shockin. Two men getting married. How's that happenin?' They're startin tae catch on tae it. And that Irish abortion thing. Ye've got fuckin Nicola Sturgeon sayin let's trust women. Ya cunt does she say let's trust women to pay the right taxes? Does she fuck! Does she say let's decriminalise murder an jist trust women tae make the right decision an' no kill somebody? Does she fuck! The fuckin SNP we aa voted fir isnae in charge. It's these fuckin liberals. An Ah'll tell ye what ye have tae watch fir an aw, an Ah've said this for years, an everybody's like. 'Fuck! Here he goes again,' eh? Ah think they're gonnae try an lower the age e consent. Watch fir that creepin slowly but surely. Break the family up. See the named person scheme; who the fuck thought that up? Aright there's a lot e vulnerable families oot there, that's what the social work department is fir, eh?

Paul: Have ye seen the latest stupidity? I can now be a woman because I say I'm a woman.

Alec: There's people behind this. Slowly but surely. Ah jist see it as a new wiy e brining communism back. Ah think that's what it is, eh? Attack the Church. Attack the family. Bring in the LGBT. Gie thame a say. Wance they get their fuckin claws intae everybody. Look at that carry oan wi that survey in Perth and Kinross back whenever it was; an noo some fuckin clown in the SNP wants tae criminalise parents who hit their bairns.

Eurig (editor):
I do not think that the section 'Producing Sociological Analysis with Associate Members' should be in the chapter. The connection with the WEA is tendentious and the

arguments do not follow. 'Alec' does not reflect a 'subaltern counterpublic' as argued in the provocation, his narrative does not address the sociological grounds for subalternity (class exploitation, British unionism) but is a defence of straight white male privilege and the promotion of injustice by pathologising black, female and LGBT representation in culture. Racism, homophobia, heteronormativity and anti-liberalism is as much to be found in middle class England, and indeed in sociological texts, and I do not think it has a place in our argument about public sociology. Introducing this narrative detracts from an interesting argument about the WEA and the post-industrial working class.

Paul: I will be in 'Alec's' company tonight so it'll be interesting to get his reaction to you calling him a racist and a representative of straight white male privilege and a promoter of injustice by pathologising black, female and LGBT representation in culture.

What I'd find helpful is if you could give me some help identifying what is counterpublic and what is subaltern? You mention in your email 'the sociological grounds for subalterneity (for example class exploitation, British unionism) and I am not sure what that means. Does it mean being working class means you qualify as being subaltern? Or only if you not only are working class but also discourse on the topic of class exploitation?

Also, can you clarify if being a British unionist means you are subaltern? Or is it that being a Scottish nationalist means you are subaltern? To me the subaltern idea is something I associate with Spivak's famous article on lower caste females in India having no voice. So some clear examples of what would qualify as a subaltern counterpublic in Scotland would be very helpful.

Another question I'd find it helpful to get clarity on is what public do you have to be against in order to be counterpublic? Could you give me a list of counterpublics? Not exhaustive obviously but a few examples that occur to you so I can get a sense of the answer.

Eurig: I think your questions are important ones in the discussions of public sociology, as indeed they are somewhat represented in the literature. What I am arguing is that the 'public' with which public sociologists (at least in the sense of Burawoy's

Organic Public sociology) engage needs to be a subaltern counterpublic. To state that, is to ask more questions than to answer – some of which you have identified. What does subaltern mean, sociologically?

Spivak's version, in 'Can the Subaltern Speak?' (Spivak, 1988) is an important contribution to this debate, which I take as a critique of Gramsci's understanding of the role of such groups in class formation and the emergence of class consciousness, at least in the post-colonial context. Spivak is, of course, located within the Subaltern Studies' group whose interest is in the history of the multitude of diverse, non-elite groups in South Asia. Others have used the term in other contexts. In Evelyn Nakano Glenn's (2007) response to Burawoy ('Whose public sociology? The subaltern speaks but who is listening?') she uses the term largely to mean women and racialised minorities in the USA, and refers to women's studies and African American studies as 'subaltern fields' and subaltern scholars within sociology. It seems to me that it is important to explore and justify the meaning of subalternity sociologically, in terms of the structures of power in societies. It is relatively clear that African Americans as a category are subaltern in the context of USA, even though some African Americans can be elite (even president). But they are not elite *as* African Americans (you might say they are elite despite being African American). So, the interconnecting sociological categories of power, exploitation of labour power, symbolic oppression in culture, discrimination etc are essential to an understanding of subalternity – this is what the intersectionality / social reproduction debate is all about.

When Nancy Fraser introduced the concept of the subaltern counterpublic it was in relation to the narratives of groups who are disempowered or under-represented within Habermas' liberal model of the bourgeois public sphere. She refers to public sphere and publics (and the nature of 'publicity') but does not really define either subaltern or counterpublic, which she appears to take as given. I would regard this as our point of departure, bringing sociological categories to analyse and justify subalternity and counter-ness.

You ask for some clear examples of what would qualify as a subaltern counterpublic in Scotland. This, I think, is part of our project of public sociology. Scotland is capitalist, and part of a global capitalist economy. It is also social democratic, having retained a good bit of the infrastructure of social democracy of the British state, but which is being dismantled in England. The working class is a subaltern class within capitalism as a result of the exploitation of its labour power, or its subordinate position in terms of life chances, or its symbolic representation in public discourse (depending on which line of sociological analysis you prefer). The British working class is a subaltern counterpublic in the sense that it has collectively challenged these forms of exploitation, subordination, misrepresentation etc. Social democracy is one of its major achievements. Black, Asian and Minority Ethnic (BAME) communities are subaltern within Scotland due to the institutional racism that is present in British institutions, the legacy of British colonialism, the symbolic under-representation of their culture, religions, visible presence, minority status, demonisation by white supremacists etc. There is much sociological literature on this. BAME communities are counterpublics in that they have collectively challenged aspects of their oppression and exploitation, and have achieved some success.

Scotland (that is the people of Scotland) is subaltern in relation to the British state since it has historically been denied the same political control over its affairs that England has enjoyed and is subject to symbolic misrepresentation through the legacy of explicit repression of culture (language, music etc) and through institutional invisibility (for example the Brexit referendum, which ignored Scotland's majority vote to remain). The people of Scotland have, collectively, challenged this subalternity through cultural revivals, the devolution movement and the ongoing campaign for independence, and thus can be regarded a counterpublic in this sense. Similarly, women are subaltern within Scotland as a result of the exploitation of unpaid labour, symbolic misrepresentation, sexual violation, the glass ceiling etc and have collectively countered these forms of exploitation with some legislative and cultural success. All of these categories of subalternity have countered the axes of their oppression, achieved some success, defend this success against reaction and continue to counter ongoing oppression. None of these categories is homogenous and they interact with one another generating conflicting interest.

So for the male white working class in Scotland, the axes of their subalternity lie in 'class' (in relation to the capitalist class / higher status classes / symbolic representation of habitus etc) and 'Scotland' (in relation to the British state, the democratic deficit and symbolic misrepresentation) but not in 'white' (since white is the hegemonic category of 'race' in Scotland), nor in 'male' (since male is hegemonic in Scotland). 'Alec's' narrative locates the source of his grievance in what he perceives as the over-representation of black and female characters in symbolically superior positions in popular culture and in society more generally. If this narrative is to represent a subaltern counterpublic then it would be challenging the causes of subalternity (in opposition to capitalism / higher status classes and the British state / British nationalism), not challenging the achievements of other subaltern groups in their struggles to challenge the over-representation of white and male characters in symbolically superior positions in society.

Some of these axes of oppression have been central to the project of the New Left movements which you critique in your chapter, although arguably the achievements have tended to be liberal rather than New Left – the New Left is an attempt to challenge the liberalism from the Left. Again I would find helpful Nancy Fraser's (1995) distinction between affirmative and transformative responses to injustice, which I think explains some of the category errors in Alec's narrative.

For most subaltern counterpublics (and indeed most public sociology worldwide) the experience of subalternity is obvious and needs little justification – experienced through poverty, hunger, violence, destitution, dispossession etc, – public sociology can contribute to analysing the particular forms and causes of exploitation in order to counter them. In post-industrial, post-colonising, social democratic, devolved Scotland, public sociology has a role, I would argue, in analysing the nature of subalternity as well as the strategies of countering (see Arribas Lozano's (2018) similar argument from South Africa).

There is a valuable sociological task in understanding why Alec's narrative challenges the achievements of other subaltern groups, rather than the axes of the subalternity of his class and nation. This may indeed be another task for public sociology. There is also a sociological task (probably not a public sociological task) in understanding the experience represented in Alec's narrative as part of a rejection of liberalism or, as you have called it elsewhere, a 'systematic integralism'. I'm not convinced that a conservative public sociology is the answer, but this is a legitimate debate.

I hope that you had a good evening with 'Alec' and would be interested to hear his response. I don't know 'Alec' of course and have no opinion about whether he is personally racist (although his wife 'Mary' seems to think he is) but I would regard his narrative as racist.

Paul: I think if you talk about a counterpublic that is working class then you have to include a sociological criticism of television as they consume so much of it. In this regards 'Alec's' rant against the public realm of television being SUDDENLY awash with ethnic minorities and sexual minorities etc from 2016/7 (who on any sociological analysis are clearly marginal and subaltern in some respects) but in the television context Alec was referring to are clearly on any sociological analysis not there to have any agenda of their own but to signal companies happy to include these people in their customer base so they are there to sell products and signal how banks and drink companies are nice inclusive neoliberal consumers and how these groups are nicely incorporated into neoliberalism. (I know you are aware of this). You disallow Alec as a counterpublic voice because he 'misinterprets the source of his grievances'. I think Alec in his own mind is criticising not ethnic minorities and homosexuals but criticising advertising as ciphers for selling liberalism. It seems you think adverts with lots of ethnic mixed couples and programmes of incompetent white men are 'representations of resistance'? Surely a sociological analysis of Alec means looking at the public sphere as reproducing tightly controlled access to it and the close policing of content? What gets allowed and what gets banned. So I'd say a plumber isn't misrecognising anything but raising the question about what changes have occurred in the British public realm recently so the public sociologist would have to reference how the social institutions that self-regulate the content of TV and radio advertisement in Britain (the Advertising Standards Authority Ltd and the Committee of Advertising Practice Ltd and the Broadcast Committee of Advertising Practice Ltd) have all made it mandatory to include the LGBT agenda and I see they have recently agreed to enforce the ban on all 'stereotyping' in adverts on the basis of sex. Now you can't watch adverts without it being a mixed race couple. Now every washing up liquid advert has a young man washing the dishes. How very progressive. How fuckin patronising to women! This fools nobody. Certainly not Alec as it changes nothing. So what is the analysis of sociology?

The interpretation of these new rules by sociologists of course will always be different. One analysis will say they give voice to the marginalised and other interpretations will say they are just more examples of the 'opportunity hoarding' by the middle class you mentioned, as liberals are the only ones who can sign off on this tokenistic bullshit. I assume you'd agree with me that liberalism is entirely functional to social groups' practice of 'opportunity hoarding'? I also think that is an interesting line of argumentation / contestation that a Marxist-inspired public sociology could pursue.

So when I listen to Alec I don't see a racist when he bemoans mixed race couples but someone who is clearly against this part of the public realm, that doesn't lay a glove on structural issues, but because it pushes other agendas it imagines itself progressive and even virtuous. And he is just venting against an agenda being pushed onto him as a viewer of this important aspect of the public realm. Some working class people have a nose for agendas being pushed onto them by more powerful others. Some don't. Alec's wife, for example, seems to have no such awareness of an agenda at work. So, we have two opposite views of two lay people. Who is right according to sociological analysis? I'd say Alec every time.

But these changes in representational regimes are sociologically interesting of course. It shows some agendas in the neoliberal order are easily incorporated and represented while others are not. There's no mention of class. I know you know this, but maybe you could strengthen the invisibility of class theme you have by developing it in the realm of television as class has been wiped clean off out screens – unless its 'consecrated' class representations like *Downtown Abbey* of course.

You say I portray the working class as having the conservative values of family, religion and locality. Yes! They are conservative. That's how I find them. You quote S1 on page 61 saying working class communities were oppressive in the 1970s and 1980s for blacks and people with diverse sexualities. And he says that representation is simplistic and retrograde. Well last year a local gay hairdresser left for Glasgow. He was, and I quote from his co-worker, 'sick e bein the only gay in the village havin to put up wi grief all the time'. Total cliché I know and then there's more examples of harassment I could easily give. And, of course, there are counter-examples such as local SNP councillor on a pride march in Kirkcaldy.

I think the whole question of what counts as counter-cultural might be more empirical. What for Fraser is counter-cultural and what isn't? What are the counter-cultural causes public sociology validates and which are the ones it invalidates. These 'impossible' questions are begging for an answer. You have to say the Left-liberal causes are fine for public sociologists to get behind and the anti-liberal conservative ones are not really public sociology, or you say both liberal and conservative ones are fine. Otherwise the whole thing is fudged. Unless you resolve it by saying as a professional sociologist you allow a broad church as sociology is a broad church and has liberals and conservative voices – that in real life most sociologists are liberal in some respects and conservative in other respects.

Conclusion

There are two aspects of how to conclude this dialogue: from the perspective of sociology and from the perspective of social justice. Advances in the representation of (some) subaltern groups in the cultural public sphere, for example on television, are certainly exploited for neoliberal gain. At the same time, the material oppression of subaltern groups continues, whilst the material exploitation of subaltern classes remains invisible. So, the debate is not so much about which groups is it legitimate for public sociologists to work with, but rather what axes of exploitation and oppression can be targeted by public sociologists in the interests of social justice.

References

Arribas Lozano, A. (2018) 'Reframing the public sociology debate: towards collaborative and decolonial praxis', *Current Sociology*, 66(1): 92–109.

Burawoy, M. (2005) 'For public sociology', *American Sociological Review*, 70: 4–28.

Burawoy, M. (2008) 'A public sociology for California', *Critical Sociology*, 34(3): 339–348.

Evans, G. and Tilley, J. (2017) *The New Politics of Class: The Political Exclusion of the British Working Class*, Oxford: Oxford University Press.

Fraser, N. (1990) 'Rethinking the public sphere: a contribution to the critique of actually existing democracy', *Social Text*, 25/26: 56–80.

Fraser, N. (1995) 'From redistribution to recognition? Dilemmas of justice in a 'postsocialist' age', *New Left Review*, 212: 68–93.

Glenn, E.N. (2007) 'Whose public sociology? The subaltern speaks, but who is listening?', in Clawson, D., Zussman, R., Misra, J., Gerstel, N., Stokes, R., Anderton, D.L. and Burawoy, M. (eds) *Public Sociology: Fifteen Eminent Sociologists Debate Politics and the Profession in the Twenty-first Century*, Berkeley: University of California Press, pp 213–230.

Hoare, Q. and Smith, G.N. (1971) *Antonio Gramsci: Selections from Prison Notebooks*, London: Lawrence and Wishart.

Sapouna, L. and O'Donnell, A. (2017) '"Madness" and activism in Ireland and Scotland, a dialogue', *Community Development Journal*, 52(3): 524–534.

Scandrett, E., Crowther, J. and McGregor, C. (2012) 'Poverty, protest and popular education: class interests in discourses of climate change', in Carvalho, A. and Peterson, T.R. (eds) *Climate Change Communication and the Transformation of Politics*, London: Cambria, pp 277–305.

Spivak, G.C. (1988) 'Can the subaltern speak?', in Nelson, C. and Grossberg, L. (eds) *Marxism and the Interpretation of Culture*, Basingstoke: Macmillan Education, pp 271–313.

Wright, E.O. (2015) 'From grand paradigm battles to pragmatist realism: towards an integrated class analysis', in Wright, E.O. *Understanding Class*, London: Verso, pp 1–18.

SECTION II

Knowledges

PROVOCATION II

'Really Useful' Public Sociology Knowledge

Eurig Scandrett

This section addresses the 'what' of public sociology education, and asks about the political and epistemological status of public sociology knowledge, including in relation to other sociological practices. What special knowledge(s) can public sociology generate? And, in particular, what constitutes the knowledge-content, or curriculum, of public sociology education? Here it is argued that a key heuristic for public sociology knowledge is its requirement to be 'really useful' in the sense that this term has developed in adult education theory (Johnson, 1976; Scandrett et al, 2010).

The concept of 'really useful knowledge' has been used in radical adult education theory to mean knowledge that is selected, critiqued and generated by communities and groups engaged in struggles against oppression. It is based on the nineteenth century British working class critique, as elaborated in the radical press of the time, of the philanthropic Society for the Diffusion of Useful Knowledge (SDUK), established in 1826 by the Edinburgh lawyer and Whig politician Lord Henry Brougham. Brougham argued, contrary to the explicit elitism of the Tories of the time, that it was important for Enlightenment knowledge in the sciences and humanities to be made available to the working class through public lectures. Following the same tradition of public education delivered by the Andersonian Institution and the Mechanics Institutes, the SDUK was based on a philosophy that knowledge held by the elite should be translated into forms that could be accessed by the working class – at least its skilled sectors.

These institutions by the educated elite for the benefit of the working class were subject to radical critique as

> organs of the middle classes [teaching students] to be subservient to the existing political and social order. All that the worker hears in these schools is one long sermon on respectful and passive obedience in the station of life to which he has been called. (Engels, 1844)

At the time of SDUK, radical working class political movements such as the Chartists and the Owenites were arguing that the working class should be in control of their own education. Mocking the SDUK, the movement for *Really* Useful Knowledge' questioned in what way this knowledge was useful: useful for whom? who is to decide its usefulness? and through its satirical press, wondered 'What is useful *ignorance*? – ignorance useful to constitutional tyrants?' (The Poor Man's Guardian September 1831, quoted in Johnson, 1976). They argued that the selective provision of education by the elite would inevitably exclude anything that would threaten their interests as a ruling class. The radicals therefore demanded full access to the sources of Enlightenment knowledge on their own terms, and that any selection for an educational curriculum should be made by the working class movements themselves, in the interests of the working class.

As Johnson (1979) points out, this early nineteenth century conflict was explicitly over knowledge in two senses. First, the working class movements accepted the dominant Enlightenment assumptions of objective knowledge to which they demanded full access. But, secondly, they also argued that some knowledge was more useful than others to the working class in their emancipatory demands. Whether knowledge was 'really useful' or not, was to be tested in the political struggles of the radical working class movements, whether for independent organisation of production (Owenites) or democratic transformation of politics (Chartists).

Various authors have noted the value of this critique for educational practice. Griffin (1983) suggests that there is a continuous line of critique from these movements for 'really useful knowledge', through the deschooling of Illich (1970) and Freire's (1972) pedagogical innovations and culminating in the Lifelong Education of Ettore Gelpi (1979, 1985). Gelpi's fundamental argument (according to Griffin) is that it is not so much the institution (*contra* Illich) or pedagogical practice (*contra* Freire) that prevents education from being liberating, but the implications of these for *knowledge*, whose usefulness can only be judged through political struggle. Really useful knowledge can be generated and contested in schools and deschooled study circles, in didactic and dialogical pedagogy, by elite classes or subalterns (although in each case, the possibilities are enhanced in the latter option); what makes it 'really useful' is the interrogation of knowledge by subaltern struggles – and the deployment of knowledge to interrogate, dialectically, these struggles. Whilst dialogical pedagogical methods facilitate the generation of really useful knowledge, as Kane (2001) points out, the methods themselves do not make knowledge 'popular' (in the interests of the popular classes) or 'really useful'. It is the knowledge, not the method of its generation, that is the subject of critical scrutiny by those engaged in struggle.

The cases in this section explore the parameters of really useful knowledge generated through a range of pedagogical practices. And, as the third section of this collection explores, whilst social movements may well be more conducive to really useful knowledge production, such is also possible within the institutions of higher education.

For public sociology education, the challenge of 'really useful knowledge' is that it is not sociologists who are entitled to select sociological knowledge for 'their' public, but rather that such curriculum is generated through a mutually critical dialogue between sociological knowledge and the knowledge demands and knowledge production of publics and, in particular, subaltern counterpublics.

The validation of knowledge is therefore subject to a dual set of criteria: firstly, the normal academic validation process of intellectual rigour and acceptance by a disciplinary epistemic community; and, secondly, critical interrogation by a public engaged in struggle against structures of oppression, exploitation and injustice. Michael Burawoy's (2005) American Sociological Association address distinguishes 'organic public sociology' that has close connections with such movements (among others) and argued that 'The project of such public sociologies is to ... validate these organic connections as part of our sociological life' (Burawoy, 2005: 8). It is argued here, that really useful (public sociology) knowledge on the contrary, would require the reverse: validation of public sociology knowledge by subaltern movements. Such validation is not a once-and-for-all event, or even an incremental accrual of truth, but a political process of constant contestation and argument, of generating 'good sense' – indeed, as Kate Crehan (2016) points out, Gramsci's subalterns are not fixed classes but historically contingent. Moreover, at any point in this contestation, public sociology has a responsibility to offer the analytical tools of our discipline for interpreting the social relations of exploitation and oppression that designate the subaltern and resources for their struggle, subject to critical engagement by such movements.

Public sociology education and, in particular, dialogical pedagogical praxis, has a role in this project. The cases that follow demonstrate how much public sociology draws on the theory and practice of dialogical education and, in particular, the work of Paulo Freire. As with Freirean education, public sociology is based on an epistemological commitment to dialogue between, on the one hand, knowledge generated by specific publics and, on the other, sociological theory. Public sociologists vary in their emphasis on either side of this dialectic, yet all are committed to engaging with the other. Many of the methods used by public sociologists, ranging from participatory action research, through critical ethnography, activist research, photovoice and so on are based on these pedagogical approaches. The focus here is on the knowledge content of public sociology education, how it is generated and validated through dialogical process with particular publics, what the implications of such knowledge generated outwith the academy is and, moreover, how this knowledge can be understood historically in relation to an abstraction of subaltern counterpublic.

In the context of teaching participatory action research, I have used a formula of the 'Five Fs' which provide its epistemological grounding: Frankfurt School; Fanon; Feminism; Freire; Foucault. I find this a useful lineage for exploring public sociology knowledge. From the Frankfurt School we take the insistence that knowledge is historical. In their challenge to the Viennese circle's empiricism, Horkheimer and colleagues insisted on the historical construction of knowledge through a dialectical process such that knowledge tends towards an epistemological totality. Thus, to these critical theorists, knowledge is always partial, not in the empiricists' sense of partially known, but in the dialectical sense of contingent and intrinsically connected with class consciousness. Whilst human society remains divided by a class structure that arises from the relations of production, then knowledge will always be embedded with class interests. Thus, the distinction between fact and value, between knowledge and ideology, so valued by the empiricists, is ultimately overcome through political emancipation in a classless society. Whilst acknowledging the limitations of class reductionism implicit in some of this analysis, the insistence on discerning class (and other social) interests in the historical process of knowledge production provides valuable insights for public sociology curriculum, as well as the requirement to engage in historical processes of struggle for knowledge validation.

For Fanon, knowledge is also colonial. The colonised subject internalises the knowledge of the coloniser, which is presumed as superior and excludes all other forms of knowledge. Liberated knowledge not so much rejects the coloniser's knowledge, still less seeks to 'return' to a pre-colonial purity, but rather is 'cleansed' through an active process of decolonisation. Political decolonisation must be accompanied by cognitive decolonisation, the latter achieved in part through the struggle for the former. In a context of neoliberal globalisation, the sociological analysis of struggles for decolonisation becomes crucial. As Raewyn Connell has argued:

> 'public sociology' ... is not an option within the metropole ... Rather it is a necessity on a world scale.
> Neoliberal globalisation itself pushes sociology into an oppositional position, since the very act of naming social structures is an obstacle to the triumph of market ideology. If sociology is not to fade into a residual science researching those who sadly fail to 'achieve' in a neoliberal world, it must connect with the energies of resistance and the intellectual critique of global domination. (Connell, 2011: 118)

Engaging in the decolonisation of knowledge, moreover, needs to draw on the sociological analysis of the disparate nature of colonialism (Bhambra, 2016). Although Fanon did not differentiate, this applies as much to the historical conditions of imperial colonisation to actually existing settler colonialism, and to the racialised social relations of the canon of academic knowledge, including sociology. By this we recognise that whilst classic imperial colonialism – the historical conquest of lands for the purposes of exploitation of resources and labour in the interests of a colonial power – has largely ended with the 'age of Empire' (Hobsbawm, 1989), nonetheless the legacy of such colonisation continues, both in neocolonial geopolitical relations, and in the forms of institutional racism and epistemological imperialism of our educational institutions – as highlighted in movements such as 'Rhodes must fall' and 'why is my curriculum white'. Meanwhile, settler colonialism – a process through which persecuted European 'surplus populations' have settled other lands for the purpose of creating new, quasi-European settlements, expropriating land and resources (but not labour) for the settler population but expelling, exterminating and ethnically cleansing the indigenous population – continues in the ongoing exploitation of First Nations, Native Americans, Australian Aborigines, the Maori of Aotearoa/ New Zealand and Palestinians. And, finally, the practice of decolonisation is not restricted to the practice of public sociology of the colonised (where it is intrinsic) but also to the knowledge of the coloniser. A public sociology is one that engages in a process of decolonisation through solidarity (Gaztambide-Fernández, 2012). For Scotland, often in denial of its relationship to colonialism as a failed imperial power in its own right and an active contributor to the British Empire following the union, there is a particular importance of exposing the necessity of this process of epistemological decolonisation.

From feminism we take the important insight that not only is knowledge gendered, but it is embedded in the gendered social world. De Beauvoir pointed out that, by default, knowledge is male in that it is degendered. In 1949 she was able to write:

> A man would never set out to write a book on the peculiar situation of the human male. But if I wish to define myself, I must first of all say: 'I am a woman'; on this truth must be based all further discussion. A man never begins by presenting himself as an individual of a certain sex; it goes without saying that he is a man. A man is in the right in being a man; it is the woman who is in the wrong.
>
> It amounts to this: just as for the ancients there was an absolute vertical with reference to which the oblique was defined, so there is an absolute human type, the masculine. (De Beauvoir, 1949: xxvii)

The epistemological assumption of the Enlightenment is that true knowledge is disinterested and abstract, a knowledge of science, free from emotion and human contamination. It is unnecessary to specify that this knowledge belongs to men. Women's knowledge requires explanation and justification. Feminists have been at the forefront of challenging this conception of knowledge by exposing the interests and situations of the genesis of knowledge, the interactions of social assumptions and emotion in the most abstract of knowledge, and the role that such constructions of knowledge plays in the reproduction of gendered violation and patriarchal epistemology. Feminist social theory emerged as much from the practice of mobilising for women's liberation as from the canon of social science literature (Mitchell, 1971). Practices such as consciousness raising enabled women's private troubles to be turned into not just public issues, but also a methodology of analysis of public issues. For feminists such as Haraway (1988), these insights dissolve knowledge into an always situated and partial process of knowing, organised not just along gendered lines but also through other socially produced axes of inequality and oppression.

Here the 'objectivity' of the Enlightenment and Durkhiem's social 'facts' can be recast as we see 'objectivity as an excuse for a power relationship' (Stanley, 1993: 163). The insight that knowledge(s) are always situated, partial, embodied and therefore political owes a particular debt to Black feminist theory, with its attention to 'ongoing epistemological debates concerning the power dynamics that underlie what counts as knowledge' (Hill Collins, 2009: 292). This means that feminist academics aim not only 'to generate more and/or better knowledge but also ... to question and transform dominant standards ... of academic knowledge production' (Pereira, 2017: 95). Here we can see that public sociology knowledge joins long-standing debates on how, and whether, the 'master's tools' can 'dismantle the masters' house' (Lorde, 1984).

Freire approaches the different ways in which oppressions and exploitations are embedded in knowledge, and knowledge generated through struggles for emancipation, and locates them in a methodology of education. Freire's dialogical pedagogy aims to synthesise the word and the world, knowledge and action, the concrete with the abstract. It contains within it the possibility that the oppressed can also be the oppressor unless the epistemological roots of oppression are systematically critiqued alongside the political–economic causes. Freire provides a fundamental methodology for public sociology, for generating the always unfinished abstract dialogue between sociological theory and the practice of liberation through the concrete dialogue between public sociologists and subaltern counterpublics.

Foucault's understanding of knowledge goes beyond the limits of structuralism without abandoning its normative positioning. Knowledge takes its place in the wider struggles over power and resistance in the everyday, in the governance of populations, of collective bodies and subjectivities, and in the discourses that shape our knowledge about knowledge. For many feminists and critical race scholar-activists, the process of emancipating knowledge from its construction in patriarchy and colonialism occurs not just in the fields of academic debate or political campaigns, but also in the everyday domestic narratives of the lifeworld, subjectivity and bodily experience.

Thus, public sociology practice and popular education (Crowther, Galloway and Martin, 2005) are both engaged in similar political processes in the context of hegemonic struggles for democratic control of knowledge. Indeed, often public sociologists need to be able to switch between the two processes on the basis of responding to changes in political contexts.

This is a risky undertaking, especially where public sociology interacts with 'policy sociology' and the 'impact' agenda, and aims to implement practical outcomes of public sociology through systems of governance. Public policy has a track history of ignoring, co-opting, controlling, or reifying public knowledge, a risk into which policy sociology can also fall. In Case II.1, drawing on her experience of research in sexual health, Jan Law looks at the interface between policy sociology and public sociology, and explores how vested interests, and marketisation of sociological labour, conspire to shift policy research away from the subaltern publics that public sociologists aim to foreground. She examines the opportunities for public sociology to problematise the disciplinary power exercised through market relations that govern the relationship between the sociologist, the public and the policy entrepreneur, over control of knowledge. By contrast, Laura Lovin's Case II.2 examines a dialectical approach to knowledge generation, through which the voices of refugee and asylum-seeking women are being recognised in public policy in Scotland. Through the work of the Scottish Refugee Council and the Refugee Women's Strategic Group, the Scottish Government's *New Scots* refugee integration strategy has embraced the intersectional context of racialised and gendered knowledge construction by refugee and asylum-seeking women. Here, Lovin argues, lies the opportunity for really useful knowledge to be embedded in public policy, and perhaps for policy sociology to be enriched by public sociology.

The focus on 'really useful' public sociology knowledge returns us to the publics with whom dialogue takes place, and the methodologies appropriate to different publics and the ways in which methodology affects knowledge production. In Case II.3, Emma Wood explores dialogical methodologies employed with teenagers in the context of shaping knowledge about alcohol consumption. Teenage alcohol use is often framed in policy terms (at least outside the cultural world of teenagers) as a public health and social order concern. Employing dialogical methodology, Wood analyses the extent to which knowledge generated by and with teenagers is 'really useful', or indeed whether it is public sociology. Maria Giatsi Clausen (Case II.4) further explores to what extent public sociology knowledge can be 'really useful' when generated in dialogue with younger children, and whether methodologies employed reproduce power relations embedded in social constructions of childhood that deny the agency of the child.

References

Bhambra, G.K. (2016) 'Postcolonial reflections on sociology', *Sociology*, 50(5): 960–966.

Burawoy, M. (2005) 'For public sociology', *American Sociological Review*, 70: 4–28.

Connell, R. (2011) *Confronting Equality: Gender, Knowledge and Global Change*, Cambridge: Polity Press.

Crehan, K. (2016) *Gramsci's Common Sense: Inequality and its Narratives*, Durham, NC and London: Duke University Press.
Crowther, J., Galloway, V. and Martin, I. (2005) *Popular Education: Engaging the Academy. International Perspectives*, Leicester: NIACE.
de Beauvoir, S. (1949) *The Second Sex*, New York: Vintage Books.
Engels, F. (1844) *The Condition of the Working Class in England*, Leipzig: Otto Wigand.
Freire, P. (1972) *Pedagogy of the Oppressed*, London: Penguin.
Gaztambide-Fernández, R. (2012) 'Decolonization and the pedagogy of solidarity', *Decolonization*, 1(1).
Gelpi, E. (1979) *The Future of Lifelong Education*, Manchester: University of Manchester Press.
Gelpi, E. (1985) *Lifelong Education and International Relations*, London: Croom Helm.
Griffin, C. (1983) *Curriculum Theory in Adult and Lifelong Education*, London: Routledge.
Haraway, D. (1988) 'Situated knowledges: the science question in feminism and the privilege of partial perspective', *Feminist Studies*, 14(3): 575–599.
Hill Collins, P. and Bilge, S. (2016) *Intersectionality*, Malden: Polity Press.
Hobsbawm, E. (1989) *The Age of Empire: 1875–1914*, London: Vintage.
Illich, I. (1970) *Deschooling Society*, New York: Harper and Row.
Johnson, R. (1976) '"Really useful knowledge": radical education and working-class culture 1790–1848', in Clarke, J., Critcher, C. and Johnson, R. (eds) *Working Class Culture: Studies in History and Theory*, London: Hutchinson, pp 7–28.
Kane, L. (2001) *Popular Education and Social Change in Latin America*, London: Latin American Bureau.
Lorde, A. (1984) *Sister Outsider*, Berkley, CA: Ten Speed Press.
Mitchell, J. (1971) *Women: The Longest Revolution*, London: Penguin, pp 75–122.
Pereira, Maria do Mar (2017) *Power, Knowledge and Feminist Scholarship: An Ethnography of Academia*, Abingdon: Routledge.
Scandrett, E., Crowther, J., Hemmi, A., Mukherjee, S., Shah, D. and Sen, T. (2010) 'Theorising education and learning in social movements: environmental justice campaigns in Scotland and India', *Studies in the Education of Adults*, 42(2): 124–140.
Stanley, L. (1993) 'On auto/biography in sociology', *Sociology*, 27(1), 41–52.

CASE II.1

Crossing the Quadrant: Policy Research and Public Sociology

Jan Law

Introduction

This chapter explores the relationship between policy research and public sociology. Sociology, as Burawoy (2007a) famously argued, has a responsibility to turn the reflexive knowledge that it produces over to the service of social and political 'progress' and has a long tradition of producing 'really useful knowledge' to address 'social problems'. Useful knowledge is subject to dialectical and dialogical processes between diverse publics and sociologists, producing open-ended, morally and politically freighted possibilities that cannot be predetermined. In terms of extra-academic knowledge Burawoy (2007a: 31) distinguishes public sociology from 'policy sociology'. The latter is characterised as the production of expert knowledge to provide recommendations or legitimate solutions defined by a non-academic client. Policy sociology aims to contribute to the public policy process by attracting research funding either directly from policy-making bodies or from third parties such as charitable foundations or other public agencies. The boundary between public sociology and policy sociology is sometimes more fluid than static ideal-types suppose. For example, policy sociology may assume the form of public sociology in cases where sociologists seek the support of non-policy publics when clients refuse to support policy proposals. Typically, policy sociology seeks to foster constructive relationships with government and policy insiders. Policy sociology is sometimes accused of reducing sociology to a form of technical expertise shaped more by the conditions of funding than the logic of scientific enquiry (Bryson, 1999). Such instrumentalism risks reducing policy sociology to a subordinate relationship to funders in the form of 'sponsor capture'.

A growing body of literature suggests that the subjective experience of researchers, especially contract researchers, within the processes of policy sociology is often neglected and marginalised by standard accounts of the research process (Bryson, 1999; Hey, 2001; Allen Collinson, 2004; Tilbury, 2007). Contract research is often viewed as a rite of passage, involving what Burawoy (2007a) describes as crossing 'the quadrants of sociology'. Burawoy's idea of a sociological quadrant refers to a four-fold division of sociological labour – professional, critical, policy, public – and the position that an individual sociologist might occupy at any particular time. Across their career trajectories sociologists will often traverse the quadrant as they attempt to balance the sociological habitus with the fractured structure of the institutional field:

> The tension between institution and habitus drives sociologists from quadrant to quadrant, where they may settle for ritualistic accommodation before moving on, or abandon the discipline altogether. Still, there are always those whose energy and passion are infectious, spilling over into the other quadrants. (Burawoy, 2007a: 40)

Burawoy (2007a: 38–40) gives examples of pioneering sociologists like W.E.B. du Bois who attempted to change policy through public sociology, with an interlude working as a professional sociologist, while Robert Park became a professional sociologist only after working as a campaigning journalist. C. Wright Mills more promiscuously moved between professional sociology, public sociology and critical sociology.

My experiences as a policy researcher inform my discussion in this chapter of policy sociology and its relationship to public sociology. In the critical discussion of Burawoy's typology policy sociology is often assumed as typically taking a pathological form, corrupted by client capture (Piven, 2007). While the number of policy researchers has mushroomed in recent decades their experience has largely been ignored in standard accounts of the research process. This chapter offers an account of how policy sociology can be shaped by clients. It concerns experiences of a government-funded evaluation of sexual health education policy. This process was fraught with tensions between the client's steering group and the academic research team in ways that broadly corroborates the experience of other researchers about how policy evaluation shapes research design and 'cherry picks' research data to service predefined political objectives (Bryson, 1999; Allen Collinson, 2004; O'Brien et al, 2008; Tilbury, 2007).

Public sociology and policy sociology

In Britain sociology developed a close relationship to policy elites, typically as gifted amateurs concerned to ameliorate appalling social conditions as problems of urbanism, industrialisation, poverty, ethnicity, deviance, labour, and conflict (Abrams, 1968). More empirical forms of sociology committed to social reform like the British social survey tradition of Charles Booth exerted only a limited influence on the policy process (Bulmer, 1985). The main approach of the British social problems tradition was to stimulate moral outrage through a factual 'exposé' of social degradation requiring the amelioration of evil conditions that would induce individuals to improve their personal moral habits and hygiene. The assumption was that poverty or slum housing only had to be brought to the public's attention by means of irrefutable, detailed empirical evidence such as Booth's social surveys for an appropriate public policy remedy to stimulate the moral reform of character (Bulmer, et al, 1991).

While these studies raised the profile of the social problems agenda in the public consciousness their effectiveness in influencing public policy was limited. As sociology became professionalised, systematic and specialised from the 1930s onwards it adopted a more detached scientific self-image. As such it was concerned to limit accusations of political or moral bias. Earlier sociological preoccupations with social problems became institutionalised and formalised. Policy sociology aimed to ameliorate social problems in partnership with the requirements of public policy (Dahrendorf, 1995). From its base in the Fabian-influenced London School of Economics (LSE), British sociology was strongly associated with social administration, social work and public service (Dahrendorf, 1995). With its close alignment to the Labour Party and commitment to social reform, post-war sociology expanded outwards from the LSE into 'the provinces'.

A strong public service ethos enabled professional sociology to function as academic, sometimes critical advisors to the establishment during the post-war welfare consensus (Halsey, 2004). The growth of state-run public services generated a demand for the academic analysis of social and public policy, centred initially on health, social work and urban deprivation. Action research evaluated policy as it was framed within the established welfare consensus. Politicians and policy makers offered up their plans to the techniques of experimental social science on the tacit understanding that if its effectiveness was not supported by valid research techniques then the plan would be reviewed, revised or changed. Such a model continued to assume that there was a political consensus about social outcomes. As Halsey (2004: 106) notes, the language of 'social problems' could disguise underlying conflicts between sociology and public policy:

> The historic role of the social scientist as critic of the social order must set limits to his or her incorporation into administration just as the maintenance of political democracy must set limits to his or her participation in the making of decisions.

Such a value consensus policed the boundaries between political involvement and sociological detachment.

Since the last decade or so of the twentieth century, the relationship between sociology and government policy in the UK has often been an antagonistic one. The Conservative governments of the 1980s and early 1990s marginalised professional sociology from the policy process. Professional sociology also remained on the periphery of New Labour policy making after 1997. Under Thatcherism, mainstream sociology was made the subject of vitriolic political attack to the extent that it maintained an independent concern for the structural basis of social problems and a critical orientation on unequal relations of power (Halsey, 2004). Neoliberalism's agenda of 'rolling back the state' and 'rolling out the market' as the best possible solution for an individual and her family to flourish meant that policy elites had less use for critical, independent professional sociology, including policy sociology. In this context of institutional marginalisation sociology re-engaged with non-state publics active in social movements and as public advocates for disenfranchised social groups.

Burawoy's (2007a) ideal-type policy sociology provides solutions to predefined problems. External clients specify the task of the sociologist within a narrowly defined contractual relationship, while other clients are closer to arm's length patrons of broadly defined policy agendas (Burawoy, 2007a: 31). Policy sociology therefore is often far removed from the ideal of sociology as an autonomous, intellectually critical endeavour (see Table 1). Policy sociology is often associated with what Morris Janowitz (1972) called an 'engineering model' of instrumental knowledge. The instrumentalism of policy sociology is determined by a form of technical expertise that policy sociologists can draw upon

Table II.1.1: Burawoy's ideal-type of public sociology and policy sociology

Criteria	Policy sociology	Public sociology
Knowledge	Instrumental	Communicative
Truth	Pragmatic	Consensus
Legitimacy	Effectiveness	Relevance
Accountability	Clients	Designated publics
Politics	Policy intervention	Public dialogue
Pathology	Servility	Faddishness

Source: Adapted from Burawoy, 2007a: 43.

rationally from their 'tool-kit' to deal with the job in hand. Its subject of this form of 'really useful knowledge' is not a 'subaltern counter-public' but an institutionally powerful client. The engineering model is often contrasted to an 'Enlightenment model' of knowledge, which develops the basic science of abstract theoretical models separate from any direct concern with practical issues. Rejecting the intoxication of theoretical speculation or ideological partisanship, the sober collection of data and measured calculations about alternative courses of action underlie the engineering ideal in policy sociology.

Nonetheless, the idea that the application of a scientific methodology will produce cast-iron results to improve society through policy manipulation has not only failed to deliver lasting or cumulative gains in terms of either social reform or scientific knowledge but is based on unchallenged value assumptions about the hierarchy of power that more critical forms of sociology would contest at root. It also presents an unrealistic picture of the research process itself, which, as John Law (2004) argues, is much messier, more confused, uncertain, and contingent than the smooth appeal to technical expertise would suggest. In the interest of maintaining an engineering façade, policy sociologists are careful to conceal problems in the research process in case it calls into question technical competence and usefulness.

Perhaps the most trenchant critique of Burawoy's treatment of policy sociology has been that of David Brady (2004). Brady is concerned that Burawoy is turning attention away from the state and relations of power at a time when the anti-state ideology of neoliberalism makes engagement with the state an imperative for sociology as a discipline. Brady (2004: 1634) argues that Burawoy constructs a false dichotomy between public and policy sociology and

> arbitrarily places success stories under the label of 'public' sociology when they could just as easily be labelled 'policy'

sociology (research on displaced workers, toxic waste, housing inequalities, and educational reform, to advocacy for public health campaigns around HIV-AIDS or needle exchange to training community organisers to deal with the media).

To see all state-funded research as requiring a servile relationship, Brady argues, promotes an unreal caricature: 'sociologists have something very different and valuable to contribute to policy. For example, status attainment stratification sociologists have provided convincing evidence that much of one's socioeconomic status is inherited' (Brady, 2004: 1635). However, Brady, in turn, borders on a caricature of Burawoy, who does in fact note the value of policy sociology when it is tempered by dialogue with other forms of sociology.

Others like Douglas Massey (2007) came to the defence of policy sociology, while being sharply critical of the politics of public sociology. While Massey is personally committed to social justice and has been a politically active sociologist on a range of contentious public issues, he rejects political partisanship within professional and policy sociology. He advances a number of familiar reasons. First, 'effective policy requires an accurate understanding of the social structures, group processes, and individual behaviours that one seeks to modify through political action' (Massey, 2007: 146). Second, sociology depends on its reputation for impartiality and objectivity, and to stick to statements of scientific fact; anything less lacks scientific legitimacy. Third, by constantly improving the standards of social investigation, sociology acquires scientific prestige and respect, which only authorised leaders in the profession can appeal to in their public pronouncements.

For defenders of policy sociology like Massey, its chief legitimation is that only by becoming a trusted insider within the networks of policy elites can sociology have a 'real' influence, rather than being ignored as irrelevant to 'real world' issues. Without this kind of insider policy engagement sociology will prove irrelevant, prone to 'abstract' theory and 'structural bias' rather than interact with the concerns of elites. For Burawoy (2007b: 248), Massey's 'confident, almost euphoric' belief in sociology's technical virtues harks back to the technocratic politics in a 'messianic defence' of what he calls 'second-wave sociology' that was dominant in the USA during the Cold War years. This moment has gone for good, Burawoy argues, undone by the public and critical sociology that emerged with 1960s radicalism.

Methodological reflexivity

My experience of a government-funded evaluation of sexual health education policy tends to confirm the tensions identified above between public sociology and policy sociology. The aim of the evaluation was to assess the progress of the aims of the policy action plan at national, regional and local level and make recommendations. A mixed methods research design combined semi-structured interviews, focus groups and surveys with key stakeholders based in urban and rural localities. My main role as a contract researcher was to conduct semi-structured interviews and focus groups with key stakeholders in the national steering group, clinical services, education, prisons and religious and non-statutory sectors. In reporting my own experiences within the policy sociology field, I take ethical account of the contested nature of knowledge, including knowledge of knowledge production. Attempts were made by the clients to control both the research design and findings. We were subjected to informal pressure from policy insiders who expected the research team to comply. Throughout the different phases of fieldwork, I was extremely active with the time-consuming routines of the research process: negotiating access, liaising with funders, conducting interviews, writing up field notes, attending meetings, and so on. As a by-product of this activity, I retained a hoard of paperwork, personal notes and electronic communications, which I draw upon to inform the following narrative.

Dorothy Smith's (1987) materialist approach to institutional ethnography has advanced the case for the necessity of reconstructing experiential accounts. This is especially significant for dealing with marginal structural positions where a documentary trail is unavailable or unlikely to reveal unequal power dynamics. Materialist feminists argue that such narratives provide meaningful reconstructions of the institutional worlds in which research gets embedded (Naples, 2003). It allows some access to local institutional practices within which policy sociology is enacted. Materialist feminism aims to produce knowledge that helps its producer understand her implicit as well as explicit position in specific institutional contexts. This complicates the idea advanced by Massey (2007) that social research involves taking an innocent stance as a neutral observer of social action. Institutional ethnography adopts an 'insider's critique' from points of view marginalised by the ruling relations that operate in local contexts (Smith, 1990).

Here I am encouraged by some of the 'confessional' narratives of contract research that are beginning to emerge (see Reay, 2000; Hey, 2001; Goode, 2006; Tilbury, 2007). However, there is a danger with the cultural fascination with the confessional. Some researchers confuse personal confession with reflexivity in the sense of an attempt to account for the structural position of the researcher in objective social space. Diane Reay (2000) described her own sense of marginalisation when, working as a contract researcher, she was stigmatised as 'dim dross'. In response, she took up a standpoint as a working class woman to raise issues around social justice, the ethics of caring and the culture of uncaring which permeates academic, as well as wider social, elites. Similarly, Patricia Hill Collins (2007: 104) acknowledges that her own marginalised social position as an African American woman in overwhelmingly white and male settings informed her intellectual and political standpoint. She felt frustrated about carrying her working class habitus into situations that 'routinely privilege the cultural (and actual) capital of middle-class families'. Since she belongs to and identifies with groups that attract little prestige within American society, she stands in a different relationship to power relations than mainstream white, middle class sociology. This helped her to develop distinctive ideas about democracy, social justice, ethnicity, and feminism.

My own experience as a researcher in the field of policy sociology in different capacities, as contract researcher, research fellow, co-investigator and consultant, may shed further light on the tensions between public sociology and policy research. The types of policy research I conducted range across social attitudes studies, child protection, school and higher education, and social aspects of health, including disability, homelessness, young people, sexual health, and smoking. While much of my experience as a policy researcher, particularly time spent in the field, was productive and rewarding, it has also been one of job insecurity, intense emotional labour and inequality of opportunity. Policy researchers may face stigmatisation and threats from more powerful clients even if the research is conducted with integrity, professionally and ethically. In this my experience closely parallels those reported by sociologists engaged in policy research (Bryson, 1999; Reay, 2000; Hey, 2001; Allen Collinson, 2004; Tilbury, 2007) and tallies with wider studies on the careers of contract researchers (Simmons and Walker, 2000; UCU, 2008a, 2008b).

At one extreme, I was employed as a contract researcher to carry out interviews for a national survey organisation. Here the work was highly impersonal, bureaucratically organised with tight controls imposed over fieldwork data collection. My job involved little in the way of personal autonomy and the work itself felt remote, isolating and automatic. Even my safety in the field was nobody's affair but mine alone (Lankshear, 2000). More usually, contract research involves a deeper intellectual and emotional commitment (Goode, 2006). In one study I was engaged as a part-time, hourly paid contract research assistant to evaluate sex education training in primary schools. Interviews were conducted with teachers in rural and urban primary schools with the aim of evaluating the extent to which training had enabled teachers to acquire the necessary confidence and skills to become effective sexual health promoters in the classroom. The policy-level interest concerned variations in classroom delivery of the programme might lead to uneven and ineffectual sex education. The richness of data that I elicited through fieldwork interviews on this highly sensitive issue made a significant contribution to national policy understanding of aspects of sex education that was otherwise shrouded in popular misconceptions.

Policy sociology and client capture

Some of the tensions of policy sociology may be illustrated by recounting my experiences of government-funded evaluation of sexual health education policy. Independent research was needed by government to provide reliable data and form policy recommendations through expert evaluation of sexual health policy. We envisaged the relationship as coming close to Massey's (2007) idea of political partnership. Perhaps naively, we assumed that since the research involved policy evaluation that it would be linked to the public interest demands of accountability. It became clear early on that we were expected to play a more subordinate role to the demands of a national steering group composed of a senior civil servant, health professionals and policy officials. This risked diluting our control over the research process. At an initial meeting significant changes were made to the research design by the steering group, who demanded that the survey instrument ought to resemble the interview schedule more closely. The steering group proposed that both research instruments should cover identical themes in order that both could be coded according to the same quantitative values and the different sources of data compared statistically. At that stage the clients were concerned to apply some form of numerical value to the qualitative as well as the quantitative research findings. This ran contrary to elementary methodological principles of inherently different research techniques. Reducing qualitative research to numerical values, we argued, would undermine the validity of the semi-structured interviews, which require a more flexible and responsive mode of investigation. Nonetheless, we reluctantly revised the research instruments.

Originally, we specified 50 people for interview, which we considered a sufficiently robust number for a six-month evaluation covering two geographical areas. However, the steering committee required an additional case study, committing us to three case studies instead of the two that we had tendered for. Members of the steering group also wanted to restrict the sample size for the survey to key stakeholders identified by them, which we argued would affect the reliability and representativeness of the data. The sample was determined in the first instance by the list of stakeholders supplied to the research team by the client, from where we would 'snowball' out to encompass wider circles of stakeholders. In fact, it was difficult to enrol certain institutional stakeholders to participate in the evaluation.

Just as O'Brien and colleagues (2008) battled with their clients to interview frontline service professionals and not just their managers, our study also depended on eliciting the views of frontline workers since they possess first-hand experience of the effective implementation of new policies. A voluble member of the steering group instructed us that frontline worker voices were not required for the evaluation contrary to our claim that any credible policy evaluation must involve the people responsible at all levels for implementing the policy. It appeared that the steering group were far from unanimous in excluding frontline staff from the policy evaluation process and had mixed understandings about the nature of the research process. It was essential to the integrity of the research design as well as a defence of the interests and voice of a group lower down the policy hierarchy (Piven, 2007). In the event, the voices of frontline staff had a major impact on the critical aspects of the findings.

As the data emerged from the interviews, it became clear that the steering group were concerned about some of the more politically contentious findings. Evidence that the policy was far too narrowly focused on clinical considerations rather than cultural and social conditions of sexual health was not well received. This reflected the main interest of steering group membership, which consisted largely of professionals with clinical backgrounds. In interviews, frontline workers in the non-statutory sector said that they felt demoralised and under-appreciated by clinical/statutory sectors. Again, issues of clinical elitism were also raised by non-statutory sectors who felt that they were being obstructed from developing any clinical strategies of their own. It became clear from the interviews that most stakeholders thought that social and cultural factors were not being sufficiently addressed and that policy tended to be far too narrowly focussed around clinical and medical models of sexual health.

For both the draft report and the ministerial presentation the contents were vetted by the steering committee. Some members of the steering group suggested that the interview data had been misinterpreted. They requested access to the original transcripts of the hundred or so interviews that I had conducted in order to reanalyse the data for themselves. We were concerned that they would 'cherry pick' from the findings and produce a report that uncritically endorsed the effectiveness of policy. Criticism was also raised about our methods and sample sizes and the data sent to a 'swat team', a government analytical services research department. By sending the report to analytical services, any findings that the policy group found objectionable could be invalidated as a technical question of scientific administration.

Funders held the reins of power over the 'product' by controlling the distribution and consumption of the report. While the findings were presented to the Minister and the national committee, to my knowledge the report never went 'live' for public viewing nor was it circulated to research participants. A circular was sent to all health boards outlining key clinical indicators and recommendations. However, no mention was made of the need to address social and cultural factors, our key finding. There was no contact or invitation by the authorities to present our findings to committees or conferences.

Conclusion

At all stages of the research process repeated attempts were made by the clients to shape the research and findings. Ultimately, the report itself seems to have fallen into a black hole and has not been widely distributed or made publicly available as far as can be discerned. This illustrates some of the implicit tensions of policy sociology. It can take the pathological form of client dependency and sponsor capture identified by Burawoy, coming under political pressure to legitimate policy. While there are examples of creative policy interventions by policy sociology, shading into more critical and public forms of sociology, too often policy sociology is prone to pathological forms of unequal imbalances of power and dependency in neoliberal conditions of market competition for research funding and career survival.

Policy sociology views the public interest as its own speciality, best advanced by working directly with powerful clients like government. This perspective has been subject to sustained critique within sociology for over 50 years, not least for its unreal image of the policy process and the role of sponsor capture of sociological research (Piven, 2007). Such critiques take aim at policy sociology for corrupting the 'real' sociology done by professionals and public advocacy. While it relies on professional sociology for legitimacy, policy sociology, like public sociology, speaks to non-academic audiences. Unlike the reflexive useful knowledge of public sociology, the useful knowledge of policy sociology is instrumental, recommending the 'best' means of engineering a given policy end (Burawoy, 2007a: 34). In this it can often find itself in a defensive alliance with policy elites against forms of critical sociology and public sociology that contest the very terms and values of the debate about the public interest. Policy sociology legitimates itself by stressing the value of research technique, its effectiveness, and its pragmatic sense of realism. Without regular contact with the creative pulse of public, professional and critical sociology, policy sociology can too easily degenerate into a narrow, pathological form of sponsor capture, as my experience testifies. Burawoy's attempt to counter-balance the instrumentalist pathologies of client-dominated policy sociology by building relationships across the reflexive knowledge quadrants of public and critical sociology suggests that the tensions and power plays of fashioning what kinds of 'really useful knowledge' lie at the heart of the sociological enterprise are unlikely to dissipate any time soon.

References

Abrams, P. (1968) *The Origins of British Sociology, 1834–1914*, Chicago, IL: University of Chicago Press.

Allen Collinson, J. (2004) 'Occupational identity on the edge: social science contract researchers in higher education', *Sociology*, 38(2): 313–329.

Brady, D. (2004) 'Why public sociology may fail', *Social Forces*, 82(4): 1629–1638.

Bryson, C. (1999) 'Contract research: the failure to address the real issues', *Higher Education Review*, 31(2): 29–49.

Bulmer, M. (ed) (1985) *Essays on the History of British Sociological Research*, Cambridge: Cambridge University Press.

Bulmer, M., Bales, K. and Sklar, K.K. (eds) (1991) *The Social Survey in Historical Perspective, 1880–1914*, Cambridge: Cambridge University Press.

Burawoy, M. (2007a) 'For public sociology', in Clawson, D., Zussman, R., Misra, J., Gerstel, N., Stokes, R., Anderton, D.L. and Burawoy, M. (eds) *Public Sociology: Fifteen Eminent Sociologists Debate Politics and the Profession in the Twenty-First Century*, Berkeley, CA and London: University of California Press, pp 23–66.

Burawoy, M. (2007b) 'The field of sociology: its power and its promise', in Clawson, D., Zussman, R., Misra, J., Gerstel, N., Stokes, R., Anderton, D.L. and Burawoy, M. (eds) *Public Sociology: Fifteen Eminent Sociologists Debate Politics and the Profession in the Twenty-First Century*, Berkeley, CA and London: University of California Press, pp 241–258.

Burawoy, M. (2009) 'Disciplinary mosaic: the case of Canadian sociology', *Canadian Journal of Sociology, Cahiers canadiens de sociologie*, 34(3): 869–886.

Coleman, J. (1979) 'Sociological analysis and social policy', in Bottomore, T. and Nisbet, R. (eds) *A History of Sociological Analysis*, London: Heinmann.

Dahrendorf, R. (1995) *LSE: A History of the London School of Economics and Political Science, 1895–1995*, Oxford: Oxford University Press.

Goode, J. (2006) 'Research identities: reflections of a contract researcher', *Sociological Research Online*, 11(2), www.socresonline.org.uk/11/2/goode.html

Halsey, A.H. (2004) *A History of Sociology in Britain*, Oxford: Oxford University Press.

Hey, V. (2001) 'The construction of academic time: sub/contracting academic labour in research', *Journal of Education Policy*, 16(1): 67–84.

Hill Collins, P. (2007) 'Going public: Doing the Sociology that had no name', in Clawson, D., Zussman, R., Misra, J., Gerstel, N., Stokes, R., Anderton, D.L. and Burawoy, M. (eds.) *Public Sociology: Fifteen Eminent Sociologists Debate Politics and the Profession in the Twenty-First Century*, Berkeley, CA and London: University of California Press, pp 101–114.

Janowitz, M. (1972) *On Social Organization and Social Control*, Chicago, IL: University of Chicago Press.

Lankshear, G. (2000) 'Bacteria and babies: a personal reflection of researcher risk in a hospital', in Lee-Treweek, G. and Linkogle, S. (eds) *Danger in the Field: Risk and Ethics in Social Research*, London: Routledge, pp 72–90.

Law, J. (2004) *After Method: Mess in Social Science Research*, London: Routledge.

Massey, D.S. (2007) 'The strength of weak politics', in Clawson, D., Zussman, R., Misra, J., Gerstel, N., Stokes, R., Anderton, D.L. and Burawoy, M. (eds) *Public Sociology: Fifteen Eminent Sociologists Debate Politics and the Profession in the Twenty-First Century*. Berkeley, CA and London: University of California Press, pp 145–157.

Naples, N.A. (2003) *Feminism and Method: Ethnography, Discourse Analysis, And Activist Research*, London: Routledge.

O'Brien, M., Clayton, S., Varga-Atkins, T. and Qualter, A. (2008) 'Power and the theory-and-practice conundrum: the experience of doing research with a local authority', *Evidence & Policy*, 4(4): 371–390.

Piven, F.F. (2007) 'From public sociology to politicized sociologist', in Clawson, D., Zussman, R., Misra, J., Gerstel, N., Stokes, R., Anderton, D.L. and Burawoy, M. (eds) *Public Sociology: Fifteen Eminent Sociologists Debate Politics and the Profession in the Twenty-First Century*, Berkeley, Los Angeles, London: University of California Press, pp 158–168.

Reay D. (2000) '"Dim dross" – marginalised women both inside and outside the academy', *Women's Studies International Forum*, 23(1): 13–21.

Simmons, P. and Walker, G. (2000) 'Contract research as interactive social science', *Science and Public Policy*, 27(3): 193–201.

Smith, D. (1987) *The Everyday World as Problematic*, Boston, MA: Northeastern University Press.

Smith, D. (1990) *Texts, Facts and Femininity: Exploring the Relations of Ruling*, London: Routledge.

Tilbury, F. (2007) '"Piggy in the middle": the liminality of the contract researcher in funded 'collaborative' research', *Sociological Research Online*, 12(6), www.socresonline.org.uk/12/6/16.html

University and College Union (UCU) (2008a) 'UCU wins landmark fixed-term employment tribunal', 5 June, www.ucu.org.uk/index.cfm?articleid=3340

UCU (2008b) *The Researcher's Survival Guide*, London: UCU Campaigns Unit, https://www.ucu.org.uk/media/4832/UCU-researchers-survival-guide/pdf/ucu_researchersurvivalguide_jul15.pdf

CASE II.2

Recreating Knowledge for Social Change: Convergences between Public Sociology, Feminist Theory and Praxis of Refugee and Asylum-Seeking Women's Integration in Scotland

C. Laura Lovin

Introduction

The explorations in this chapter are guided by shared affinities between public sociology and feminist theory. Whereas public sociology is committed to dialogic knowledge production, bringing sociological theory into conversation with the voices of marginalised groups, feminist examinations of social, political, economic and cultural practices that produce racialised, gendered and sexualised subject positions have produced analytical categories that enhance understandings of relations of domination and subordination as well as subsequent policy making and service delivery. Together, public sociology and feminist theory share a commitment to unveiling power structures through knowledge that is collaborative, inclusive and relevant to individual and collective efforts to create social change. In my explorations, I use textual data gathered from project reports produced by the Scottish Refugee Council (SRC) and the Refugee Women's Strategic Group (RWSG) between 2011 and 2016 to analyse their efforts toward refugee and asylum seeker integration in Scotland.

The SRC's commitment to grounding their services and policies in participatory knowledge production is visible throughout their projects. This methodological orientation has enabled the SRC to capture the links between sociocultural and economic structures and the personal problems experienced by refugees and asylum seekers in their everyday lives and, most importantly, it has foregrounded the intersectional analytics articulated by the refugee and asylum-seeking women participating in SRC programmes. The RWSG was thus formed by the SRC in 2015 following the realisation of the significance of the inquiries, concepts and visions for social change put forth by refugee and asylum-seeking women. RWSG's main goal would ultimately become the development of a strong collective voice that would impact refugee and asylum policy making and politics. To illuminate why the goal of impacting policy change is yet to be achieved and as a way of framing the particular trajectories of the SRC, the RWSG and their partners, the first part of the chapter revisits the exclusionary relations that have shaped conceptualisations and practices of citizenship historically. The second part of the chapter unfolds by following the work of SRC and the RWSG and tracing the connections among their praxis, public sociology and feminist theory: frameworks of participatory knowledge production, intersectional analysis, women's experience centred analysis, and the employment of women's voice toward transformative change.

Contexts: from geographic scale to conceptual frameworks

New Scots, Scotland's refugee integration strategy, signals by name and content an orientation toward inclusion into the nation's body politic. The strategy is led by the Scottish Government, the SRC and the Convention of Scottish Local Authorities (COSLA), who partner with other local organisations and community groups that support refugees and asylum seekers in rebuilding their lives. The SRC, the Scottish Executive and their partner organisations operate in the framework set up by the United Nations in the 1951 Convention Relating to the Status of Refugees and the 1967 Protocol Relating to the Status of Refugees. The UK is a signatory party and has integrated them into domestic law, specifically through the 1993 Asylum and Immigration Appeals Act and the 1996 Asylum and Immigration Act (Palavra, 2016/2017). According to these documents, a refugee is a person who owing to a well-founded fear of being persecuted for reasons of race, religion, nationality, membership of a particular social group, or political opinion, is outside the country of his nationality and is unable or, owing to such fear, is unwilling to avail himself of the protection of that country; or who, not having a nationality and being outside the country of his former habitual residence as a result of such events, is unable or, owing to such fear, is unwilling to return to it. (UN High Commissioner for Refugees, 2011)

One is a refugee based on a declarative claim. However, the status of a refugee is granted by state institutions of the country entered. Thus, a person who has fled their country due to fear of persecution and asked the government of the country they entered to recognise them as a refugee is an asylum seeker. Upon the evaluation of the asylum seeker's claims, in accordance to parameters set up in the 1951 Convention and its 1967 Protocol, asylum seekers may be given refugee status.

The figures of the refugee and the asylum seeker have been central to the media and political debates of the past decade, foregrounding questions of integration and achievement of citizenship in the UK. These conversations unfolded in considerably different registers in England and Scotland. Whereas immigration is an issue reserved to Westminster, Scottish ministers have consistently and increasingly distanced themselves from Westminster's hostile position to immigration, on many occasions demanding powers to be devolved in order to address Scotland's demographic and employment issues through a Scottish-specific immigration policy (BBC News UK, 2017). The latest New Scots strategy for 2018–2022

> commits to better access to essential services such as education, housing, health and employment, […] recognises the skills, knowledge and resilience which refugees bring and aims to help people to settle, become part of the community, and pursue their ambitions. (Scottish Government, 2018)

Most asylum seekers arrive to Scotland from Afghanistan, Albania, Eritrea, Iraq, Iran, Somalia and Syria. In spite of the official position of the Scottish Executive, asylum seekers who were perceived as non-White were likely to encounter hostility. In 2002, the results of an attitudinal survey showed that 24 per cent of its Scottish respondents considered verbal attacks toward asylum seekers who receive housing and benefits in Scotland justifiable (Charlaff, 2004). Needless to say, this was at a time when refugees and asylum seekers had no platform through which they could make their stories heard by the local population or confront media distortions and political discourses that portrayed them through unrecognisable traits.

As this chapter explores the scope of interventions made by both governmental organisations (GOs) and non-governmental organisations (NGOs) and their ability to produce knowledge that challenges institutional and everyday practices of exclusion and marginalisation in an effort to transform them, it is important to note that the boundaries of citizenship are dynamic markers that delineate the nation's demographic inside. Whereas the category of asylum seeker has been constructed to exclude from citizenship, the ultimate recognition of refugee status and asylum seekers' journeys toward citizenship are determined by objective requirements and subjective criteria that remain informed by racialising discourses and gender- and class-normative notions of 'good' and 'bad' character (Kapoor and Narcowicz, 2017). Next, I turn a feminist lens to discussions of citizenship in order to analyse the genealogies that inform the intersectional exclusions and marginalisations experienced by refugees and asylum seekers today. Because the meanings of citizenship are as diverse as the places, times, ideologies and legal frameworks that fall under scrutiny, theories of citizenship explore specific articulations among the roles of individuals, collectivities, communities and nation-states. For instance, the ancient Athenian version of participatory citizenship came to be viewed as pure democracy because Athens' free adult men came together regularly to decide the affairs of the city-state. The Roman Empire developed a modality of citizenship reliant on legal status and specific rights and duties. At the time of the French Revolution, citizenship became tied to the nation-state and signified the relationship between individuals and the polity. In the German context, the ethnic national collectivity rather than the individual became the locus of citizenship rights. Nowadays, in the age of globalisation and supranational governance through human rights discourses, many nation-states feel pressured to extend membership rights to immigrants, a change that has co-existed with resurgent nationalist ideologies and border refortifications. Feminists thinkers have long cautioned that universalistic criteria of inclusion pertaining to citizenship tend to hide masculine privileges (Pateman, 1988). Under their scrutiny, Athenian 'purely' participatory democracy was shown to have been sustained through the extraction of privatised work from disenfranchised women, immigrants and slaves (Gielan, 2011). In later times, women, undocumented immigrants, imprisoned people and workers in informal economies are likely to be disadvantaged when full citizenship rights are conditioned by active participation, for instance, in paid employment.

Feminist Marxists revealed that the capitalist order of the liberal state is founded on patriarchal structures that have normalised the sexual division of labour and has obscured the fact that equality requires the reorganisation of productive and reproductive work (Eisenstein, 1978). Later on, Carole Pateman proposed a conception of citizenship that rejected the unitary conception of the individual as an entity abstracted from embodied existence and called for the simultaneous recognition of the specificity of women's experiences and the common humanity of women and men (Pateman, 1988). Yet, a sexually differentiated model of citizenship poses problems in relation to the specific duties that would be expected of women and men as well as their equal valuation by the state (Mouffe, 1995). Dissatisfied with the framework of liberalism, feminist thinkers also turned to civic republicanism, hopeful about the inclusive potential of a conception of citizenship that foregrounds political participation and non-individualist notions of the common good. However, its reliance on shared moral values proved incompatible with pluralism and the substantive diversity of contemporary polities, rendering particularly vulnerable the groups constructed as ethnic minorities as well as those heteronormatively constructed as 'immoral other' (Evans, 1993).

Writing from within the context of the UK, Nira Yuval-Davis (2007) noted that an intersectional approach to citizenship is essential to comprehending the unstable and contested locations that emerge at the intersection of multiple social divisions and structures of power, ie gender, class, race, age, nationality, disability and sexuality. Over the past several years, the British national community has been discussed simultaneously in two opposing registers: a progressive Britishness that endorses human rights, cosmopolitanism and civic democratic values, or a Britishness concerned with origins, whiteness and imperialist identities (Gardner, 2017). In resurgent nationalist contexts, an intersectional analysis of citizenship holds the potential to move past a homogenised British citizenship that is constructed against other citizenships and thus reach a point where it can differentiate among locations, identities and political values while being fundamentally non-racist and non-sexist (Yuval-Davis, 2007: 572).

While public policy has become avowedly gender- and colour-blind, Mary Hawkesworth (2016: 85) calls attention to the multiple ways in which 'embodied power continues to structure government interventions whether the domain involves poverty, social services, environmental degradation, economic incentives for businesses, education, immigration, or securitisation'. For instance, the production and circulation of racialised and gendered group memberships such as 'Muslim women', 'Blacks', 'Middle Eastern countries', 'Eastern Europeans' or 'women of the global South' cluster together people from different regions, nation-states, cultures and traditions who may have little to nothing in common. Such categorical formations rely on stereotyping and are mobilised in the construction of target populations for 'differential treatment, marginalisation, and exclusion of particular racialised groups; silencing; withholding epistemic authority and political recognition; surveillance; detention; death and collective extermination' (Hawkesworth, 2016: 5). The value of intersectional analytics reaches past challenging unidimensional categories by unveiling the complexity of lived experience within social groups (McCall, 2005: 1786). It is important to stress that processes of racialised gendering and gendered racialising are integral parts of imperial and contemporary war-making enterprises that construct 'enemies' and divide the globe into 'stable' and 'failed' states through the recirculation of the old binary of civilised/barbaric. In addition to revealing intracategorical variations, an intersectional approach can also render visible the points where institutional power arrangements, interwoven with structures of domination and subordination, 'confound and constrict the life possibilities of those who already live at the intersections of certain identity categories, even as they elevate the possibilities of those living at more legible (and privileged) points of intersection' (Cooper, 2016: 392).

From participatory knowledge production to shaping a 'strong voice' to influence policy and politics

The five reports introduced below inform the second part of my chapter. Because most of the SRC's policy documents use the categories of 'refugee' and 'asylum seeker' together, I will proceed by using the phrase 'refugees and asylum seekers' throughout this chapter, while I remain fully cognisant of the legal and experiential differences that these categories entail.

1. *The Struggle to Contribute: A Report Identifying the Barriers Encountered by Refugee Women on Their Journey to Employment in Scotland* (STC, 2011). STC consolidates the input of 40 refugee and asylum-seeking women who participated in the Women's Employment Information Event (WEIE) in February 2011 in Glasgow. The event was organised by the RWSG in partnership with the SRC, the

Poverty Alliance and the Women's Support Project, with funding from the Women's Voluntary Sector Network and the SRC. It aims to respond to refugee and asylum-seeking women's need for information and to provide a forum to discuss their experiences of employment.

2. *One Step Closer: Confidence Building and Employability Skills for Refugee and Asylum-Seeking Women* (OSC, 2014). OSC reports on a ten-week skill development course in confidence and employability developed to address refugee and asylum-seeking women's needs identified in the framework of the STC. Implemented by the RWSG, the SRC and the Glasgow English as a Second Language (ESOL) Forum, the courses were funded by the SRC, the Scottish Government and Glasgow ESOL Forum.

3. *Speak for Yourself: Report from Our Engagement with 100 Refugee and Asylum-Seeking Women between June and November 2013* (SFY, 2014). Speak for Yourself (SFY) is RWSG's first large-scale initiative aimed at collecting refugee and asylum-seeking women's accounts of encounters with barriers to integration though one-on-one interviews, focus groups, meetings with refugee community organisations, and workshop discussions. Developed with support and funding from the SRC Comic Relief, SFY established the RWSG as an important partner in the development of Scotland's new refugee integration strategy alongside the Scottish Government, the SRC and COSLA Strategic Migration Partnership.

4. *Raising Refugee Women's Voices: Exploring the Impact of Scottish Refugee Council Work with the Refugee Women's Strategic Group 2011–2015* (RRWV) (Qunitero et al, 2016). RRWV draws from 19 interviews with key stakeholders, members of the RWSG, representatives of Glasgow Violence Against Women Partnership, UK Visas and Immigration Scotland and Northern Ireland, Asylum Aid and Queen Margaret University, as well as from other GO and NGO reports in an effort to provide a model of intervention that combines 'community development with policy influencing and development' (2016: 5). It received support and funding from Comic Relief and the Women's Voluntary Sector Network.

5. *Sharing Lives, Sharing Languages: A Pilot Peer Education Project for New Scots' Social and Language Integration* (SLSL) (Hirsu and Bryson, 2017) reports on a peer education pilot project that aimed to supplement ESOL training with learning experiences undertaken alongside other non-native English speakers and local community members. The goal was to develop social connections and language and cultural exchange between multilingual peers (2017: 5).

The programme was implemented by the SRC with advisory contributions from the Vulnerable Persons' Resettlement Scheme for Syrian Refugees.

It is important to underline that the RWSG initially functioned as an integral part of the Scottish Refugee Policy Forum. It became an independent group in 2015 and was soon recognised as 'the most authoritative voice among refugees' (RRWV, 2016: 12). The organisation brings together refugee and asylum-seeking women who aim to make their views heard, to represent their communities in dialogues with key decision makers and to influence the policies and practices that impact their lives. The programmes developed by the SRC in collaboration with the RWSG operate with the understanding that refugee and asylum-seeking women have gender-specific experiences and encounter gendered barriers throughout their flight, journeys to safety and resettlement. Employment and education emerged as key priority areas, and the presentation of these women's intricate articulations of marginalisation and exclusion constitute the main focus of the remainder of this section.

From the perspective of employment and education, nation-states respond to the presence of refugees and asylum seekers with specific interventions that range from, on the one hand, proactive interventions, cultural inclusion, providing equitable access to education, offering skill development and employment opportunities, and the recognition of academic credentials and qualifications to, on the other hand, marginalisation, the rejection of qualifications and academic credentials, the withholding of epistemic authority and a lack of respect for the newcomers' culture. These latter responses constitute major hindrances to social integration and upward economic mobility. Eleanor L. Brown (2013) has pointed out that exclusionary measures cultivate economic disadvantage and dependence, psychological insecurity, academic failure, cultural isolation and an overall loss of human potential. The type of response offered by a nation-state is nevertheless determined by national commitments to multiculturalism or conversely to non-differentialism, demographic goals, resources that are allocated to refugees, the number of received refugees and, last but not least, the ideological positions of those in political, governmental and administrative power (Krasteva, 2013). Anna Krasteva (2013: 11–12) notes that, after 1980, the UK moved to make legal entry more difficult, restrict social and legal rights (right to work, benefits and higher education) and increasingly refuse to grant refugee status.

In Scotland, *The Struggle to Contribute* (STC) shows that refugee and asylum-seeking women face the greatest disadvantage in employment relative to white women and British women of colour (STC, 2011: 4). Refugee and asylum-seeking women have drawn attention to the fact that the employment and information and services they accessed were inadequate in relation to the complexity of the benefits and entitlements system and the asylum process (STC, 2011: 8–10; SFY, 2014: 5). Insufficient space in ESOL programmes further limited their access to jobs and Job Centre Plus services (STC, 2011: 11; SFY, 2014: 5). Employers' racist and discriminatory attitudes based on gender, race, foreign accents, foreign names and/or disability status during job interviews, along with their lack of knowledge about immigration status and work permits, led to poor employment outcomes (STC, 2011: 8–9; SFY, 2014: 4). Various participants emphasised that, although they had been able to access multiple volunteering positions, they could not get secure paid employment because white Scottish candidates were preferred (SFY, 2014: 5). They felt pressured into taking 'cleaning jobs or jobs which did not recognise their skills and experience', and deskilling was a significant problem for them (SFY, 2014: 5).

The scarcity of affordable childcare also hampered their access to secure employment. Due to their childcare responsibilities, many women were offered only part-time positions lacking job security. The lack of affordable childcare also prevented them from pursuing educational opportunities, ESOL, professional training or activist work (STC, 2011: 8). Childcare was a gendered barrier, which in the view of one participant men did not experience:

> A man has a higher chance to succeed in a new environment than women [...]. For instance if you do not have childcare, you cannot go to study. The man can think about his career, there will not be many family obstacles preventing him from going far. If I had come here alone, I would have gone to university; but I had to take care of my two boys. (RRWV, 2016: 7)

Women also connected their deskilling and underemployment in the feminised sectors of social care, catering and cleaning to the recognition of qualifications for skilled employment or postgraduate training in pursuit of new high-skilled specialisations (STC, 2011: 10; SFY, 2014: 5). The participants also signalled that vocational training for occupational niches deemed open to them – childminding as a social enterprise and customer services – was unavailable (STC, 2011: 10; SFY, 2014: 5). In relation to education, refugee and asylum-seeking women shared a positive view of the Scottish Government's policy of granting young asylum seekers access to tuition-free full-time further and higher education (STC, 2011: 11). But ultimately, downward occupational mobility, limited employability, restrictions to their right to work and experiences of discrimination proved to be damaging to the mental health of the participating refugee and asylum-seeking women, their partners and children (SFY, 2014: 4).

The participants' analyses of barriers to integration make apparent an intersectional methodology that foregrounds significant differences among the lived experiences of those identified by the phrase 'refugees and asylum seekers'. Their examinations of education and employment shed light on institutional arrangements that derail their life goals, threaten their overall well-being and keep them from full public participation, be it within the realm of employment, education or activism. Moreover, they expose the points at which institutional forces converge with economic and sociocultural structures of domination (racism, gendered divisions of work, informal economies and the reliance on gendered and racialised migrant work in particular economic sectors) to produce refugee and asylum-seeking women as low-skilled feminised workers. Finally, they show that if such hidden structural arrangements and cultural mechanisms of exclusion and marginalisation are not made clearly visible, discourses and representations that construct refugees and asylum seekers as unassimilable are bound to remain in circulation. The insights gathered by foregrounding the perspectives of refugee and asylum-seeking women have led SRC and RWSG to prioritise developing their 'strong voice', with a view to effecting change in service delivery, policy making and politics. Their vision is predicated on collaborations among communities, stakeholders and political actors and, most importantly, on the empowerment of refugee and asylum-seeking women in relation to their own epistemological authority and co-ownership of the construction of representational narratives.

The projects developed by the RWSG and the SRC demonstrate a gradual incorporation of the knowledge produced by refugee and asylum-seeking women into GO and NGO policy and practice, thus perhaps signalling a shift from an integration paradigm reliant on the reproduction of dominant norms to more dialogic processes that are inclusive of and responsive to refugees and asylum seekers. A host of such adjustments followed *One Step Closer* (OSC): the RWSG and the SRC provided childcare services during their programmes, timed courses to fit with school hours and reimbursed travel expenses. Organisers and trainers also took into account that the incomprehensibility of the 'language of jobs' is not always due to lack of linguistic competency but also to unfamiliarity with rather localised cultures of human resources (OSC, 2014). It was thus acknowledged that there are subtle skill-development needs that are specific to newcomers and that are most often taken for granted by more settled populations. For instance, vocabulary tackled in the ESOL portion of the programme (such as 'good team player', 'able to work on your own initiative' and 'eager attitude') could be seen as dimensions of performative or affective work and need to be understood as components of new subjectivities. *Sharing Lives, Sharing Languages* (SLSL) linked language barriers and the need for better dissemination of information about local services through the framework of mutual integration, thus foregrounding the facilitation of social connections with natives of Scotland. This approach eventually led to improved confidence in communicating in English, better knowledge of local services, more diverse social connections and enriched understandings of other groups' cultural heritage.

Through its consultations with refugee communities, RWSG continued to refine understandings of why services for refugees and asylum seekers require a gender-sensitive approach. However, its goal of using its 'strong voice' to influence decision makers and thus create 'measurable policy change' proved difficult to achieve (RWSG, 2017: 11). The RWSG encountered numerous challenges to being heard or having refugee and asylum-seeking women's voices valued by stakeholders who were able to effect change in the very politicised area of refugee and asylum policy: 'The doors are not always open for us. We are fed up with hearing that they will take things into consideration' (RRWV, 2017: 17). Some of the hindrances were posed by Scotland's specific conditions, which require working across devolved and reserved competencies, with asylum policy reserved at the level of the UK Government and refugee integration policy and implementation to some extent devolved within the powers of Scottish Government. RWSG's incremental improvements and accomplishments are nevertheless impressive and deserve mentioning: temporarily introducing childcare for asylum interviews (a change that was reversed due to budgetary constraints); receiving requests for consultation and invitations to stakeholder fora; securing statements of commitment from ministers; introducing gender training for decision makers; including asylum-specific actions in the Home Secretary's Call to End Violence against Women and Girls; and prioritising gender as an area for improvement by the Home Office. And, locally, they developed a new women's page on the Scottish Refugee Council's website; closely collaborated with Glasgow City Council to inform women about their entitlement to school clothing grants; and developed a rights pamphlet for women claiming asylum (RRWV, 2017).

The context for the RWSG's limited success in changing policy should be understood as transcending the local scale of Scotland, particularly because the policies that govern the lives of refugees and asylum seekers are shaped at the intersection of interests, ideologies, agencies and agendas that are 'highly politicised' as well as 'subject to rapid and complex shifts at the whim of governments of the day' (RWSG, 2017: 11). Policy making and policy change are rooted in the normalisation and contestation of power, which produce certain issues and groups as 'problems' and others as 'non-problems' (Bacchi, 2009). The agents and institutions of hegemonic power reproduce prevailing economic, gender, heteronormative and racial hierarchies through long-established discourses and practices. The UK's current longing to restore its prominence in the world has resuscitated colonial undercurrents, including desires for racial hierarchy and racist domination, and has legitimised its attempts to turn its geographical insularity into a political vision for a retreat from globalisation (Virdee and McGeever, 2017). Ultimately, it is important to acknowledge that the RWSG and the SRC, along with their partners and collaborators, are essential agents who contest, subvert and expose the stigmatising representations and marginalising practices that target refugees and asylum seekers. Such alterations can certainly interrupt and undermine the circulation and persistence of exclusionary normative frameworks through the introduction of new vocabularies and practices (Butler, 1993).

Despite their limited success in changing policy, many women pointed out the inestimable value of bringing together diverse communities to facilitate dialogue, to share their experiences and to listen to one another. A few statements quoted below relay the scope of their thoughts and feelings about what it means to be be part of the RWSG:

> Look, we are in a new country, we don't know the country, and the people here don't know us. I think we need to organise ourselves, so that our voice can be heard. (RRWV, 2017: 5)

> We can say these are the lived experiences of women, they are irrefutable, they are not anecdotal, they are not hearsay, they are real, they are lived. (RRWV, 2017: 12)

What is special about us is that we get to speak for ourselves. […] If I go there and tell my story, my way, it is going to have an impact unlike if you are telling my story. That's what is special about us ... we tell our stories as they are. (RRWV, 2017: 13)

We see the wider picture presenting common concerns rather than focusing upon their own individual concerns. (RRWV, 2017: 13)

Exercising their own representational agency was an important accomplishment among the RWSG members. Many collaborating service providers, partner organisations and governmental representatives recognised the value of hearing their voices and acknowledged the RWSG's representativeness, diversity and credibility. Service providers confessed to better understanding the shortcomings of their services. Small steps were made toward changing the negative media rhetoric and public outlook on refugees and asylum seekers. Whereas communicating with the Home Office remained a daunting prospect for refugees and asylum seekers, on critical occasions RWSG intervened on their behalf (RWSG, 2017: 16). The importance of the opportunity to hear directly from refugee voices at the National Asylum Stakeholder Forum was acknowledged by the participating Home Office representatives and appraised as a useful first-time occurrence.

Conclusion

The establishment of the RWSG highlights an interest in incorporating refugee and asylum-seeking women's knowledge into Scotland's integration strategy. Knowledge constitutes the building blocks of what comes to be recognised as valuable or true by the members of particular societies, and the absence of particular groups from the ranks of knowledge producers is a symptom of their marginalisation and exclusion. Feminists of colour and third-world feminists contend that marginal positions can in fact constitute an epistemological privilege as they provide a better location from which to grapple with structures of oppression sustained by patriarchal, colonial, heteronormative, capitalist or nationalist ideologies (Spivak, 1988; Collins, 1990; Narayan, 1997). The category of 'women's experience' raises important epistemological issues of difference, eliciting careful consideration of women's potentially divergent positions in relation to gender, sexuality, race, class, heteronormative and colonial structures (Harding,

1993; Hesse-Biber and Leavy, 2007). The dialogic methodologies of the RWSG and the SRC and the reciprocal integration approaches that emerged through their interventions distribute epistemological authority to all parties involved. By highlighting refugee and asylum-seeking women's experiences, and by foregrounding these women as active knowledge producers, their stories and examinations become a source of knowledge that can be counterposed to media, official, expert or male-centred accounts, and, most importantly, this knowledge can be mobilised toward the creation of a feminist strategy to rebuild the lives of refugees.

A strong current of participatory and gender- and culture-sensitive approaches to service provision, education and advocacy is noticeable throughout the documents available in the SRC's archive. Whereas the title of Scotland's integration strategy, New Scots, might signal a monocultural approach to integration yet a diachronic approach to Scottishness, the concrete projects implemented under its umbrella have gradually created forms of mutual integration that have allowed for the affirmation of difference and diversity, for dialogues to take place (both among different groups of refugees and between refugees and natives) and for the formulation of common concerns as the first steps toward policy change. At the same time, the 'strong voice' developed by the RWSG also functions as proof of the active participation of refugee and asylum-seeking women in the life of their new polity, countering representations promulgated by the anti-immigration media and political establishment, which construct them as unassimilable due to their supposed traditionalism and lack of civic involvement or public participation. This is a significant intervention in conversations that focus on the cohesion of societies as a whole, since in such contexts, specific articulations of difference can lead to the identification of commonalities that give grounds for inclusion, and other articulations of difference can be perceived as irreconcilable with the body politic and thus justify exclusion from it.

References

Bacchi, C.L. (2009) *Analysing Policy: What's the Problem Represented To Be?*, New South Wales: Pearson.

BBC News UK (2017) MPs to study effect of immigration policy on Scotland, www.bbc.co.uk/news/uk-scotland-scotland-politics-41682584

Brown, E.L. (2013) 'Volume introduction', in Brown, E.L. and Krasteva, A. (eds) *Migrants and Refugees: Equitable Education for Displaced Populations*, Charlotte, NC: Information Age Publishing, Inc.: xii–xix.

Butler, J. (1993) *Bodies That Matter: On the Discursive Limits of 'Sex'*, New York: Routledge.

Charlaff, L. (2004) *An Audit of the Skills and Aspirations of Refugees and Asylum Seekers Living in Scotland*, Scottish Executive in partnership with the Scottish Refugee Council, Scottish Executive and Scottish Refugee Council.

Collins, P.H. (1990) *Black Feminist Thought: Knowledge, Consciousness, and the Politics of Empowerment*, Boston, MA: Unwin Hyman.

Cooper, B. (2016) 'Intersectionality', in *The Oxford Handbook of Feminist Theory*. New York: Oxford University Press.

Eisenstein, Z.R. (ed) (1978) *Capitalist Patriarchy and the Case for Socialist Feminism*, New York and London: Monthly Review Press.

Evans, D. (1993) *Sexual Citizenship: The Material Constructions of Sexuality*, London: Routledge.

Gardner, A. (2017) 'Brexit, boundaries and imperial identities: a comparative view', *Journal for Social Archaeology*, 17(1): 3–26.

Gielan, P. (2011) 'The art of democracy', *Krisis*, 3: 4–12.

Harding, S. (1993) *Feminism and Methodologies: Social Science Issues*, Bloomington: Indiana University Press.

Hawkesworth, M. (2016) *Embodied Power: Demystifying Disembodied Politics*, New York: Routledge.

Hesse-Biber, S.N. and Leavy, P.L. (2007) *Feminist Research Practice*, London: Sage.

Hirsu, L. and Bryson, E. (2017) *Sharing Lives, Sharing Languages: A Pilot Peer Education Project for New Scots' Social and Language Integration*, Glasgow: Scottish Refugee Council and Scottish Government, www.scottishrefugeecouncil.org.uk/wp-content/uploads/2019/10/Sharing_Lives_Sharing_Languages_REPORT.pdf

Kapoor, N. and Narkowicz, K. (2017) 'The character of citizenship: denying the rights of asylum seekers and criminalising dissent', in *Open Democracy*, 20 May 2017, www.opendemocracy.net/uk/kasia-narkowicz-nisha-kapoor/character-of-citizenship-denying-rights-of-asylum-seekers-and-crimin

Krasteva, A. (2013)'Integrating the most vulnerable: educating refugee children in the European Union', in Brown, E.L. and Krasteva, A. (eds) *Migrants and Refugees: Equitable Education for Displaced Populations*, Charlotte, NC: Information Age Publishing, Inc.: 3–28.

McCall, L. (2005) 'The complexity of intersectionality', *Signs: The Journal for Women in Culture and Society*, 30(3): 1771–1800.

Mouffe, C. (1995) 'Feminism, citizenship, and radical democratic politics', in Nicholson, L. and Seidman, S. (eds), *Social Postmodernism: Beyond Identity Politics*, Cambridge: Cambridge University Press: 315–331.

Narayan, U. (1997) *Dislocating Cultures: Identities, Traditions, and Third-World Feminism*, New York: Routledge.

One Step Closer: Confidence Building and Employability Skills for Refugee and Asylum-Seeking Women (2014) Glasgow: Refugee Women's Strategic Group, Scottish Refugee Council, Glasgow ESOL Forum, file:// staff-data/homedirs/escandrett/Downloads/slidelegend.com_one-step-closer-scottish-refugee-council_59dcafc41723dd2a0e8c7db2.pdf

Palavra, V. (2016/2017) 'The legal context', in *Refugees in Scotland: Understanding the Policy Domain*, Edinburgh: University of Edinburgh.

Pateman, C. (1988) *The Sexual Contract*, Cambridge: Polity.

Quintero, M., Murray, N., Connely, E. and Ballantyne, F. (2016) *Raising Refugee Women's Voices: Exploring the Impact of Scottish Refugee Council Work with the Refugee Women's Strategic Group 2011–2015*, Glasgow, www.scottishrefugeecouncil.org.uk/wp-content/uploads/ 2019/10/Scottish-Refugee-Council_s-Women_s-Project-Impact-Report.pdf

Scottish Government (2018) *Refugees and asylum seekers*, https://www.gov.scot/policies/refugees-and-asylum-seekers/ new-scots/#:~:text=The%20New%20Scots%20refugee%20 integration,%2C%20housing%2C%20health%20and%20employment

Speak For Yourself (2014) *Conference Report*, Glasgow: Scottish Refugee Council.

Spivak, G.C. (1988) *Can the Subaltern Speak?* Basingstoke: Macmillan.

UN High Commissioner for Refugees (UNHCR) (2011) The *1951 Convention Relating to the Status of Refugees and its 1967 Protocol*, www.refworld.org/docid/4ec4a7f02.html

Virdee, S. and McGeever, B. (2017) 'Brexit, racism, crisis', in *Ethnic and Racial Studies*, 0(0): 1–18.

The Struggle to Contribute: A Report Identifying the Barriers Encountered by Refugee Women on their Journeys to Employment in Scotland (2011): Refugee Women's Strategic Group, Glasgow: Scottish Refugee Council.

Yuval-Davis, N. (2007) 'Intersectionality, citizenship and contemporary politics of belonging', *International Social and Political Philosophy*, 10: 561–574.

List of abbreviations

COSLA   Convention of Scottish Local Authorities
ESOL   English as a Second Language
GO   Governmental organisations
NGO   Nongovernmental organisations

OSC　One Step Closer: Confidence Building and Employability Skills for Refugee and Asylum-Seeking Women
RRWV　Raising Refugee Women's Voices: Exploring the Impact of Scottish Refugee Council Work with the Refugee Women's Strategic Group 2011–2015
RWSG　Refugee Women's Strategic Group
SFY　Speak for Yourself: Report from Our Engagement with 100 Refugee and Asylum-Seeking Women between June and November 2013
SLSL　Sharing Lives, Sharing Languages: A Pilot Peer Education Project for New Scots' Social and Language Integration
SRC　Scottish Refugee Council
STC　The Struggle to Contribute: A Report Identifying the Barriers Encountered by Refugee Women on Their Journey to Employment in Scotland
WEIE　Women's Employment Information Event

CASE II.3

Young People, Alcohol, Dialogical Methods

Emma Wood

Introduction

This chapter introduces a model of critical dialogue designed to create a brave space in which previously ignored, silent or marginalised young people can together develop a critical awareness of potentially harmful attitudes and behaviours (often accepted as normal within their social group or national culture) and be inspired to act in solidarity as allies to bring about positive social change. It focuses on a study of the AlcoLOLs project. One headteacher in this study described her typical Monday mornings as 'picking up the pieces of family or pupil relationships' damaged by alcohol-fuelled behaviour over weekends. The risks incurred by adolescent drinking make a significant topic on which to focus – not only because of its impact on young people's social context, but also because alcohol use is the leading risk factor for premature death and disability worldwide for people aged 15–49 years old (Griswold et al, 2018; WHO, 2018). In addition, there is increasing evidence that alcohol may have acute and prolonged neurobiological effects on developing adolescent brains (Clark, 2008; Squeglia, 2009 in Cukier et al, 2018) and alcohol use is linked to over 200 health conditions, including heart disease, stroke, diabetes and seven types of cancer (Morey et al, 2017).

The AlcoLOLs approach was premised on views that resonate with those of the lobby group Alcohol Focus Scotland:

> Young people are under a lot of pressure to start drinking at a young age. Alcohol today is cheap, readily available and heavily marketed. As a result, young people are growing up in a pro-alcohol society where drinking is seen as the norm. (Alcohol Focus Scotland, 2019)

It was informed by research suggesting that young people drink to get drunk (Seaman and Ikegwuonu, 2010; Percy et al, 2011) and teenage discourse is dominated by the view that excessive consumption is admirable and the key to accumulating social and cultural capital and thus access to 'insider' or popular friendship groups (Jackson et al, 2000; Järvinen and Gundelach, 2007; Percy et al, 2011; Atkinson et al, 2014). This perspective was very much reflected in the evaluation of the AlcoLOLs project: 'Popular people drink ... you want to be like the older ones – get invited to parties ... everyone does it, you feel left out if you're not' (Pieczka, Wood and Castelrione, 2016: 4). Consequently, at an age of transition, young people are seen to use alcohol as part of a process of creating a social identity (Jackson et al, 2000; Percy et al, 2011; Atkinson et al, 2014) and 'it is the cautious drinkers, and not the experienced ones, who risk social marginalisation by their peers, described as not being "in", and as persons "nobody knows" and "nobody invites"' (Järvinen and Gundelach, 2007: 68). As a result, at a time when young people navigate their route into adulthood, these perceptions can prevent them from openly discussing their fears about excessive drinking (Percy et al, 2011; Atkinson et al, 2014). In the evaluation of the AlcoLOLs project, the teenage co-producers explain this as 'You need to be swag ... you can't show vulnerability ... it's hard to tell people serious stuff' and 'You don't understand what you're feeling – can't speak properly because you might be judged' (Pieczka, Wood and Castelrione, 2016: 4). Consequently, despite that, by the age of 18, most young people are able to make confident decisions about how to drink for pleasure, this is realised through a process of trial and error that exposes them to significant risk (Percy et al, 2011). So, the idea behind the AlcoLOLs project was that if young people could challenge a discourse in which the voice of cautious drinkers is silenced, they could share insights and develop knowledge that could cut out the trial and error process and enable participants to adopt drinking behaviours that did not incur unwanted risk. To do this, we selected a diverse range of young people (in terms of levels of confidence, gender, social, economic and ethnic background) and designed a series of dialogic experiences aimed at enabling them to hear and explore a wide range of perspectives about drinking in what dialogue theory terms a 'safe space' free from judgement (Bohm, 1996). In a current context, the term 'brave space' (Arao, 2013) seems more apt and to capture Bohm's intentions more accurately. We were clear that dialogue would only work if we had a range of differing views, so we asked for pupils who were not part of the same friendship groups and who may have different attitudes towards drinking. As one of the AlcoLOLs explains: 'We're not like brainiacs ... some of us are a bit stupid and we're not all like the most popular pupils in the school either. We're not all the same – that's better' (Pieczka, Wood and Casteltrione, 2016: 15).

Seventeen pupils from Portobello High School (Edinburgh), aged 14–17 years old, participated in an initial small-scale project. However, they reported themselves to be so transformed by the experience that they persuaded their headteacher to contact the academics at Queen Margaret University (QMU) to help them co-produce a bigger intervention that they could use to duplicate their dialogic experience for their peers at school. The project grew to involve 3,000 young people in six north-east Edinburgh schools over three years[1] taking part in two dialogue groups (each consisting of around 15 S2 and S4[2] pupils facilitated by four AlcoLOLs and no adults present in the room). It delivered a number of outcomes across individual, school, and community levels (Pieczka and Wood, 2013; Pieczka, Wood and Casteltrione, 2016) but this chapter will focus on what may have motivated the young people to risk the social condemnation of their peers by actively seeking to talk about drinking in a way they knew could attract ridicule.

The dialogue process created a critical awareness of what can be argued as the young people's oppression, which then motivated them to involve their peers (in Freirean terms, their allies) to 'struggle for liberation' (Freire, 1970: 36) and speak freely so they could make informed choices about drinking and getting drunk. Clearly, in terms of a scale of oppression, this is different from that to which Freire refers in colonised and dominated countries in South America and Africa where people are experiencing extreme poverty. In a number of ways, however, our data and experience suggest that these young people were, to some level, oppressed – by a hegemonic drinking culture that equates drinking with social success and non-drinking as social failure; a powerful drinks industry that invests heavily in producing drinks and marketing / media strategies aimed at manipulating young people; and being at a life stage where young people often do not experience themselves as powerful, valuable, contributing members of society (see Nguyen, 2010, and Rinaldi, 2005, quoted in DeJong and Love 2015). This vulnerability, exploited by the alcohol industry to fuel a teenage drinking culture, creates a form of everyday oppression for these young people. This is illustrated by headteacher, Peigi MacArthur, in her comment:

> As someone who has worked with teenagers all my professional life I realise what a torrid troubled time adolescence is ... You're crippled with fear about the judgements you ... have to make ... You're under so much peer pressure ... because you're just lacking in confidence at that stage in your life and I think what was good about the AlcoLOLs ... they heard from other people about the decisions that they'd made ... and that allowed them to think about what they might do in a similar situation. (Pieczka, Wood and Casteltrione, 2016: 34)

Context

Scotland's drinking culture

Although the idea of entire nations having a particular 'drinking culture' can be seen as controversial (Savic et al, 2016), we argue that positioning Scottish young people as dominated by what we view as a hegemonic drinking culture is helpful in terms of recognising that their social environment could be preventing them from being free to make confident, informed, decisions about drinking. The idea of a national drinking culture can be seen to be supported by the Scottish Social Attitudes Survey (2007), based on annual rounds of interviews with 1,600 people, which suggests that while there may be different drinking cultures within Scotland in terms of the patterns of drinking, types of alcohol consumed or the contexts in which alcohol is drunk by different groups, there is relatively strong agreement across all groups that drinking is both a problem for Scotland as a whole and a central part of the country's culture. This research shows that two-thirds (64 per cent) agreed or agreed strongly that drinking is a major part of the 'Scottish way of life', and a similar proportion agreed that other Europeans tend to drink more sensibly than Scottish adults. The idea of hegemony can also be reinforced by the research, which shows that these views were shared by men and women, respondents in different age groups and respondents in urban and rural areas. Agreement across all class and educational groups was also high. Other statistics also suggest heavy drinking is not limited to one or two social groups across Scotland or to a particular gender – working Scots (particularly high-income earning managerial/professional workers) drink more heavily and frequently than those who are unemployed or economically inactive; but immediate health impacts are greater among poorer groups (Institute of Alcohol Studies, 2014). The prevalence of drunkenness among young people is also amongst the highest in Europe with drunkenness in Scots aged 15 being the sixth highest (out of 36 countries) with very little difference between drunkenness of girls and boys (Inchley et al, 2014).

Power of the drinks industry

The power of the drinks industry is also significant to the construction of young Scots as oppressed. In 2018, the market value of alcoholic beverages in the UK reached around 62 billion euros (Euromonitor, 2019) and the spirit industry alone contributes approximately 3 per cent to total Scottish GDP (O'Connor, 2018). However, as Jackson et al (2000) point out, alcohol is a global enterprise and recent consolidation means that it is controlled by a decreasing number of expanding multinationals. The alcohol industry spends about USD 1 trillion annually worldwide to market its products (Institute of Alcohol Studies, 2013) so can allocate significant resources to researching consumer preferences and developing new products (for example, producing 'alcopops' disguising the taste of alcohol to appeal to a child's palate, produced in child-friendly packaging at pocket money prices). Highly sophisticated marketing techniques (Hastings et al, 2005) embrace sponsorship of major sports teams (who wear alcohol logos on their shirts), music festivals, well-resourced content creation on social media designed to encourage user-generated sharing as well as celebrity and influencer endorsement and character drinking on television. A growing body of research shows a significant link between young people's exposure to this type of sophisticated alcohol marketing and the development of pro-drinking attitudes, social norms and subsequent drinking behaviour (Anderson et al, 2009; Smith and Foxcroft, 2009; Engels et al, 2009; Moreno and Whitehill, 2014; Morey et al, 2017; Cukier et al, 2018).

In this context, then, Freire's conceptualisation of oppression seems useful in interpreting young people's apparent lack of agency in challenging their immersion in a culture of excessive drinking because 'their perception of themselves as oppressed is impaired by their submersion in the reality of the oppression' (Freire, 2017: 19). Consequently, Freire's (2017) pedagogy of oppressed can help identify what influenced the young people in our study to become conscious of their situation and organise to resist it (Freire's process of conscientisation, which will be illustrated later in the chapter).

Analysis

This analysis is based on my experience as a co-producer of the AlcoLOLs project from 2010 to 2016, working closely with an initial group of 16 AlcoLOLs (and subsequent 184 who joined in from 2012 to 2015) as well as providing support and researching impact (which involved spending around one day a week in schools from 2012 to 2016). The AlcoLOLs project was conceived with QMU colleague Dr Magda Pieczka and we have worked as partners on it from the very beginning in 2010. We were joined by research assistant Dr Paolo Casteltrione in 2014. We have previously theorised the design of the project as action research (Pieczka and Wood, 2013) and this chapter also draws on our analysis of data used to evaluate the project, consisting of field notes, 21 individual interviews and three focus groups with 40 AlcoLOLs, interviews with five teachers and one with a community police officer based at three of the schools, comments written by AlcoLOLs and participants on tablecloths during world café sessions and 1,402 questionnaires completed by in-school group participants to evaluate the impact of the in-school dialogue after they had participated in AlcoLOLs sessions (Pieczka, Wood and Castelrione, 2016).

We designed four two-hour sessions when 17 young people (selected according to diverse criteria as outlined above) came to QMU and we used a variety of approaches to facilitate and develop critical dialogue including a world café, storytelling, and citizens' jury (see Pieczka and Wood, 2013). A major obstacle to dialogue experienced during the first session seemed to be our role as adults and educators. As adults, it seemed that initially the young people felt that our views were irrelevant to them (which makes sense if they are viewing their use of alcohol as a way of creating a social identity for themselves with their peers). We also found it difficult to engage a number of them as they seemed intent on rolling their eyes, pulling faces behind our backs and trying to involve their peers in this process of undermining us. Freire's (2017) conceptualisation of a 'banking model of education' was helpful in explaining and countering this behaviour. By distinguishing our dialogic approach from the traditional teacher / learner dichotomy usually experienced at school, Freire's banking model posits education as a process by which the teacher acquires knowledge that they then invest or deposit into the learners who then memorise and regurgitate it. In this way the teacher has all the power and knowledge (and the pupils are 'doers' rather than 'thinkers'). If the young people were used to that model and to only being able to exercise power within it by subverting the power of the teacher, this could help explain their refusal to engage seriously with us. We clearly could not achieve dialogue within this dynamic and Freire's alternative pedagogy of the oppressed is a useful way of distinguishing our different approach. Consequently we explained that we were not teachers but co-learners. Freire values intuition and what he calls concrete knowledge and we explained that only their lived experience could deliver the knowledge and understanding we needed in this situation. So we would not be transferring or even just sharing, but creating new knowledge as a result of dialogue. As young people they were the experts about underage drinking and how to affect it, not us. We also ensured that the young people understood our different ethical guidelines[3] – that as researchers, not teachers, we were allowed to hear about illegal behaviour and were not required to take action unless we believed someone was about to cause immediate harm to themselves or others.

First session: world café approach used to affect Freire's stage of problematisation

The first session aimed to challenge the young people's social norms about how much it is 'normal' and admirable to drink by developing a critical lens through which they could view Scotland's drinking culture. To achieve this, we needed, in Freirean terms, to problematise the situation:

> The starting point for organising the program content of education or political action must be the present, existential, concrete situation ... utilising certain basic contradictions, we must pose this existential, concrete, present situation to the people as a problem which challenges them and requires a response – not just at an intellectual level, but at the level of action. (Freire, 2017: 69)

We problematised on several levels – including an analysis of the external, cultural and political context of alcohol consumption, but also considered more personal factors such as their own ability to communicate honestly with each other at school and about alcohol. So, at the external level, the problem we posed was the costs of managing the impact of Scotland's drinking culture (£3.6 billion a year according to the Societal Cost of Alcohol Misuse in Scotland for 2007), and how

60 per cent of young offenders were drunk at the time of their offence and may not have committed a crime if they had been sober (Prisoners Survey, 2015 – Young People in Custody). We also demonstrated how unusual our Scottish attitude to drinking is in a worldwide context, with young people not getting drunk in the vast majority of countries, and shared our view that Scottish drinking culture was manipulated by a drinks industry that wielded significant power.

We also explored what could be seen as a more personal or internal level of problematisation during the world café activity, whereby pupils were asked to question how alienated (Freire, 2017) they felt – or constrained in communicating their real feelings about their attitudes to the culture of underage drinking they were experiencing. To do this, we adopted a 'world café' format whereby in groups they moved round a series of three tables facilitated by an academic and each focussed on asking a series of questions about a particular phenomenon. One of these prompted the young people to analyse how they routinely communicate with their peers and in class at school and another focussed on how they routinely talked about alcohol – what people would say (and not say) about drinking. Rather than just describing these, they were asked to critically reflect on the answers – for example when someone wrote on the tablecloth 'I never say what I really think at school, I say what I think I need to say to fit in' (written on tablecloth in world café) everyone was asked if they identified with the phenomenon or could further elucidate it; to describe how it feels; to identify what could have caused it; what constricted them and so on. Some of the insights gained from this are included in the introductory section of this chapter referring to feeling vulnerable and in fear of being 'judged', and more can be seen in the full AlcoLOLs Project report (Pieczka, Wood and Castelrione, 2016: 4–5).

Throughout the three sessions, and beginning here, one of the key triggers for motivating the young people to become AlcoLOLs could be seen as their recognition of their own role as oppressors. In Freirean terms 'during the initial stage of the struggle, the oppressed, instead of striving for liberation, tend themselves to become oppressors or 'sub oppressors' (Freire, 2017: 19). This type of 'sub oppression' can be interpreted as the way that pupils report being judged or laughed at by their peers for what they say or how they behave at school resulting in the feeling of not being able to talk authentically, as previously described. It can also be relevant to the way that young people can use discourse to curate their image as being socially successful through reference to excessive drinking. In this way they can be seen as complicit in encouraging younger siblings or pupils at school to follow their example and blindly decide they also need to drink excessively to 'fit in' or to keep silent about not wanting to drink for fear of social stigmatisation or judgement (AlcoLOLs film; Percy et al, 2011). During our storytelling session our dialogue participants became aware of this role when stories were told of younger pupils scrutinising older teenagers' social media posts for clues about the type of behaviour they needed to copy to gain access to the popular groups. This realisation of what is termed here as sub-oppression is often reported in our data as a key trigger for young people becoming AlcoLOLs to take action to run dialogue groups in order to 'liberate' these younger peers.

In terms of praxis, this process can be interpreted as what Freire refers to as conscentisation: 'To surmount the situation of oppression, people must first critically recognise its causes, so that through transforming action they can create a new situation, one which makes possible the pursuit of a fuller humanity' (Freire, 2017: 21). In this respect, Freire's process of humanisation is also significant – and something that can be seen as particularly relevant during our second stage of dialogue – our storytelling session.

Second session: storytelling approach used to affect Freire's stage of conscentisation

Having viewed Scotland's drinking culture, their role in it and their levels of agency, authenticity and power at school through a critical lens – perhaps detecting oppression, or beginning the process of conscientisation – the pupils were given a month to think about a story that would illustrate their experience of or views about drinking. It did not have to be negative or positive or even about them; but it did have to accurately reflect something they would really like to share with the group. In this way, the young people were in control of identifying the issues they wanted to explore (a key aspect of critical pedagogy). We worked on creating a brave space (Bohm, 1996; Pieczka and Wood, 2013) to enable this to happen – and to do this, the young people decided they wanted to produce a contract whereby they specified the behaviours necessary for them to be able to speak honestly. This process of producing a contract was continued throughout the years in which the project developed – and although the contracts adopted varied, they always included key tenets of dialogue, focussing on suspending judgement, not laughing at each other, trust (not sharing their stories outwith the circle), responding to their stories face to face so that the teller knows what the others think (even if they disagree or do not rate the point made). One of the AlcoLOLs describes how this felt: 'I thought "Well, if everyone else is opening up, it's OK if I can open up as well", and I didn't feel like I was being judged ... and the more I spoke the better I felt' (Pieczka, Wood and Casteltrione, 2016: 21). Our data show that the young people find this quality of conversation– dialogue or authentic talk – unusual and the stories told makes the biggest impression on participants (Pieczka, Wood and Casteltrione, 2016).

This session is similar to Freire's culture circles – diversity in the group means that a range of different stories is shared and the 'brave space' enables them to be interrogated and interpreted from multiple perspectives. Common stories involved seemingly popular, confident pupils retelling tales of drunken behaviour that their peers have always found funny. Often, however, these stories are no longer told as posturing 'badges of honour' but from a new perspective, with the teller revealing their vulnerability, the pressure they felt to perform so that others have a good time and their feeling that people are laughing at them but not liking them. Conversely, some participants shared stories of drunken behaviour as something to be proud of, and others responded to these by revealing their previously secret view that actually they do not find drunkenness funny, and hate having to deal with it – some go as far as saying drunkenness is attention seeking and tiresome. Pupils disclosing that they do not drink and are happy not drinking always invoked an interesting response.

A number of aspects of Freire's pedagogy are useful here in terms of interpreting what could be happening and how this leads to the young people developing praxis and organising themselves to create change. The storytelling can certainly be seen as a way of breaking the behaviour Freire sees as typical of the oppressed:

> the oppressed who have adapted to the structure of domination in which they are immersed, and have become resigned to it, are inhibited from waging the struggle for freedom as long as they feel incapable of running the risks that requires. ... they prefer gregariousness to authentic comradeship; they prefer the security of conformity with their state of unfreedom. (Freire, 2017: 21)

The storytelling can be seen to break this security of conformity (through the admission of not drinking or not enjoying drunkenness) and puncture the gregariousness (posturing about the joy of drunkenness) either by pupils revealing their own feelings of vulnerability or by feeling safe enough to be honest with each other about how others' drunken behaviour really makes them feel. This resonates with Frieire's notion that risk taking (sharing these views openly feels like a risk for these young people) is key to the process of liberation. And risk taking like this is felt to be bound up with other key aspects of praxis; notions of trust and comradeship or community, love and hope (Freire, 2017: 64). This can be seen in a series of quotes from one of the AlcoLOLs in a film they made to show to their peers in school to stimulate dialogue:

> I thought I'd let them down if I wasn't drunk ... that they'd have nothing to laugh at ... I didn't know other people didn't drink ... didn't want to drink. It was so refreshing to be around that ... I want to be myself and not in a blueprint somebody else has created for me ... if this had happened when I was in 3rd year I would be a different person, I would have been much happier ... I'd love to rewind and start again. (*The AlcoLOLs*, 2011)

The storytelling session does not consist just of sharing and listening – it is a critical dialogue. We reflected on and analysed the stories together – creating knowledge by articulating and debating responses and insights and interpreting meaning. This process also involves an element of identifying ways in which we can learn from the stories, about how to treat each other differently, about how to create what Freire would term a better 'human–world relationship' (Freire, 2017: 79). A typical question here following a story about a young person feeling social pressure to drink excessively would be 'what could we do to help X not feel that it's her duty to get drunk so that everyone has something to talk about?' Freire would refer to this process as co-investigators joining in analysis and decoding a coded situation (Freire, 2017: 78). The coding of an existential situation is the representation of that situation (in our case the stories): 'Decoding is the critical analysis and involves moving between the concrete to the abstract' (Freire, 2017: 78). Asking what happened; analysing why it might have happened; and thinking about how we could act together to prevent it from happening again – all relate to historical and cultural context. In thinking about praxis, though, and how this storytelling process can be seen as part of this process, it is useful to consider Freire's views on how the decoding creates new knowledge and a new 'real consciousness of the world' (Freire, 2017: 88). In the process of decoding, the participants begin to see how they themselves acted whilst actually experiencing the situation they are now analysing and thus reach a 'perception of their previous perception. By achieving this awareness, they come to perceive reality differently ... decoding stimulates the appearance of a new perception and the development of new knowledge' (Freire, 2017: 88). This could certainly be seen as evident with the first group of AlcoLOLs who, having returned to school after our intervention, lobbied their headteacher to contact us and persuade us to work with them to devise a way for them to extending critical dialogue into their schools. This was articulated as the pupils saying that the dialogue process changed them, and we could not leave them like that – they needed to change things for their peers too.

The very personal storytelling (and decodification of the stories) could be seen to engender compassion among the group and build a feeling of community – the stories transformed what had previously been anecdotes to be laughed at into stories with human consequences – in Freirean terms then, part of the dialogic process of humanisation brings about solidarity 'when he [sic] stops regarding the oppressed as an abstract category and sees them as persons who have been unjustly dealt with and deprived of their voice' (Freire, 2017: 24).

This was a powerful effect of the storytelling session both at QMU and later in the sessions run by the AlcoLOLs in schools where they told their stories in a 'talking film' aimed at modelling and stimulating dialogue. After one of the participants in an in-school session heard her friend talking about how it felt to feel pressured to get drunk to entertain her friends, one young woman was literally moved to tears. She sought me out and explained how hearing the story had made her reframe her behaviour (laughing at the drunkenness) as bullying. She was adamant that everyone in her school should see the film and take part in dialogue. This seems to be a clear example of humanisation in action. Freire refers to Buber's (1958) work in this respect. Using Buber's terms, previous to the dialogue, the drunken friend had merely been viewed as an 'it' an instrumentalised object (Freire, 2017) or dehumanised character in a story; but following the dialogue she was 'humanised' and became Buber's 'thou' – a real person in an 'I–thou' relationship with her friend. The effect on the pupil dialogue participant also demonstrates the solidarity this type of humanisation process encourages, as well as showing how storytelling (coding and decoding) can bring into focus the condition of oppression and sub-oppression (what the friend described as bullying).

Third session: citizen's jury

The AlcoLOLs became thirsty for more and different types of knowledge once they started seeing their world through a critical lens and they had developed their own in-depth understanding of the complex range of their peers' experiences of drinking. During the third session we presented them with a whole range of 'experts' to interrogate using a 'citizen's jury' approach whereby each expert witness gave a short testimony about their credentials and the insights they wanted to share. The young people (the jury) interrogated them, attempting to create dialogue to explore their views. The experts talked about a range of issues and included biochemists (talking about the impact of alcohol on the body and brain), sociologists (about the power and manipulative techniques of the drinks industry), the Justice Minister (about how many young people in prison were drunk at the time of offending), mental health nurses (about how to set a drinking plan) the police (about drunkenness being no defence in cases of sexual assault and the technicalities of rape) and so on (Pieczka and Wood, 2013).

In Freirean terms, the citizens' jury session embeds into the dialogue process his view that concrete or experiential knowledge does not displace or subvert technical or scientific knowledge in his critical pedagogy. Rather it demonstrates that these different types of knowledge should not operate as a dichotomy 'Neither objectivism nor subjectivism, nor yet psychologism is propounded here, but rather subjectivity and objectivity in constant dialectical relationship' (Freire, 2017: 24). The AlcoLOLs did not privilege either type of knowledge when they designed their own two-step dialogue programme for schools. Their first session focussed on subjectivism in terms of encouraging and analysing their own and their participants' stories (and they incorporated their expert witnesses' stories and information into this too); and their second session focussed on scenario planning and 'facts' (for example about units of alcohol, its comparative strength, how it affects the brain or affects women differently at different stages of their menstrual cycle).

The AlcoLOLs reported a number of impacts on their drinking behaviour as a result of the dialogue (ranging from developing the confidence to start drinking as well as say no when they did not want to drink and drinking more safely). They had learned a way of making decisions that involves talking through options and making confident choices. But the AlcoLOLs did not just enjoy their own newly confident state; they opted to take what Freire refers to as 'liberating action' to enable their peers to experience a similar transformation. In Freirean terms, then, they had a stark choice to remain oppressed or take action, a choice 'between human solidarity or alienation; between following prescriptions or having choices; between being spectators or actors … between speaking out or being silent' (Freire, 2017: 22) and this is what the author argues makes the project public sociology.

The process and methods elucidated in this chapter and used to operationalise Freire's theory (informed by his philosophy) are mapped below in a 'theory of change' model. It shows how each of Freire's stages (problematisation, conscientisation, humanisation and praxis) can be addressed. The model is currently being transferred into a very

Figure II.3.1: Model of critical dialogue for youth solidarity

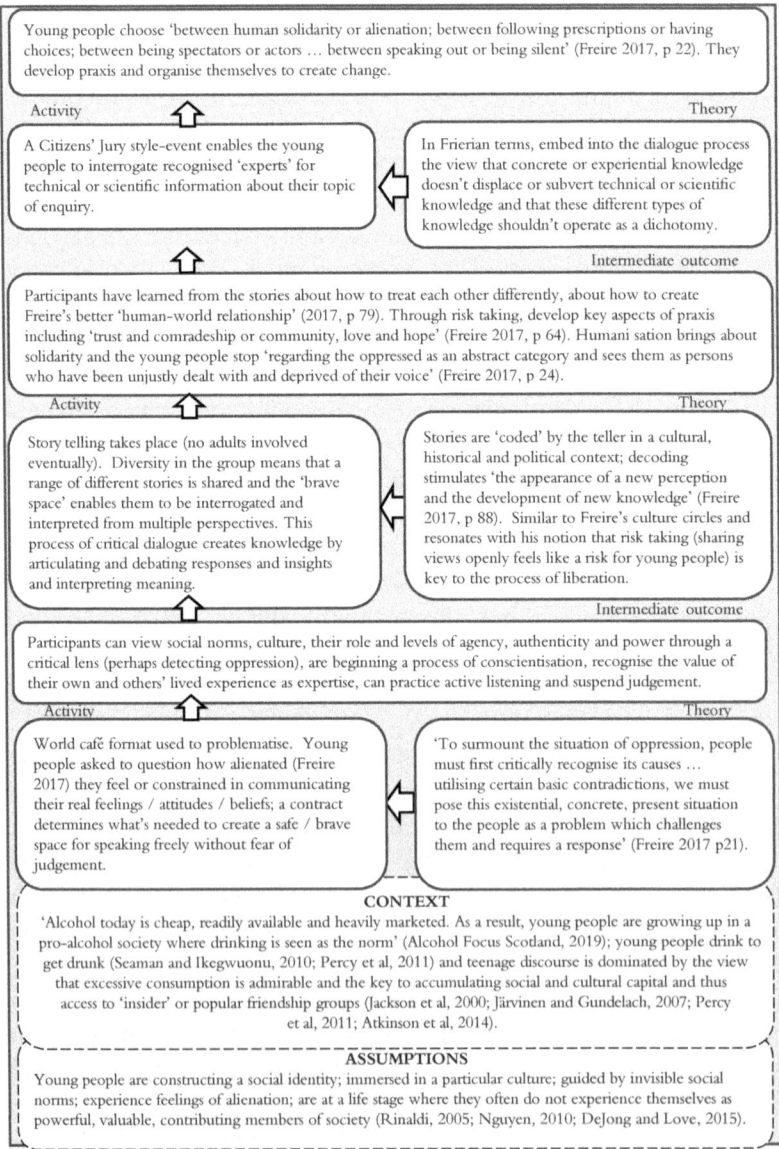

Source: author's own

different context, empowering marginalised young people in Malawi to lead critical dialogue groups with young Scottish visitors to challenge social norms embedded in voluntourism trips. Although the context in Malawi is different, and the meaning of oppression apparently more familiar in relation to Freire's conceptualisation, the assumptions about young people remain the same, as argued in this chapter – that Freire's conceptualisation of oppression is relevant because of their life stage, feelings of alienation and lack of agency.

Notes
1. Castlebrae Community High School, Drummond Community High School, Holyrood RC High School, Leith Academy, Portobello High School and Trinity Academy.
2. These refer to the year groups at senior school in Scotland. S2s are usually 13/14 years old and S4s are 15/16.
3. Based on the United Nations Convention on the Rights of the Child (1989) which includes the right of participation and a child's right to have a say in decisions which affect them. And the Children (Scotland) Act 1995 which clearly states that children should be given an opportunity to have a say on matters which affect them.

References

Alcohol Focus Scotland website, 'Alcohol and young people', www.alcohol-focus-scotland.org.uk/alcohol-information/alcohol-and-young-people/

AlcoLOLs, The (2014) [DVD] Ciara Merouan.

Anderson, P., De Bruijn, A., Angus, K., Gordon, R. and Hastings, G. (2009) 'Impact of alcohol advertising and media exposure on adolescent alcohol use: a systematic review of longitudinal studies', *Journal of Alcohol and Alcoholism*, 44(3): 229–243.

Arao, B. and Kristi, C. (2013) 'From safe spaces to brave spaces: a new way to frame dialogue around diversity and social justice', in Landreman, L.M. (ed) *The Art of Effective Facilitation*, Sterling, VA: Stylus Publishing: 135–150.

Atkinson, A., Ross, K., Begley, E., Sumnall, H. (2014) *Constructing Alcohol Identities. The Role of Social Network Sites (SNS) in Young Peoples' Drinking Cultures*, Centre of Public Health, Liverpool John Moores University, www.basw.co.uk/system/files/resources/basw_20150-7_0.pdf

Bohm, D. (1996) *On Dialogue*, New York: Routledge.

Buber, M. (1958) *I and Thou* (2nd edn, trans R.G. Smith), New York: Charles Scribner's Sons.

Clark, D.B., Thatcher, D.L. and Tapert, S.F. (2008) 'Alcohol, Psychological Dysregulation, and Adolescent Brain Development', *Alcoholism: Clinical and Experimental Research*, 32: 375-385, doi:10.1111/j.1530-0277.2007.00601.x.

Cukier S., Wettlaufer A., Jackson K., Minozzi, S., Bartholow, B.D., Stoolmiller, M.L. and Sargent, J.D. (2018) 'Impact of exposure to alcohol marketing and subsequent drinking patterns among youth and young adults', *Cochrane Database Syst Review*, 8: CD013087, doi:10.1002/14651858.CD013087, www.ncbi.nlm.nih.gov/pmc/articles/PMC6326175

DeJong, K. and Love, B.J. (2015) 'Youth oppression as a technology of colonialism: conceptual frameworks and possibilities for social justice education praxis', *Equity & Excellence in Education*, 48(3): 489–508.

Euromonitor, 'Market value of alcoholic drinks in the United Kingdom (UK) from 2013 to 2018 (in million euros)', in *Statista – The Statistics Portal*, https://www.statista.com/chart/12808/the-value-of-the-uk-alcoholic-drinks-market/

Freire, P. (2017) *Pedagogy of the Oppressed*. London: Penguin Books.

Griswold, M.G., Fullman, N., Hawley, C., Arian, N., Zimsen, S.R., Tymeson, H.D., and Abate, K.H. (2018) 'Alcohol use and burden for 195 countries and territories, 1990–2016: a systematic analysis for the Global Burden of Disease Study 2016', *The Lancet*, 392(10152): 1015–1035.

Hastings, G., Anderson, S., Cooke, E., and Gordon, R. (2005), 'Alcohol Marketing and Young People's Drinking: A Review of the Research', *Journal of Public Health Policy*, 26: 296-311, 10.1057/palgrave.jphp.3200039

Inchley, J., Currie, D., Vieno, S., Torsheim, T., Ferreira-Borges, C., Weber, M.M., Barnekow, V., and Breda, J. (eds) (2014) 'Adolescent alcohol-related behaviours: trends and inequalities in the WHO European Region, 2002–2014, Observations from the Health Behaviour in School-aged Children (HBSC)', WHO collaborative cross-national study.

Institute of Alcohol Studies (2014) 'Socioeconomic groups and alcohol', www.ias.org.uk/uploads/pdf/Socioeconomic%20groups/Socioeconomic%20groups%20and%20alcohol%20factsheet%20February%202014.pdf

Jackson, M.C., Hastings, G., Wheeler, C., Eadie, D., and Mackintosh, A.M. (2000) 'Marketing alcohol to young people: implications for industry regulation and research policy', *Addiction*, 95 (Suppl 4), S597-608, https://doi.org/10.1080/09652140020013809, https://abdn.pure.elsevier.com/en/publications/marketing-alcohol-to-young-people-implications-for-industry-regul

Järvinen, M. and Gundelach, P. (2007) 'Teenage drinking, symbolic capital and distinction', *Journal of Youth Studies*, 10: 55–71, https://doi.org/10.1080/13676260701196137

Morey, Y., Eadie, D., Purves, R., Hooper, L., Rosenberg, G., Warren, S., Hillman, H., Vohra, J., Hastings, G. and Tapp, A. (2017) 'Youth engagement with alcohol brands in the UK', Cancer Research UK, www.cancerresearchuk.org/sites/default/files/youth_engagement_with_alcohol_brands_in_the_uk.pdf

Moreno, M.A. and Whitehill, J.M. (2014) 'Influence of Social Media on Alcohol Use in Adolescents and Young Adults', *Alcohol Research*, 36(1):91–100.

O'Connor, A. (2018) 'Brewing and distilling in Scotland – economic facts and figures', The Scottish Parliament, https://sp-bpr-en-prod-cdnep.azureedge.net/published/2018/10/11/Brewing-and-distilling-in-Scotland---economic-facts-and-figures/SB%2018-64.pdf

Percy, A., Wilson, J., McCartan, C. and McCrystal, P. (2011) *Teenage Drinking Cultures*, Joseph Rowntree Foundation, www.jrf.org.uk/sites/files/jrf/teenage-drinking-culture-full.pdf

Pieczka, M. and Wood, E. (2013) 'Action research and public relations: dialogue, peer learning, and the issue of alcohol', *Public Relations Inquiry*, 2(2): 161–181, https://doi.org/10.1177/2046147X13485955

Pieczka, M., Wood E. and Casteltrione, P. (2016*) AlcoLOLs: Final Report*, Edinburgh: Queen Margaret University.

Prisoners Survey (2015) *Young People in Custody*, www.sps.gov.uk/Corporate/Publications/Publication-3908.aspx

Rutger, C.M.E., Engels, R.H., van Baaren, R.B., Hollenstein, T. and Bot, S.M. (2009) 'Alcohol portrayal on television affects actual drinking behaviour', *Alcohol and Alcoholism*, 44(3): 244–249, https://doi.org/10.1093/alcalc/agp003

Savic, M., Room, R., Mugavin, J., Pennay, A. and Livingston, M. (2016) 'Defining "drinking culture": A critical review of its meaning and connotation in social research on alcohol problems', *Drugs: Education, Prevention and Policy*, 23(4): 270–282, https://doi.org/10.3109/09687637.2016.1153602

Scottish Social Attitudes Survey (2007) 'Something to be ashamed of or part of our way of life? Attitudes towards alcohol in Scotland', www2.gov.scot/Publications/2008/08/01112431/0

Seaman, P., and Ikegwuonu, T. (2010) 'Drinking to belong: Understanding young adults' alcohol use within social networks', Joseph Rowntree Foundation, www.jrf.org.uk/sites/default/files/jrf/migrated/files/alcohol-young-adults-full.pdf

Smith, L., and Foxcroft, D. (2009) 'Drinking in the UK: an exploration of trends', Joseph Rowntree Foundation, www.jrf.org.uk/sites/files/jrf/UK-alcohol-trends-FULL.pdf

Societal cost of alcohol misuse in scotland for 2007, www.webarchive.org.uk/wayback/archive/20170701074158/http://www.gov.scot/Publications/2009/12/29122804/0

World Health Organization (2018) *Global Status Report on Alcohol and Health. World Health Organization*, Geneva: World Health Organization, http://apps.who.int/iris/bitstream/handle/10665/274603/9789241565639-eng.pdf?ua=1

CASE II.4

Young Children and Participative Research Enquiry: A Case for Active Citizenship

Maria Giatsi Clausen

This chapter enquires into possibilities for young children's active citizenship as provoked through their involvement in participative research enquiry. It is the main crux of this chapter that learning that happens though experiencing authentic participation, for example participative research, creates possibilities for young children's active citizenship. My interest in these possibilities is based on my work and interaction with children both in my capacity as a researcher and paediatric practitioner throughout my professional life. The potential that participative research enquiries hold is based on my observation and interaction with children around their perceptions of their *rights* (for example, children understand their rights to protection and to provision; although they emphasise their participation rights, they find that these are not always respected); agency (children find that their moral status is often questionable in the eyes of adults; they are often not believed, or are wrongly blamed); self-realisation and adult dominance (constant negotiation with adults in order to have time for oneself and to resist adult demands, at home and at school; pursuing own interest against arguing against control and supervision).

Active citizenship refers to being a social agent expressing opinions, and initiating social actions. The concept of agency is central to active citizenship. Hannah Arendt (1998) argued that to be agentic one must initiate action with other people, that emerges from new ideas from our interactions with other people. The intention of this chapter is to provide discussion and understandings about theories and pedagogies that are applicable to research that is democratic in its process, relevant to its young participants, and one that grants their authentic voice, recognises their agency, and can bring about action and change.

Research with children is viewed often as, potentially, different from research with adults, mainly because of adult perceptions of children and children's position in adult society or because children are viewed to be different. Those that argue for adapted research techniques for work with children also emphasise the competence of children. There, however, lies also a potential controversy and a question on why, if children are indeed competent social actors, there is a need to use 'child-friendly' methods to communicate with them. Research with children is influenced by the way in which researchers perceive the status of children; this then influences the choice of epistemological approach and methods of a study (Punch, 2002). In the field of occupational therapy, my professional background, participation in various occupations is considered a fundamental right and a pre-condition to leading a good life. Yet, occupational therapy practice has often been criticised as 'adult-centric', practitioner and/or parent-led, with clinicians and researchers often underestimating children's abilities, or not providing children with the opportunity to participate in goal setting (Royeen, 2004).

This chapter first presents current debates on children's participation starting with the children's rights movement. A critique of the movement follows, based on the work of Foucault on power and domination, to illustrate the obstacles we still face towards achieving an authentic intergenerational dialogue, based on current views on childhood. Pedagogical approaches, mainly the work of Paulo Freire on active citizenship, is then argued as an avenue to achieve meaningful participation of children in the public life domain and, particularly, in consultancy and research. The main notions of Hannah Arendt's theorising on power, agency, action and relationality are then presented as a relevant framework applying to participatory research with children. The chapter concludes with the discussion of specific methodological considerations for this type of research enquiry.

Participation as a children's right

Participation rights have become the norm in child rights practice and policy. This also extends to participatory methods in research, as it is now widely recognised that stakeholders who have the most at stake, eg the more vulnerable, should be able to exert an influence over the choices we make in terms of priorities, strategies and directions and partners (Cornwall, 2002). One cannot argue strongly enough the centrality of participation, and the call for change for organisations and institutions involved in children's lives, with the advent of the UN Convention of the Rights of the Child. Article 12 of the UN Convention states that:

> parties shall assure to the child who is capable of forming his or her own views the right to express those views freely and in all matters affecting the child, the views of the child being given due weight in accordance with the age and maturity of the child. (UNICEF, 1990)

This unequivocal commitment to capturing children's authentic voice and granting participation rights, marked by the Convention, was the product of a specific historical period, and a set of social conditions that led to liberal thinking in the nineteenth century. Albeit widely celebrated, however this commitment may not be sufficient to interrupt common patterns of intergenerational interaction and deeply habituated power relations that can emerge in a dialogue, and influence its course (Gadda, 2008; Taft, 2015).

Work on children's participatory rights requires paying very close attention to adult–child relationships (Mayall, 2000). The idea of an egalitarian intergenerational collaboration, whether this relates to research and consultation, policy making, or decision making at everyday settings, such as the school, is very difficult to implement given the broader social context of age-based inequality, and the deeply structured patterns of behaviour that give adults power (Clark, 2011; Taft, 2015). The complex endeavour that is to bring together social actors with unequal social and political status, such as children and adults, has to be acknowledged, and the tensions and challenges need to be addressed prior to celebrating a dialogical approach as a successful avenue to enacting authentic child participation.

Albeit the optimism surrounding the importance of children's voice and the declaration of their participation rights, scholars also challenge whether dialogical opportunities always give rise to the identification of the children's concerns (Harris and Maniatakis, 2013). To be meaningful, consulting with children must be based on Freirean active citizenship principles and the condition that the participants become conscious of their presence in the world (Freire, 2017). It is through this actualisation, and an open dialogue that interrogates different possibilities in the societies we live in, that things become transformative in nature (Freire, 2017). Taft (2015) argues that in an intergenerational habitus where adults speak and children listen, a simple emphasis on focusing on the child's voice is not enough to create an egalitarian approach and dialogic relationship; on the contrary, sometimes, it can provide a narrative justification for an implicit continuation of adult dominance.

Genuine attempts are being made to address rigour and quality of research with children. Addressing tokenism and tackling ethical issues, attention to sampling and recruitment techniques to safeguard for representativeness of membership, adult researcher leading or speaking less in the process to avoid reaching false consensus are now, as practices, often the norm. These attempts are, however, qualitatively very different to the big issues that remain around ownership of research, authenticity in the dialogue, relational power between the social actors involved, the dynamics of power, and the difference between voice and agency (Punch, 2002; Alderson, 2008; Taft, 2015). The notion of agency in particular has to be further explored and advocated, as participation with a focus on agency, is 'not only being able to speak, but also, having one's identity, status, opinion recognised as worthy of respect and consideration' (Taft, 2015: 462).

Critique of the children's rights movement

The construct of 'childhood' is artificial and is a product of social and socioeconomic circumstances. Previously developmental psychology, and now the rights discourse, normalise the child and reinforce a Western adult world's idea of a perfect childhood, leading to marginalisation of the child in the community. Researchers carefully need to, at the outset of any research that may involve children, reflect on their views on what childhood means and fundamentally question, before anything else, the right of an adult to search for children's point of view. Participation of children in research and consultation, for its own sake, and without genuine and authentic interest in agency and citizenship of the child, can become misappropriation.

Before considering research with children, one needs to critically engage and reflect on dominance paradigms and what children's right movements, in general, can represent. In the first place, childhood is a political issue:

> Theories about what children need, about how they develop and what input from adults is therefore appropriate, are indeed theories or stories (rather than facts) and practices

that derive exclusively from adult perspectives. They derive
from adults' study of children, contextualised and structured
by adults' social and economic goals in specific societies.
(Mayall, 2000: 245)

Gadda (2008) argues that developments such as the UN Convention, albeit a step towards upholding some children's rights, especially around protection and provision, are not necessarily a step towards children's participation, and can serve as a consolidation of institutional power in its existing forms. The modern humanitarianism emerging in the nineteenth century ('living a good life') was a result of better material conditions, but the liberal theory and its notion of the capable citizens who can exercise their rights led to a new form of dominance. The views of the eighteenth century of the child as a 'savage' that needs control were replaced by the romantic child who needs protection; with this leading to a new form of dominance. The notions of vulnerability and competence emerged, which led to a new hierarchy; the one between the adult citizen who is active and rational, and the passive child as a citizen awaiting making (as an extension of being an adult in awaiting, due to the child's special developmental needs). Childhood has been constructed, and still at large remains, the opposite of adulthood with established hierarchical relationships, characterised by power differentials (Gadda, 2008). Critical reflection on adult dominance is required when conceptualising and conducting research with children. Foucault's views on dominance paradigms and oppression offers a useful, critical lens when reflecting on children's rights movements, which supposedly grant them the right to participation in consultation and research. 'Supposedly' refers to the fact that such developments are not necessarily great steps towards authentic participation but can retain and consolidate power of adults over children. Views of children as needing protection are profoundly influenced by colonialist European expansionism of the eighteenth and nineteenth centuries, an analogy also supported by Hannah Arendt's analysis of the social construction of the individual and of totalitarianism that grounds relationships of undifferentiated equality (Arendt,1998).

The need to view and study children as social actors, separate and extricated from their parents, family, teachers, has been stressed often as an important enterprise towards including them in the 'writings' of the social order. According to Mayall (2000: 243) 'children's welfare in the last 100 years has been inextricably woven into women's welfare and women's social condition'. Social order requires consideration of all its members, and that we need to acknowledge that children, like other minority groups, have a right to be heard. It is then only through understanding the social condition of childhood that children's rights can be implemented. In the twentieth century, children and childhood have become the objects of interventions in the name of addressing their needs and protecting their rights, all on the basis of expert professional opinion, in the fields of education, health promotion, social work practice etc. The need, in particular, to monitor children's development has led to unprecedented surveillance at school and at home. At the same time children's presence has been excluded from other aspect of public life and from public spaces. The scholarisation of childhood, with distinct developmental sequelae and descriptors resembles rather an apprentice model towards adulthood, alongside an acquisition of knowledge and skills, which simply respond to modern societies' demands and are characterised by affluence, status and consumerism (Mayall, 2000).

Education and legal systems normalise this power system all on the basis of the 'truth' produced by disciplines such as developmental psychology, around the developmental needs and capacities of the children. Clark (2011) contributes further to this point by asserting that research even about, let alone with, children, is a result of this child theorisation. Children are viewed as a universal, homogeneous group, according to the orthodoxy of developmental theories. Research on children is often less threatening, neutralised or even playful topics, or a sentimental child utopia, something that further endorses the view that 'their issues' cannot be the same as 'adult issues'. This patronising attitude also transpires into the way research is conducted and affects children's agency and potential to act as social actors.

Right to participate as an opportunity for learning, action and citizenship

The case for arguing for participative research enquiry as a unique way to conduct research with young citizens draws on the fundamental principles of Freire's work, and the right to participate and learn as an avenue for action and citizenship; also, the work of Hannah Arendt on agency and action.

Paulo Freire argues that 'no one's born fully informed; it is through self-experience in the world that we become what we are'. Children's participation in public life is about enacting citizenship; and participative research enquiry could be another such opportunity for enacting citizenship. The child, as a citizen, has the ability to have a voice and participate in influencing public policy and social determinants within a community. Children are viewed as competent human beings, key informants and experts in their own lives with the view that they can express these views with an insight for matters affecting them (Harris and Maniatakis, 2013). These principles are also core to the paradigm of participative research enquiry, as an open, participant-led, democratic way to conduct research that is relevant for, and beneficial to, the group (Koch and Kralik, 2006). Key to any such involvement is the view of the child as a 'citizen'. A social-political interpretation of the UN Convention becomes therefore imperative (Roose and Bouverne De Bie, 2008). The authors argue that conceptions of citizenship assume the existence of a conciliatory concept as the norm, somewhere in between 'non-citizenship' and 'citizenship'. Research and pedagogical practices are often applied on the basis of that norm. Pols (2004) argues that 'relational citizenship', citizenship that is developed through dialogue and interaction with the 'other', is often neglected. Citizenship is a developing concept and experience and that is actualised in activities and relationships (Cox, 2018). Such a position could impact significantly on pedagogical and research practice, as the child is not expected to be guided towards full citizenship but researchers and pedagogues are simply adults who enter into a dialogue with the child. However even in the case of such a realisation, ie that becoming a citizen is a learning process, the wide variety of social norms in a society, and the power that lies in the interpretation of what constitutes a dialogue, on the side of the adult researcher or pedagogue, implies that there can be great variation in what different children eventually experience.

The point of departure when conducting research with children ought to be critically considering why children are, first and foremost, invited to participate. It is not uncommon that the right to participate often dominates the agenda, to the expense of carefully considering how the young participants' voice is amplified, and their agency is endowed. For this to be the case, not only the notion has to be present that children are competent actors but also that, from a Freirean perspective, active democratic citizen in that they participate in the world in order to transform it, with a sense of social justice and self-awareness of one's presence in the world, not simply expressing civic responsibility by expressing ideas (Harris and Maniatakis, 2013). Cornwall (2002) stresses the importance of shifting the frame of participatory practice beyond 'invited participation' in predetermined spaces and with predetermined agendas to enable people to define for themselves key points for change. According to Cornwall (2002), the vision of participation should be less about institutions involving citizens in the design or delivery of programmes, but participation to initiate social change that is needed for self-determination and, potentially, self-governance. In the case of children and research, early public involvement and dialogue in the community could serve as 'organised efforts to increase control' (21), which could in turn potentially inform research undertaken on issues that matter to them under the maxim of 'for, by and with' the children.

A prime example of intergenerational dialogue and an exploration of the role of children and youth in social change is the work of Jessica Taft. Her work focuses on the political lives of children and youth in South America. It researches a movement that is committed to children's leadership and seeks to create egalitarian relationships between working children and adults. Starting from the theoretical position that childhood is a socially constructed category whose meaning varies by context, the research explores the possibilities for non-hierarchical intergenerational relationships. The work is based on a model of collaboration between adults and children, found in the Peruvian working children's movement. Although quite unusual and non-normative, the movement and the participative enquiries around it certainly push the boundaries of 'normal' or hegemonic paradigms of childhood, and allow for exploration of the dynamics between the intergenerational dialogues in this non-normative contexts. It most certainly calls for the meaning of childhood to be constantly revisited and redefined, and can have important implication for possibilities in children's participation in research, social change and decision making. The author herself states that it allows for careful consideration of the plasticity of the meaning of childhood (Taft and Hava, 2013; Taft, 2015).

In addition to adding to the theoretical debate and need for constant reconfiguration of the meaning of childhood, Taft's work unravels ample opportunities to facilitate children's agency and participation as engaged citizens. Participative research enquiries could serve as an opportunity to full participation in everyday community life and decision making, when these decisions are viewed as of importance to the young participants. It is important to explore how the researcher and the child participant interact and generate knowledge in that space in an open communicative manner.

Interaction between the child and the adult researcher: relationality; plurality and solidarity

On the point of interaction between the adult researcher(s) and child participants in a participative research enquiry, with a focus on action and/or change, Hanna Arendt's work on power, action and agency is of elementary importance.

According to Penta (1996), two key concepts are in the heart of Arendt's notion of power: potential for action, and the relational constitution of one's political self. These could be of relevance to research with children. According to Arendt, potential for action is present when people gather together 'under uncorrupted condition of communication' (Penta, 1996). A participative research enquiry is one such opportunity. Action is then connected to the disclosure of the 'who', of the agents involved: a human being who is not simply 'the other' but distinct (Arendt, 1998). In the case of the child participant; the disclosure of 'who' is different to 'what' the person, here the child, is (in terms of shortcomings, gifts, talents). We argue that research with children has focused exponentially into the 'what' of the child; their special characteristics or shortcomings, often determined by developmental theories, leading to viewing research with child participants as fundamentally different to research with adults. This universal way of viewing childhood can be challenged in open, democratic enquiries, where the focus is on everything somebody does and says. This is, according to Arendt, essential and explicit to action.

Another notion, in Arendt's work, undeniably related to action, is relationality. She stressed that plurality and solidarity among the actors are key. Although tension does often exist between human distinctiveness and human collectivity, action can emerge from this tension as the actors move from the 'who' (the unique; 'plurality'), to the 'we' (collectivity), which is required for action. According to Arendt, power does not inhere necessarily in the actors themselves. It exists between those who act, as the condition of their action, ie it is a phenomenon of reciprocal rationality (Penta, 1996). The implication of this realisation for adult–child interactions during research could be withdrawal of instrumental control; providing information about a broad research interest or area, which is not followed by further analysis by the adult researcher, as this could infer how knowledgeable and, therefore, dominant the adult is. This could potentially lead to the openness and unpredictability of the communicative relationship. This does not mean that one such open, authentic interaction that occurs during that adult–child dialogical opportunity leads automatically to child sovereignty and empowerment. There is, as it has been argued before, inequality between adults and children prior to such an encounter. Penta (1996) argues that if we accept Arendt's assertions that power lies in the 'in between' space of the actors, in their relational constitution of themselves when they come together, and is not inherent in them, it is possible that we can have asymmetry, or even inequality, among the actors (adult researcher; young participants) prior to the meeting; however, a democratic space can lead to isonomy of power when they – politically – constitute themselves face to face in relation to each other. This also agrees with the Freirean perspective of active citizenship through self-awareness of one's presence, in the world, in relation to others (Freire, 2017). In other words, such dialogical opportunities albeit not leading to the empowerment of the child, they can be an empowering experience for the active child citizen, in that there is possibility for change, through their engagement, within the plurality (of those involved) in the 'we' (solidarity) of the action.

Participative research enquiry

Participative research enquiry with children, as with adults, must tend to creating a dialogical opportunity to give rise to the children's thematic concerns and broad problem posing question, as these interrogate possibilities and enquire what we want for the future (Harris and Maniatakis, 2013). A careful co-constructed exploration of the general themes of relevance to the child is therefore a precondition. Participative enquiries should aim at not only amplifying children's voice at the point of data collection and analysis, but the outset of the enquiry, with an emphasis to gain access to key events and ideas of children (Punch, 2002; Clark, 2011). By definition it should focus on children's salient concern and issues. Attention has to be exercised, however, that there is no filtering of the issues children raise as of interest to them. Clark (2011) argues that even those who are committed to this type of research may still, non-intentionally, treat children as a group to be symbolical, protected from behaviours adults regularly practice, for example consumption; and therefore ignore that the topic may be of significance to a child for the same reason it is of significance to an adult.

Most issues relating to research with children relate to methodological considerations and predominantly enhancing the validity and trustworthiness of studies' findings. The goal and challenge, as with any other research, are how to maximise participants' ability to express themselves at the point of data gathering but, also, when analysing and interpreting data. Amplifying their voice and expression by employing multiple methods has, however, been misappropriated to often safeguard for validity and reliability of research with children, or as an attempt to cross-check and triangulate. Children are viewed often as prone to exaggeration in their narratives, limited vocabulary, or as reaching false consensus in discussion with adults in order to please them (Punch, 2002; Clark, 2011). Such 'concerns' expose the hypocrisy around the statement that children are indeed competent actors and undermine the very purpose of participative enquiry. Attention to what children wish to talk about, eg a particular experience, how they named it, how significant it was etc, is what should be rather of concern to researchers, with the selection of data collection method being of secondary significance, as it is the former that safeguards for authentic participation and expression.

Considering multiple methods of expression, which can also be non-literal, and include creative arts, storytelling, brainstorming, writing, drama, arts etc, should be negotiated with the young participants and be considered only if they can enhance active control, more forthcoming, widen the latitude for expression of meaning (Alderson, 2008; Harris and Maniatakis, 2013) Irrespective of research methods deployed, however, research with children that has a transformative potential should involve analysis of reality, and should not shy away from 'key words' which allow the introduction of children's reflections on the social world that surrounds them (Andreola, 1993). Freire, in the book *Cultural Action for Freedom*, notes than in literacy 'creating a problem around a word which came from the popular classes means to create a problem for the themes it refers to, which necessarily involves analysing reality'. (Freire, 1977 in Andreola, 1993: 230).

References

Alderson, P. (2008) 'Children as researchers', in Christensen, P. and James, A. (eds) *Research with Children: Perspectives and Practices*, New York: Routledge: 276–290.

Andreola, B.A. (1993) 'Action, knowledge and reality in the educational work of Paulo Freire', *Educational Action Research*, 1(2): 221–234.

Arendt, H. (1998) *The Human Condition* (2nd edn), Chicago. IL: University of Chicago Press.

Clark, C.D. (2011) *In a Younger Voice: Doing Child-centred Qualitative Research*, Oxford: Oxford University Press.

Cornwall, A. (2002) *Beneficiary, Consumer, Citizen: Perspectives on Participation for Poverty Reduction*, Sida Studies no. 2, Gothenburg: Elanders Novum AB.

Cox, P. (2018) 'Children and relational citizenship: a history', in Shaw, M. and Bailey, S. (eds) *Justice for Children and Families: A Developmental Perspective*, Cambridge: Cambridge University Press.

Harris, P. and Maniatakis, H. (2013) *Children as Citizens: Engaging with the Children's Voice in Educational Settings*, Abingdon: Routledge.

Freire, P., Bergman Ramos, M. and Macedo, D.P. (2017) *Pedagogy of the Oppressed* (30th anniversary edn), New York: Bloomsbury Academic.

Gadda, A. (2008) *Rights, Foucault and Power: A Critical Analysis of the United Nation Convention on the Rights of the Child*, Edinburgh: Working Papers in Sociology no. 31.

Koch, T. and Kralik, D. (2006) *Participatory Action Research in Health Care*, Oxford: Blackwell.

Mayall, B. (2000) 'The sociology of childhood in relation to children's rights', *International Journal of Children's Rights*, 8: 243–259.

Penta, L.J. (1996) 'Hannah Arendt: on power', *Journal of Speculative Philosophy*, 10(3): 210–229.

Pols, J. (2004) *Good Care. Enacting a Complex Ideal in Long-Term Psychiatry*, Utrecht: Trimbos-Instituut.

Punch, S. (2002) 'Research with children: the same or different from research with adults?', *Childhood*, 9: 321.

Roose, R. and Bouverne De-Bie, M. (2008) 'Do children have rights or do their rights have to be realised? The United Nations Convention on the Rights of the Child as a frame of reference for pedagogical action', *Journal of Philosophy of Education*, 41(3): 431–443.

Royeen, C.B. (2004) *Pediatric Issues in Occupational Therapy: A Compendium of Leading Scholarship*, Bethesda, MD: American Occupational Therapy Association: 38.

Taft, J.K. (2015) 'Adults talk too much: intergenerational dialogue and power in the Peruvian movement of working children', *Childhood: A Journal of Global Child Research*, 22(4): 460–473.

Taft, J.K. and Hava, G. (2013) 'Youth activists, youth councils, and constrained democracy', *Education, Citizenship, and Social Justice*, 8(1): 87–100.

UNICEF (2000) *The United Nations Convention on the Rights of the Child*, London: UNICEF UK.

CASE II.5

English Last: Displaced Publics and Communicating Multilingually as Social Act and Art

Alison Phipps, Tawona Sitholé, Naa Densua Tordzro and Gameli Tordzro

once in a while
i hear the comment
you speak good english
in my school days
it was a compliment
but at some point it got a bit complicated

Tawona Sitholé

Introduction

None of the authors of this chapter are sociologists. All of them have featured in a major international, sociological keynote and public lecture. Each has been, and may still claim to be, an indigenous person (one, somewhat tenuously). Each is a migrant. Each is a multilingual. Each is an artist.

There is something strange, consequently, for each to be invited to contribute to a volume on public sociology education without actually having any of the qualifications. For Alison, this was made particularly stark at the Australian Sociological Association's 2017 conference in Perth, Western Australia. She had been invited to give the public keynote lecture, perhaps the highest guest honour. In the opening sessions all delegates were given the task of asking themselves the question, 'When did you give your first sociology paper at a sociology conference.' Everyone had an example, except for those just starting out, and they were given a warm welcome as they made their rite of passage into the scholarly communities of sociologists.

Alison was the imposter, and the materials in her bag for her public lecture were those of equal imposters, the co-authors of this chapter. She wore a suit made by the sociology imposter Naa Densua Tordzro for the occasion. It was hand woven, and tailored, and it was a research output. This was not a normal piece of 'data' or 'result' or 'finding' for the sociologists gathered together. Nor was it a normal for a middle-aged public lecture to be given by a white, educated women wearing kente cloth. The cloth was also to become the design for the book cover of the anthology of poetry written by the next imposter, Tawona Sitholé, whose work with Alison would also feature in the public lecture. Finally, there was the music, composed by the final imposter, Gameli Tordzro. All of this was public, in a setting marked up as the most sociological of sociological spaces by the doyens of sociology, able to designate, or otherwise, what it means to be a sociologist.

Alison began her lecture laughing at the fact that her answer to the question, 'When did you give your first paper at a sociology conference?' was 'I'm just starting to give it now.' But for all the joking this was an important move, a signal to the different nuances, and phrases, the jargon of different disciplines, to which she would have recourse. It was also a nod to the way in which her form of lecture would differ, having, as Williams notes, its own 'active material base' (Williams, 1977), and it was a public attempt at a performance of some humility, in front of a kindly but nonetheless terrifying prospect, of 400 plus professional sociologists, all waiting to be entertained, to learn something new perhaps.

To have become something of a public intellectual affords many such occasions to be an imposter. The capital – cultural, symbolic and financial – of many different disciplines and fields, is spent inviting Alison to take part in a range of public forums – form media through to academic conference keynotes. It makes for a gruelling, nerve-wracking, exhilarating, intellectually stimulating and, at times, very boring, series of experiences. It means being itinerant, compromised – and compromised in myriad ways. Much of the time she has the sense that she is gate-crashing a whole series of weird and wonderful parties. And it is her work as a scholar and her ontological placement deeply within a refugee family, with skin in the game, that seems to be her meal ticket. She is legitimised as a public sociologist, and many other diverse things, like an ambassasor, a chair, a gardener and mother that bring a smile, and increasingly an acceptance, as part of the way disciplines and institutions both seek out cultural capital, perform their genuine if compromised moral purposes, and renew or expand the stock of resources within their own disciplinary spaces (Bourdieu, 1988).

She has agonised about the politics of representation in this space. A white woman speaking about refugees is a critiqued and vilified figure in the world of intersectional politics – usually by other scholars, often white themselves. Her team is one of the most diverse in the university. This too is a cause for much agonising as she considers the way diversity plays itself out. She is invited onto Black History Month committees and there are no people of colour. She points this out. People of colour are drafted in to be diverse, and worry at their own lack of qualifications or time for another such position, and the newly created exigencies that Sara Ahmed (Ahmed, 2012) has documented so compellingly, which create their own new complicities with institutions legal and market-driven requirements to be seen to be diverse and equal. Such is the double bind Spivak speaks of (Spivak, 2012). There is no pure place to work from. And to keep silence, or course, when she – Alison – does, brings the accusation from those of refugee background, rightly, that she is not speaking out on their behalf.

So, the question for Alison has become how to work through the politics of this sociological space in such a way that it might offer educational models of alternatives. For Alison this comes under the rubric of Freire's phrase, '

> *Nao e possivel a pronuncia do mundo que e um ato de criacao e recriacao, se nao ha amor que a infunda.* [It is not possible to pronounce (many translations have 'name') the world, which is an act of creation and recreation, if it is not infused with love.] (Freire, 2006: 78–79)

This chapter examines how the fraught intersectional sociological politics of education and representation have led to a team working to attempt new forms of multilingual pronunciation as acts of creation and recreation, amongst diaspora, those seeking refuge, and those migrating. It does so by drawing on a range of research council funded projects, which have produced creative and empirical work over the last four years, have involved attempts to work and research multilingually, as the borders of the body, language, law and the state, and have intersected with questions pertinent to sociology in particular. It also works from the practices of indigenous practice, which intersect, especially in the African diasporic context, strongly with the experience of multilingualism being a mother tongue, an ever-widening practice of spoken life. The discussion of refuge and exile also necessitates a starting point within indigeneity, placement, rootedness, for displacement and loss to be understood within both social and cultural contexts of heritage.

Pronuciar do mundo

Sociological space is, amongst many other things, acoustic, though you would not know this from the output or theorising, the methodological approaches or the conceptualisations for society that dominate the literature. Sociological research, like the majority of work published in academic journals worldwide, is Anglo-normative and, whilst it focuses on the social categories of race, gender and class, it has failed utterly, to incorporate language as a social category of import into its theorisation or into its methodological frameworks, even in its reflexivity.

Research is increasingly, under the neoliberal paradigm, written and published in English and those who speak English as an additional or second language and work as sociologists will chose to write and publish largely in English in order to ensure their work has the audience it requires for citation indexes, even if that is not the best way to engage, check, co-design, co-interpret their research. A full discussion of the monolingual paradigms and Anglo-normativity can be found in Gramling (Gramling, 2016). All sociological research is multilingual. A founding father of the discipline – Durkheim – constructed his theoretical base in French. That he is widely cited in English points to the extent of the Anglophone monopoloy and the political economy of Anglo-normative research. As such, monolingual research is a fallacy. That sociological research does not even countenance the ways in which working multilingually, living through different languages and inhabiting social space in languages that are other than that of the dominant social group – and in sociological terms that is Anglo-normative – renders sociological research linguistically mute.

To this end the AHRC Large Grant Researching Multilingually at the Borders of Language, the Body, Law and the State 014-2017 was co-designed, multilingually, to examine how researchers engage with the social category of language, how they 'research multilingually' at every level of their research, not simply in multilingual attempts at dissemination or communication. This research focused, in particular, on categories of people seeking asylum from persecution, where the role language places in their agency, resistance and social security and protection can be a matter of life and death.

Through this research the epistemocide created by the epistemic violence done by monolingual assumptions in sociological research, but also in research across the academy, was revealed in stark relief. This included interesting, language-focused disciplines such as modern languages, with their focus on 'world languages' or languages of political power, where the majority of the languages through which societies form and are contested, worldwide, are invisible. In short, following on from Freire's injunction to 'pronounce' the world, it became clear from our reflections and research across multiple disciplines (Gramling, 2016; Phipps, 2018, 2019) that the sociological world was being pronounced, in research terms, in English first, and often in English only.

In order to begin tackling this lacuna, the project employed three consulting artists from the Global South who spoke approximately 20 different languages themselves, and were particularly focused on the preservation and use of languages from their own societies as a way of preserving both tangible and intangible cultural and artistic heritage. At a time when debates around xenophobia in the UK in particular, and around refugee integration, focus on deficit models of spoken and written English in migrants, or on often violent challenges to anyone heard speaking a language other than English in public space, the need to engage with this social acoustic is pressing.

A way of beginning this process was through discussions multilingually, about indigenous languages and ways in which multilingual societies function. This is a transcript from one such discussion and attempt to hear each other 'pronounce' our worlds, valenced in English but multilingually.

> G: That has to do with how language has been diluted among the younger generations but the other things is that … who said this …? In Cape Coast he was referring to Fanti language, he was saying there is Fanti and deep Fanti. All the languages are like that, we in Ewe have what we call adagana that is vocabulary that is not available for everyone but for older people who have a bigger wider control over the language so you can sit among older people and they will be speaking your language, you can hear the words but the way they are using the words is above your head.
>
> Z: We call that Mdmikira at home, Mdimikira because its about the vocabulary and the way of expressing, that you will sit there and you will not hear anything.

G: And the same thing can have two three different names depending on the context its being used. e.g. A bat is called abuto and that is what everyone knows but amongst poets ... older people they will say Sapwatoi [R&G chorus] [laughter] so unless you know that a bat is also call sapwatokwi they are speaking about a bat you will never know what they are talking about.

R: It's the same in Gha as well we can be sitting here and they will be speaking, I remember your mum did the same thing to me some time ago, and we were sitting there and they were speaking the Ewe language, the one that I understand, the simple one he was talking about, and then from a pause to the next one and asked if I understand, and her mum chuckled and laughed and she laughed and laughed and told the woman and that she can take me to Kaswa and sell me a bag [laughter].

G: Kaswa is a market.

Z: Ahhh.

R: And she will not get a word out of her.

Z: No but this thing about words what you are talking about.

[As I – Alison – transcribe the text at this point I am really noticing something about pace here – Z speaks very quickly, so do I – I cannot keep up when typing, but R & G speak almost at touch-typing pace, with more space between words.]

[...] like we will say, when it is raining we will say Nvura, and everyone understands that but when elders are speaking they will say Nonodzo and Nonodzo to us literally it is just sort of to cool something down, but they are talking about the rain Nonodzo so it's another level that you have been jumped but one interesting thing that I discovered recently from my mum a few months ago, there is one proverb because when you are talking about inaccessibility of for the purposes of that situation they are kids, so there is one saying that I didn't realise had 4 different meanings so even if you think you know [R what] what the proverb [R comes in and joins the sentence and completes it] tells you they are using the third meaning that you only know the first one, you have not even got to the second stage, so now they are on the third meaning, so even if you think you are reading it you are still not reading it.

G: You know one very interesting example is using the expression of somebody eating salt to mean does a person not understand the language.

R: Uh hu.

Z: [laughter]

G: so for example [R – laughter] if R and I are speaking my language and she is not sure whether you understand or not or yeah if she is not sure, she will ask me Adujah – has he eaten salt. And the same thing in my language, if I am speaking with him I will ask in my language, [... okoloay ashe.] does his lagoon go into [G: Reach] to the sea.

Z: Ahhh.

R: But if I ask [okoloay asheom ...] you will not know what we are talking about because you don't know.

Z: It's interesting because we might say are we climbing mountains here, like we are getting away, yeah yeah yeah ... [laughter].

R: Okoloay ashe.

Experiencing the multilingual repertoires of transcribing and listening to this is a little as early anthropologists must have transcribed words when writing them down and transliterating. So, what I am doing here is how the verbal is made literate and transposed in a particular way, but the same researching multilingually method is being used and is being traced again. If I go back to Z/R/G and ask for corrections – which I can and will – this is still working in a specific somewhat positivistic set of parameters, which are trying to get the language 'right', and it will mean they have to fit it into codifications that were laid down originally through transliterations of missionaries and linguistics and anthropologists. Linguistic incompetence is present but even more so the need to account ethically for how, what and whether we strive for an accuracy that is a code and construct.

It is important to note here that whilst Alison was present and an equal partner in this conversation, she was silent. She had nothing to add from her own stock of English, French, German and Portuguese monolingualisms. She did not understand many of the words, or the social references and the context was a defamiliarisation from the office at the University of Glasgow where this discussion took place. The silence is important as it offers a glimpse into the linguistic incompetence of the researcher (Phipps, 2013) and why it is that the surrendering of linguistic power in research interactions, and in social space, comes with a cost – epistemic, spatial, ontological. As she transcribed the conversation the silence broke, and the synchronicity of the transcription with greater time for reflection than is afforded in conversation brought two elements of commentary where by the positivistic and imperial epistemologies of the work of transcript come into view, and begin to be problematised.

'Criacao e recriacao'; an act of creation and recreation

The transcript shows how attempts at multilingual research destabilise many dominant research assumptions.

Firstly, the discussion is largely opaque for the majority of Western academics operating not just in English but even in French, German, Spanish, Italian, Portuguese or any other colonial language. Colonial languages were themselves formed as a result of the colonisation of precisely such peoples and languages as those in discussion in the transcript. These languages thus strengthen conceptual and spatial dominance. David Gramling (Gramling, 2016) documents the many achievements of monolingualism in his book, *The Invention of Monolingualism*, and also Foucauldian disciplinary powers of monolingual assumptions, which fit, naturally, into those of colonial and imperial settlement.

Secondly, the transcript reveals levels of metaphoricity and linguistic maturity that are involved in understandings and in generational use of language, and in the way language is used even internally, within age-related settings, to veil and render opaque, as much as it is to convey meaning and act transparently. The qualities and uses of languages, in this short transcript, already reveal ways of operating socially, through language, in ways that are strange and unfamiliar to monolingual framings of social space.

Thirdly, the interplay between the speakers demonstrates an ease with operating in a world that has a high level of multilingual fluidity. There is no puzzled struggle or shock at the use of a word from another linguistic tradition. The insertion of that word into a sentence 'we say'; 'in my language we say' acts like a modal particle, a piece of punctuation, because it has been normalised to speak multilingually. Indeed, it has been said that for the majority of the world's population, the mothertongue is multilingual.

Fourthly, this conversation, when played out against the backdrop of a project where people seeking sanctuary are at the centre as subjects and agents, takes on a particular comparative dimension. It becomes illuminating. When set against, for instance, the transcripts of asylum interviews, or the ways in which people will speak of their lives, the metaphoricity and the different ways in which understanding and misunderstanding, opacity and transparency will interplay, reveals how language acts as both cloak and a revealer. In social contexts where transparency, coherence, and efficiency are the prized bureaucratic values dominating every form and every form-filling of social life in the West, each designed to render everything transparent and coherent, the metaphoricity of language dissembles and disguises, operating as a counterpoint to the form.

The transcript could allow for further commentary but these four examples suffice for us to make our case for the acts of creation and recreation that have their source in languages, their interpretations, their manifold deployments, and their instantiations in everyday multilingual conversation. Multilinguality provides an endless well for the work of translation and interpretation, for the engagement with difference, agency and diversity when it is engaged within the typical multilingual spaces of sub-Saharan Africa, south-east Asia and with the social groupings of refugees in the spaces of dispersal, and integration assigned to people seeking refuge in the West, and in the corridors and vehicles of stasis and movement that carry them. It is particularly true given the way that nationality and language, whilst they may, under the intervention of monolingualism (Anderson, 1991; Gramling, 2016) have become synonymous and singular, remain in the majority world, diverse and connected to land, ethnic group, and shared through translation and cohabitation.

In our transcript of our conversation we see an example of this 'act', which Freire speaks of 'e um ato de criacao e recriacao' as what we might also term a speech act (Austin, 1975). These are social moments signaling an interplay of performativities whereby the subject is interpolated by the acts of translation and interpretation in the social space, moderating and modifying their own speech, offering examples as gifts for resourcing and replenishing the conversation. Multilingual speech – translanguaging as Creese and Blackledge (Creese and Blackledge, 2010) refer to it, or translingual practice (Canagarajah, 2013) – in the same ways as the arts opens out the familiar and defamiliarises such that diversity is made manifest, and palpable and has to be engaged. These everyday instances of multilingual pedagogies, of what Alison has termed elsewhere as intercultural listening and speaking (Phipps and Gonalez, 2004), are where the language-labour, which enables us to live together in diversities of language and culture, is undertaken.

It is at this point that, in contexts designed for monolingual practices, which render invisible or are simply unprepared to acknowledge the importance of language for the construction of world views and cosmologies, the social space becomes contested. In the present debates about English language and integration, Baroness Casey, in the Casey Review (Casey, 2016), has correctly identified the role language plays in enabling social bonds (Ager and Strang, 2008) to be forged and for people to play a role in society. Here the recommendation is made for England and Wales, that a date be set by which time everyone will speak English. It is as if language is made into a silver bullet for frictionless refugee integration. What is missing from the contentious recommendation is the understanding that it is not fluency in a language that makes the difference, but rather the labour with linguistic difference on a continual basis. There is no doubt that fluency in English is highly desirable for many new arrivals, and for employment and social purposes, as well as being especially prized by security services for whom it renders the subject transparent. However, it is the ongoing, everyday, ordinary acts of linguistic hospitality that create and recreate the sources of intercultural listening and speaking through which dialogue becomes normalised, and is practiced well. What the glossophobia (linguaphobia) of the present day reveals is not any lack on the part of the refugee, in monolingual contexts, but the lack of multilingual social practice that has been afforded to majority monolingual subjects, in the monolingual state. Much of this is structural, relating to educational policy and, increasingly, the stigmatising of the languages as 'foreign', but also regularly as 'difficult' and subjecting them to what Deborah Cameron terms 'hygiene practices' that show much about attitudes to languages, in the ways they are variously marked, discursively, as other, or as wrong or as out of place (Cameron, 2013).

The differences between England and Wales, and Scotland, in policy terms have been noted elsewhere (Phipps, 2018), given that Scotland is officially a multilingual country with language plans in place for both Gaelic and, emerging, for British Sign Language. The New Scots Refugee Integration Strategy 2018–2022 has moved from previous strategies where language barely featured to now having multilingual language sharing, as a mutual, integrating practice, at its heart, alongside the provision of English language classes and support, albeit still at minimal levels.

For the everyday linguistic practice of intercultural listening and speaking to function well in society, it needs sociology to embrace multilingual research. From our practice-led work in the Reserching Multilingually at Borders project, a large grant project funded by the Arts and Humanities Research Council, we would wish to recommend this as a creative and artistic approach, first and foremost, rather than a requirement of grammar, syntax and language learning, at least not in the first place. Our starting point for this recommendation comes first of all, from within psychotherapy and the work of Dewaele and Costa (Costa and Dewaele, 2012).

Se nao ha amor que a infunda; if it is not infused with love

Jean Marc Dewaele and Beverley Costa (Costa and Dewaele, 2012) have written and researched the sociolinguistics and psychodrama of multilingual encounters in the peculiar, Western social space and practice of the therapy session. In addition, they have considered how translation and translators' presence in the triadic relationships of translation in encounters with professionals and statutory services (lawyers; health care; social work) change dynamics of trust. In particular, Costa has shown how professionals, when they do not understand language being spoken or transactional features in conversations where they are not privy to the exact content, can shift from a position of experienced privilege to one where they feel victimised and excluded. For Costa, this understanding dynamics of exclusion around markers of identity – race, gender, class and, importantly, language – accounts for many of the conflicts and dis-ease produced within the power structures of social interactions.

Whilst Dewaele and Costa's work analyses the situation in the triadic counselling and translation situations, this dynamic is also writ large socially, where Anglo-normative assumptions relating to linguistic practice dominate. Where researchers of social phenomena and social practice exclude the multilingual dimension from analysism this exclusionary dynamic can be understood, following Dewaele and Costa, as both consequence and also as cause. No one voluntarily places themselves in a situation where they might feel victimised, and so it is vital that a shift to understanding and applying the insights of research into researching multilingually can also bring with them ways of mitigating the consequences of such dynamics. What the transcript of the discussion earlier demonstrates is how this dynamic is mitigated when multilingual conversations take place, and translingual practice occurs, whereby the exclusionary dynamic is mitigated with intra-conversational translation and pedagogy.

In the Arts and Humanities Research Council project we were able to trial many different approaches, and space prohibits a detailed exposition of the many errors, aborted attempts and even limited successes we had in practising multilingual research across different disciplines and different stages from research design and to research dissemination (http://researching-multilingually-at-borders.com). An important element in our explorations, was, however, the inclusion, and consequent production and normalisation, of multilingual, multiethnic, non-academic working relations across the project and the invitation to the artists working with us, to bring the arts into relationship and dialogue or even confrontation with our normative research practices, especially our chosen language.

An early contribution to this was an ironic, gentle, and, following Freire, 'loving' response to the way the English language had colonised the people of Zimbabwe, through its use in schools, and then, for the poet, in everyday comments and compliments. Sitholé's poem, in the epigraph, begins 'Once in a while, I hear the words, you speak good English.' The poem then deconstructs the many problems with such a 'complicated compliment'. In the spoken word film of this poem, the smile and gentle irony, the shaking head but non-assignment of blame, together with the deliberate naming of the many instances of confusion and outright oppression mean that the political issues are in no way side stepped, but there is, in the poem and performance, a 'third term' inserted into the social interaction around which change and understanding can begin to cluster.

> Was it a 'minute' silence we were meant to be observing, to reflect on our loss [...] but in the end it's just a smile, my little awkward smile, a euphemism for words. (Tawona Sitholé)

The poem draws the heat from the fraught, exclusionary spaces of multilingual practice in Anglo-normative contexts and then concentrates it into the poetic, highly sophisticated English language form, in order to show, rather than to attack, to humour, rather than harangue, to help show, through the use of greetings made in 'amor – love'.

In educational terms this work also reflects bell hook's (hooks, 1994) observations in *Teaching to Transgress* on the vital element of eros in all processes of educational change that wish to effect change non-violently and to enable the constructive engagement of issues that are personally and socially fraught. Whilst there is no need for this to be the case, social space has, in the present times, constructed those seeking sanctuary, those speaking in accents and languages other than a highly codified norm, as threats and subjects for multiple exclusion. hooks would argue, and our researching multilingually work would bear out, that to bear fruit, any radical sociological critique of this situation has to work through the dynamics of eros. 'When eros is present in the classroom', says hooks 'love is bound to flourish' (hooks, 1994: 198). If we are to follow pedagogies of freedom and hope, then this erotic element is crucial. When groups cluster around new, strange, humours, affecting artefacts – like the poem 'Good English' or the words shared as a call and response of every speech in our transcript – then the erotic, in its widest, life-creating sense, is required and can both transform and transgress the norms.

For the poet, here, critique of Anglo-normativity and the exclusionary forces which nest into nuances of dialect and centre-periphery assumptions that intersect with categories of race and class, has to be offered with a love of the world, of life, of people, if dialogue is to be possible, to paraphrase Freire's original: 'Se nao amo o mundo, se nao amo a vida, se nao amo os homens, nao e possivel o dialogo.'

Across the 'researching multilingually' explorations these were crucial elements in the challenges we made and enactments that shifted Anglo-normative practices. Here, the example is of a poem, but in our wider work with artists the 'third term', inserting new dynamics into fraught social relationships of power and often extreme marginalisation, it could have come from across the panoply of artic genres and linguistic forms. Rather as our transcript demonstrates the range of linguistic borrowings and insertions, defamiliarising the grammatical norms, which translanguaging allows, rely on the 'third term', the defamiliarising instance or object being regularly and repeatedly present in social interactions for the work of understanding, of learning and of comparison to be undertaken. And when this work is undertaken, and normalised, it serves to create conditions for the continual enactment of humility, in the ways Freire, suggests: 'Nao ha, por outro lado, dialogo se nao ha humilidade [On the other hand, you cannot have dialogue if you do not have humility]' (Freire, 2006).

Conclusion

> *Was tun dann als Soziologen?*
> *Mir waere es recht wenn Ich ohne Englisch, zum Schlüss kommen dürfte, ohne Redaktion.*

What do public sociologists do? Well, for us the answers are in working through and embedding as an everyday research practice the defamiliarisation of privileged practice, the gentle loving use of humour and third terms that can create dialogue, reveal diversity, and allow others to take their turns, often by placing English in last place in multilingual research encounters and design, and not, at best, in first with translation and, at worst, as the only language in place. Building in regular, reflection on the place and need for love and humility if conditions of dialogue and creativity are to be possible is now, for us, a central working method.

We are a very long way from changing the dominance of English as a language of teaching and research, of decision-making and of publication in the academy. We are starting from an extremely low base, but we take heart from both feminist and post-colonial studies (Fanon, 1965; Kristeva, 1998; Ahmed, 2000; Irigarary, 1994, 2007; Mbembé, 2000) and the progress made by raising these questions of social categories repeatedly and across many dimensions of work. We are fully aware of the irony, even hypocrisy, in writing this article in English. The editor did not stipulate we should, but the call was made in English, and so were the provocations. This is, indeed, the double bind which Spivak speaks of so well (Spivak, 2012) and which Ngougi wa T'hiongo outlined and radically upended with his artistic critique and practice in *Decolonising the Mind* (Ngugi wa, 1986).

We were given a provocation and have responded with a provocation of our own. And in this spirit, we would wish to conclude as follows:

Chitsva chiri mutsoka

Find out what it means. Learn of the heritage of these words. Discover its speakers. Be humble in the face of its wisdom.

Chitsva chiri mutsoka

References

Ager, A. and Strang, A. (2008) 'Understanding integration: a conceptual framework', *Journal of Refugee Studies*, 21(2): 166–191.

Ahmed, S. (2000) *Strange Encounters: Embodied Others in Post-Coloniality*, London: Routledge.

Ahmed, S. (2012) *On Being Included: Racism and Diversity in Institutional Life*, Durham, NC: Duke University Press.

Anderson, B. (1991) *Imagined Communities: Reflections on the Origin and Spread of Nationalism*, London and New York: Verso.

Austin, J.L. (1975) *How to do Things with Words*, Cambridge, MA: Harvard University Press.

Bourdieu, P. (1988) *Homo Academicus*, Cambridge: Polity.

Cameron, D. (2013) 'The one, the many and the other: representing multi-and mono-lingualism in post-9/11 verbal hygiene', *Critical Multilingualism Studies*, 1(2): 59–77.

Canagarajah, S. (2013) *Translingual Practice: Global Englishes and Cosmopolitan Relations*, London: Routledge.

Casey, L. (2016) *The Casey Review: A Review Into Opportunity and Integration*, London: UK Government.

Costa, B. and Dewaele, J-M. (2018) 'The talking cure – building the core skills and the confidence of counsellors and psychotherapists to work effectively with multilingual patients through training and supervision', *Counselling and Psychotherapy Research*, 19: 231–240.

Costa, B. and Dewaele, J.-M. (2012) 'Psychotherapy across languages: beliefs, attitudes and practices of monolingual and multilingual therapists with their multilingual patients', *Language and Psychanalysis*, 1: 19–41.

Creese, A. and Blackledge, A. (2010) *Multilingualism: A Critical Perspective,* London: Continuum.

Fanon, F. (1965) *The Wretched of the Earth*, Grove Press: New York.

Freire, P. (2006) *Pedagogia do Oprimido*, 43. São Paulo: Paz e Terra.

Gramling, D. (2016) *The Invention of Monolingualism*, New York and London: Bloomsbury.

hooks, b. (1994) *Teaching to Transgress: Education as the Practice of Freedom*, London and New York: Routledge.

Irigarary, L. (1994) *Thinking the Difference: For a Peaceful Revolution*, London: Athlone.

Irigarary, L. (2007) *Je, Tu, Nous*, London: Routledge.

Kristeva, J. (1998) *Étrangers à nous-mêmes*, Paris: Librairie Arthème Fayard.

Mbembé, J.-A. (2000) *De la postcolonie: essai sur l'imagination politique dans l'Afrique contemporaine*, Paris: Karthala Editions.

Ngugi wa, T. o. (1986) *Decolonising the Mind: The Politics of Language in African Literature*, Kampala: East African Educational Publishers.

Phipps, A. (2013) 'Intercultural ethics: questions of methods in language and intercultural communication', *Language and Intercultural Communication*, 13(1): 10-26.

Phipps, A. (2018) 'Language plenty, refugees and the post-Brexit world: new practices from Scotland', in Kelly, M. (ed) *Languages after Brexit: How the UK Speaks to the World*, London: Plagrave Macmillan.

Phipps, A. (2019) *Decolonising Multilingualism: Struggles to Decreate*, Bristol: Multilingual Matters.

Phipps, A. and Gonzalez, M. (2004) *Modern Languages: Learning and Teaching in an Intercultural Field*, SAGE Publications: London.

Spivak, G. (2012) *An Aesthetic Education in an Era of Globalization*, Cambridge, MA: Harvard University Press.

Williams, R. (1977) *Marxism and Literature*, Oxford: Oxford University Press.

CASE II.6

The Construction of 'Public Knowledge' within Community Planning Partnerships: Reducing Structurally Embedded Inequalities at Local Level?

Marion Ellison

Introduction

The concept of 'public knowledge', how it is created, its role and influence has become central to understandings of forms of democratic community engagement, which are designed to address economic, social and economic inequalities at local level (Fraser, 1990; Williams, 2008; Bivens et al, 2015; Hall et al, 2015). Whilst there is substantive theoretical and empirical evidence elevating the role of public knowledge in building social capital, and equipping people with citizenship skills that are central to community building, the role and potential of transformative forms of public knowledge co-generated by people experiencing inequalities as 'cognitive praxis' is less understood (Eyerman and Jamison, 1991). As a recent World Science Report argues:

> There are key opportunities for a transformative knowledge agenda that is co-constructed with those who are experiencing inequalities and are in a position to influence change through policies, practices and politics ... In a world in which knowledge shapes power and voice, and vice versa,

> the fundamental inequality in the production of knowledge about inequality itself must be addressed. (International Social Science Council, 2016: 275)

The co-generation of knowledge between 'publics' at community level, academics, and policy makers has been central to recent place-based approaches to joint planning, resourcing and delivery across Scotland's local authority areas. The notion of 'community empowerment' legally constituted with the Community Empowerment (Scotland) Act (Scottish Government 2015) is pivotal to these approaches. Underlining this, the social rationale for place-based approaches is rooted in ideals of 'democratic engagement', 'accountability' and 'greater responsiveness in decision making' (Scottish Government, 2016).

Critically, however, whilst these principles are firmly cemented into the policy architecture of community planning partnerships (CPPs), the operationalisation of these principles raises a number of questions. Exemplifying this, the concept of 'democratic engagement' is located within a wide continuum of interpretations. Here, 'democratic engagement' may be limited to a dialogical process enabling communities to clearly articulate welfare needs and priorities to local and national government. At the other end of the continuum, notions of 'democratic engagement' may enable communities to actively challenge the external causes of inequalities, which have created these welfare needs and priorities in the first place (Revell and Dinnie, 2018). Thus the process of 'democratic engagement' may be limited to the assimilation of community voices within existing institutional frameworks or actively operationalised as a vehicle to encourage communities to challenge wider structural inequalities that lie at the heart of welfare needs and priorities (Brandsen, Verschuere and Steen 2018; McCrea and Finnegan, 2019). For Crowther and Shaw (2018) community engagement is conceptualised as 'a moment of realisation', which enables publics to turn 'private troubles' into 'public issues'. Here, the methods used to implement community engagement are designed to promote 'collective actions to achieve social justice' (Crowther and Shaw, 2018). The role and construction of knowledge within this process is pivotal. In particular, it is argued that collective action requires shared understandings of public issues. A growing body of research evidences that the generation of these shared understandings is facilitated by giving people the tools they need to critically analyse the causes of the problems they face (Christens and Speer, 2006; Brandsen, Verschuere and Steen, 2018; McCrea and Finnegan, 2019).

Whilst recent evidence indicates that the majority of place-based approaches adopt a holistic approach, directed at reducing inequalities and supporting people, families and communities, what constitutes public knowledge, how it is created, its role and, most particularly, its influence in reducing structurally embedded inequalities at local level are little understood.

Drawing upon recent research conducted in Edinburgh, this chapter provides an analysis of the construction, role and influence of 'public knowledge' within the implementation of the 'community planning partnership' policy framework in Scotland. The initial stage of this research has involved a critical review of existing theoretical and empirical knowledge in the field and documentary analysis of legislative publications. In addition, semi-structured interviews with policy makers at national and local authority level and with a range of community planning partnership participants including members of Edinburgh Voluntary Organization Council (EVOC) have been undertaken. The chapter also critically examines the current and potential role of public sociology education in facilitating transformative knowledge agendas that address structurally embedded inequalities at local level in Scotland.

Theoretical considerations

Conceptualising the construction and role of public knowledge

The construction and role of knowledge within a societal context has been elucidated by a range of contributions through the theoretical lens of socioconstructivism (Heath, 2007; Williams, 2008; Abrell et al, 2009; Bivens et al, 2015; Hall et al, 2015). These contributions are unified by the view that the development of knowledge involves an intricate and dynamic relation between individual perception and the lived experience of collective issues. Here personal constructions of knowledge are located and restructured within specific societal contexts. Knowledge is thus simultaneously constructed as a social product and personal reconstruction (Sanchez and Escrigas, 2014). Ecological approaches locate the development of human knowledge within the physical reality of unique places inhabited by people. Importantly, the social world involves collective or public knowledge that groups of people have developed to explain the ecological world or place in which they live. Leff (2015) has argued that cultural rationality emerges from collective knowledge. This form of rationality is central to the legitimation of the relationship between people and their immediate environment. Critically, the social sphere encompasses governmental politics and institutions that create structural conditions, which may limit or enable the development of collective intelligence. Here dialogical forms of governance facilitate collective knowledge (Hall et al, 2015; Hall and Tandon, 2017). Within this theoretical context collective or public knowledge may be regarded as a form of solidarity among social actors or groups. Thus, whilst each person's lived experience may be defined by a unique configuration of biographical, educational and geographical contexts combined with cultural experiences of communities and social relationships, it may be argued that public knowledge has a transformative capacity. In particular, it may be argued that public knowledge may be regarded as a form of 'collective intelligence' capable of solving collective issues. Recent ideational expressions of the value of public knowledge in reshaping 'how people think' have emphasised its transformative capacity:

> The commons offer the same promise of uniting people concerned about the common good in many forms into a new kind of movement that reshapes *how people think* about the nature of ownership and the importance of collaboration in modern society. It's not necessary that everyone adopt the word commons. What matters is that people understand that what we share together (and how we share it) is as important as what we possess individually. ... That's how the commons has worked throughout history, fostering democratic, cultural, technological, medical, economic, and humanitarian advances. (Walliasper 2010: 103)

The role of public knowledge within place-making theory

Place-making is a concept central to community planning in Scotland and across a growing number of national and local settings. It describes a dialogical process enabling collaborative, inclusive approaches to advancing the quality of lived experiences within geographical spaces. Here geographical spaces or communities are regarded as physical and socioemotional spheres of activity (Proshansky, Fabian and Kaminoff, 1983; Gieryn, 2000; Hidalgo and Hernandez, 2001). Critically, the socioemotional spheres of activity, which define place, are constructed through human interaction and experience. As Relph (1976: 47) argues: 'While place meanings are rooted in the physical setting and its activities, they are not a property of them but a property of human interaction and experiences of those places.' Thus, it may be argued that meaningful community planning requires the collaborative and inclusive participation of members of the community as a collective process of place making. The production of public knowledge through dialogue is central to this collective process. Importantly, place is thus socially contested involving learning, movement and fluidity. The realisation of public knowledge thus relies on partnership. As Rule (2015) argues:

> Dialogue is an unfolding process, a search or quest for knowledge and understanding usually through the medium of spoken language, but not excluding written and visual codes, *involving partners who are committed to this quest*. Thus, dialogue assumes relationship and is impossible without it. This is one of the differences between dialogue, on the one hand, and monologue and diatribe, on the other. (Rule, 2015: 2) (my emphasis)

The concept of partnership is thus central to meaningful and productive dialogical processes. As a contested concept partnership has been theorised and evidenced and problematised as a collaborative, fluid and dynamic relationship between stakeholders within and across communities and societies (Christens and Speer, 2006; McCrea and Finnegan, 2019; Vanleene and Verschuere, 2018). A number of theorists have identified the central characteristic of partnership as being a collaborative relationship leading to innovative approaches and outcomes through unpredictable, fluid forms of decision-making (Chandler, 2019; Gilchrist, 2019; Rees, Mullins and Bovaird 2012). A central concern of recent research has been the influence of power dynamics within collaborative partnerships within and across communities and societies (Mackintosh, 1992; Gray and Purdy, 2018). Growing emphasis on the involvement of communities in Scotland in governance mechanisms has undoubtedly created possibilities for publics to express their welfare needs and priorities. However, it may be argued that the central focus on place-based approaches limits the capacity of publics to articulate their lived experiences of issues such as poverty and social exclusion, marginalisation and description. Here, space-based approaches to community engagement offer the possibility of enabling people within social spaces to develop collective and cooperative ways to identify communal values and actively seek socioeconomic rights. Of critical importance is the role of power within this distinction. For example, place limits the notion of community engagement by focusing on geographically predefined communities. Here a focus on developing the integration of geographically defined communities may fail to take account of power relationships between publics and groups with conflicting interests. Moreover, the influence of power and resourcing in the operationalisation of CPPs in Scotland is determined by the degree to which public involvement is initiated as a top-down or bottom-up process. As a number of authors have argued, the technocratic, agenda-setting, managerial procedures that characterise top-down initiatives developed by state agencies predefines procedures for participation, thereby limiting the ability of communities to develop relevant bottom-up approaches that create the 'space' for collective social and political practice (Cooke and Kothari, 2001; Christens and Speer, 2006; Brandusescu and Sieber, 2018).

The construction and role of public knowledge within community planning partnerships in Scotland

Social, economic and policy context

The central role of CPPs as a central pillar of national governance in Scotland was largely developed in response to growing financial, social and demographic challenges. The UK government's imposition of severe austerity measures in 2010 combined with considerably reduced budgets for public services in Scotland elevated the significance of strategic community planning as a way of mitigating the full impact of UK-wide welfare reforms and austerity measures on people who live in the most deprived areas of Scotland. Professor Philip Alston, United Nations, has most recently illustrated the gravity of the lived experience of poverty and the impact of welfare reforms in the UK as a whole:

> The results? 14 million people, a fifth of the population, live in poverty. Four million of these are more than 50% below the poverty line, 1 and 1.5 million are destitute, unable to afford basic essentials. ... The Institute for Fiscal Studies predicts a 7% rise in child poverty between 2015 and 2022, and various sources predict child poverty rates of as high as 40%. For almost one in every two children to be poor in twenty-first century Britain is not just a disgrace, but a social calamity and an economic disaster, all rolled into one. (Alston, 2018: 1)

The statement also underlines the profound impact of welfare reforms and austerity measures since 2010:

> [G]reat misery has also been inflicted unnecessarily, especially on the working poor, on single mothers struggling against mighty odds, on people with disabilities who are already marginalised, and on millions of children who are being locked into a cycle of poverty from which most will have great difficulty escaping. (Alston, 2018: 2)

UK-wide welfare reforms and budgetary constraints have thus placed considerable pressure on the provision of public services in Scotland, exacerbating social and geographic inequalities. Recent figures indicate that 19 per cent of people in Scotland were living in relative poverty after housing costs between 2014 and 2017. More strikingly, the Palma coefficient, which measures income inequality, indicates that the top 10 per cent of the population in Scotland had 24 per cent more income in 2014–2017 than the bottom 40 per cent combined. This compares to 21 per cent more income in 2013–2016 (Scottish Government, 2018a). In Edinburgh, 22 per cent, or approximately 20,000, children live in relative poverty living in households where total household income is below 60 per cent of national median income (Scottish Government, 2018b). The Scottish Index for Multiple Deprivation (SIMD) reveals that six of the most deprived areas of Scotland are located in Edinburgh (Scottish Government, 2018). In addition, the existence of wide inequalities in Edinburgh is evidenced by the variation of poverty rates at ward level between 5 per cent and 29 per cent (EVOC, 2018). The contours of these inequalities have also been shaped by historical transformations in Scotland's industrial and demographic landscape.

The construction of community planning partnerships as a place-based response to inequality

The rationale underpinning CPPs in Scotland is that new pressures on public services have also arisen as a result of 'failure demand', the demand for public services, which could have been avoided by earlier preventative measures, and 'rising demand' of services from an ageing population (Scottish Government, 2018). The development of CPPs is part of a broader government strategy to address these pressures by providing 'place-based' innovative approaches delivering preventative programmes and measures tailored to local priorities and needs.

Here, the Scottish Government argues that:

> Evidence clearly demonstrates that improved outcomes for people and better use of resources can be achieved when local services are planned and delivered through effective place-based partnership and integrated service provision. In many instances, truly preventative approaches are only possible when organisations work together in collaboration and plan budgets jointly. (Scottish Government, 2011: 10)

The central requirement of CPPs is to ensure that public bodies collaborate with local communities to co-construct and deliver better services to make a positive difference to people's lives (Scottish Government, 2015). Partnership working is thus tailored to specific local circumstances providing innovative programmes, which improve local services and ensure that they meet the needs of local people particularly those who are most socioeconomically disadvantaged within the community. The Scottish Government works with each CPP to deliver local outcome improvement plans. A crucial requirement of all CPPs is to deliver the Scottish Government's national priority to reduce inequality. Here the strategic role of CPPs is firmly embedded with the Scottish Government's 'Solidarity Purpose' with the central ambition to ensure that Scotland ranks in the top-performing quartile of OECD countries in terms of having the lowest levels of inequality. The Scottish Government argues that increasing economic growth and reducing inequality are mutually supportive. CPPs play a direct strategic role in helping to achieve solidarity targets by facilitating local partnerships designed to support people into work by providing effective public services to meet their needs:

> Our strategic priorities now are economy, health, children and then the community safety partnership includes alcohol and drugs, housing and repeat re-offending. All these partners sit on the lead officer's groups some are community partnerships and others include public bodies such as the Police and NHS. But things like poverty and inequality that cuts across all the groups. Everything moving forward has poverty and inequality written through it as the main focus of community councils. (Interview 2, Policy Maker B; Edinburgh City Council)

The adoption of innovative place-based programmes at local level is integral to the reform of public services in Scotland. Place-based approaches integrate and operationalise the key principles of public sector reform: participation, partnership, prevention and performance as outlined by the Christie report (Scottish Government, 2011). Here, a key recommendation of the Christie Commission, which was set up by the Scottish Government in 2010 to examine the future delivery of public services in Scotland, was to focus on place in the reform of public services as a reorientation towards locality. This reorientation provides a focus for local people through public knowledge to improve communities whilst also moving away from silo working by individual service providers. Thus, the Christie Report (Scottish Government, 2011) argued that:

> Many effective solutions to the complex challenges we face – from tackling crime to improving public health – lie locally. The best ideas and most effective solutions will often come from those with the most direct experience of the issues at hand – that is, users of services and frontline workers. (Scottish Government, 2011: 10)

Here, as Dorling (2001) argues, the lived experiences of people living in areas of socio-economic disadvantage are 'largely controlled and constrained by life places in which they grow up, the local expectations, resources, schools, job opportunities, child-care expectations, and housing opportunities' (Dorling, 2001: 1338). The Scottish Government's 'Solidarity Purpose' agenda clearly brings a social, economic and moral rationale for a focus on improving the lived experiences of the places in which we live. Critically, people living in absolute or relative poverty are often trapped in areas of socioeconomic deprivation. It may be argued that community-based approaches to inequality acknowledge the impact of situational constraints imposed by the political economy in which people live. In contrast, focusing on the impact of poverty on individuals in society can lead to the pathologisation of individual behaviours and choices when understanding the underlying causes of poverty. Here, 'peoples have freedom within the limits of a situation' (Satre, 1946), and that living within an area of socioeconomic inequalities creates a deprivation of capabilities. Critically as Sartre (1946) argues: 'The exercise of this freedom may be considered as authentic or inauthentic according to the choices made in the situation. Authenticity, it is almost needless to say, consists in having a true and lucid consciousness of the situation' (Sartre, 1946: 27). The co-generation of public knowledge as a useful knowledge has an important role to play in true and lucid consciousness of wider structural factors generating inequalities at local level. Awareness of place as being characterised by a 'deprivation of capabilities' (Sen, 2004) promotes possibilities for the raising of public consciousness and awareness of the collective intelligence and voice of communities. Exemplifying this it may be argued that the profoundly unequal distribution of resources and power across different communities in Scotland limits the capacity and motivation of people to participate in community planning. The Scottish Government has sought to address this issue by advocating a dialogical bottom-up approach to community planning. Crucially, however, it may be argued that in recognising the need to ensure that people have 'authentic' and 'true and lucid consciousness' of their situation elevates the central importance of the role of public knowledge as collective intelligence of wider structural factors generating inequalities at local level.

Nevertheless, a strategic priority for the Scottish Government is to facilitate a shift from top-down service led, reactive delivery towards more tailored, preventative and collaborative ways of working at local level requiring a dialogical, bottom-up approach to reducing inequalities. Here, innovative place-based approaches have been developed at neighbourhood level by most CPPs in response to the requirements of Audit Scotland and the Community Empowerment (Scotland) Act. The Community Empowerment (Scotland) Act bestowed statutory powers on CPPs designed to facilitate their role in reducing inequality and enhancing community participation (Scottish Government, 2015). The Act establishes a legislative requirement that CPPs ensure that communities are central to the community planning process. This involves effective collaboration and joint resourcing amongst partners. From the perspective of a leading policy maker in Edinburgh City Council, the operationalisation of this approach involves the adoption of models of co-production and democracy at local level expressed below:

> It's about finding out what users needed, and this is what we do with communities. We engage with people and look at the best models available and support available. And it is going quite well. So, co-production is our core contract and we then follow up with a dedicated partnership scheme. So, for example the funding is there and people in the community can vote on how that money is spent in the community. So, it's about having a flexible approach and ensuring that each CPP utilises the model which is right for them. (Interview 3, Policy Maker A; Edinburgh City Council)

Importantly, in recognising a central source of structural inequalities this policy maker goes on to explain the importance of ensuring that quality jobs are provided within the labour market in Edinburgh. Here, there is a clear shift away from a focus on responsibilisation, employability and activation towards a focus on addressing the structural conditions of the labour market in Edinburgh: 'So, the emphasis is on how we can shift the priorities to ensure that the labour market has quality jobs. In the past the emphasis was on ensuring that people were actively looking for jobs in the labour market' (Interview 3, Policy Maker A; Edinburgh City Council). The role of community planning in reducing inequalities is a statutory requirement. Here the Community Empowerment (Scotland) Act 2015 details a legislative requirement to achieve 'a real and sustainable reduction in socio-economic inequalities' (Scottish Government, 2015: 16). The Act states:

> In carrying out functions conferred by this Part, a community planning partnership must act with a view to reducing inequalities of outcome which result from socio-economic disadvantage unless the partnership considers that it would be inappropriate to do so. (Scottish Government, 2015: 27)

Here, CPPs can generate public knowledge, which provides an insight into the impact of socioeconomic disadvantage on the lived experiences of people in the community. Further, priority can then be given to innovative programmes and preventative measures, which alleviate the worst dis-welfares of these inequalities. However, it may also be argued that the central generating mechanisms of these inequalities are largely external to the community and that a broader conceptualisation of the role of public knowledge as a form of social learning and empowerment is needed. The Scottish Government has articulated a clear commitment to the concept of empowerment as:

> Supporting our communities to do things for themselves, and to make their voices heard in the planning and delivery of services ... The Community Empowerment (Scotland) Act 2015 aims to raise the level of ambition for community planning, setting out a legislative requirement to improve outcomes and ensure that: communities are central to the process; effective collaboration and joint resourcing takes place among partners; a robust evidence base is used

to ensure efforts are targeted on areas of greatest need; a real and sustainable reduction in inequalities is achieved. (Scottish Government, 2015)

Here the focus is on supporting communities to do things for themselves ensuring that their 'voices are heard in order to bring about a real and sustainable reduction in inequalities'. It may be argued that public knowledge in the form of collective intelligence is critical to this transformative agenda; it is also important to ensure public knowledge at community level is part of a broader dialogic processes across Scottish society and beyond. Critically, however, this transformative agenda intrinsically requires a dialogical process, which is fully inclusive of people within communities. As a leading representative of EVOC argues, representing the voice of small organisations is problematic. Whilst people may feel consulted, the degree to which they feel they have been heard depends upon whether they feel their priorities or concerns have been acted upon particularly in relation to citywide agendas:

> It's very difficult for one organisation to represent the voice of all these smaller organisations so that's why we also have the thematic groups and local groups to ensure that there are other avenues and there is more chance that the voice of local organisations will be heard. And we will then feedback what happened within the Edinburgh Partnership meeting to the third sector organisation and community groups and say you know this is what has come out of the citywide forum and these are the decisions that were taken: is there anything you want us to take back to the Edinburgh Partnership at the next meeting. *So, I think people feel consulted as organisations. Whether they feel it has happened after that or how well they have been heard, that can be an issue.* (Interview 4, EVOC leading representative) (my emphasis)

The need to ensure that the existing model of community partnerships fully engages all groups within communities has also led to an increased focus on *using* public knowledge at local level:

> We also have an example in Wester Hailes. It is a smaller group of people but it is the same model. We are trying to get local organisations to work together. You know taking

> it out of the wider context and *making it about using public knowledge at local level*. (Interview 4, Third Sector)

Critically, this observation illustrates the central limitation of place-based approaches – focusing the voice of pre-established organisations and groups within geographically defined communities may fail to take account of power relationships between publics and groups with conflicting interests. Moreover, the institutional and governance arrangements for representation have in fact led to the reproduction of power imbalances between smaller and larger organisations. In addition, the perception that whilst people may be consulted the degree to which they feel they have been heard depends upon whether they believe that their priorities or concerns have been acted upon, particularly in relation to citywide agendas. This suggests that smaller organisations and groups feel that their influence is limited by agenda setting, managerial procedures that characterise top-down initiatives at citywide level. Here, whilst there are clear institutional avenues through which the voices of thematic and local community groups may be heard, the degree to which conflicting interests are negotiated at local level and national level is highly dependent on the methods adopted by local CPPs and by citywide agendas. Here, it may be argued that an increased focus on bottom up approaches creating the 'space' for collective social and political practice across a range of 'publics' at local level would enable the development of negotiating mechanisms between conflicting interest groups. In addition, space-based approaches would facilitate shared understandings of community through cooperative approaches that encourage the development of communal values, shared understandings and action for socioeconomic rights (Cooke and Kothari 2001; Christens and Speer 2006; Brandusescu and Sieber, 2018).

Conclusion

Public knowledge with community planning partnerships: a transformative knowledge agenda?

Recent research has informed the potential of CPPs to utilise public knowledge at local level to identify and prioritise community needs and concerns.

The potential of transformative forms of public knowledge co-generated by people experiencing inequalities, as 'cognitive praxis' is less understood (Eyerman and Jamison, 1991) and likely to involve local action and articulation to challenge inequality in the creation of subaltern counterpublic spheres. It may be argued that universities have an important role to play in this dialogical process within a much broader transformative agenda. The role of universities as co-generators of public knowledge within communities is directed at facilitating social and structural change underpinned by values of social justice. Critically, however, the meaningful co-generation of public knowledge requires full cognisance of explicit and implicit power differentials between collaborative partners within this dialogical process. This is a contested, dynamic and fluid arena of decision-making in which public knowledge is centrally generated by a synthesis of each person's unique lived experience and collective social and cultural relationships of communities. Here, it may be argued that public knowledge as 'collective intelligence' capable of solving collective issues is given priority within this dialogical process. Recent contributions have argued for higher education institutions to co-generate public knowledge through reciprocal mutual respect as equal partners in the social co-creation of public knowledge (Sanchez and Escrigas 2014; Hall and Tandon 2017).

Public knowledge may be regarded as a special knowledge within broader transformative and democratic approaches to knowledge democracy. Sources of public knowledge include images, texts, stories, music, poetry, drama, and numbers and are inclusive of a range of ways of knowing or epistemologies. The transformative potential of public knowledge with CPPs in Scotland is deepened by raising awareness of its value as a politically strategic way to reduce inequalities that are generated by economic and political structures and process that are external to the community, ensuring 'authentic, true and lucid consciousness' of the situation (Sartre, 1946). As Tremblay, Gutberlet and Bonatti (2015) argue:

> Transformation happens, I believe, when you realise your potential and act on it in *an authentic way*. Methods such as CBR [community-based research], PAR [participatory action research] and other CUE [community– university engagement] approaches often inspire these types of inner discovery, and mutual learning – changing the way we see oneself and each other, and in the end value other knowledge. (Tremblay, Gutberlet and Bonatti, 2015: 81)

Strengthening the connection between people and the places they share, place making refers to a collaborative process by which we can shape our public realm in order to maximise shared value. More than just promoting better urban design, place making facilitates creative patterns of use, paying particular attention to the physical, cultural, and social identities that define a place and support its ongoing evolution. It may be argued that the special role of public knowledge within this process is as transformative knowledge. As Sanchez and Escrigas (2014) argue, transformative knowledge requires dynamic changes in how we understand, create and value knowledge. Centrally this involves a movement from monoculture scientific, descriptive knowledge to integral human, holistic and complex knowledge, which emerges through social co-creation of knowledge (Sanchez and Escrigas, 2014). Further, for CPPs, the construction of public knowledge, meaningful collective participation and collective intelligence to support social change requires a shift from a focus on community in itself towards a community for itself. Here it may be argued that the situational constraints of 'place' reveal entrenched and complex inequalities bringing urgency to work with communities rather than imposing solutions on them. Whilst there is a clear policy commitment to dialogical and bottom-up approaches to the reduction of inequalities at local level in Scotland the extent to which 'public knowledge' co-generated by people experiencing inequalities as 'cognitive praxis' is evidenced by CPPs in Scotland requires further co-generated research. Here, it may be argued that public sociologists and communities have the potential to co-generate authentic knowledge, which enables 'true' and 'lucid consciousness' of the wider structural factors that contribute to the generation of inequalities at local level. Critically, whilst the Scottish Government requires that universities in Scotland engage with communities as a core activity it may be argued that this requirement should place greater emphasis on encouraging universities to identify relevant ways to ensure the co-generation of authentic knowledge with local communities. As has been argued, this can be achieved through the adoption of methods that enable people within communities to develop critically reflexive and analytical skills such as participant action research (PAR) and participatory action learning and action research (PALAR) (Kearney, Wood and Zuber-Skerritt, 2013; Brandsen, Verschuere and Steen, 2018). In this way universities in Scotland can play an active role in developing a transformative knowledge agenda by working with local communities to achieve 'space' through shared understandings of community as a cooperative endeavour towards the realisation of communal values and socioeconomic rights.

References

Abrell, E., Bavikatte, K.S., Cocchiaro, G., Jonas, H. and Rens, A. (2009) *Imagining a Traditional Knowledge Commons: A Community Approach to Sharing Traditional Knowledge for Non-Commercial Research*, Rome: International Development Law Organization.

Alston P. (2018) 'Statement on visit to the United Kingdom by Professor Philip Alston, United Nations Special Rapporteur on extreme poverty and human rights', London, 16 November 2018, www.ohchr.org/Documents/Issues/Poverty/EOM_GB_16Nov2018.pdf

Bivens, F., Haffenden, J. and Hall, B. (2015) 'Knowledge, higher education and institutionalization of community university research partnerships', in Hall, B., Tandon, R. and Tremblay, C. (eds) *Strengthening Community University Research Partnerships: Global Perspectives*, Victoria: University of Victoria, pp 5–30.

Brandsen, T., Verschuere, B. and Steen, T. (eds) (2018) *Co-production and Co-creation: Engaging Citizens in Public Services*, Abingdon: Routledge.

Brandusescu, A. and Sieber, R.E. (2018) 'The spatial knowledge politics of crisis mapping for community development', *GeoJournal*: 1–16.

Chandler, S.M. (2019) *Making Collaboratives Work: How Complex Organizational Partnerships Succeed*, Abingdon: Routledge.

Christens, B. and Speer, P.W. (2006) 'Review essay: tyranny/transformation: power and paradox in participatory development', in Forum Qualitative Sozialforschung/Forum: *Qualitative Social Research*, 7(2).

Cooke, B. and Kothari, U. (eds) (2001) *Participation: The New Tyranny?*, London: Zed Books.

Crowther, J. and Shaw, M. (2018) 'Community engagement: a critical guide for practitioners', *Concept*, 9(1).

Dorling, D. (2001) 'Anecdote is the singular of data. How much does place matter?', *Environment and Planning A*, 2001, 33: 1335–1369.

EVOC (2018) 'A strategy to tackle poverty and inequality in Edinburgh', 29 January 2018, Edinburgh Voluntary Organisations Council (EVOC), www.evoc.org.uk/updates/strategy-tackle-poverty-inequality-edinburgh/

Eyerman, R. and Jamison, A. (1991) *Social Movements A Cognitive Approach*, Cambridge: Polity Press.

Fraser, N. (1990) 'Rethinking the public sphere: a contribution to the critique of actually existing democracy', *Social Text*, 25/26: 56–80.

Gieryn, T.F. (2000) 'A space for place in sociology', Annual Review, *Sociology*, 26: 463–496.

Gilchrist, A. (2019) *The Well-connected Community: A Networking Approach to Community Development*, Bristol: Bristol University Press.

Gray, B. and Purdy, J.M. (2018) *Collaborating for Our Future: Multistakeholder Partnerships for Solving Complex Problems*, Oxford: Oxford University Press.

Hall, B., Tandon, R., Tremblay C. and Singh, W. (2015) *Challenges in the Co-construction of Knowledge: A Global Study for Strengthening Structures for Community University Research Partnerships*, http://unescochair-cbrsr.org/unesco/wp-content/uploads/2014/05/Hall.pdf

Hall, B.L. and Tandon, R. (2017) 'Decolonization of knowledge, epistemicide, participatory research and higher education', *Research for All*, 1(1): 6–19.

Heath, R.D. (2007) 'Rethinking community collaboration through a dialogic lens creativity, democracy, and diversity in community organizing', *Management Communication Quarterly*, 21(2): 145–171.

Hidalgo, M.C. and Hernandez, B. (2001) 'Place attachment: conceptual and empirical questions', *Journal of Environmental Psychology*, 21: 273–281.

International Social Science Council (2016) *World Social Science Report*, ISSC, IDS and UNESCO, www.worldsocialscience.org/activities/world-social-science-report/

Kearney, J., Wood, L. and Zuber-Skerritt, O. (2013) 'Community–university partnerships: using participatory action learning and action research (PALAR)', *Gateways: International Journal of Community Research and Engagement*, 6(1): 113–130.

Leff, E. (2015) *Political Ecology: A Latin American Perspective*, 35, UFPR, file:///C:/Users/New%20User/Downloads/44381-168655-1-PB%20(2).pdf

Mackintosh, M. (1992) 'Partnership – issues of policy and negotiation', *Local Economy*, 7(3): 210–224.

McCrea, N. and Finnegan, F. (eds). (2019) *Funding, Power and Community Development*, Cambridge: Policy Press.

Proshansky, H.M., Fabian, A.K. and Kaminoff, R. (1983) 'Place identity: physical world socialization of the self', *Journal of Environmental Psychology*, 3: 57–83.

Rees, J., Mullins, D. and Bovaird, T. (2012) 'Third Sector Research Centre Research Report (88)', Partnership working, Birmingham: TSRC Publications.

Relph, E. (1976) *Place and Placelessness*, London: Pion Limited.

Revell, P. and Dinnie, E. (2018) 'Community resilience and narratives of community empowerment in Scotland', *Community Development Journal*, 55: 218-236.

Rule, P.N. (2015) *Dialogue and Boundary Learning*, Rotterdam: Sense Publishers.

Sanchez, J.G. and Escrigas, C. (2014) 'The challenges of knowledge in a knowledge democracy', in *Global University Network for Innovation. (2014). Higher Education in the World 5: Knowledge, Engagement & Higher Education: Contributing to Social Change*, Basingstoke: Palgrave Macmillan.

Sartre, J.P. (1946) *Existentialism Is a Humanism, Les Editions Nagel*, Paris: Methuen and Co.

Scottish Government (2011) 'Report on the future delivery of public services by the commission chaired by Dr Campbell Christie', Local Government and Communities Directorate.

Scottish Government (2015) 'Community Empowerment (Scotland) Act 2015', Scottish Government www.legislation.gov.uk/asp/2015/6

Scottish Government (2016) *Scottish Open Government National Action Plan: 2016–2017, Scottish Government*, https://www.opengovernment.org.uk/resource/scottish-open-government-national-action-plan-2016-2017/

Scottish Government (2018a) *Poverty & Income Inequality in Scotland: 2014–17*, Scottish Government Statistics, https://www.gov.scot/publications/poverty-income-inequality-scotland-2014-17/

Scottish Government (2018b) *Scottish Index of Multiple Deprivation 2018*. Scottish Government Statistics, http://simd.scot/2016/#/simd2016/BTTTFTT/9/-4.0000/55.9000/

Sen, A. (2004) 'Capabilities, lists, and public reason: continuing the conversation', *Feminist Economics*, 10(3): 77–80.

Tremblay, C., Gutberlet, J. and Bonatti, M. (2015) 'Celebrating community–university research partnerships: experiences in Brazil', in Hall, B., Tandon, R. and Tremblay, C. (eds) *Strengthening Community University Research Partnerships: Global Perspectives*, Victoria and New Delhi: University of Victoria Press and PRIA: pp 73–94.

Vanleene, D. and Verschuere, B. (2018) *15 Co-Production in Community Development. Co-production and Co-creation: Engaging Citizens in Public Services*, Abingdon: Routledge.

Walliasper, J. (2010) *All That We Share: How to Save the Economy, the Environment, the Internet, Democracy, Our Communities, and Everything Else That Belongs to All of Us*, New York: New Press.

Williams, M. (2008) *The Roots of Participatory Democracy*, London: Palgrave Macmillan.

DIALOGUE II

'Really Useful' Public Sociology Knowledge

Eurig Scandrett, Marion Ellison and C. Laura Lovin

This dialogue includes an engagement between the author and two of the case contributors, both of whom are operating at the boundaries of policy sociology. Whilst this has perhaps underrepresented those working in other spheres of knowledge co-production – research, art, behaviour – it has allowed a focus on the kinds of knowledge that find their ways into the process of policy development and, more generally, what knowledge is valued in the public sphere.

The section starts with Jan Law's case study of a particular practice of sociology, driven by the needs of policy. Policy formation and implementation, with its associated discourses of politics, influence, interests and media narrative, constitutes an important public sphere in which public sociology might occur, as well as a branch of sociology with the particular combination (according to Burawoy's (2005) categorisation) of instrumental knowledge aimed at an extra-academic audience. Jan's experience of the challenge to the academic integrity of the sociologist in this context, especially from sponsor capture, leads her to 'cross the quadrant' towards public sociology. The key issue that this policy-to-public sociology raises is not so much sociological practice as knowledge – who is able to control the knowledge generated by sociological practices. By contrast, Laura Lovin's experience of policy sociology accounts for a context in which that challenge has been met, relatively successfully, by the integration of the knowledge contribution of refugee and asylum-seeking women into a gendered and racialised policy discourse which otherwise seeks to devalue that knowledge. The combination of a conducive policy context (the Scottish Government's 'New Scots' integration strategy) and implementation by NGOs sensitive to dialogical practice within 'invited participation' (Cornwall, 2002) has achieved a degree of affirmation of the knowledge contribution of refugee women. This is an unfinished and ongoing project and, as Laura acknowledges, constitutes 'first steps toward policy change', unlike in Jan's case where she encountered fierce resistance to policy change from clients with vested interests in existing sexual health policy. The contrast between these cases may suggest a dynamism in the relationship between policy and public sociology, contingent on power relations and appetite for policy change amongst key stakeholders, requiring sociologists to cross back and forth across Burawoy's quadrants in response to political opportunities and challenges. The constitutional politics of the policies driving the research may also be significant, in which asylum policy remains reserved at the UK national government level whereas refugee integration allows for some devolved and distinctive policy implementation within Scotland. Sexual health policy on the other hand is fully devolved within the powers of the Scottish government.

Marion Ellison also comments on Laura Lovin's revelation that a conducive policy context is integral to the affirmation of public knowledge. More broadly it may also be argued that public knowledge is intrinsically a 'special knowledge' within broader transformative and democratic approaches to knowledge democracy. Here, a dynamic and encompassing conceptualisation of public knowledge may be regarded as a knowledge 'in itself' and a knowledge 'for itself' enabling a more politically transformative agenda to emerge. Here, the co-generation of public knowledge by publics and public sociologists may be analysed within a broader conceptualisation of public knowledge as a special knowledge that intrinsically raises awareness of the value of public knowledge as a politically strategic way to reduce inequalities and forms of social exclusion and marginalisation generated by wider economic and political structures and processes. Illustrating this, whilst the Scottish Government has created a supportive policy context for the development of public knowledge within community planning partnerships in Scotland, the transformative potential of this knowledge is expanded and deepened by an approach that encourages individual and collective understandings of personal and community issues within wider economic and political inequities. This 'active public knowledge' would, Marion argues, encourage the emergence of more democratic and transformative forms of public knowledge.

The significance of dialogue in generating and valuing knowledge from subaltern publics whose knowledges are routinely excluded from the public sphere is well made by Lovin, and dialogical methodologies (and especially the pedagogical insights of Paulo Freire) continue to be a key methodological theme embraced by the cases addressing forms of public sociology knowledge. Similarly excluded publics include children and young people who present particular methodological challenges to sociologists: how should such knowledges be treated? In these contexts, invited participation is often (although not always) a necessary but insufficient requirement for public sociology practice to take place, which make dialogue a vital methodology. Emma Wood and Maria Giatsi Clausen demonstrate the importance of dialogue with teenagers and younger children respectively, at the same time recognising power differentials. Dominant discourses of participation are filtered through perceptions of agency shaped by narratives of children's vulnerability and competence, and teenage deviance and gullibility – discourses that dialogical methodologies are able to undermine.

The dominant institution of education in society – the school – is significant in the construction of knowledge and its value. Children and young people are almost defined by school: as 'schoolchildren', level or grade at school, 'still at school'; and this is replicated in higher education, which is largely orientated towards 'school leavers'. Moreover, as Maria points out, schooling is dominated by developmental psychology, in which learning is understood as incremental and sequential, dependent on psychological understandings of competence, rather than dialogical. The school curriculum is selected by adults from 'what there is potentially to learn', and largely by a select gatekeeper caste of knowledge-holders. The contribution of children's knowledge to the public sphere is diminished and distorted by narratives of childhood that structure the selection of knowledge required for the curriculum. In this context, as researchers, Emma and Maria have been able to negotiate spaces for dialogue and respect for the agency of children and young people. Ettore Gelpi (1979; see also Griffin, 1983) in his conception of lifelong education has rejected age-related developmental categorisations of education but rather sought to reorientate education towards a social understanding of knowledge content (curriculum) that is generated by the struggle for dignity in social conflict – irrespective of age.

Exploring the contribution to knowledge of such marginal groups as children refocuses public sociology away from the risk of reifying the subaltern counterpublic, and recognising the dynamic nature of agency in both subalternity and its counter-force. Subalternity might be analysed from the outside by sociologists, but recognised differently, in different and changing ways, or not at all, by the subaltern groups and especially the diverse people who constitute these groups. The act of recognising, interpreting and analysing subalternity requires agency on behalf of the subaltern, not a passive reception of the analysis of the outsider, whether sociologist or not. Dialogue occurs between active agents, and this requires a recognition of the agency – and the different ways in which agency is understood – by publics (asylum-seeking women, young children, teenagers) as well as professionals. Under certain sets of conditions, such imminent analysis generated through dialogue can lead to mobilisation to counter the sources of that subalternity. Knowledge generation in the sociological encounter with subaltern counterpublics is dynamic, contingent and ongoing.

Furthermore, the focus on knowledge reinforces the sociological insight that interests are embedded in knowledge. Both material and symbolic interests are reflected in the situated knowledge of all social groups, whether or not they are analytically subaltern, or experiencing subalternity. That includes the interests embedded in sociological knowledge. Whilst this can be seen explicitly in the context of sponsor capture in policy sociology, it is implicit in all forms of sociological knowledge, including professional sociology. The sociological encounter with publics and the dialogical pursuit of really useful knowledge requires a hermeneutic of suspicion on both sides.

One of the ways in which interests are embedded, imperceptibly, in knowledge is through the language in which knowledge is expressed. Alison Phipps, Tawona Sitholé, Naa Densua Tordzro and Gameli Tordzro draw attention to the language of knowledge, the dominance of colonial languages, and particularly English, in academic publication, and, moreover, the dominance of monolingualism. The experience of knowledge, and hierarchies of knowledge, is different in a context in which multiple languages are the norm, compared to the presumption of monopoly language with translation. As Alison and her colleagues describe it, the 'disciplinary powers of monolingual assumptions, which fit, naturally, into those of colonial and imperial settlement'. The power exerted by the dominance of monolingual languages is reflected in the power attached to knowledge meanings. What implications this has for a provincialised (Burawoy, 2005: 20) really useful public sociology knowledge is barely understood. In their insistence on the arts as bearers of knowledge, Alison and her colleagues echo the insights of Raewyn Connell (2007) that the expression of public sociology knowledge in most of the world, outwith the hegemonic metropole, is not through academic publications but through a far wider range of cultural forms.

It is valuable to return to the question posed by Ballantyne et al in section I (chapter I.1) – how sociological is public sociology knowledge? In pursuing really useful knowledge, subaltern counterpublics draw on academic and other forms of knowledge that may or may not include sociology. To insist that subaltern counterpublics engage in dialogue with *sociological* knowledge undermines the claim to really useful knowledge, in which it is the action of the subaltern in countering the sources of their oppression and exploitation, that discern the usefulness of the knowledge. The cases represented here demonstrate that practitioners are not necessarily sociological – contributors' professional disciplines range from Occupational Therapy to Modern Languages – but all utilise concepts that may be understood as the sociological imagination. All, in fact, require an insistence that the social is not ignored or dismissed in exploring the experiences of people.

In dialogue, C. Laura Lovin highlighted the explicit involvements with feminist theories as well as perhaps more implicit resonances in the works of the authors included in the section. In the analytical space opened by questions such as: 'What counts as knowledge?' 'Who count as knowers?' And 'How do we know in public sociology and when public sociology works alongside policy making?' the authors included in this section position knowledge production as a significant building block in structures of value recognition, truth production, and boundary-making across particular contexts.

The absence of particular groups from among the knowledge makers of a particular society is a symptom of their marginalisation, exclusion, oppression or subordination within larger frameworks of power. Black feminists and third world feminists such as, but not exclusively, Patricia Hill Collins, Rey Chow, Chandra Talpade Mohandy, Umma Narayan, Chandra Sandoval, and Barbara Smith, have contended that marginal positions could in fact function as a spaces for the production of better, and certainly useful knowledge as their dwellers grapple on an everyday basis with structures of patriarchal, colonial, heteronormative, capitalist or nationalist domination. Furthermore, methodologies and methods that promise neutrality, objectivity and bias-free knowledge (as in Haraway's 'God trick' (1988)) were exposed as mythologies produced, legitimised and circulated by the privileged or the ruling capitalist classes. Alongside with critical theorists, feminist theorists call for considerations of how complex assemblages of conscious and unconscious orientations, intentional and unintentional vectors of desire, structures of interest, hegemonic discourses, feelings of identity and belonging, manifestations of agency and material conditions shape particular instances of knowing and visions for social transformation.

Laura notes that,

when asked about their expectation or the reasons why her students found themselves in a class of feminist social theory, many of them would contextualise their curiosity about 'how societies work' within their commitments to future careers in service of social justice causes. Concepts and inquiries into articulations of social change, individual and collective agencies and the social structures harbouring inequality, discrimination, marginalization, symbolic hierarchies and economic stratification are central to the feminist social theory classroom. I believe that the section Knowledges would enhance the syllabi of many such class and attest for convergences between feminist theory and public sociology as well as for their relevance and participation interdisciplinary quests. The commitment shared by the authors of this section to documenting, unveiling, critically interrogating, and even actualising modes of knowing and learning that are inclusive, relevant to individual and collective visions for social, institutional and political change, and generative of nonhierarchical and egalitarian learning environments, where the learners' voices and experiences are respected, valued, and mobilised toward collaborative modalities of knowledge production will inspire students to recognise and hopefully engage in the production of useful knowledge.

Laura also draws attention to the analytical currents that juxtapose public sociology with policy sociology and foreground dialogical and participatory knowledge production and dialectical sociocultural analysis. The authors included in the Knowledge section of the volume show that stakeholders' ideological allegiances, political and economic interests shape categories and norms that frame policy problems and policy solutions. Notions of neutrality, objectivity, and an abstract or disembodied citizenry continue to inform policy making. Dialogical knowledge production, participatory research, and emplaced community planning bring to the fore the voices, experiences, and visions for change of people whose lives are shaped by intersecting inequalities – for instance in explaining how many policies add layers of stigmatisation rather than provide relief, and contributing to important public debates over contextualised definitions of people's needs. The inclusion of policy concerns and visions for policy making of non-hegemonic groups is an invaluable issue for the public agenda. What further scholarly convergences and dialogues are necessary so that policy instruments are deployed toward addressing complex forms of inequality?

One final insight that this collection highlights is the political economy of knowledge. Sociological knowledge, and the interests embedded in it, is determined by questions of who funds what research and education and how (sponsorship, contract, peer review), and who decides what is published (publishers, peer review) under whose names. Many of the contributors to this publication have invested considerable effort into negotiating authorship of chapters in which the author(s) of the words constitute only a small proportion of those who have contributed the knowledge content. What counts as knowledge in academic terms is what is published, largely in English. Behind this published (reified) knowledge lies a labour process of knowledge production, which includes tendering for policy research, discerning eligible expenditure for publicly funded research, contestations over academic freedom and research impact, and the activities of academics in legitimising time for unfunded research in the increasingly neoliberal discipline of the university (see section III).

References

Burawoy, M. (2005) 'For public sociology', *American Sociological Review*, 70: 4–28.

Connell, R. (2007) *Southern Theory*, Cambridge: Polity Press.

Cornwall, A. (2002) *Beneficiary, Consumer, Citizen: Perspectives on Participation for Poverty Reduction*, Sida Studies no. 2, Gothenburg: Elanders Novum AB.

Gelpi, E. (1979) *The Future of Lifelong Education*, Manchester: University of Manchester Press.

Griffin, C. (1983) *Curriculum Theory in Adult and Lifelong Education*, London: Routledge.

Haraway D. (1988) 'Situated knowledges: the science question in feminism and the privilege of partial perspective', *Feminist Studies*, 14(3): 575–599.

SECTION III

Practices

PROVOCATION III

Public Sociology Practices, Privatising Universities

Eurig Scandrett

This section is concerned with the *how* of public sociology education, what public sociologists do and how this is shaped by – and in some ways works to transform – the contexts in which we do it. It is therefore also about the *where* of public sociology. In relation to which locations and institutions does the practice of public sociology education take place? Here we analyse the contexts of public sociology and how these mediate the practices and possibilities of public sociology education. The case studies in this section continue to explore what public sociologists *actually do*, and illuminate the ambivalent institutional locations of public sociology. This prompts dialogue on, and analysis of, how such located-ness and institutional status is marked by the power relations previously considered in the constitution of publics and the production and validation of knowledge in public sociology.

Turning to practice here, and asking where public sociology takes place, means raising and responding to the following questions:

- How is public sociology practised in different places, spaces, contexts, and organisations? Where do public sociologists locate their practices of educational dialogue in relation to communities, social and political movements, and educational institutions?
- How is the practice of public sociology education – (what public sociologists actually do, including particular research methods, pedagogies, collaborations, political and epistemological commitments) – legitimised, recognised, and valued in different locations and institutions?
- What do the practices and contexts of public sociology education tell us about the constitution of publics and the validation of knowledge in public sociology? What do they tell us about the relationships between 'publics' and 'sociologists' and between public knowledges and sociological theories?

Not all public sociology takes place within universities, and many cases in this volume acknowledge and aim to understand the different locations that shape and are shaped by public sociology practice – expanding and questioning assumptions about where public sociology takes place. However, much public sociology does have a connection to higher education institutions (HEIs), and the case studies in this section reflect upon public sociology education practices connected to HEIs, in Scotland and England in particular.

The marketisation of UK higher education (HE) is well established (for example Canaan and Shumar, 2008), and this raises some significant issues and challenges for the practice of public sociology education in increasingly neoliberal universities whose status as public institutions – despite resistance (eg Holmwood, 2011) – is being eroded. Public sociologists can find themselves and their work uncomfortably implicated in the proliferation of pay-walled publications, pay-to-publish 'open access' journals, unaffordable conference fees, league tables, quasi-competitive metrics (in the UK, the Research and Teaching Excellence Frameworks [REF and TEF] and National Student Survey [NSS]), 'impact' agendas, and income generation and commercialisation via 'knowledge exchange', just as inflated senior management remuneration packages come under criticism and working conditions are eroded. In the neoliberal, performative, and entrepreneurial university (Gill, 2010; Pereira, 2018), where students and publics alike are positioned as knowledge *consumers*, public sociology education is vulnerable to co-option as an impactful sub-discipline with appeal to fee-paying students and the potential for income-generating, commercialised knowledge exchange. In such a formulation public sociology can be incorporated into the academy, whereby publics become co-opted as commodifiable and measurable evidence of 'research impact' for the entrepreneurial university (Sprague and Laube, 2009).

For practitioners, doing public sociology in the context of HE can bring access to important resources like jobs, a career path, funding, institutional and epistemological legitimacy, and enthusiastic partners in the shape of students and colleagues. However, such access is partial and contingent on an uneasy congruence with the demands of neoliberal HEIs. Sprague and Laube identify two 'institutional barriers to doing public sociology: the culture of professional sociology and the standards we use for evaluating scholarship' (Sprague and Laube, 2009: 249). The cases in this section build upon and stretch their question: 'What are the institutional arrangements that make doing public sociology difficult, and thus less likely?' (Sprague and Laube, 2009: 249) to discuss also the various ambivalent relations that public sociology has with HEIs, particularly in the context of Scottish and English universities, and to understand the tensions, complicities, and opportunities of such a relation. Practitioners of public sociology education might seek to gain access to HEIs, and/or to negate and subvert the surveillance and audit cultures of contemporary UK HE, and/or to intervene in and rework the hierarchies, power relations, culture, structure, and functions of HE.

To understand the relationships between public sociology and its institutional contexts, we need to attend to how English and Scottish HEIs are foundationally implicated in multiple axes of inequality and oppression, often precisely the forms of inequality and oppression that public sociology seeks to challenge. Universities reproduce structures of exclusion by race, gender and class, Universities act as agents of border control (in the UK, the monitoring of Tier 4 visa students, and requirements to report under the Prevent 'anti-radicalisation' programme), and environmental destruction (eg fossil fuels, investments).

The editor and most contributors to this volume are located in Scottish universities in which these issues are manifest through the particularities of Scotland's history and 'civic' nationalist present. Cooke (2006) has pointed out that, at the time of the Act of Union with England (1707), Scotland's five universities (three fifteenth century and two sixteenth century) educated a higher proportion of its population than England's two older institutions (Wales had no university until the nineteenth century). The establishment of the Andersonian Institution in Glasgow in 1795 for working class adults prefigured the British Mechanics Institutes and, in 1868, the Argyll Commission reported that 'in Scotland, six times as many students per head of population received a university education as in England and that something like one-fifth of all Scottish university students had working class origins' (Cooke, 2006: 119). As late as 1919, the post-war Ministry of Reconstruction report on adult education noted that, by contrast with England, the working class in Scotland 'have little difficulty in finding the way to the universities' (quoted in Cooke, 2006: 140–141). Cooke notes that the report concludes that this explains the dearth of adult education classes in Scotland, yet neglected to take into account some 2,500 students enrolled in John McLean's independent Marxist working class educational bodies.

The twentieth century saw many trends towards harmonisation of Scottish and English HE, including an increase in specialisation and the decline of Scotland's distinctive philosophy-based 'Democratic Intellect' (Davie, 1961, 1986). The Robbins report led to the expansion of participation in HE in the 1960s across the UK, and the 1992 Act turned the English polytechnics, Scottish central institutions and colleges of higher education into a single tier of universities. Nonetheless, elements of distinctiveness remained, such as the undergraduate university degree being three years in England and four years in Scotland, reflecting the different emphases on specialism and generalism, south and north of the border. The devolution of HE policy to the Scottish Parliament in 1999 somewhat reversed the trend towards convergence, with debate being somewhat dominated by the introduction of student fees in England (but not, for local and EU students in Scotland), and respective governance reforms motivated by democratic accountability in Scotland (2016 Act) and marketisation in England (2017 Act).

Scotland's (somewhat overstated) self-image as avowedly more 'tolerant' and 'welcoming' than England (cf. Davidson et al, 2018) is accompanied by a very small minority ethnic population (4 per cent in 2011, according to census data). This is complicated by Scotland's historically disproportionately prominent role in the expansion of the British Empire – a key motivation for the union with England – in tension with a relationship to Europe which has declined, since the union, to a peripheral status, and a national imagination that foregrounds both emigration (particularly to British settler-colonies) and a fraught union with England. Scotland's Enlightenment, the 'Democratic Intellect' and the generalist tradition of the 'lad o pairts' inflects the current HE imaginary landscape (Brotherstone and Mathison, 2018). The central belt contains ancient, elite universities (the University of Edinburgh, University of Glasgow (which together, in 2014–2015 accounted for 41 per cent of the entire sector's income (Audit Scotland, 2016)) as well as modern, 'recruiting' universities. Here too universities draw on histories of working class education (the University of Strathclyde's origins in the Andersonian Institute) and women's education (Queen Margaret University's roots in the Edinburgh Association for the University Education of Women). Scotland's universities, therefore, offer a distinctive and contested location approximating to a European social democratic 'public good' model of HE but heavily dominated by an English sector aligned with a neoliberal 'private investment' model.

Since Burawoy's high profile case for public sociology (2005), and the debates that followed (Calhoun, 2005; Etzioni, 2005; Inglis, 2005; Kalleberg, 2005; Scott, 2005; Lal, 2008) there are signs that public sociology is moving closer to the centre of the discipline in the UK and other dominant Anglophone contexts. For instance, the British Sociological Association's 2016 and 2017 event programme featuring public sociology symposia, the development of undergraduate and postgraduate programmes with a public sociology focus (at Birmingham City, Nottingham Trent and Queen Margaret Universities), and indeed this Public Sociology series at Policy Press. However, as Connell and others have argued, public sociology has always been central to the discipline in much of the Global South, linked to anti-colonial struggles and an intellectual project of decolonisation (Connell, 2007, 2011).

In the UK, we can look to movements like popular education, workers education, adult education and community education to contextualise the history of public sociology (for example Thompson, 2000; Crowther et al, 2003; Cooke, 2006). Likewise, we can trouble the Eurocentric 'founding fathers' narratives of sociological theory, of the discipline's origins in Comte and following a lineage through Durkheim, Weber and Marx, ignoring, for instance, Ibn Khaldun's work in the fourteenth century on a science of society. As Southern theory (Connell, 2007) and post-colonial critique (Bhambra and De Sousa Santos, 2007) make clear, these disciplinary self-understandings silence and 'other' marginalised voices and epistemological antecedents. The twentieth century saw many diverse initiatives for universities to engage 'publics' and organic intellectuals to make demands on universities, ranging from the departments of adult and continuing education, through the settlement movement, Workers' Educational Association, science shops, folk colleges, independent adult education colleges and community-based research. In 2012, internationally, UNESCO appointed two co-chairs in community-based research and social responsibility in higher education. Attempts by academics in a range of disciplines to make the resources of the university accessible and relevant to communities engaged in mobilisation and struggle has always been a priority for some, who have found new and innovative ways to practise this commitment, with varying degrees of success. From the end of the twentieth century, these initiatives have increasingly faced the pressures of neoliberalism, with marketisation, metrics of performance, commercialisation and managerialism becoming everyday experience of university workers.

Here we can ask further questions:

- How do public sociologists work in relation to increasingly privatised HEIs?
- What do public sociologists do within, outside, at the edges of, despite, because of, and against HEIs?

- How is public sociology implicated in, complicit with, constituted and limited by, and transformative of neoliberal, performative, and entrepreneurial HEIs?

These questions draw our attention to the ambivalent location of public sociology practice in relation to HE, as well as to mainstream, professional, academic and policy sociology. As with other disciplines and sub-disciplines concerned with emancipatory education and social justice, public sociologists can find themselves in contexts where trying to *play the game* and *change the rules* of academic work, sociological research and teaching, and 'knowledge exchange' takes place at the same time (Burawoy, 1979; Res-sisters, 2017).

The example of the partial institutionalisation of women's, feminist, and gender studies (WFGS) in the UK and Europe (Pereira 2018) is instructive here. An uneasy congruence with the performative demands of the neoliberal university is visible in a 'paradoxical' expansion of Women's Studies through the 'rapid growth' in student numbers (Skeggs, 1995: 465). The recognition of feminist scholarship's financial value can be essential to its institutionalisation (Pereira, 2015: 287), which is often contingent on the publishing and income-generating performance of *individual* feminists (Pereira, 2018). Likewise, we can look to feminist knowledge production, and draw parallels between the uneasy tensions and complicities that arise when this takes place in relation to academic contexts.

Like public sociology education practice, academic feminist knowledge production encounters the epistemological problem of how to make convincing, valid, useful knowledge claims whilst shifting the definition of 'valid knowledge'. Feminist knowledge production, for instance in social science, is usually critical of dominant epistemological paradigms, at the same time as orientating towards them in some way. This aspect of feminist intellectual labour can be found in methodological text books (see for instance, Ramazanoglu and Holland, 2002: 15–16) and the emergence of feminist epistemologies as critical of androcentric 'malestream' biases in the guise of 'objective' social science, indeed of 'objectivity as an excuse for a power relationship' (Stanley and Wise, 1993:163), whilst also needing to make a convincing and authoritative case for generating some kind of truth about the gendered realities of the social world.

This connects to the arguments and cases in sections I and II of this book, which together advance the case for how public sociology education is concerned with knowledge that is validated not by academic institutions and conventions, but by the subaltern counterpublics with whom such knowledge is produced in dialogical process. This tension can be traced through the emergence of feminist epistemology and the stance that women's embodied experiences of the everyday could form the primary basis for sociological knowledge and the development of feminist standpoint theory (for example Harding, 2004), and Black feminist thought (Crenshaw, 1989; Hill Collins, 1990). Black feminist thought in particular 'addresses on-going epistemological debates concerning the power dynamics that underlie what counts as knowledge' (Hill Collins, 2009: 292), and makes it clear that 'feminist knowledge' and 'women's experience' have never been innocent, homogenous, or unmarked by unjust (raced, classed) power relations.

Attending to the practice of public sociology education and the contexts in which such practice takes place, means therefore asking how power and knowledge co-constitute each other in the details of what public sociologists actually do. Raising and responding to such questions can be informed by a range of traditions, from the sociology of knowledge, through science and technology studies, to post-structural theory. In light of the ambivalent relationship to HEIs discussed above, here it is particularly useful to think through well-established working class and Black feminist understandings of the uncomfortable complicities, and possibilities for change, of 'being an outsider within' the academy.

Contemporarily, we can see how the language of social justice and equality can be co-opted by educational institutions keen to promote themselves as 'diverse' and 'inclusive' (Ahmed, 2017) without meaningfully working to – and often actively refusing to – address the class–race–gender exclusions and stratifications reproduced in HE and the role HE plays in reproducing structures of exploitation and oppression. Relatedly, we can see how, while the twentieth century has seen large increases in student numbers across the UK, current policy emphasises 'widening access', and Scotland, in 2016, appointed a Commissioner for Fair Access. This is accompanied, however, by worrying trends in decreasing numbers of part-time and mature students, and the loss of initiatives that facilitate access for community groups, trade unions, students from working class and low income backgrounds outwith the walls of the university.

'Diversity' is measured, in initiatives such as Athena SWAN, and becomes a metric of institutional differentiation. Here, student and staff identities and personal stories become evidence, promotional material, for the commodified 'happy diversity' of the institution. While the 'language of diversity' becomes a 'holy mantra', diversity practitioners can experience HEIs as resistant to their work, and there is a significant gap between symbolic institutional commitments to 'diversity' and those students and staff who embody 'difference' (Ahmed, 2012). Ahmed (2012) argues therefore that institutional commitments to 'diversity' can be understood as 'non-performatives', in the sense that such commitments do not bring about the 'diversity' they name; the institutionalisation of 'diversity' can paradoxically work to obscure institutional class elitism, whiteness, racism and sexism (Ahmed, 2012).

Inquiry as to the context and location of public sociology education practice is necessarily also a question about which bodies get to enter into which institutions and how, as well as which public spaces are academics located in their practice of public sociology. Who, therefore, has access to public sociology education? What are the conditions of entrance? And how does 'widening access' and 'equality and diversity' in universities relate to structural change?

Despite (because of?) this, universities and educational institutions remain sites of possibility for emancipatory forms of education, and collective action in the face of individual competition. Public sociologists who work in universities in the UK are likely implicated in, and invested in, the managerialist audit and surveillance regimes that govern our working lives, encourage us to compete with our colleagues for artificially limited resources, and position us as service providers for students-as-consumers. While it is tempting to locate the public sociologist as separate from and resistant to the neoliberal university, in practice it seems clear that we are thoroughly entangled in the performative, entrepreneurial governance of academic labour. It is from this scene of implication – and resistance to it – that practices of public sociology education might emerge as an opportunity for a revival of the spirit of initiatives of the past – the workers' colleges, university settlements, science shops, adult and community education departments that have been closed, curtailed or co-opted – as a prefigurative politics, which might imagine alternative possibilities to neoliberal business as usual. To explore this potential, we need to attend to our own ambivalent investments in and constrained agency within, the structures of the contemporary academy.

Considering the practice of public sociology in education means attending to the situatedness of public sociology knowledge production as well as contested and political distinctions between public/private and political/personal spheres. In these ways, exploring the located practice of public sociology education in this section enables a synthesis of previous sections on who (which publics) gets to know what (knowledges) and how (practices).

The cases discussed here explore the opportunities and risks involved in public sociology within, at the margins of and outwith HE. Case III.1 provides some analytical context to the nature of the neoliberal university. Mignot and Gee's research into students in the highly marketised English university sector explores the production of vulnerability as students become competitive consumers of services in an 'employability' market, and of precarity as students are workers in the neoliberal economy. The relationship between the political economy of the university and of wider society provides the context in which other cases in this section explore possibilities for praxis.

Johnson (Case III.2) explores the implications of public sociology education at the heart of the work of university academics, that of the students who, it is claimed, are the 'first public' (Back, 2016). Drawing on his own recent experience of being a working class mature student from rural Shetland, he explores the implications of the widening access agenda in Scotland, where a no fees policy and targets for particular 'non-traditional' categories of student, provides opportunities and challenges for public sociologists engaging with subaltern counterpublics that such categories reflect.

The following three chapters explore different relationships between the university and the wider social context of community. Whilst Docherty-Hughes et al (Case III.3) engage with a community in order to conduct sociological education, Crowther and Shaw (Case III.4) draw on their work with students of community education to employ the sociological imagination in order to critique community engagement, and Hutchings and Lyons Lewis (Case III. 5) provide a self-critical analysis of seeking to employ service-based learning.

These authors argue that, despite the neoliberal trend in university education, there remain spaces for public sociology education within and at the margins of the university. Such spaces can be created, not only through the pedagogical practices in university teaching, community-based education and research, but also through academics' engagement in industrial struggles as workers. In Case III.6, returning to a political economy analysis, Wånggren finds that the neoliberal trend generates opportunities for public sociology education in and against the university through the resistant praxis of campus trade unions.

References

Ahmed, S. (2012) *On Being Included: Racism and Diversity in Institutional Life*, London and Durham, NC: Duke University Press.

Ahmed, S. (2017) *Living a Feminist Life*, London and Durham, NC: Duke University Press.

Audit Scotland (2016) *Audit of Higher Education in Scottish Universities*, Edinburgh: Audit Scotland.

Back, L., (2016) *Academic Diary: Or Why Higher Education Still Matters*, London: Goldsmiths Press.

Bhambra, G.K. and de Sousa Santos, B. (2007) 'Global futures and epistemologies of the south: new challenges for sociology', *Sociology Special Issue*, 51(1).

Brotherstone, T. and Mathison, M. (2018) 'Higher education in turbulent times', in Bryce, T.G.K., Humes, W.M., Gillies, D., Kennedy, A. (eds) *Scottish Education* (5th edn), Edinburgh: Edinburgh University Press: pp 661–671.

Burawoy, M. (1979) *Manufacturing Consent: Changes in the Labor Process under Monopoly Capitalism*, Chicago, IL: University of Chicago Press.

Burawoy, M. (2005) 'For public sociology', *American Sociological Review*, 70: 4–28.

Calhoun, C. (2005) 'The promise of public sociology', *British Journal of Sociology*, 56(3): 355–363.

Canaan, J.E. and Shumar, W. (2008) *Structure and Agency in the Neoliberal University*, Abingdon: Routledge.

Connell, R. (2007) *Southern Theory*, Cambridge: Polity Press.

Connell, R. (2011) *Confronting Equality: Gender, Knowledge and Global Change*, Cambridge, Polity Press.

Cooke, A. (2006) *From Popular Enlightenment to Lifelong Learning: A History of Adult Education in Scotland 1707–2005*, Leicester: NIACE.

Crenshaw, K. (1989) 'Demarginalizing the intersection of race and sex: a Black feminist critique of antidiscrimination doctrine, feminist theory and antiracist politics', *University of Chicago Legal Forum*: Article 8.

Crowther, J., Galloway, V. and Martin, I. (2003) *Popular Education: Engaging the Academy. International Perspectives*, Leicester: NIACE.

Davidson, N., Liinpaa, M., McBride, M. and Virdee, S. (2018) *No Problem Here: Racism in Scotland*, Edinburgh: Luath Press.

Davie, G.E. (1961) *The Democratic Intellect: Scotland and her Universities in the Nineteenth Century*, Edinburgh: Edinburgh University Press.

Davie, G.E. (1986) *The Crisis of the Democratic Intellect*, Edinburgh: Polygon.

Etzioni, A. (2005) 'Bookmarks for public sociologists', *British Journal of Sociology*, 56(3): 373–378.

Gill, R. (2010) 'Breaking the silence: the hidden injuries of the neoliberal university', in Ryan-Flood, R. and Gill, R. (eds) *Secrecy and Silence in the Research Process: Feminist Reflections*, Abingdon: Routledge: pp 228–244.

Harding, S.G. (2004) (ed) *The Feminist Standpoint Theory Reader: Intellectual and Political Controversies*, Abingdon: Routledge.

Hill Collins, P. (1990) *Black Feminist Thought*, Boston, MA: Unwin Hyman.

Hill Collins, P. (2009) *Another Kind of Public Education: Race, Schools, the Media and Democratic Possibilities*, Boston: Beacon Press.

Holmwood, J. (2011) 'Viewpoint – the impact of 'impact' on uk social science', *Methodological Innovations Online*, 6(1): 13–17.

Inglis, C. (2005) 'Comments on Michael Burawoy's ASA Presidential Address', *British Journal of Sociology*, 56(3): 383–386.

Kalleberg, R. (2005) 'What is "public sociology"? Why and how should it be made stronger?', *British Journal of Sociology*, 56(3): 387–393.

Lal, J. (2008) On the domestication of American public sociology: a postcolonial feminist perspective, *Critical Sociology* 34(2): 169–191.

Pereira, M. do M. (2015) 'Higher education cutbacks and the reshaping of epistemic hierarchies: an ethnographic study of the case of feminist scholarship', *Sociology*, 49(2): 287–304.

Pereira, M. do M. (2018) 'The institutionalisation of gender studies and the new academic governance: longstanding patterns and emerging paradoxes', in Kahlert, H. (ed) *Gender Studies and the New Academic Governance: Global Challenges, Glocal Dynamics and Local Impacts*, New York: Springer, pp 179–199.

Ramazanoglu, C. and Holland, J. (2002) *Feminist Methodology: Challenges and Choices*, London: Sage.

Res-Sisters, The (2017) '"I'm an early career feminist academic: get me out of here?" Encountering and resisting the neoliberal academy', in Thwaites, R. and Godoy-Pressland, A. (eds) *Being an Early Career Feminist Academic: Global Perspectives, Experiences and Challenges*, London: Palgrave Macmillan: 267–284.

Scott, J. (2005) 'Who will speak, and who will listen? Comments on Burawoy and public sociology', *British Journal of Sociology*, 56(3): 405–409.

Skeggs, B. (1995) *Feminist Cultural Theory: Process and Production*, Manchester: Manchester University Press.

Sprague, J. and Laube, H. (2009) 'Institutional barriers to doing public sociology: experiences of feminists in the academy', *The American Sociologist*, 40(4): 249–271.

Stanley, L. and Wise, S. (1993) *Breaking out Again Feminist Ontology and Epistemology*, Abingdon: Routledge.

Thompson, J. (2000) *Stretching the Academy: The Politics and Practice of Widening Participation in Higher Education*, Leicester: NIACE.

CASE III.1

Precarity as an Existential Phenomenon within a Post-industrial Labour Market

Philip Mignot and Ricky Gee

Introduction

This chapter argues from a neo-Marxist perspective that precarity is an existential phenomenon, whereby economic actors experience a state of productive anxiety within a post-industrial labour market. In this sense, all who labour are positioned on a spectrum of vulnerability to precarity; a positionality that is both individuated and collective, constantly producing capital gain. Furthermore, that precarity as a state of existence provides capital with a mechanism to appropriate the commons of the life-world; that personhood is progressively given up to capital through the extensification and intensification of economic labour. In order to develop these critical points, the chapter will utilise particular examples of the precarious interrelationship between individuals and collectives within the labour market in the UK, focusing initially on the nascent labour of students in the marketised university. The examples will be drawn from case studies produced via a longitudinal research project undertaken by one of the authors (Gee, 2017). The chapter will conclude by considering how, through solidarity, individuals and collectives might become less vulnerable to the processes of producing precarity outlined above. As will be discussed, solidarity is understood to be the collective experience of precarity made manifest in the minds of economic actors; a precursor of the formulation and enactment of a practical politics for change (Spivak, 1990).

The research project

The focus of the research project was on undergraduate transitions toward the labour market and beyond, three years on from graduation (Gee, 2017). During the course of the project participants provided accounts of how their 'career' had unfolded as an undergraduate and subsequently as a graduate; critically, the accounts included concerns about enacting career in a precarious post-financial crash labour market. The participants had studied a course in the social sciences at a post-1992 university in the East Midlands region of England; many of the participants were the first generation of their family to experience higher education (HE). Participant accounts were gathered and analysed in three stages. As a first stage, the participants as undergraduates engaged in a writing task (as part of a summative reflexive worksheet assignment for a second-year module); these written accounts were supplemented by oral accounts gathered via semi-structured interviews. In stages two and three, semi-structured interviews were conducted with participants two years after graduation, and then subsequently a further year on from graduation. Extracts from the participant accounts taken from the various stages of the project will be used to illustrate key points in the analysis that follows.

Productive anxiety, learning to labour, and labouring to learn

Against a backdrop of concern about the mental health of university students (The Guardian, 2017), a form of endemic anxiety within the student body emerges. As Macaskill (2013) has observed, the incidence of mental health issues amongst students in English universities is approaching parity with that of the general population; the massification and marketisation of HE being key contextual issues, both leading to the student body having increasing resemblance to the body of society as a whole. As we shall see, although this pattern of resemblance is not restricted to mental health, nevertheless it does serve to locate the subjective experience of the student at the heart of this analysis. Here, the potentially anxious mind of the student within the institutional body of the marketised neoliberal university is the initial focus of attention. This will afford opportunities to extend the analysis given that universities encapsulate the key features of a society driven by neoliberalism (Brown, 2011).

As a number of commentators have observed (Naidoo and Jamieson, 2005; Molesworth et al, 2009; Furedi, 2011; Maringe, 2011; Brown and Carasso, 2013), the policy-driven commitment of universities towards enhancing the student experience inevitably has a raft of consequences, if not anticipated then not always desirable. For example, Williams (2011) has observed that a process of 'infantalisation' can be found in contemporary HE, whereby childhood is maintained amongst young people within an extended period of transition to adulthood (Berrington et al, 2014), the continued proximity of 'parenting' being a feature here. It is noted at this point that the present focus is on young people as students, acknowledging the prominent decline of mature and part-time students since the tripling of tuition fees in England and Wales since 2012 (HESA, 2018). According to Williams, the infantalisation of students has been prompted by the progressive marketisation of the sector and the associated imperative that universities must be committed to a provider–consumer relationship with their students (and indeed their parents as co-consumers). This relationship in English and Welsh HE institutions has been secured and intensified legally and institutionally through consumer protection law (Competition and Markets Authority, 2015) and the development and implementation of the Teaching Excellence and Student Outcomes Framework (Department for Education, 2017). Universities therefore have both a legal and commercial duty of customer care which requires an intense, indeed often intimate, focus on the student experience, culminating in close scrutiny of National Student Survey (NSS) results. This can be found in the proliferation and promotion of student services operating as a form of parenting by proxy, giving a level of 'care' and attention that has the potential to provoke a weakening of resilience and a sense of *vulnerability* within the mind of the student (Williams, 2011; Mignot, 2017). Thus, the infantalised student may come to accept, indeed expect, to feel vulnerable and fragile; a sense of vulnerability that becomes normalised amongst a student body that has consumer rights of access (rather than being afforded rites of passage) to tangible products of support. This is augmented by a governmental and therefore institutional concern with student outcome metrics designed to measure postgraduate employment characteristics and earnings. At the time of writing the metrics are based on the Longitudinal Educational Outcomes dataset (LEO), which seeks to connect and correlate HE and tax data in order to focus upon the economic transition of graduates from HE into the labour market. The dataset includes the personal characteristics of graduates and their educational experiences (including further education (FE) and HE providers attended, qualifications achieved), employment history and income (Department for Education, 2017: 34).

The level of scrutiny applied to graduate transition into the workplace, evidenced by the LEO, serves to introduce the strategic significance of 'employability', a contested concept but nonetheless a phenomenon that embodies a sense of institutional vulnerability associated with student outcomes, particularly outcomes that may harm the reputation of the institution concerned. Vulnerability is once again a key concept here, connecting the individual with institutional mechanisms of measurement and control. The etymology of vulnerability, from the Latin 'vuln', means both the propensity to be harmed as well as producing harm. To develop this point, institutional vulnerability can be seen to be coterminous with student vulnerability in the sense that both have provoked concerns about the processes of learning to labour (*pace* Willis, 1977): the student being concerned about the prospect of becoming employable as a graduate; the university having concerns about its ability to produce work-ready graduates in order to maintain market position within an increasingly volatile and metricised higher education sector. Here, student and institutional vulnerability is mobilised for productive purposes. As Mignot (2017) has observed, under these conditions vulnerability transmutes to *productive anxiety* within the encapsulated capitalistic space that is the marketised university. This is exemplified in the following statement made by a second-year undergraduate student who participated in the research project: 'I feel very protected right now, I'm not going to when I have finished when I don't have a job' ('Rachel', in Gee, 2017: 57). Here, the student expresses infantalised feelings of being protected, a word that connotes a sense of vulnerability, a connotation that can be found immediately in the student's expressed anxieties about her future in work held in the same sentence. Here, the speed of the transmutation from a vulnerable to a productively anxious state of mind is notable. Indeed, the statement demonstrates a co-existence of vulnerability and productive anxiety in the existential experience of the student. This is evidenced further in an interview with the same participant two years after graduation; here the participant was asked to recall her thoughts about finding employment once graduating:

> When I was at uni I was worried about not being able to get a job as soon as I moved ... as people struggle to get employment after uni, yeah so I was excited to actually get a job and going into something full time. ('Rachel', in Gee, 2017: 58)

This recollection reveals that the participant's anxiety about getting work was intensified by a provoked sense that it was necessary to compete with her peers to gain access to the labour market. Furthermore, it is noted that the phrase 'to actually get a job' reveals an anxiety that is productive in the following terms: that under competitive HE and labour market conditions, the perceived achievement of gaining employment produces a productive mindset irrespective of the prospect of earnings. As Mignot (2017) has observed:

> Under competitive market conditions it is perfectly possible to de-couple productivity from earnings ... Simply put, by flooding the labour market with a reserve army of graduates (and prospectively postgraduates), productivity may become incentivised by the mere fact of having a job and under these conditions Capital clearly gains. (Mignot, 2017: 133)

What is being highlighted by the participant accounts presented thus far is a process of individuation that is a key requirement of flexible capitalism; to be productively anxious is to be fit for the purposes of capital gain, a principle that applies to both individuals and institutions as individuated economic actors. It therefore follows that productive anxiety is a concomitant of economic labour, a proposition that allows perspectives on precarity to be brought within the scope of this analysis.

Precarity and productive anxiety at work

As a point of departure for what follows, precarity will be regarded as an existential phenomenon, not solely as the substantive positioning of economic actors in a flexible labour market (see Standing, 2011 for such a wider discussion). Based on the analysis thus far, it is argued that precarity is experienced existentially as a state of productive anxiety, a dynamic force that is generated by a provoked sense of vulnerability to capital. As such, given the proposition that productive anxiety is a concomitant of economic labour, then all who labour are positioned on a spectrum of vulnerability to precarity. This is not a tautological claim, rather it invites attention to the particular contexts and conditions that provoke such a sense of vulnerability; a vulnerability that initiates a process whereby social actors are reconstructed as economic actors. As we have seen in the context of higher education, the vulnerability of students and institutions is provoked in part by a set of market conditions laid down by government. Under these conditions, universities function as an encapsulated capitalistic space for learning to labour, wherein the life-world of social actors are first made vulnerable and then appropriated for the benefit of capital (Mignot, 2017). Thus, the student and institutional body is brought to labour. This *bringing to labour* is reflected in the following account given by a participant of the research project:

> I might turn out to be not a very good person to employ was what my worry was, then I think that I worried that I wouldn't be able to put theory into practice and there is a lot pressure put on you by education to be able to go into full time employment and I think they measure, yeah HE places seem to measure success and their success by students going into full time employment, which I was very aware of and that made me quite anxious about things. ('Adam', in Gee, 2017: 60)

In addition to the presence of productive anxiety in this account, it is also important to note the anxious reference to 'theory into practice'. Here the graduate is implicitly acknowledging a tension between what might be termed the 'academic' and 'vocational' aspects of a HE. This tension is exemplified in the following research participant account:

> I felt like as doing a degree what was expected as a student and what would get you the grades to be successful would be able to write a good essay, because our course was 100% assignments so I was very aware that I was good at writing and I didn't have that much experience, I had limited experience of working in primary schools and things, but I didn't have that much experience anywhere on the ground. ('Chris', in Gee, 2017: 62)

The tensions and anxieties evident in these two participant accounts can be related to the long-standing and ongoing concerns amongst the academy about curriculum relevance (to the needs of industry and commerce) and the promotion of the student as an economic resource (Mignot, 2017). As Foskett (2011) has observed, the debate about the appropriateness of an economistic approach to education is of historical and contemporary significance, the Callaghan Ruskin College speech in 1974 being seen as a watershed moment in the formulation of educational policy. Such wider concerns about vocationalism reveal a sustained belief within the academy that HE has an essence that needs to be protected from market forces. Although this belief has been met with some scepticism (see, for example, Love, 2008; Maton, 2015), there is wider evidence to show that university life continues to be existentially experienced as a place that is independent from the prurience of the market (McCulloch, 2009; Streeting and Wise, 2009). The dates of the following student observations drawn from the work of O'Regan (2009) and Mignot (2015) illustrate this:

> The 'mass' nature of our universities are suffocating to a person like me, at least. The joy of learning is fragile, easily lost and put aside and needs to be cared for and encouraged in the right environment. ('Kate' in O'Regan, 2009: 9)

> [U]niversity is not all about gaining a career, but about gaining knowledge, an education. ('Grace' in Mignot, 2015: 16)

What the students observe here resonates with the neo-Marxist analysis of capitalism offered by Fleming (2009). Drawing significantly from the work of Hardt and Negri (1994), Fleming draws attention to how the reproduction of capitalism is dependent on the sustained appropriation of the 'commons', which is conceptualised 'first and foremost as a kind of non-commodified labour that exists outside of the realms of Capital' (Fleming, 2009: 10). In these terms, universities can be seen as 'social factories', where production is no longer fixed in time and space (as in the traditional factory) but moves to cover the entire social body, thus bringing the 'commons' progressively within its reach (Hardt and Negri, 1994). In the university as a social factory, academic life and work is appropriated and transformed into economic labour, characterised by a sense of productive anxiety and, therefore, a vulnerability to precarity. In the university as a social factory, learning becomes laborious in both its intensification and extensification within the life-world of the economic actor; a life-world where 'time and motion' performance measures in the form of assessment and engagement metrics are constantly applied to students and academics alike. As the participant accounts presented thus far show, with the spectre of (un)employability ever-present in university life, the labour of learning can be seen as precarious work, with no guarantee of a return from an investment in a HE. This is exemplified in the following reflections given by 'John', a recent graduate and participant of the research project:

> I think that, I think sometimes I do get frustrated, I think why have I got myself into all this debt with a degree when

> I could of maybe worked my way up, it's catch 22 because
> I think I did need that degree at the time, me personally,
> but I think honestly I don't think, I think people overplay
> degrees nowadays I don't think you need a degree you can
> work you work your way up, three years of a degree you
> can do three years at a place and be at the same level. ('John'
> in Gee, 2017: 67)

Furthermore, in order to undertake the labour of learning, many students are also *labouring to learn*; this is to acknowledge the significant number of university students who undertake part-time work whilst studying (Taylor, 2017). Drawing once again from the work of Hardt and Negri (1994), such work can be regarded as an economic *externality* of the university production process; rather than being directly accounted for by HE performance measures, the effects of part-time working are offloaded into the private lives of students and, as will now be discussed, the wider body of society.

Precarious work and the paradox of precarity

As explained earlier, the foregoing analysis is based on the premise that the student body has an increasing resemblance to the body of society as a whole. To in part reiterate, at an objective substantive level a pattern of resemblance can be found in the massification of HE, where around 47 per cent of the general population are students of some description (Brown and Carasso, 2013). This is augmented by the marketisation of HE, whereby the dynamics of competition, commodification and consumer identity that are integral to the wider market economy find their place in the university. At a subjective existential level, a pattern of resemblance can be found in a vulnerability to precarity, characterised by a sense of productive anxiety within and amongst students and the wider population of economic actors (a population made up increasingly of graduates). It is under these circumstances that students come to resemble precarious workers, productively anxious in their resolve to make their lives less vulnerable to the vagaries of the working world.

It is important at this point to consider how the productively anxious mind of the economic actor is manifested in the form of a precarious worker. In so doing it needs to be acknowledged that for some who labour there may be perceived benefits associated with working precariously; here the mind of the precarious worker is made manifest in alienated form. As Edgell (2006) has observed, under capitalism those who are content with their work are no less alienated, no less vulnerable to capital than any other worker. This serves to introduce a paradox in the existential experience of some who undertake precarious work. For students who labour to learn, the flexibility offered by precarious work may be regarded as beneficial; under such circumstances the substantive precarity of a casualised contract, zero-hour or otherwise, may not be experienced as a contractual vulnerability: 'It was part time but it was a zero-hour contract, so they kept me on the books even when I was at university' ('David' in Gee, 2017: 88). At the same time, by definition, the student who is labouring to learn is also learning to labour, a form of learning that is precarious in terms of the sense of vulnerability and productive anxiety that it engenders. Under these circumstances the student is willingly brought to a substantively precarious position in the wider labour market, to work flexibly around the productive demands of the factory of the university. Hence the paradoxical nature of precarity, where the benefits and costs of precarious work co-exist circumstantially, substantively, and existentially for the economic actor. Whilst it may be said that paradoxically all waged labour carries with it both benefits and costs by degree, it is important to reiterate that the paradox of precarity points to the significance of productive anxiety, an existential experience that is itself paradoxical: to have a sense of being both productive and anxious at the same time.

The paradox of precarity can be found in the circumstances of many who labour flexibly and therefore precariously. For example, those with family and care commitments may also be willingly brought to a substantively precarious labour market position. Under such circumstances it is the unpaid family work of care that engenders an existential sense of vulnerability and productive anxiety amongst those brought to labour precariously. Here, in similar vein to the lives of students, capital succeeds in appropriating the commons of family life, capitalising on unpaid familial work; a form of work that serves to produce a reserve army of labour (Edgell, 2006) whilst at the same time being an externality that is of no cost to capitalist production. This relates to the labour market positioning of women in particular, a paradoxical position where the benefits of flexible work delivered through precarity come at the cost of continued work inequalities for women collectively (Fawcett Society, 2014). This, in turn, highlights the Janus-faced aspect of capitalism, where the effects of undertaking precarious work are both individuated and collective, with the former having primacy in the existential experience of the economic actor. In other words, to be productively anxious diminishes the collective aspect of experience, thus diminishing the potential to be collective in response to the demands of capital. Evidence of this can be found in the research participants' accounts, where reference to the student body was framed solely in terms of competition; the need to compete with fellow students for access to what is perceived to be a graduate labour market. Under these individuated conditions a sense of collective interest as a basis for solidarity can be seen to evaporate, with self-interest predominating.

Reclaiming the collective experience of precarity

This final part of the chapter is concerned with how a collective experience of precarity might be reclaimed for the purposes of solidarity. This endeavour is informed by the principle already articulated: that whilst the effects of undertaking precarious work are inevitably both individuated and collective, it is the former that predominates in the existential experience of economic actors. As such, the potential to be collective rather than competitive in response to the demands of capital is diminished. It is also important to reiterate the significance of government policy in setting the social and economic conditions for the accumulation of capital. As the case of the quasi-marketisation of HE discussed earlier demonstrates, a neoliberal state can be found at work here (Brown, 2011). This is exemplified in the current policy interest in promoting 'good work' (Taylor, 2017), which can be regarded as a revisionist approach guided by an unwavering commitment to flexible capitalism:

> Our goal of good work for all is ambitious and involves concerted action ranging from specific changes in the short term to longer term strategic shifts. We advocate change but in doing so we seek to build on the distinctive strengths of our existing labour market and framework of regulation; the British way. National labour markets have strengths and weaknesses and involve trade-offs between different goals but the British way is rightly seen internationally as largely successful. We believe it is possible to build on that success without undermining its foundations. (Taylor, 2017: 7)

Whilst revisions to regulatory frameworks may well be welcome in the moment of implementation, their longevity is inevitably undermined by the flexibility of capitalism itself. This beckons a distant reminder from Marx (1894) that capitalists are no less vulnerable to the vagaries of capitalism than their workers. In the context of a marketised society

(Sandel, 2012), where public goods such as education and educational institutions become corporatised, such a reminder brings the entire domain of the corporation within the purview of the collective; a potential point of solidarity between all who labour irrespective of their position within the corporate structure (see Hall and Bowles, 2016, for a related discussion of solidarity within the academy). Solidarity here is understood to be the collective experience of precarity made manifest in the minds of economic actors. To become conscious of the collective experience of precarity is at the same time to be conscious of one's own individuated experience. By reclaiming the collective experience, a shared understanding of how we become vulnerable to precarity is made possible (see the Better Than Zero Campaign, 2019, for a specific example). Under these circumstances the possibility is also opened up for us to be productively anxious for both ourselves and others, rather than living an individuated life driven by competition against others. Such a form of productive anxiety might contribute to what Spivak (1990) has conceptualised as a practical politics of the open end, where the politics of the everyday is brought together with a wider politics (revisionist or otherwise), bringing each to productive crisis. As a final point a thought experiment comes to mind: imagine a moment when a call to 'just say no' is taken up collectively by economic actors at the point at which a revisionist labour market policy is about to be implemented. What might this act of practical politics open up for precarious workers?

References

Berrington, A., Tammes, P. and Roberts, S. (2014) *Economic Precariousness and Living in the Parental Home in the UK*, University of Southampton, ESRC Centre for Population Change, Working Paper 55.

Better Than Zero (2019) *Scotland's Movement Against Precarious Work*, www.betterthanzero.scot/

Brown, R. (2011) 'The march of the market', in Molesworth, M., Scullion, R. and Nixon, E. (eds) *The Marketisation of Higher Education and the Student as Consumer*, Abingdon, Routledge: 11–24.

Brown, R. and Carasso, H. (2013) *Everything for Sale? The Marketisation of UK Higher Education*, Abingdon: Routledge.

Competition and Markets Authority (2015) *UK Higher Education Providers: Advice on Consumer Protection Law,* https://assets.publishing.service.gov.uk/government/uploads/system/uploads/attachment_data/file/428549/HE_providers_-_advice_on_consumer_protection_law.pdf

Department for Education (2017) *Teaching Excellence and Outcomes Framework Specification,* https://assets.publishing.service.gov.uk/government/uploads/system/uploads/attachment_data/file/658490/Teaching_Excellence_and_Student_Outcomes_Framework_Specification.pdf

Edgell, S. (2006) *The Sociology of Work: Change and Continuity in Paid and Unpaid Work,* Sage: London.

Fawcett Society (2014) *The Changing Labour Market 2: Women, Low Pay and Gender Equality in the Emerging Recovery,* www.fawcettsociety.org.uk/Handlers/Download.ashx?IDMF=0ad02d8e-0445-4b8d-bfc1-1ae54407f139

Fleming, P. (2009) *Authenticity and the Cultural Politics of Work: New Forms of Informal Control,* Oxford: Oxford University Press.

Foskett, N. (2011) Markets, government, funding and the marketization of UK higher education', in Molesworth, M., Scullion, R. and Nixon, E. (eds) *The Marketisation of Higher Education and the Student as Consumer.* Abingdon: Routledge: 25–38.

Furedi, F. (2011) 'Introduction to the marketisation of HE', in Molesworth, M., Scullion, R. and Nixon, E. (eds) *The Marketisation of Higher Education and the Student as Consumer,* Abingdon: Routledge: 2–7.

Gee, R. (2017) *Exploring Career as a Lived Experience Via the Lens of Paradox, Document 4 of Professional Doctorate,* Nottingham Trent University.

Guardian, The (2017) 'Mental health: a university crisis', www.theguardian.com/higher-education-network/2017/sep/07/its-time-for-universities-to-put-student-mental-health-first

Hall, R. and Bowles, K. (2016) 'Re-engineering higher education: the subsumption of academic labour and the exploitation of anxiety', *Workplace,* 28, 30–47.

Hardt, M. and Negri, A. (1994) *The Labour of Dionysus: A Critique of the State Form,* Minneapolis: University of Minnesota Press.

HESA (2018) 'Research update: part-time data analysis from HESA and CFE', www.hesa.ac.uk/insight/26-02-2018/OFFA_research_update

Love, K. (2008) 'Higher education, pedagogy and the 'customerisation' of teaching and learning', *Journal of Philosophy of Education,* 42(1): 15–34.

Macaskill, A. (2013) 'The mental health of university students in the United Kingdom', *British Journal of Guidance and Counselling,* 41(4): 426–441.

Maringe, F. (2011) 'The student as consumer: affordance and constraints in a transforming higher education environment', in Molesworth, M., Scullion, R. and Nixon, E. (eds) *The Marketisation of Higher Education and the Student as Consumer*, Abingdon: Routledge: 142–154.

Marx, K. (1894) *Capital: A Critique of Political Economy. Volume III*, International Publishers: New York: 171.

Maton, K. (2005) 'A question of autonomy: Bourdieu's field approach and higher education policy', *Journal of Education Policy*, 20(6): 687–704.

McCulloch, A. (2009) 'The student as co-producer: learning from public administration about the student university relationship', *Studies in Higher Education*, 34(2): 171–183.

Mignot, P. (2015) 'Critical perspectives on employability. Keynote presentation to the Learning and Teaching Conference', Lincoln, Bishop Grosseteste University, 23 June.

Mignot, P. (2017) 'Young people as consumers – the construction of vulnerability amongst consumers of higher education', in Hawkins, C. (ed) *Rethinking Children as Consumers: Valuing Children and Young People in Society*, Abingdon: Taylor & Francis.

Molesworth, M., Nixon, E. and Scullion, R. (2009) 'Having, being and higher education: the marketisation of the university and the transformation of the student into consumer', *Teaching in Higher Education*, 14(3): 277–287.

Naidoo, R. and Jamieson, I. (2005) 'Empowering participants or corroding learning? Towards as research agenda on the impact of student consumerism in higher education', *Journal of Educational Policy*, 20(3): 267–281.

O'Regan, M. (2009) *Career Pursuit: Towards an Understanding of Undergraduate Students' Orientation to Career*, University of Reading, summary report adapted from PhD thesis.

Sandel, M. (2012) *What Money Can't Buy: The Moral Limits of the Market*, London: Penguin.

Spivak, G. (1990) *The Post-Colonial Critic: Interviews, Strategies, Dialogues*, London: Routledge: 105.

Standing, G. (2011) *The Precariat: The New Dangerous Class*, London: Bloomsbury Academic, 102.

Streeting, W. and Wise, G. (2009) *Rethinking the Values of Higher Education: Consumption, Partnership, Community?*, Gloucester: Quality Assurance Agency for Higher Education.

Taylor, M. (2017) *Good Work: The Taylor Review of Modern Working Practices*, https://assets.publishing.service.gov.uk/government/uploads/system/uploads/attachment_data/file/627671/good-work-taylor-review-modern-working-practices-rg.pdf

Williams, J. (2011) 'Constructing consumption: what media representations reveal about today's students', in Molesworth, M., Scullion, R. and Nixon, E. (eds) *The Marketisation of Higher Education and the Student as Consumer*, Abingdon: Routledge, 170–182.

Willis, P.E. (1977) *Learning to Labour: How Working Class Kids Get Working Class Jobs*, Farnborough: Saxon House.

CASE III.2

Student–Public–Sociologist: On Dialogue with our First Public, and in Widening Access to Higher Education

Karl Johnson

Introduction

By some measurements, I should not be in a position where I can contribute a chapter to an academic text. I entered university as a mature, working class, first generation student from a rural background, with less than impressive school attainment and a menial employment history. Here, as an early career lecturer experiencing culture shock, imposter syndrome and struggling with my mental health at time of writing, I reflect on the impact of dialogue on the Scottish widening access agenda and of students as arguably our first and most important public.

If Burawoy's address acts as a foundation of discussion here then let us consider his thesis on 'The multiplicity of public sociologies' – where perhaps lost among assertions of traditional and organic public sociology, Burawoy (2005: 9) describes students as 'carriers of a rich lived experience' and of 'ambassadors of sociology'. Back (2016: 46) is more straightforward, identifying students as 'our first public and often our most important audience and some of them are also our future colleagues'. Rather than simply a homogeneous mass, students experience their degree careers in the public sphere as a collective of diverse backgrounds and private issues.

The UK widening access agenda seeks to move beyond the traditional white middle class student population, and the Scottish approach has been to reduce financial and attainment barriers to entering higher education (HE), to instil a greater sense of meritocracy and social equality in society (Iannelli, 2011; Tigh, 2012; Lasselle, 2016; Rainford, 2016; Sosu et al, 2016). Friedman (2016), Reay (2017) and others can evidence and attest to the fact however, that this simplistic and short-sighted numbers management has thus far served only to perpetuate class and minority inequality, and further stratify HE. Decision makers have ignored 'the complexities of the [social] mobility experience' (Friedman, 2016: 145) and significance of forms of capital available – or not – to students from different backgrounds. At times the politicised goals of reducing inequality and increasing social mobility have become conflated with achieving targets and success in league tables (Ianelli 2011; Gallacher 2014; Weedon 2016).

Defining widening access/widening participation (WP) and the groups to which it refers in Scotland varies across governmental policy (Scottish Government, 2016), sectoral direction (HEA, 2013) and academic literature. Typically, though, it includes examples of Fraser's (1990) subaltern counterpublics – 'women, lower socio-economic groups, mature adults, and ethnic minorities' (Tight, 2012: 211), disabled people, care leavers and those who are the first in their family to enter HE (Roberts, 2011; Meharg et al, 2017). As the Scottish Government pursues the broadening of the widening access agenda (Weedon, 2016), it requires consideration in terms of how the habitus of future colleagues from so-called non-traditional backgrounds are impacted upon by their experience of HE.

Still seen and felt by most to be a middle class (or elite) environment, in which access to and aptitude in forms of capital is to an extent predetermined, the mere admission to university does not solve social inequalities (Ianelli, 2011; Lasselle, 2016; Reay, 2017). If we can agree that one of the inherent tasks of the public sociologist is to critique and counter this, then where better to begin than in the lecture, the seminar, the workshop, the supervisory meeting?

This chapter positions WP activities and engaging so-called non-traditional students in meaningful dialogue as public sociology practice, exploring and addressing the exclusion of WP groups from the dominant public sphere via the field of education. I draw upon some of my own experience as a student from a working class, rural background and transitioning into being employed as a lecturer with responsibility for WP at Queen Margaret University (QMU).

Student

Increasingly, research conceptualises the student sense of belonging and their experience of transitioning into, through and out of HE – the experience of social mobility, in part – in Bourdieusian terms of habitus and capital (Reay et al, 2009; Lehmann, 2013; Alexander, 2016; Friedman, 2016; Abrahams, 2017). Although certainly adaptable, the habitus (its resilience and the extent of its malleability) is largely the result of parent culture and early socialisation (Bourdieu, 1984, 1993). Students entering the university environment already equipped with substantial reserves of social and cultural capital to draw upon will be in a stronger position to accumulate further and more broadly than those students whose socioeconomic and/or cultural backgrounds are not as typically accommodating (Bourdieu, 1984; Bourdieu and Wacquant, 1992).

Students are typically expected to move away from home to transition into an independent student identity which aligns with their chosen institution. This ritualised process of financial and geographical mobility inherently assumes the youth, lack of responsibility, monetary security and ease of travel that working class rural applicants do not necessarily have (Abrahams and Ingram, 2013; Alexander, 2016; Lasselle, 2016). Applicants from the Scottish islands are immediately disadvantaged by geography: the physical distance required to travel to a mainland higher education institutions (HEI), the time and cost involved; as well as the distance from support networks, cultural belonging and well-being associated with home (Abrahams and Ingram, 2013; Alexander, 2016; Lasselle, 2016).

Linguistics create further barriers. To the lament of my grandmother, I have spent years curbing my distinctive Shetland accent and dialect in order to be understood in mainland (particularly central) Scotland and better fit in. I am not alone. It is commonplace for students transitioning into HE to develop a chameleon-like approach to their new environment and what they perceive to be the right ways to sound and behave in order to be successful (Abrahams and Ingram, 2013; Addison and Mountford, 2015). Accents and ways of talking are burdened by associations with class, intelligence and value and therefore of insider/outsider status in certain contexts. HE staff and students have been commonly found altering their own speech to align with a form of Standard English and its perceived middle class legitimacy and cultural connotations (Abrahams and Ingram, 2013; Addison and Mountford, 2015; Donnelly, 2018; Donnelly et al, 2019).

This is known in the Shetland tongue as 'knappin'', where dialect speakers switch to Standard English for a variety of reasons and in specific situations, most commonly when speaking to persons unfamiliar with Shetland dialect (Karam, 2017). Knappin' perpetuates an insider/outsider dichotomy and in some circumstances delegitimises the capital and experience of Shetlanders in favour of dominant structural discourse.

'They [mainlanders]'ll just have to learn', my grandmother said, and, of course, she was right. If the institution is to reflect society, then the institution is to be a place where the student population is a plurality of diverse, intersecting publics – subaltern, counter, or otherwise – in which some dominant forms of capital are abandoned where they serve no constructive purpose. Rather than filtering the student public, as it has historically done, it must explore and appreciate the multiplicity of the student public in discourse and collaboration (Fraser, 1990; Glenn, 2007). Opportunities for staff and students to present research, take part in knowledge exchange, debate, etc, in their native dialect would for example create academic environments where publics could palpably enter and be included in HEIs.

Public

For a brief passage in Burawoy's (2005) eleven theses, he walks through the centre of a Venn diagram of practicality, pastoral work and opportunism. Readily available, in some institutions growing, and occasionally even an avid audience – the student public is oftentimes overlooked where academics view lecturing as a chore rather than a privilege (Back, 2016). Undertaking an undergraduate degree is not merely a process of learning for the student, of the input of knowledge and intellectual expansion as new ideas are grappled with – but a transitional life experience in every sense of the word (Light et al, 2009; Lehmann, 2013; Reay, 2017). The skills and conceptualisations that sociology students acquire should better equip them to navigate the complexities of social and organisational control they encounter outside the HEI (Nyden et al, 2012), and so it is the responsibility of educators to appreciate the power and influence they wield.

'Education', Burawoy (2005: 9) says, 'becomes a series of dialogues on the terrain of sociology that we foster …'.

… a dialogue between ourselves and students …

Whether taking direction from Simmel or Burawoy (2005), Gouldner or Hartmann (2017), or whoever else inspires, the public sociologist within the HEI has the opportunity to use the relative freedom they have as educator. Bringing professional debates, sector challenges, personal concerns and above all, honesty, into class discussion as part of a reflexive process of demystifying HE and the discipline can serve as an engaging and self-affirming process for student and lecturer alike (Dallyn et al, 2015; Kane, 2016). Kane (2016), for example, has been contributing to this process for some time in her teaching – bringing public sociology from the staffroom to the classroom as an embedded feature of a module – exploring together the realities of how HE reaches and collaborates with communities, how sociology as a profession is structured and operates, and the inequalities found within academia itself.

Improving dialogue between academics/lecturers and first public, balancing the power dynamic and demystifying HE can also begin to be achieved via institutionally embedded WP initiatives as well as simple, individual changes to teaching (Sosu et al, 2016; Thomas et al, 2017; Breeze et al, 2018). Some students find lecturers stand-offish and are put off asking for help due to difficulties in establishing trusting enough relationships with them (HEA, 2013; Meharg et al, 2017). Recently, Public Sociology masters students at QMU highlighted the difficulty they had had transitioning into HE and acclimatising to not just the academic terminology, but also some of the professional language and formality found at an institutional level. Long before Burawoy (2005) and since (Besbris and Khan, 2017; Healy, 2017), professional and critical sociology has been criticised for its introspection, over theorising and impracticality. In a small, post-92 university like QMU – the kind of institution where the larger share of so-called non-traditional students are enrolled (Ianelli, 2011; Gallacher, 2014) – dialogue with students ought to be in terms and contexts that they can understand and engage with. That is by no means to suggest that dumbing down is required, but rather by having a greater awareness of the demographics of the lecture hall and appreciation of the publics that make it, academics and others may find common ground and engage in a more reciprocal form of teaching that focuses more on empirical description as Besbris and Khan (2017) suggest.

The lessons from feminism that Fairbairn (2019) discusses as aiding public sociology bridge the gap between university and community, of reflexivity, praxis and interdisciplinarity, are at their core further evidence of the need to engage in dialogue that is accessible and honest. I attempt to conduct lectures, facilitate seminars, write papers and book chapters in a tone that is as accessible to all as possible, while recognising that an appropriate amount of academic challenge and dissemination is still necessary. I have been in discussion elsewhere

(Christie and Johnson, 2017; Breeze et al, 2018) about the academic and personal labour one must invest, however, in this occasionally more informal and fluid pedagogical approach.

One more institutionally structured WP approach to engaging our first public, challenging perceptions and power dynamics between lecturers and students has been developed with colleagues (Breeze et al, 2018). We undertook a longitudinal induction project that assessed the main aptitudes and anxieties of students in their first week at university, in order to better accommodate them as much as practically possible in the semester ahead. Establishing informal face-to-face contact and talking honestly about expectations in a university degree can serve as a stepping-stone to students at risk feeling comfortable in approaching individual staff – whether in open drop-in sessions, skills workshops, by email or at the end of lectures – and working to support, signpost appropriate services and find solutions to their issues (HEA, 2013; Breeze et al, 2018; Meharg et al, 2017; Thomas et al, 2017).

… between students and their own experiences, among students themselves …

Transitions into, through and out of HE can be fraught with anxieties, expectations, uncertainties, information overload and loneliness (HEA, 2013; Christie et al, 2013; Christie and Johnson, 2017). Facilitating student peer interaction is of course part of the everyday work of lecturers, but important too is that students have discursive spaces of their own, whether created by or provided for them. Institutions such as QMU – which may be described as less prestigious, or in the terminology of Boliver et al (2018), less likely to be 'nationally selective' universities and certainly not 'globally competitive' – are doing the heavy lifting in WP as 'social groups with historically low participation rates are least well represented in the more prestigious universities' (O'Sullivan et al, 2019: 2). WP groups such as direct entrants via college articulation, mature students, lone parents, disabled people, care leavers, Black, Asian and Minority Ethnic (BAME) students, those from low socioeconomic backgrounds, etc, form the multiplicity of subaltern publics that contest the historically dominant homogeny of middle class and elite HE (Fraser, 1990; Glenn, 2007; Reay, 2017).

Certain HEIs thus become opportunities for the experiences, identities and knowledge of publics to be shared with one another, heard perhaps for the first time and challenged by each other. As Fraser (1990) expands, by accommodating a diverse variety of competing subaltern counterpublics, a small post-92 university such as QMU may better promote and progress participative equality.

Small steps may be taken in learning and teaching to lay foundations. Peer assisted learning support (PALS) schemes train students to facilitate informal additional revision and review classes, where lecturers have no input or presence (Packham and Miller, 2000; Colvin and Ashman, 2010). In some sense professionalising the common base form study group, PALS schemes leave students free to explore their own pedagogies while legitimising and expanding the aptitudes and capital brought into the institution from their own publics.

This does, however, highlight the impact of structural constraints on individual agency and success. PALS schemes – such as that recently begun with our own sociology programmes at QMU – rely on availability and attendance. Students with jobs and/or children and/or restrictive disabilities and health concerns and/or live outside of urban areas with reliable (and affordable) transport infrastructure are highly unlikely to engage with additional voluntary class time. This is especially true of commuter institutions such as QMU and it remains to be seen how successful PALS will be for student peer engagement in the long term.

... and finally a dialogue of students with publics beyond the university

Engaging our first public with public sociology literature, the realities of HE and academia, and with the lived experiences and personal troubles of their peers may initially seem like a labour of Hercules in itself, 'but there is a more difficult task of building a dialogue with the publics outside the universities' (Scott, 2005: 408).

It stands to reason, then, to begin taking steps towards the apprenticeship of students as public sociologists as early as possible. Part of the challenge of public sociology is in communicating it with citizens outside of academia; thus if we can successfully engage our students then they are better equipped and positioned to return to their own parent cultures and publics to begin the conversation between communities and public sociologists (Kalleberg, 2005; Hartmann, 2017; Wingfield, 2017). How exactly this takes shape in practice will be at the discretion of those involved, but we may return to Kane (2016) for an example. Having engaged her students in debates around public sociology, they then had opportunities to work with local publics through community-based research projects – during which time they were tasked with collaborating on beneficial issue-based outcomes.

A similar module is run at QMU, to which I have had the pleasure of contributing teaching. Engaged Sociology involves the close reading of Burawoy's (2005) address and the critique that followed, as well as exploring the contributions of Freire, Gramsci, Elias, Bourdieu and Wacquant and more. Alongside these classroom discussions students are offered the chance of various local voluntary opportunities, on which they then write reflections as part of their assessment. I have rather taken the opening line of the module handbook for Engaged Sociology literally, as it states: 'This module marks a key moment in your apprenticeship as a Public Sociologist.'

Quaye and Harper (2015) rightly state, though, that we cannot simply expect students to take full responsibility in engaging themselves in their education and activities such as those outlined above. It is up to academics to 'foster the conditions that enable diverse populations of students to be engaged' (Quaye and Harper, 2015: 5); which for our first public requires lecturing teams and accompanying degree programmes that are honestly and explicitly dedicated to the ethos of public sociology, and institutions that focus on customised practices to ensure success rather than league tables (Etzioni, 2005; Quaye and Harper, 2015; Reay, 2017).

Sociologist

Nyden et al (2012) believe that the key to ensuring successful graduates lies in the encouragement and resourcing of academics with proven track records of public sociology scholarship and engagement with learning and teaching. What that looks like is debatable, however, as the neoliberal university will likely measure it by impact and output, Research Excellence Framework (REF) and Teaching Excellence Framework (TEF) in the UK, and table achievements; while individual public sociologists – indeed academics of any discipline – may quite rightly take a more holistic, person-centred view. It matters because increasingly the face of the current and future generation of academic staff is one of anxiety, imposter, precarity and detrimental fetishisation of the doctorate (Logan et al, 2014; Dallyn et al, 2015; Breeze, 2018; Loveday, 2018).

I am in my 30s, I do not have a doctorate and up until a few years ago had never had a job that allowed for sitting down for extended periods of time. The meetings, policies and bureaucracy (a word I still cannot spell correctly on first attempt) of working in a HEI baffle and frustrate me; yet I contribute to it in my efforts to level the playing field for all students – regardless of background, though perhaps admittedly with some bias towards those similar to myself – and further cement my experience and credentials as a member of staff worth keeping under contract.

Just as the casually employed academic staff of Loveday's (2018) research, I have pressured myself into trying to become the kind of lecturer that gets noticed by management, that students seek out for support, who works over and above their contracted parameters, whose mental health has been negatively affected as a result, and perpetually does not feel they belong to their institution and profession in any case. The short-sighted approach of the neoliberal university (and target-driven political sphere) is harmful to the staff it so heavily relies upon – staff who function as a result of institutionalised anxiety, as well as in spite of it (Loveday, 2018). Just as it is harmful to the students to whom it claims to open its doors, while determining which particular doors are available.

My employment has, however, afforded me the opportunity to be part of tangible and long-term institutional change in contributing to the development of QMU's contextualised admissions (CA) policy. CA is an increasingly popular tool in opening doors to university, where admissions decisions are taken on comparable merit to standard admissions, with an appreciation of an individual's attainment in relation to their school, social background and personal status (for example, having experience in a care background) (Boliver et al, 2018; O'Sullivan et al, 2019). The removal of unconsciously biased 'one size fits all' minimum entry requirements – which favoured applicants with greater amounts of capital – aims to better accommodate students based on their drive and potential (Weedon, 2016; Boliver et al. 2018; Rainford, 2016; Sosu et al, 2016). In the case of QMU, our research into WP and review of internal data has had the added benefit of evidencing the flaws in the dominant approach to university admissions; in many cases applicants with lower attainment or that had taken non-traditional entry routes were just as, if not more, likely to successfully complete their degree as their paradigm-fitting peers.

Conclusion

Sociology as a discipline is 'in constant need of revitalisation' (Hartmann, 2017: 14) in order to keep pace with society itself. Making a dedicated effort to engage the current and potential next generation of academics in public sociology scholarship means making a parallel dedication to rethinking our degree programmes, pedagogies and embedding WP approaches for all students (Nyden et al, 2012). Dialogues, competing discourses both in and outside of the university walls, are crucial to not just the revitalisation of public sociology as our discipline but also to the parity of educational participation as our responsibility.

As Glenn (2007) foresaw, my background informs my sense of responsibility, or accountability, to other students from subaltern publics. Surely, then, it is as a public sociologist that I may begin to highlight and address the inequalities in HE, at least at a local level – at a public level? Perhaps I can still identify myself as part of the working-class rural public I was when I was a student? By embracing the identity of cultural outsider with a conflicted (chameleon) habitus crossing a divide, I can work towards becoming something in the vein of a Simmel-esque Stranger who is in the university, but not *of the institution* (Dallyn et al, 2015). An academic who prioritises their lecturing, tutoring and student pastoral support, with a temperament that does not conform to the professionalism of the sector and chooses to write in an accessible way.

References

Abrahams, J. (2017) 'Honourable mobility or shameless entitlement? Habitus and graduate employment', *British Journal of Sociology of Education*, 38(5): 625–640.

Abrahams, J. and Ingram, N. (2013) 'The chameleon habitus: exploring local students' negotiations of multiple fields', *Sociological Research Online*, 18(4).

Addison, M. and Mountford, V.G. (2015) 'Talking the talk and fitting in: troubling the practices of speaking 'what you are worth' in higher education in the UK', *Sociological Research Online*, 20(4).

Alexander, R. (2016) 'Migration, education and employment: socio-cultural factors in shaping individual decisions and economic outcomes in Orkney and Shetland', *Island Studies Journal*, 11(1): 177–192.

Back, L. (2016) *Academic Diary: Or Why Higher Education Still Matters*, London: Goldsmiths Press.

Besbris, M. and Khan, S. (2017) 'Less theory. More description', *Sociological Theory*, 35(2): 147–153.

Boliver, V., Powell, M. and Moreira, T. (2018) 'Organisational identity as a barrier to widening access in Scottish universities', *Social Sciences*, 7(9).

Bourdieu, P. (1984) *Distinction: A Social Critique of the Judgement of Taste*, Cambridge, MA: Harvard University Press.

Bourdieu, P. (1993) *The Field of Cultural Production: Essays on Art and Literature*, Cambridge: Polity Press.

Bourdieu, P. and Wacquant, L. (1992) *An Invitation to Reflexive Sociology*, Cambridge: Polity Press.

Breeze, M. (2018) 'Imposter syndrome as a public feeling', in Taylor, Y. and Lahad, K. (eds) *Feeling Academic in the Neoliberal University*, London: Palgrave Studies in Gender and Education.

Breeze, M., Johnson, K. and Uytman, C. (2018) 'What (and who) works in widening participation? Supporting direct entrant students in transitions to higher education', *Teaching in Higher Education*, www.tandfonline.com/

Burawoy, M. (2005) 'For public sociology', *American Sociological Review*, 70: 4–28.

Christie, H., Barron, P. and D'Annunzio-Green, N. (2013) 'Direct entrants in transition: becoming independent learners', *Studies in Higher Education*, 38(4): 623–637.

Christie, H. and Johnson, K. (2017) 'Don't panic: common sense and the student voice in a transitional guide', *Journal of Perspectives in Applied Academic Practice*, 5(2): 66–72.

Colvin, J.W. and Ashman, M. (2010) 'Roles, risks, and benefits of peer mentoring relationships in higher education', *Mentoring & Tutoring: Partnership in Learning*, 18(2): 121–134.

Dallyn, S., Marinetto, M. and Cederström, C. (2015) 'The academic as public intellectual: examining public engagement in the professionalised academy', *Sociology*, 49(6): 1031–1046.

Donnelly, M. (2018) 'Inequalities in higher education: applying the sociology of Basil Bernstein', *Sociology*, 52(2): 316–332.

Donnelly, M., Baratta, A. and Gamsu, S. (2019) 'A sociolinguistic perspective on accent and social mobility in the UK teaching profession', *Sociological Research Online*, https://journals.sagepub.com/doi/10.1177/1360780418816335

Etzioni, A. (2005) 'Bookmarks for public sociologists', *The British Journal of Sociology*, 56(3): 373–378.

Fairbairn, J. (2019) 'The public sociologist as a university–community hybrid: lessons from feminism', *Critical Sociology*, 45(2): 285–304.

Fraser, N. (1990) 'Rethinking the public sphere: a contribution to the critique of actually existing democracy', *Social Text*, 25/25: 55–80.

Friedman, S. (2016) 'Habitus clivé and the emotional imprint of social mobility', *Sociological Review*, 64(1): 129–147.

Gallacher, J. (2014) 'Higher education in Scotland: differentiation and diversion? The impact of college–university progression links', *International Journal of Lifelong Education*, 55(1): 96–106.

Glenn, E.N. (2007) 'Whose public sociology? The subaltern speaks, but who is listening?', in Clawson, D. (ed) *Public sociology: Fifteen Eminent Sociologists Debate Politics and the Profession in the Twenty-First Century*, California: California University Press, pp 213–230.

Hartmann, D. (2017) 'Sociology and its publics: reframing engagement and revitalizing the field', *Sociological Quarterly*, 58(1): 3–18.

HEA (2013) *Learning Journeys: Student Experiences in Further and Higher Education in Scotland*, Edinburgh: Higher Education Academy.

Healy, K. (2017) 'Fuck nuance', *Sociological Theory*, 35(2): 118–127.

Ianelli, C. (2011) 'Educational expansion and social mobility: the Scottish case', *Social Policy & Society*, 10(2): 251–264.

Kalleberg, R. (2005) 'What is "public sociology"? Why and how should it be made stronger?', *British Journal of Sociology*, 56(3): 387–393.

Kane, E.W. (2016) 'The baby and the bathwater: balancing disciplinary debates and community engagement to advance student interest in publicly engaged sociology', *Humanity & Society*, 40(1): 43–63.

Karam, K. (2017) 'Knappin: standard versus dialect speech modification in Shetland', University of Aberdeen (PhD thesis).

Lasselle, L. (2016) 'Barriers to higher education entry – a Scottish rural perspective', *Scottish Educational Review*, 48(1): 78–88.

Lehmann, W. (2013) 'Habitus transformation and hidden injuries: successful working-class university students', *Sociology of Education*, 87(1): 1–15.

Light, G., Cox, R. and Calkins, S. (2009) *Learning and Teaching in Higher Education: The Reflective Professional* (2nd edn), London: SAGE.

Logan, P.A., Adams, E., Rorrison, D. and Munro, G. (2014) 'Exploring the transition to becoming an academic: a comparative study of Australian academics with and without a doctorate', *Journal of Perspectives in Applied Academic Practice*, 2(3): 34–47.

Loveday, V. (2018) 'The neurotic academic: anxiety, casualisation, and governance in the neoliberalising university', *Journal of Cultural Economy*, 11(2): 154–166.

Meharg, D., Taylor-Smith, E., Varey, A., Mooney, C. and Dallas, S. (2017) 'An enhanced route from FE to HE graduation?', *Journal of Perspectives in Applied Academic Practice*, 5(2): 85–92.

Nyden, P., Hossfeld, L. and Nyden, G. (2012) *Public Sociology: Research, Action, and Change*, London: SAGE.

O'Sullivan, K., Bird, N., Robson, J. and Winters, N. (2019) 'Academic identity, confidence and belonging: the role of contextualised admissions and foundation years in higher education', *British Educational Research Journal*, 45(3): 554–575.

Packham, G. and Miller, C. (2000) 'Peer-assisted student support: a new approach to learning', *Journal of Further and Higher Education*, 24(1): 55–65.

Quaye, S.J. and Harper, S.R. (2015) *Student Engagement in Higher Education* (2nd edn), New York: Routledge.

Rainford, J. (2016) 'Targeting of widening participation measures by elite institutions: widening access or simply aiding recruitment?', *Perspectives: Policy and Practice in Higher Education*, 21(2–3): 45–50.

Reay, D. (2017) *Miseducation: Inequality, education and the Working Classes*, Bristol: Policy Press.

Reay, D., Crozier, G. and Clayton, J. (2009) ' "Strangers in paradise"? Working-class students in elite universities', *Sociology*, 43(6): 1103–1121.

Roberts, S. (2011) 'Traditional practice for non-traditional students? Examining the role of pedagogy in higher education retention', *Journal of Further and Higher Education*, 35(2): 183–199.

Scott, J. (2005) 'Who will speak, and who will listen? Comments on Burawoy and public sociology', *British Journal of Sociology*, 58(3): 405–409.

Scottish Government (2016) 'A Blueprint for Fairness: the final report of the commission on widening access', Edinburgh: The Scottish Government.

Sosu, E.M., Smith, L.N., Mckendry, S., Santoro, N. and Ellis, S. (2016) *Widening Access to Higher Education for Students from Economically Disadvantaged Backgrounds: What works and why?*, Glasgow: University of Strathclyde.

Thomas, L., Hill, M., O'Mahony, J. and Yorke, M. (2017) *Supporting Student Success: Strategies for Institutional Change. What Works? Student Retention & Success Programme Final Report*, Higher Education Authority.

Tight, M. (2012) 'Widening participation: a post-war scorecard', *British Journal of Educational Studies*, 60(3): 211–226

Weedon, E. (2016) 'Widening access to higher education in Scotland, the UK and Europe', in Riddell, S., Weedon, E. and Minty, S. (eds) *Higher Education in Scotland and the UK*, Edinburgh: Edinburgh University Press: 90–109.

Wingfield, A.H. (2017) 'Public sociology when the 'public' is under attack: response to Hartman', *Sociological Quarterly*, 58(1): 24–27.

CASE III.3

Experts by Experience: Art, Identity and the Sociological Imagination

John R. Docherty-Hughes, Elaine Addington, David Bradley, Linda Brookhouse, Jenny Bunting, Lorna Cosh, John Dane, Robert Lindsay and Christine Raffaelli

Introduction

This chapter offers a reflexive account of a co-produced, multisectoral, community-based project between Glasgow Open Museum (OM), Glasgow Association for Mental Health (GAMH) and Queen Margaret University (QMU). The project is framed around an accredited Public Sociology module, Identity Community & Society, in which participants explore sociological explanations of identity, community and society whilst engaging with and interpreting art and artefacts from the OM collections. We share our experiences of reaching over the chasms between the worlds of museums, mental health advocacy and higher education. Crucially, we hear from student participants, as co-authors, about the increased self-confidence and reflexive knowledge resulting from participation in the project. In interpreting different art works, participants consider a range of sociological concepts, debates and theories, that frame their interpretation of art, but also facilitate the development of a critical consciousness about social issues that they have direct experience of themselves or that impact participants' communities.

Widening participation is at the heart of this project; the adult learners, most of whom have limited recent experience of formal learning, became associate students of QMU, with full access to institutional resources whilst learning in a safe community space. In the presentation of our narrative here, we draw upon a combination of personal reflexive accounts, participant feedback and theoretical inspirations. More specifically, later in the chapter, we unpack the underpinning ethos of the project as theoretically framed by Freire's (1970) dialogical 'pedagogy of the oppressed', and we conceptualise the practice of our participants as Gramscian organic intellectuals (Gottlieb, 1989). We take the opportunity to weave critical reflection on the utility of Burawoy's (2005) theses for public sociology as a channel through which to interpret and problematise 'for whom' and 'for what' public sociology is, as well as our positions as value committed, partisan public sociologists, who are committed to creating a sociological space in which community-based adult learners mobilise their own sociological praxis. The focus in this chapter is explaining the meaning of (and need for) a public sociology as a particular style of practising sociology in an engaged, community-focussed way; and which speaks to, for, and with publics in their own communities.

The project

To contextualise, the OM is Glasgow Museums' outreach service and is based at Glasgow Museums Resource Centre (GMRC). The GMRC is a repository for the city's museums' collections when they are not on display for the public. It takes Glasgow's museum collections beyond the city's museum spaces and into communities, reaching people who may not regularly visit Glasgow's nine civic museums, or to further engage those who do. GAMH is an independent Scottish charity, providing more than 2,000 hours of community support every week to people in Glasgow. GAMH supports people who are recovering from mental health problems to live the lives they want to live, encouraging personal development and self-confidence. This project takes the study of sociology beyond the lecture theatre, and encapsulates the practice and style of an emerging community-focussed, community-based public sociology that characterises the small team at the university.

As matriculated associate students of QMU, participants developed sociological explanations of three central themes: identity, community and society. The associate students were all members of GAMH, and the module was delivered at the GMRC in Glasgow. Whilst learning about sociological concepts and theories, the module participants revelled in the historical and theoretical roots, and substantive applications, of an *engaged*, public sociology, whilst identifying and recognising the different 'communities' and 'publics' for whom public sociologists can, and perhaps ought, to represent (Burawoy, 2005). Whilst participants were all being supported by GAMH, this project is not solely focussed on making sociological sense of mental health and well-being per se; there is already exceptional work in this regard (Spandler et al, 2015). However, we are inspired by work that, rightly, acknowledges that engaging with art enhances mental health well-being (Sagan, 2012), acknowledging evidence that learning in community contexts is a positive experience for students (Reed-Bouley et al, 2012). Furthermore, the 'reflexive project of the self' (Giddens, 1991: 164) is inevitable when doing public sociology and, as is illustrated by the narratives below, a heightened sense of reflexive self amongst participants is clear, incorporating concepts of self-image and self-esteem, which were refined through engagement with others (Falk and Miller, 1998), with art and with sociology throughout the project.

On a practical level, the module consisted of six day-long sessions at GMRC, and a series of informal drop-in sessions at GAMH and in some of Glasgow's public libraries, for participants to seek advice on coursework. During the sessions at GMRC, mornings were spent engaging with sociological theory and research on a range of issues, characterised by open dialogue on the relationship between identity, community and society. Topics included the diversification of family life, poverty and social exclusion, social class as a key determinant of life chances, the social construction of gender and sexuality, and mental health stigma. During afternoons, we explored the vaults of the GMRC archives, to enjoy the art and artefacts on display but, most crucially, to reflect on how we might use the theories, concepts and research explored in the morning, to help interpret the art and artefacts before us. Participants interacted with a wide range of the museum's resources, including fine art, applied art such as pottery and metalwork, natural history, costumes, armour, vehicles and machinery.

This was far from a linear, harmonious process; it was unpredictable and sometimes involved difficult discussions, since much of the art and artefacts with which we engaged, and the sociological ideas we mobilised, elicited participants' personal troubles in a very public way (Wright Mills, 1959), and quiet, personal emotions, became publicly visible and open to sociological scrutiny. Such emotional reactions were no surprise to those of us who have had sociology in our lives for some time. Arlie Hoschchild (1983) reminds us that emotional expression is a social experience, involving a complex process of drawing upon emotional resources that we learn, hold and keep in the private sphere and which we, from time to time, acknowledge, expose and present in public contexts; this was very much the essence of the debates in our morning sessions, in the archives and in the subsequent written sociological narratives developed by participants. Throughout, participants were supported emotionally by experienced mentors from GAMH, whilst tutors from QMU guided sociological debate, and colleagues from GMRC offered expert, encouraging advice on making meaning from art and the museum's other resources. There was disagreement amongst participants about what each piece of art represented and about which sociological ideas might meaningfully facilitate artistic interpretation.

The critical, questioning mind inspired by the sociological imagination encouraged participants to challenge and deconstruct the multiple, contested barriers (Fuller et al 2008) to participating in education. It also encourages us to reboot the discipline as one that is deeply entrenched in public consciousness and claims for social justice (Trimikliniotis, 2018). The critical, questioning mind found further expression in the 1,000-word, written sociological interpretations of art that were developed by participants, which was the assessment for the module. On successful completion of the assessment, participants achieved 20 credit points at level 7 of the Scottish Credit & Qualification Framework (SCQF) (equivalent to one-sixth of the first year of a Scottish university undergraduate degree). Specifically, participants identified a sociological topic that most resonated with their own experience, identity or community, read sociological literature on their chosen topic, developed detailed written sociological narratives and related their stories to one piece of art from the museum's collections. Supported by staff from GMRC, GAMH and QMU participants transformed their work into an exhibition, entitled *Experts By Experience*, which has been displayed at Glasgow City Chambers, Glasgow's Mitchell Library and QMU. At the launch, participants presented their sociological interpretations of various pieces of art to an audience of invited guests, including friends, family, local councillors, members of the UK and Scottish Parliaments, and practitioners from the museum, health and higher education sectors. The exhibition received extensive positive media coverage at local and national levels. Furthermore, together, we have presented our work at academic and museum practitioners' conferences in Scotland and internationally.

Below, we consider extracts from participants' sociological interpretations of art, in which the struggle between private concerns and public issues, so integral in doing public sociology, are evident.

The participants whose narratives are presented are co-authors of this paper, therefore pseudonyms are not used. Participants' sociological narratives are interspersed with some personal reflections elicited from informal interviews with participants. The interviews were conducted as part of the development of a short film about the project, in which participants reflected on their experiences of learning about sociology, engaging with museum art and artefacts, as well as overall reflections on the project.

So, in the spirit of co-production, what follows combines extracts from participants' written sociological narratives, quotes from participants' informal interviews, which further contextualise these narratives, and an overarching, collective authorial voice that represents the shared positions of all contributors to this paper. Extracts from participants' sociological narratives are indented and presented in italics, quotes from informal interviews are indented in standard text, and the shared narrative is presented as standard text

Stigma, labels, mental illness, society and me (Linda)

> *The piece of art I have identified which best defines my experiences with mental health stigma is* No *by Stephen Sutcliffe. This image, I believe, identifies the effects of stigma on opportunities for employment after being labelled a mental health patient. Glasgow based artist Stephen Sutcliffe's work is a pastiche of a range of media, including British film, television and spoken words, which he has gathered throughout this life. His work is a commentary on many aspects of British society and culture, and he is particularly focussed on issues related to class-consciousness and the role of power in everyday culture.*

> *My interpretation of* No *by Stephen Sutcliffe relates to the effects of mental illness and the impact it can have when trying to gain security or promotion in work. From my own experience, the attitudes of employers and colleagues to people who have experience of accessing mental health services and support are often extremely negative; the barriers to employment are often insurmountable for those stigmatised and labelled for having lived experience of mental health challenges. Indeed, throughout my own life I have been subjected to various forms of stigma. My paper is a sociological reflection on how I feel society has*

Figure III.3.1: *No* **by Stephen Sutcliffe**

Source: copyright, and reproduced courtesy of, Stephen Sutlcliffe.

stigmatised me, by engaging with some of Becker's (1973) key contributions to labelling theory and Goffman's (1963) seminal work on stigma. I have experienced mental health problems most of my life; this has resulted in me being ostracised and marginalised in the community in which I live. In fact, the attitudes and opinions of people in my own community have often left me feeling degraded and demoralised, impacting my ability to function normally in my community. The past five years of my life have been extremely traumatic and emotionally challenging, and the devastating events were often compounded by the attitudes of others to my struggle to cope with and recover from mental health difficulties. Goffman (1961) reminds us that being admitted to a mental health care institution often means being 'turned out' by society on the grounds of socially unacceptable behaviour. Hence, as a former mental health patient, I can see

> *that I have been the occupant of an undesirable, discredited social position and identity.*

Linda was apprehensive about engaging with a project involving art, a world that was alien to her:

> We were told it involved art and I thought, well, I didn't really know anything about art. I was like, no, I'm not really interested, but I must admit it's opened, it's opened my eyes to different types of art. If you look at a picture and you think, phew, what's this, but this has got us to understand what people were thinking when they (the artists) were actually creating that kind of thing. So, it's not just looking at a picture; it's seeing the whole lot in context, so it's been great.

Here, Linda articulates a sense of 'bonding' with art, which is critical for breaking down barriers to participation in artistic cultural practices and places (Stenglin, 2007). Of course, barriers to engagement with art are not limited to a perceived lack of knowledge or confidence on the part of potential participants; of equal significance are concerns around entrance fees and transport costs and logistics, as well as worries about knowing how to look or act in museums and galleries (Alexander and Bowler, 2014). Linda's bond with Sutcliffe's work is clear:

> My piece of art is a bit of art by Stephen Sutcliffe. And it's based on week 5, which is stigma, social stigma, and I chose that because I related mostly to that through my own experiences of being stigmatised because of my mental health. So I felt that this kind of thing can inspire me, and it made me more interested in the different sociological approaches to stigma, and how to, em, how we can try and change people's opinions, change people's views.

Linda's bond is more than aesthetic pleasure, but Sutcliffe's work has inspired a sociological imagination that seeks positive social transformation for people living with mental health difficulties, and challenges the people and processes who, Linda feels, have 'discredited' her identity. In response to Burawoy's (2005) call to reflect on 'Sociology for what?', Linda's is clear; sociology needs to be put to work in effecting positive change in people's lives. Noy (2009: 235) has raised doubts about whether public sociology 'rhetoric' is productive or necessary, and has called on public sociologists to resist the role of 'partisan representatives of civil society or marginalised peoples'. However, for Linda, the labour of partisan sociologists (Burawoy, 2005) in this project is worthwhile:

> In a nutshell, it's been an absolutely life changing experience, because, em, basically I had no education, I had no real knowledge, I didn't have much schooling, no, no qualifications and, eh, then I had mental illness before I came to the class. Basically, I hadn't read, or opened a book in seven years. Coming here has brought back memories, brought back learning, and realising my abilities.

Propaganda (David)

One of my earliest memories is of watching Western movies and cheering as the brave and good cowboys overpowered the inhuman savages who tortured and scalped their victims. Then came the cavalry – almost evangelical in their role – representing authority. This was the Hollywood version of 'how the west was won'. I now know a very different version of this truth; a story of how the people native to America were slaughtered and displaced from their homes. At four years of age I was already being manipulated by the propaganda machine, and I believed that the people who held the power were 'the good guys'.

The art I want to explore is The Blind Leading the Blind *by Laila Shawa. In this painting, the subjects can be seen as a group of people being led, not by their own wit, but by another's. In so doing, they give away the freedom to think for themselves. I recognised these ideas when reading Klaehn and Mullen's (2010) work on the sociological Propaganda Model as a means for understanding media in society. The paper explores how propaganda is woven into the fabric of society, particularly focussing on the media as a means of social control.*

These ideas are exemplified in Herman and Chomsky's (1995) Manufacturing Consent. *The Propaganda Model illustrates how citizens internalise a false set of beliefs which are manufactured by powerful political elites. The model suggests that the rich and powerful perpetuate their own agenda to maintain domination*

Figure III.3.2: *The Blind Leading the Blind* **by Laila Shawa**

Source: © Laila Shawa, reproduced by kind permission.

> *in capitalist society. This manipulation was, in my opinion, widespread in the lead up to the Scottish independence referendum in 2014, and is typical of many political debates, with accusations of media bias in favour of a status quo position, which is often convenient for the political elite.*

David is an artist, but learning about sociology and using sociological ideas to interpret art, awakened an interest in concepts of false consciousness:

> I do a bit of art myself. So, I thought I might gain a wee bit of knowledge about how they [experts on art], how they see pictures. The one I done was The Blind Leading The Blind. It was like somebody leading all these other people, following. You know, and that made me think all about propaganda. People just follow on without knowing if it's the best thing for them.

Given the proliferation of sociological research that raises critical questions about the extent to which mainstream media assumes

Figure III.3.3: *Exiled* **by Jo Spence**

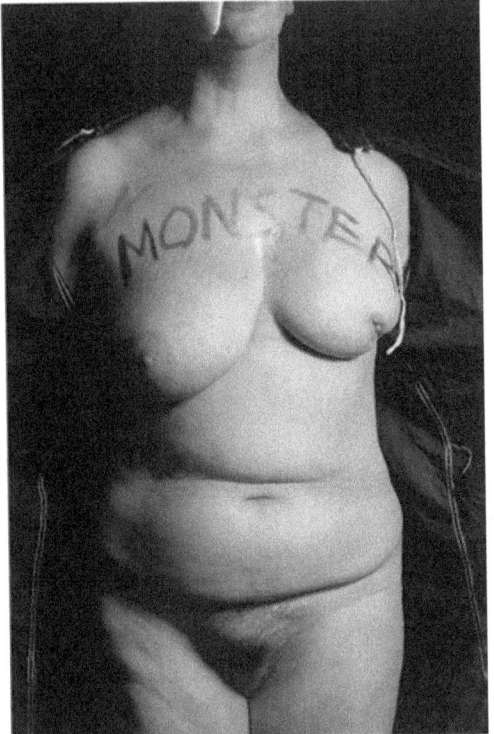

Source: copyright: The Estate of the Artist. Courtesy of Richard Saltoun, London.

objective positions (Miller, 2006), David's narrative lends further credence to Burawoy's (2012: 741) call for public sociologists to be mindful of Weber's work on value relevance and value commitment in articulating the 'relation between sociology *of* society and sociology *in* society'. In the face of a mainstream media which for David, at best, obfuscates reality, a value committed public sociology is necessary *in* society for 'people being led, not by their own wit, but by another's'.

The politics of women's bodies (Lorna)

> Exiled *by Jo Spence is a photograph that resonates with the emotions I have about my own body. Jo Spence was a feminist photographer. In 1982, Jo was diagnosed with breast cancer. Before the cancer diagnosis, her work often focussed on weddings and family portraits; following the cancer diagnosis, Jo's work focussed on women's post-surgery bodies. The change in direction*

is documented in the exhibition entitled A Picture of Health, in which Exiled *featured.*

Jo felt that she had limited control over what was happening to her body and her work allowed her to exert some power and control in her life again. The photograph is a self-portrait of Jo Spence with the word 'monster' written above her breasts. For me, this photograph challenges idealised images of what is considered normal and desirable in terms of women's bodies, and smashes through the pressures on women to conceal disfigurement. Nine years ago, when I was 48, I had a hysterectomy. As a result of what I considered medical negligence, I required emergency surgery after my bowel perforated. Following a series of infections, I was left with an open wound on my stomach. I am now left with a horrendous scar. I also have to face life with a stoma and a colostomy bag stuck to my stomach like an alien. I am still unable to look at my body in a mirror because, like Jo, I feel like a monster and undesirable.

Jo's work has encouraged me to think about the pressures faced by women to maintain the ideal body. The constant pressures for young and older women to achieve the perfect body has resulted in increased body dissatisfaction, which impacts on the emotional and physical heath of women. Body dissatisfaction is associated with depression and low self-esteem, and is a predictor of dieting, binge eating and eating disorders (Stice and Shaw, 2002). Furthermore, Puhl and Brownell (2001) suggest the stigmatisation of obesity often gives rise to discrimination in education, employment and health care and is linked to depression and low-esteem.

For Lorna, participating in the project was a new and unexpected experience: 'I left school when I was 16, and I didn't do any other education, I just worked at the time.'

Lorna's engagement with sociology evokes an emotive response to a subject that is close to her own lived experience. Much like the students who participated in Stephenson and Stirling's (2015) research on auto/biography in the development of the sociological imagination, Lorna's analysis of Spence's *Exiled* facilitates an acknowledgement of the complexity and rewards of achieving a symbiosis of personal experience and troubles, with issues of public sociological concern:

There was a time when I wanted to throw in the towel and forget all about Sociology. I would have, if it wasn't for the tutors on the course, who helped me to unscramble my ideas and write my paper. It was a miracle; this was my work on a subject close to me, and nobody could take it away from me. I never, ever imagined that I would have anything to do with a University, and I am just so proud.

Tenement living (John Dane)

> Andrew Hay is a self-taught artist with no art school training, who emerged from the Glasgow scene in the late 80s and early 90s. Two pieces of work are Springburn Tenement *(1990) and* Bute Mansions, Gibson Street, Glasgow (1990). *These works have inspired me to look at how, in tenement living, there was a class structure. I was born in December 1957, where my mum and dad stayed in a single end in an old grey tenement building in Partick, Glasgow.*
>
> *From the late nineteenth century into the early twentieth century Partick transformed into a bustling burgh with a diverse community, including many migrant workers. To house the expanding industrial community, tenements were built. These became overcrowded and, to address this, 'Ticket Houses' were introduced. This entailed a metal disc being attached to the outside door of a property to officially record the area size and the number of adults and children it could legally accommodate.*

> *The Public Health Department was founded in 1863 to combat the spread of disease. Its main function was to exercise control over the moral and hygienic standards of the rapidly expanding working class (Damer, 2000); in essence, this was a form of surveillance. In the context of Foucault's work, this was all about exercising and forcing a form of capitalist discipline amongst the local working class (Foucault, 1979) in Glasgow and was part of the process of punishing the working class after the defeats of the general strike of 1926 (Damer, 2000).*

John reflects on presenting his work at the exhibition launch, and at conferences and public events: 'Six or seven months ago, I wouldn't have got up and spoke. Now I've found a voice, and it's just great.'

Figure III.3.4: *Bute Mansions, Gibson Street, Glasgow* by Andrew Hay

Source: copyright, and reproduced courtesy of, Andrew Hay.

Sharing this experience with people from familiar backgrounds, all of whom have had lived experiences of mental health challenges was significant:

> The fact that we've all had mental health issues means that we were able to support each other through the highs and lows of the course. Achieving the qualification is not something that would have happened for us in a formal setting. We would have found it difficult to participate or even enter a room full of strangers and hard to believe in our own abilities.

Learning and sharing ideas in familiar places, with people with similar life experiences in common, were critical in emboldening participants to enter the body of the culturally hegemonic (Gramsci, 1971) beast of higher education. However, far from fostering tacit consent for cultural hegemony in all its forms, sociological debate and dialogue in safe spaces fosters deeply counter-hegemonic, critical narratives, from powerful positions of lived experience and theoretical engagement.

The cage: the consequences of conforming (Robert)

Alexander Guy's Madame X symbolises, for me, the essence of the concept of 'hegemonic masculinity' (Connell and Messerschmidt, 2005), which is the central focus of the sociological narrative presented here.

My interpretation of this painting has emerged by looking through the prism of cultural manifestations of hegemonic masculinity. The painting depicts a confined empty space, a cage constructed of iron in a masculine form, and which communicates a sense of imprisonment. All of this resides in a metaphor for conforming to the hegemonic ideals of masculinity, ideals that for most men, are unattainable and do not result in true fulfilment or freedom. The consequences of hegemonic masculinity mean that some men will live a life unfulfilled because of the restrictive dimensions of the social rules governing men and masculinities.

With significant research by the likes of Connell and Messerschmidt (2005), Elliott (2016) and Kimmel (2013), we acknowledge the symptoms of the unrealistic expectations engendered by hegemonic masculinity, and the detrimental effects on the health and wellbeing of both women and men. This research would be meaningless unless it is put to work to create a fairer, healthier life for men and women.

Having engaged critically with the academic literature on hegemonic masculinity, a focus on equality is the most fundamental key to achieving the humanisation of men and empowerment of women. Equality is intrinsically connected to humanisation, and is the most productive way to neutralise the destructive impacts of hegemonic masculinity, in which men are no longer under pressure to conform to the unattainable ideals of power, physical and emotional fortitude (Connell and Messerschmidt, 2005). Elliott (2016) calls for a reframing of the sociology of masculinities to understanding 'caring masculinities'. Masculinities are capable of reform and, as such, it can surely become more socially acceptable for men to actively engage in caring work, such as child care. Such a culture of care can only have positive effects on relationships and family life.

Figure III.3.5: *Madame X* by **Alexander Guy**

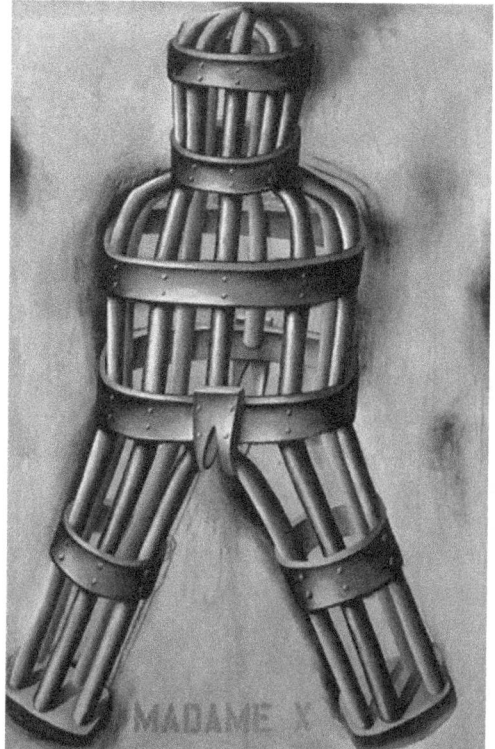

Source: copyright, and reproduced courtesy of, Alexander Guy.

It is clear from Robert's interpretation of Guy's work that he and the other participants in the project engaged in a wholesale 'reflexive project of the self' (Giddens, 1991):

> My chosen subject was hegemonic masculinity and, em, it's something I've struggled with my whole life. I've never really conformed to the hegemonic ideal. The image itself looks, actually, masculine. It's like a masculine shape, kind of, but I think that's obviously to throw you off. The closer you look at it you see the feminine dimension of the picture ... a lot of men live inside this kind of cage.

The reflexive project of the self, for Falk and Miller (1998), denotes an ability to engage in an internal conversation with oneself as subject and object of sociological analysis. The flip side of the internal conversation is in engaging with, absorbing, challenging or rejecting the perceptions of others, whether those opinions come from what we read in sociological text, from those we learn with, or those we live our lives with beyond sociology. Notwithstanding the emotional challenges of such a sociological exercise, it is not without personal and intellectual reward: 'I mean, through the course, I realised I don't live inside there. I'm actually outside looking in; I realised that I'm actually a lot freer than I thought I was when I started the course.'

Reflections

This project represents a particular style of practising public sociology; a sociology beyond the academy, outside the university, doing sociology in a community-focussed way, engaging 'multiple publics in multiple ways' (Burawoy, 2005: 1). In reflecting on our work together, we have often turned to Burawoy's ideas to help us make sociological sense of the project. Of course, we are mindful not to accept Burawoy's work in an uncritical way. Our appreciation of his manifesto for public sociology should be read in the context of our own acknowledgement that there are dissenting voices who are critical of Burawoy's work, calling for careful reflection on the 'geopolitics of knowledge' and the need to decolonise social science generally and public sociology specifically (Lozano, 2017), as well as those who caution against a partisan public sociology and argue for political neutrality in the organisation and practice of Sociology (Holmwood, 2007; Noy, 2009). We are supportive of Lozano (2017) in that public sociology ought to be for publics beyond the Global North, but we reject the idea that public sociology practice can by anything but value committed and, to coin Burawoy's (2005) final thesis, 'partisan'; such value commitment is clear to see in participants' narratives and in the motivations for designing this project.

Inspired by Freire's (1970) 'pedagogy of the oppressed', we co-created a learning environment that was dialogical, where participants were encouraged to debate and be respectfully critical of facilitators' narratives, of each other's interpretations of art and sociological theory, and of the academic literature that was identified as pertinent to each participant's sociological interpretation of artwork. We witnessed a rejection of a passive, uncritical 'banking' approach to 'expert' knowledge consumption and participants embraced the challenges of generating public sociological knowledge through the process of 'conscientisation' (Freire, 1970). This process was often perilous;

practising public sociology in this way is not for the faint-hearted, and making sense of art through sociology, and vice versa, triggered the exposure of personal, emotional experiences, which were often indistinguishable from our deliberations on the merits of this or that sociological perspective, or in interpreting or appraising particular pieces of art. Emotional connection, however, fuelled participants' desire to know more about their chosen sociological topics and artworks, and further fuelled their commitment to developing partisan, value committed public sociological narratives, all of which offered clear prescriptions for positive social transformations. In developing and refining a public sociological imagination through engagement with art, with each other, with higher education, museum and mental health advocacy practitioners, participants exercised considerable agency in arguing for social change. Such agency is often lost in a contemporary neoliberal higher education landscape that is results focussed, rather than experience focussed (Petray and Halbert, 2013), which lies at the heart of the transformative value of this project. Gramsci (1971) argued that, unlike 'traditional intellectuals', 'organic intellectuals' are able to generate counter-hegemonic forces that can effect social transformation from a position of knowledge based upon lived experience of, broadly speaking, marginalisation and oppression. The powerful synthesis of art, sociological imagination, commitment to social justice, openness to challenge and willingness to reflect on personal troubles in a transparent, public way in the sociological praxes of participants in this project encapsulates the spirit of the Gramscian 'organic' public sociologist.

References

Alexander, V.D. and Bowler, A.E. (2014) 'Art at the crossroads: the arts in society and the sociology of art', *Poetics*, 43(1): 1–19, doi: 10.1016/j.poetic.2014.02.003.

Becker, H. (1973) *Outsiders*, New York: Free Press.

Burawoy, M. (2005) 'For public sociology', *American Sociological Review*, 70(1): 4–28.

Burawoy, M. (2012) 'From Max Weber to public sociology', in Soeffner, H.G. (ed) *Transnationale Vergesellschaftungen*, Springer VS: Wiesbaden.

Connell, R. and Messerschmidt, J.W. (2005) 'Hegemonic masculinity: rethinking the concept', *Gender and Society*, 19(6): 829–859, doi: 10.1177/0891243205278639.

Damer, S. (2000) 'Engineers of the human machine: the social practice of council housing management, 1895–1935', *Urban Studies*, 37(11): 2007–2016, doi: 10.1080/713707224.

Elliottt, K. (2016) 'Caring masculinities: theorizing and emerging concept', *Men and Masculinities*, 19(3): 240–259, doi: 10.1177/1097184X15576203.

Falk, R.F. and Miller, N.B. (1998) 'The reflexive self: a sociological perspective', *Roeper Review*, 20(3): 150–153, doi: 10.1080/02783199809553881.

Foucault, M. (1979) *Discipline and Punish: The Birth of the Prison*, New York: Vintage Books.

Freire, P. (1970) *Pedagogy of the Oppressed*, New York: Herder and Herder.

Fuller, A., Foskett, R., Paton, K. and Maringe, F. (2008) '"Barriers" to participation in higher education? Depends who you ask and how', *Widening Participation and Lifelong Learning*, 10(2): 6–17.

Giddens, A. (1991) *The Consequences of Modernity*, Cambridge: Polity Press.

Goffman, E. (1961) *Asylums: Essays on the Social Situation of Mental Health Patients and Other Inmates*, New York: Anchor Books.

Goffman, E. (1963) *Stigma: Notes on the Management of a Spoiled Identity*, New York: Anchor Books.

Gottlieb, R. (ed) (1989) *An Anthology of Western Marxism: From Lukacs and Gramsci to Socialist-Feminism*, Oxford: Oxford University Press.

Gramsci, A. (1971) *Selections from the Prison Notebooks of Antonio Gramsci*, New York: International Publishers.

Herman, E. and Chomsky, N. (1995) *Manufacturing Consent: The Political Economy of the Mass Media*, New York: Pantheon Books.

Holmwood, J. (2007) 'Sociology as public discourse and professional practice: a critique of Michael Burawoy', *Sociological Theory*, 25(1), 46–66.

Hoschchild, A. (1983) *The Managed Heart: Commercialization of Human Feeling*, Berkeley: University of California Press, doi: 10.1111/j.1467-9558.2007.00297.x.

Kimmel, M. (2013) *Angry White Men: American Masculinity at the End of an Era*, New York: Nation Books.

Klaehn, J. and Mullen, A. (2010) 'The Propaganda Model and Sociology: Understanding the Media and Society', *Sociology Faculty Publications*, 5.

Lozano, A.A. (2017) 'Reframing the public sociology debate: towards collaborative and decolonial praxis', *Current Sociology*, 66(1): 92–109, doi: 10.1177/0011392117715897.

Miller, D. (2006) 'Propaganda and the "terror threat" in the UK', in Poole, E. and Richardson, J.E. (eds) *Muslims and the News Media*, London: IB Tauris.

Noy, D. (2009) 'The contradictions of public sociology: a view from a graduate student at Berkeley', *The American Sociologist*, 40: 234–248, doi: 10.1007/s12108-009-9074-1.

Petray, T. and Halbert, K. (2013) 'Teaching engagement: reflections on sociological praxis', *Journal of Sociology*, 49(4): 441–445, doi: 10.1177/1440783313504055.

Puhl, R. and Brownell, K.D. (2001)'Bias, discrimination and obesity', *Obesity Research*, 9(12): 788–805, doi: 10.1038/oby.2001.108.

Reed-Bouley, J., Wernli, M. and Sather, P. (2012) 'Student employment and perceptions of service learning', *Journal of Service-Learning in Higher Education*, 1: 6–29.

Sagan, O. (2012) 'Connection and reparation: narratives of art practice in the lives of mental health service users', *Counselling Psychology Quarterly*, 25(3): 239–249', doi: 10.1080/09515070.2012.703128.

Spandler, H., Anderson, J. and Sapey, B. (2015) *Madness, Distress and the Politics of Disablement*, Bristol: Policy Press.

Stenglin, M. (2007) 'Making art accessible: opening up a whole new world', *Visual Communication*, 6(2): 201–213, doi: 10.1177/1470357207077182.

Stephenson, C., Stirling, J. and Wray, D. (2015) '"Working lives": the use of auto/biography in the development of a sociological imagination', *McGill Journal of Education*, 50(1), 161–180, doi: 10.7202/1036111ar.

Stice, E. and Shaw. H.E. (2002) 'Role of body dissatisfaction in the onset and maintenance of eating pathology: a synthesis of research findings', *Journal of Psychosomatic Research*, 53(5): 985–993, doi: 10.1016/S0022-3999(02)00488-9.

Trimikliniotis, N. (2018) 'Public sociology, social justice, and struggles in the era of austerity-and-crises', *International Social Work*, 63(1), 5–17, doi: 10.1177/0020872818782324.

Wright Mills, C. (1959) *The Sociological Imagination*, New York: Oxford University Press.

CASE III.4

Community Engagement: Cultivating Critical Awareness

Jim Crowther and Mae Shaw

Introduction: theorising practice

We are writing as teachers and academics with substantial experience over many years (50 years combined) on undergraduate and postgraduate programmes of professional community education. This chapter is derived from that experience and developed from *Community Engagement: A Critical Guide for Practitioners* (Shaw and Crowther, 2017), a practical resource intended to guide workers as they confront the contemporary challenges of community engagement.

The formation of professional community education services in Scotland was an outcome of the 1975 Alexander Report on Adult Education: The Challenge of Change (Scottish Education Department, 1975), which was adopted by most local authorities. It was not until early 2000 that the term went largely out of favour in the context of local government reform. Whilst the term 'community education' has been largely abandoned in policy in Scotland, and other parts of the UK, it still carries historical resonance as a form of educational work rooted in the lives of real people, whatever the contingencies of context. It therefore continues to raise expectations of a curriculum that draws creatively on people's experiences in order to enlarge the space for cultivating and sustaining critical community engagement.

These aspirations, however, are increasingly subject to competing rationalities. First, they are at odds with the realities of contemporary higher education in the UK. We are based in a research-intensive university, operating within a wider system of marketised higher education. In this context, the professional locus of our work, and the ideological commitments that inform it, tend to be marginal at best; at worst, surplus to institutional requirements. In addition, changing terms and conditions of employment – towards casualisation and competitiveness – do not engender confidence in the future of such programmes. On the other hand, legislative arrangements that have embedded 'community engagement' in much public policy (see Scottish Government, 2015 Institute for Government, 2015) continue to sustain a 'market' for these kinds of programmes, whilst policy commitments to 'widening access' and 'lifelong learning' continue to receive at least rhetorical support within the university sector.

Universities have always been contradictory places, harbouring critical knowledges as well as commodified ones and, whilst the space of the former is constantly under threat, it has not yet been entirely eliminated. Indeed, nationally and internationally, there are challenges to the instrumentalism of commodified education in universities (Cowden and Singh, 2013; Collini, 2018; Darder, 2018). In our own context, undergraduate and postgraduate Programmes of community education have historically been validated both by the university and the appropriate professional body, so they are firmly located at the interface between academic and vocational standards; between theory and practice. We have found over time that these different, sometimes divergent, demands at best create a productive tension that has been at the core of our teaching, our writing and our relationships with the broader field of practice. This dynamic forces us to be dialectical in our thinking and in our practice – a discipline we have endeavoured to pass on to our students.

One way in which we characterise this dialectical relationship is through the notion of 'theorising practice': the role of theory in problematising practice and vice versa. Except in the most instrumental of cases, practitioners do not put theory into practice in any straightforward way; they put themselves into practice. This suggests a need to think critically and carefully about what role community education fulfils in particular times and places; in whose interests, who benefits, and with what implications. Such reflexivity presupposes the capacity to think politically and to engage in ideological analysis. It also means that practitioners need to develop the confidence, skills and knowledge to apply these critical understandings in and to practice. In general terms, we consider that an engagement with significant theoretical frameworks, an awareness of important historical traditions and an empathetic identification with the social reality of marginalised groups are all key elements in cultivating the kind of critical awareness that is necessary for practitioners to engage with changing communities of place, interest or identity.

Many of our students are non-traditional in the sense that they come to higher education after, or at the same time as, activism in their own communities. This experience provides a rich and diverse fulcrum for exploring the critical connections between personal experience and political structures; macro-level decisions and micro-level consequences; the potential for personal agency within structural constraints of power. We regard the role of practitioners in seeking to make these connections to be a core feature of competent professional practice. In this interpretation, the community education practitioner is conceived as an active educational agent rather than simply an agent of various policy interventions. This position necessarily creates tensions and dilemmas that need to be confronted, requiring practitioners to engage strategically and creatively with the politics of policy, whilst simultaneously attempting to enlarge the democratic spaces available for genuine community engagement. It also has particular implications for the university curriculum within which it is located.

A critical curriculum for community engagement

In its deceptively simple sense, community engagement is at the heart of any community education endeavour, projecting an image of mutuality and collectively determined action. It is a basic tenet of both professional practice and academic study in this area. However, community engagement in policy and practice must be seen as historically specific, ideologically contested and contextually specific. In this sense, it needs to be explored before it is 'espoused' (Plant, 1974). As a policy framework, for example, it has become increasingly attractive to a range of institutions and interests for a variety of reasons that have as much to do with 'efficiency savings' as democratic purpose. But it is also potentially an important component of local democracy. The parameters of such potential are necessarily contingent on the wider politics of the state, and it is now evident that the changed nature of the contemporary state has dramatically reconfigured relations between state institutions (including those that employ professional practitioners) and communities.

Many commentators argue that we are now living through a 'late' neoliberal economic phase in the UK, as in other 'mature' liberal democratic states, which has very particular consequences for processes of community engagement (for example Byrne, 2017). This account suggests a move beyond the now common introduction of markets and market principles into all aspects of social and democratic life, to a context in which many civil society organisations (including community groups) themselves reflect, and in some cases project, the characteristics and preoccupations of finance capital; where all activities are justified against a template of accruing economic advantage for individuals as economic actors. In this sense, social investment, austerity and localism could be said to operate in conjunction to construct a financialised identity amongst community groups, a precondition for assuming their 'responsibilised' status. As Meade (2017:226) warns, however, insufficient attention has been given to what the 'subjectifying force' of such practices *does* both to communities and to practitioners in terms of 'knowing' community engagement 'as a means by which communities are problematised, targeted and mobilised in the name of outcomes such as empowerment'.

According to McGimpsey (2017) there are two distinct elements in this subjectifying process: first, the definition of local organisations as public service providers in competition with each other; second, co-production: an injunction to make greater use of voluntary effort, community organisation and local social relations. A wide range of policy tools and practices has been devised by government think tanks and consultants to 'roll out' co-producing processes – variously involving communities in commissioning, budget-setting and funding, 'incorporating user knowledge and experience in service design, transfer of public assets or managerial responsibilities, and direct participation in the provision of services' (71). In this model, 'resilience', for example, is framed as a personalised trait for coping with misfortune, which teaches people 'how to invest in themselves so that they are a better and more marketable product than their [more vulnerable] neighbour' (Tronto, 2017: 33). Community engagement offers the same benefits via 'citizen sourcing' (Byrne, 2017: 355), which brings 'added value' to managing service delivery – or deciding where austerity cuts should fall! In this context, community engagement might be seen as a convenient means of mediating transactions between civil society and government rather than offering any serious democratic potential. Furthermore, as government comes to resemble merely 'a platform' that provides resources (typically, information and communications technology) that can help citizens better govern themselves and others, 'utility maximisation' comes to be seen as a credible objective.

The ideological elasticity of 'community', and the historical predilection of government to seek 'community solutions' to seemingly intractable social and economic problems, can all too easily facilitate serious slippage between 'engagement' (enacted as a managerial procedure) and 'democracy' (as a political process), with the former ultimately undermining the possibility of the latter. As Brown (2015: 128) argues, 'Democracy defined as inclusion, participation, [engagement] ... [excludes] all concern with justice and the designation of purposes, along with pluralistic struggles over these things.' In this way, she argues, democracy is reduced to a means of managing competitive relations, and stripped of its historical potential for political contestation about the terms on which public life is organised. Significantly for our argument, this happens 'not just through the mere *application* of market principles to nonmarket fields, but also through the *conversion* of political processes, subjects, categories, and principles to economic ones' (158). In addition, economisation replaces a political lexicon with a market one so there is no available language in which to express dissatisfaction, never mind dissent: 'vanquishing a vocabulary of power' in favour of a spurious consensus (129).

Against what might be regarded as 'overwhelmingly pessimistic' assessments of the democratic potential of relations between civil society organisations and state institutions, however, O'Hare (2018: 211) warns that 'outright dismissal of community engagement as a cynical attempt to neutralise local activism or to simply extract legitimacy for regeneration programmes' seriously underestimates the potential for autonomy by community actors by framing them as 'entirely passive subjects' of governance mechanisms. He argues instead for a more nuanced approach to community engagement that limits the risk of 'capture'. In any case, ceding agency too readily ignores the fact that 'activation of the citizenry, however narrowly conceived, always carries within it the seeds of resistance and counter-conduct' (Meade, 2017: 239).

Community engagement, historically, is positioned at the interface between civil society and the institutions of the state: subject both to the imperatives of policy and the demands of politics. Practitioners must learn, therefore, how to negotiate the choices and dilemmas this inevitably creates, and to assess the extent of relative autonomy available to themselves and the communities with which they work. It is a perpetual challenge to avoid being either naively optimistic or despairingly pessimistic. Engagement strategies can either co-opt and neutralise political action by communities, or proceed in ways that further their social, economic and political interests. A curriculum that sufficiently addresses the politics of democratic participation must therefore seek to problematise the framing of 'community' in policy, so that student practitioners can begin to critically assess the parameters of political agency for community groups as a necessary precondition for formulating appropriate responses. In practice contexts, this may mean developing the tools to translate community engagement strategies creatively, or to oppose them imaginatively and resolutely. The terrain of community engagement might usefully be seen, therefore, as an 'incubator for politics' (Hoggett et al, 2008): the site in which grievances are generated and responses devised; where local activists and politicians develop; where struggles for social justice grow and decline, and where reasonable differences can be negotiated.

We argue that in order to expand the democratic imaginary that animates this strategic approach, it is necessary to cultivate what the American sociologist C. Wright Mills (1959) calls the 'sociological imagination': the skill and determination to make the critical connections between 'private troubles' and 'public issues'; between personal experience and the wider society; between cause and effect. Such an expanded vision immediately raises critical questions about how community engagement as a policy discourse is framed in the current context, by whom, to what ends, in whose interests and with what effects. In our view, a curriculum that adequately prepares community-based practitioners for the politics of practice should seek to resource this kind of critical approach. Such an approach is intended both to encourage students to engage with theoretical frameworks that enable them to take into account the 'big picture', whilst also modelling an approach they can adopt in critically analysing the 'small picture' that confronts the communities in which they practise.

Framing problems and formulating solutions

Community education practitioners today work primarily across a range of voluntary sector projects (though some local authorities continue to provide educational opportunities) concerned with policy priorities such as mental health, disability, employability, literacy, wellbeing, housing, homelessness, social inclusion and diversity. Whilst such organisations often claim (and aspire) to engage with communities to identify their needs, concerns and problems, the reality is clearly that needs and problems have often already been defined elsewhere. Problem definition is a process of image-making or 'framing', to do with attributing cause, blame and responsibility (Manning, 1987). Definitions reflect wider social, political and economic concerns, and are calculated to gain support for particular interests, which are not always visible. Framing problems in particular ways means that some factors, which might be very relevant to why something is seen or presented as a problem, are deliberately left out of the picture. In the process of policy formation, the boundaries of response become established, influencing to a greater or lesser extent the ways in which people make sense of their own and others' lives.

Much has been written about the ways in which pejorative images of those most removed from power, particularly the poor, have been strategically mobilised to justify punitive measures. Such images can become normalised and internalised in mutually reinforcing ways (for example Tyler, 2013; Hanley, 2016). At the same time, it is evident that the demonisation of the poor, and the reality of their deteriorating material circumstances, have also produced counter-narratives that shine a spotlight on the inevitable social consequences of a corporate culture that enriches an increasingly small proportion of people at the top at the expense of the vast majority of those at the bottom (for example Institute for Fiscal Studies, 2018). This has arguably begun to shift public perception of what constitutes the 'deserving' and 'undeserving', offering fertile ground for critical educational engagement around the politics of claims-making.

It is clear that the way in which social problems are framed inevitably determines their potential solutions: if 'the problem' is framed in terms of personal behaviour, the solution is behavioural change; if it is framed in terms of inadequate institutional responses, the solution is institutional change; if it is framed in terms of structural inequality, the solution is wider economic and political change. Conversely, 'available' political solutions are active in determining what are presented as social problems. In reality, most problems have personal, institutional and political dimensions, but if policy frameworks limit discussion to the micro (private) level of personal experience, this makes macro (public) analysis almost impossible because it is put largely beyond consideration. Most importantly, once a particular 'discourse' has been established and entered into the public consciousness, it is very difficult to shift or challenge, since people begin to internalise it, without necessarily recognising they are doing so.

A potentially significant role for educational work with students and practitioners in the field is to begin to reframe *in political terms* those issues that are currently presented as social problems: to talk and think about problems as if they are political issues and not just personal characteristics. Community engagement lends itself well to this kind of analysis: if community engagement is the solution, what is the problem perceived to be? If lack of community engagement is seen as the problem, what is the cause, who is to blame and whose responsibility is it to rectify the situation? Are significant f/actors omitted from the picture? If community groups were to address these wider political questions before responding to pleas or demands for 'engagement', their response may be more circumspect and strategic. They may also be more effective in amplifying their own counter-claims and concerns into the public sphere, as has been the case with the recent Grenfell fire tragedy in London, which exposed the politics of housing in a very public way, arguably changing the parameters of the debate – at least in the short term. Such occurrences can also present moments of recognition, when what people think, experience and see around them seems to contradict how such things are presented in policy (and in the media). This kind of cognitive dissonance can be the beginning of politicisation. What this example reveals is a fundamental dynamic between what is understood as private and what is regarded as public.

There is a useful distinction to be made between 'open' and 'closed' social problems (Manning, 1987). Open social problems occur when different groups are competing for the right to define the problem. Closed social problems occur when political debate no longer occurs (or is ruled out) and only one definition prevails. There is of course some productive tension between open and closed social problems. What has been closed can be opened up (for example reproductive rights) and vice versa. In addition, 'new' public issues are discovered as groups gain confidence and the opportunity to collectively voice their personal experience of gender, sexuality, or disability, for example (Beresford, 2016). Conversely, issues such as poverty, health or housing can be turned back into 'private troubles' if people come to see it as 'normal' that they make their own private arrangements in place of what were once thought of, and funded, as public services. This suggests a strategic role for practitioners in ensuring that what are presented and normalised as 'private troubles' for those most removed from power are also kept alive as 'public issues'. This might involve creating collective opportunities for people to develop their analytical and presentational skills so that they can develop a shared understanding of the causes of the problems they experience and project them effectively onto a wider stage.

Whatever their limitations, community education practitioners are often still in an advantageous position to provide increasingly rare collective and prefigurative spaces for people to think for themselves by thinking together, offering resources to challenge negative or disempowering images, and supporting their self-organisation.

Education for citizenship or learning for democratic engagement

The challenge for professional practitioners then involves working between the intentions of policy and the needs and demands of communities, whilst seeking to introduce, where necessary, a critical perspective to both in a way that widens the scope for collective autonomy and agency. In the Scottish context, the historical legacy of building democracy from the grassroots has been, even if only at a rhetorical level, regarded as important to the philosophy and policy of community education (see Crowther et al, 2017). The previously mentioned Alexander Report, for example, argued the need to educationally resource dissent from established practices, because expressions of difference were vital to a thriving, pluralistic, democratic way of life. One way in which contemporary policy has framed and, arguably, depoliticised the democratic agenda has been in the focus on 'education for citizenship' as distinct from 'learning for democracy'. Whilst there may be common features between the two, we would argue that they are very different in terms of purpose, process and curriculum.

Education for citizenship as a policy imperative can act to reduce the notion of citizenship to one of civic-minded behaviour, focussing primarily on motivating and resourcing voluntary effort. Whilst the development of a culture of support and mutuality in and across communities is a necessary resource for democratic life, the 'turn' to citizenship-as-volunteering, particularly in the context of austerity, can simply substitute state withdrawal from public life with the more limited resources which communities might struggle to offer. The logic of this position is that the quality of community life may be overly assessed through the prism of 'civic mindedness', with education for citizenship aimed at addressing (or, in some cases, disciplining) so-called hard-to-reach, apathetic and demotivated groups.

In addition, education for citizenship is primarily concerned with rights and responsibilities; procedures and participation in established processes and institutions. Its frame of reference tends to be the formal rights ascribed (or denied) to those eligible to vote in the context of liberal representative democracy. The problem, according to some contemporary versions of this model, is seen in terms of protecting democratic institutions from either 'too little participation' (thereby undermining the legitimacy of these institutions) or 'too much participation' (which might end up challenging the basis of representation). The charge of too little participation tends to be framed largely in terms of voter apathy – as distinct from the unresponsiveness of the political system to a genuine plurality of interests – thus personalising the political (see Lawrence, 2015). On the other hand, the narrative of 'too much participation' draws upon a more optimistic but no less problematic estimation of political agency, which is seen to lead to populist participation of the 'wrong' kind. Responses to Brexit in the UK and Trump in the USA are regarded as the most obvious examples of this version of populism, with both said to represent a critique of mainstream elites. It could be argued, however, that anger directed towards political parties and institutions might constitute a very rational and legitimate response to conventional democratic processes that have serially failed to adequately protect people's interests – the rightful 'return of the repressed' as Streeck (2017) puts it.

Gramsci's (1971) notion of the interregnum may be a fruitful way of thinking about the current context and its contradictions. According to Gramsci, an interregnum is an indicator of the decline of hegemony of the ruling forces and a stalemate in the assertion of a counter-hegemony: 'The crisis consists precisely in the fact that the old is dying but the new cannot yet be born; in this interregnum a great variety of morbid symptoms appear' (1971: 276). Notwithstanding divergence or dispute about what constitutes the current interregnum, the volatility of the contemporary context can certainly be said to offer a space where something new can emerge, as can be seen in many parts of the world for good and ill. In this scenario, critical community engagement presents possibilities for developing counter-hegemonic visions of social organisation in which communities of endurance and struggle have a part to play as torchbearers for the 'new yet to be born'.

Reframing 'education for citizenship' in terms of 'learning for democracy' can potentially provide a more open educational agenda that is concerned with extending the ways in which citizens can imagine and begin to actively shape the type of society they want to live in, and to reject unacceptable alternatives. Fundamentally, this involves the capacity to understand and challenge wider relations of power, not least how they work on and in us. Learning for democracy involves exploring how unequal relations of power shape what we mean by democracy as well as expanding on what it might mean to address these inequalities.

Conclusion: cultivating critical awareness

In seeking to provide opportunities for student practitioners to gain access to a broad range of perspectives and arguments – and to develop and share their own – we aim to cultivate a critical culture that encourages them to theorise practice and to identify the dilemmas and choices with which they are presented. There is no option of a politics-free education. As Freire (1972) taught, education is never neutral: it is always selecting particular aspects of culture as significant and worthy, whilst making invisible whole areas of human experience that are not valued. Seeking to make power visible may be one practical way in which people can cultivate the critical awareness required to enact democracy as a political process of contestation.

In conclusion, if community engagement is to be part of a genuinely progressive mode of social organisation, there is a need to generate pre-figurative spaces – democratic, collective, convivial, compassionate, supportive – where the previously unthinkable can become the basis of a critical awareness that can make a positive difference. This suggests that students and practitioners need to practise critical engagement themselves: engaging dialectically with policy in ways that strengthen democratic political processes; engaging reflexively with communities so that problem-solving policy imperatives do not become a substitute for problem-posing; and engaging honestly and strategically with the problems and possibilities of their own professional position in difficult times.

References

Beresford, P. (2016) *All Our Welfare: Towards Participatory Social Policy*, Bristol: Policy Press.

Brown, W. (2015) *Undoing the Demos: Neoliberalism's Stealth Revolution*, Cambridge, MA: Zone Books.

Byrne, C. (2017) 'Neoliberalism as an object of political analysis: an ideology, a mode of regulation or a governmentality?', *Policy & Politics*, 45(3): 343–360.

Collini, S. (2018) 'In UK universities there is a daily erosion of integrity', *The Guardian*, 24 April.

Cowden, S. and Singh, G. (2013) *Acts of Knowing: Critical Pedagogy In and Against the University*, London: Bloomsbury Press.

Crowther, J., Ackland, A., Petrie, M. and Wallace, D. (2017) 'Adult education, community and learning for democracy in Scotland', in *Oxford Encyclopaedia of Education*, Oxford: Oxford University Press, doi:10.1093/qcrefore/9780190264093.013.253.

Darder, A. (2018) *A Student Guide to Pedagogy of the Oppressed*, London: Bloomsbury Press.

Freire, P. (1972) *The Pedagogy of the Oppressed*, London: Penguin.

Gramsci, A. (1971) *Prison Notebooks*, London: Lawrence and Wishart.

Hanley, L. (2016) *Respectable: The Experience of Class*, London: Penguin.

Hoggett, P., Mayo, M. and Miller, C. (2008) *The Dilemmas of Development Work: Ethical Challenges in Regeneration*, Bristol: Policy Press.

Institute for Fiscal Studies (2018) *Poverty and Inequality in the UK*.

Institute for Government (2015) *Smarter Engagement: Harnessing Public Voice in Policy Challenges*, PWC.

Lawrence, M. (2015) *Political Inequality*, London: Institute for Public Policy Research.

McGimpsey, I. (2017) 'Late neoliberalism: delineating a policy regime', *Critical Social Policy*, 37(1): 64–68.

Manning, N. (1987) 'What is a social problem?', in Loney, M. et al (eds) *The State or the Market: Politics and Welfare in Contemporary Britain* (1st edn), Sage: London: 18–23.

Meade, E. (2017) 'The re-signification of state-funded community development in Ireland: a problem of austerity and neoliberal government', *Critical Social Policy*.

O'Hare, P. (2018) 'Resisting the 'long-arm' of the state? Spheres of capture and opportunities for autonomy in community governance', *International Journal of Urban and Regional Research*, 42(2): 210–225.

Plant, R. (1974) *Community and Ideology: An Essay in Applied Social Philosophy*, London: Routledge & Kegan Paul.

Scottish Education Department (1975) *Adult Education: The Challenge of Change*, Edinburgh: HMSO.

Scottish Government (2015) *Community Empowerment (Scotland) Act*.

Shaw, M. and Crowther, J. (2017) *Community Engagement: A Critical Guide for Practitioners*, concept.lib.ed.ac.uk

Streeck, W. (2017) 'The return of the repressed as the beginning of the end of neoliberal capitalism', in Geiselberger, H. (ed) *The Great Regression*. Cambridge: Polity Press: 157–172.

Tronto, J. (2017) 'There is an alternative: *homines curans* and the limits of neoliberalism', *International Journal of Care and Caring*, 1(1): 27–43.

Tyler, I. (2013) *Revolting Subjects: Abjection and Resistance in Neoliberal Britain*, London: Zed Books.

Wright Mills, C. (1959) *The Sociological Imagination*, Oxford: Oxford University Press.

CASE III.5

Reflections on our Critical Service Learning Provision: Is it Critical or Are We Social Justice Dreamers?

Sharon Hutchings and Andrea Lyons Lewis

Introduction

In 2013 we ran a small but successful service learning pilot in the department of sociology at Nottingham Trent University (NTU). Immediately following the pilot, service learning was added to our BA Sociology, BA Criminology and MA Public Sociology provision as core modules. In brief, we argue our version of service learning sits within a social justice orientation, often referred to as critical service learning. Simply put, this involves students working in partnership with our not-for-profit community on social justice issues for the purpose of social change and mutual benefit for community partners and students. These are big claims. Whether the service learning we do at NTU genuinely extends beyond the dream of social justice is at the heart of this chapter.

The chapter begins by defining service learning followed by an exploration of the traditional versus critical service learning debate, an overview of our practices and values and why and how we do it. To illustrate and interrogate our practices we introduce three projects to highlight the traditional-critical learning debate and, finally, offer ideas for discussion on how to build sustainable and critical service learning. In presenting these reflections we hope to re-energise our social justice aspirations, share our practices and extend opportunities for critical dialogue with those engaged in public sociology education.

Defining service learning and introducing the traditional versus the critical debate

There are many schools, colleges and universities delivering many versions of service learning. Students provide a 'service' to the community for a specific purpose or goal and, in return, learn through the experience. Service learning can be embedded within the curriculum for disciplinary connections, with or without academic credit and/or part of volunteering strategies. At the *least* critical level, it can be described as an experiential learning opportunity; students learn whilst providing a 'service' for, or determined by, the community. The 'service' can take a variety of forms including traditional research, planning an event, promoting/evaluating new initiatives for partners. Whilst relatively new to the UK, service learning has a long history in North American universities where it is largely embedded and resourced as a university-wide endeavour. In other words, it has become institutionalised (Furco, 1996; Jacoby, 2014). Importantly, we recognise the label of service learning as new to the UK, but acknowledge the practice is not. There are many models of experiential, radical, liberatory and community education; therefore, a challenge is to express with clarity what we do and why we do it to minimise any 'conceptual imprecision' (Mooney and Edwards, 2001: 181). This, we hope, will encourage dialogue and practices facilitating intentional movement towards critical service learning.

For our version of service learning we invite the not-for-profit sector in the city to put forward projects they would like students to work on and, in return, students engage in live projects gaining experience and disciplinary insights along the way. To illustrate with an example: in 2017 a group of students worked with an organisation to produce a welcome pack for new migrants moving to the city. They were tasked with creating a 'welcome pack' for new arrivals so the new arrivals could become orientated and well informed about living in Nottingham in a useful and inclusive way. The students were able to make disciplinary connections, develop new skills, appreciate the issues within our city and gain an experience that was situated in the world of their discipline, studies, city and, for one of them, their lived experience. The community partner had a group of students that were able to research and develop the welcome pack that otherwise may not have been produced. This example meets the particular criteria of *mutual benefit* that Furco argues makes service learning distinctive from other forms of experiential education:

> Service-learning programs are distinguished from other approaches to experiential education by their intention to equally benefit the provider and the recipient of the service as well as to ensure equal focus on both the service being provided and the learning that is occurring. (Furco, 1996: 10)

In addition to mutual benefit we claim a social justice and change orientation to guide our service learning practices. This is the key distinction between traditional and critical service learning.

Traditional service learning emphasises the change experienced by students as they engage in their service. The arguments presented here often parallel those directed at the charity/voluntary sector; whilst arguably essential in a neoliberal world, they offer limited critique or challenge to the conditions creating the need for charity/volunteering. This is mirrored in traditional service learning experiences. Students may experience difference through their service, develop interpersonal skills, have increased awareness of inequalities and make disciplinary connections – but movement towards social change is not the key purpose. The traditional approach is 'depoliticised' (Mitchell, 2008: 51) in so far as there is no expectation of a structural or critical exploration of the root causes of the service (Mitchell, 2008; Butin, 2010; Petray and Halbert, 2013; Barrera et al, 2017). This absence of attention to the root causes is problematic; it may reinforce privilege or worsen the issue (Marullo, 1999; Mitchell, 2008; Butin, 2010; Jerome, 2012; Ledwith, 2015).

Critical service learning is best defined as 'a critical approach that is unapologetic in its aim to dismantle structures of injustice.' (Mitchell, 2008: 50) Whilst there are concerns over the term 'service' in much of the literature, something the chapter returns to, the emphasis is on social change within the community *and* the student (Mooney and Edwards, 2001; Mitchell, 2008; Butin, 2015; Martin and Pirbhai-Illich, 2015). Beyond the explicit change orientation, two further elements need to be present and they are critical reflection and mutual benefit (Asghar and Rowe, 2016). By reflecting on the 'service' experience, students may develop what Freire refers to as 'conscientização', critical consciousness, 'a level of insight at which people recognise oppression as a structural problem rather than an individual failing' (Ledwith, 2015: xi).

Both traditional and critical service learning emphasise the student experience which is also firmly at the forefront of the higher education (HE) employability agenda. Here there are some tensions for us. Whilst we recognise the possibilities of service learning and employability outcomes, we do not prioritise student experience over partner experience and social change. Additionally, our concerns resonate with those fears expressed by Giroux (2014) that the impact of the employability agenda has

> reshaped the connection between knowledge and power while rendering faculty and students as professional entrepreneurs and budding customers. The notion of the university as a center of critique and a vital democratic public sphere that cultivates the knowledge, skills, and values necessary for the production of a democratic polity is giving way to a view of the university as a marketing machine essential to the production of neoliberal subjects. (Concannon and Finely, 2015: 12)

These are some of our worries if we do not maintain a social justice focus and work towards a critical approach.

The aspirations we hold for our service learning are therefore challenging in the current HE environment and, as Butin (2015) rightly clams, often results in social justice dreaming. Our claims that it is situated towards the critical, social justice end, that student engagement is politicised and understood within a broader social, political and economic context, needs to be reflected upon and challenged. Whilst we explicitly set out the social justice dream in the learning and teaching, the assessment criteria and the partnership work it is at times a dream rather than a reality – it is a struggle. If we accept Burawoy's passing reference to service learning as 'the prototype' for bringing 'sociology into a conversation with publics' (2004: 7) it brings allies and a welcome community of practice for service learning and the struggle feels less isolating. This is the kind of sociology we want to do but we must be honest – there are times when our service learning reflects Butin's concerns that; 'what educators dream of – a critical service learning able to ameliorate real-world inequalities may be a case of their dreaming being fulfilled, rather than their dreams' (Butin, 2015: 5).

Why critical service learning?

The answer is threefold. Firstly, Nottingham city faces significant social and economic problems; it is one of the most deprived cities in England (Department for Communities and Local Government, 2015). Secondly, we want opportunities for our students to engage practically and with agency in their community and their disciplinary understandings. Thirdly, it is the kind of sociology we want to do: 'Sociological imagination may expose social structures as the source of our malaise, but it is not sufficient for political action. We also need a political imagination to turn personal issues into public issues' (Burawoy 2012: x).

When we ran the service learning pilot, awareness of public sociology was emerging in our department and austerity measures were in full force; this was the backdrop to the introduction of service learning. It provided a disciplinary focus and a political energy for service learning. We hoped students would engage and, in doing so, 'gain a public voice and come to grips with their own power as individuals and political agents' (Giroux, 2002: 105). For us it presented the opportunity to align the values we hold alongside what feels like 'a natural extension of the sociological enterprise' (Nyden et al, 2012: 13).

How do we practice service learning?

Following the successful but very small pilot in 2013 we immediately scaled up to three core modules across the department numbering 300 year 2 students, 15 postgraduate students and approximately 30 partners. We work to a calendar, not academic year, as the partners and projects need to be in place for the beginning of each new academic year leaving us only the summer to build relationships with our community. This does, however, place significant demands on time and resources and should not be underestimated. In term one students encounter the literature, ideas and challenges of service learning within the context of our city, social justice and sociology. Late in term one, partners introduce their projects to students and, shortly after, students select and begin work on them in term two. The actual service varies according to the organisation, but examples include:

Nottingham Citizens:	researching Islamophobia, participation and public life
Himmah:	gathering data to evidence racist attacks on taxi drivers in Nottingham
Nottinghamshire Sexual Assault Centre:	raising awareness of rape and sexual assault
Renewal Trust:	building support mechanisms for new arrivals to the city
Mojatu:	campaigning to end female genital mutilation

Ideally, students do not fill core business nor draw resources from the organisation. During their period of service, they are supported by academic staff and community partners through structured workshops and meetings. We do not expect organisations to dedicate resources to assessing or intensively supervising the work of students. During the service period, students might typically dedicate 5–10 hours a week to the service activity.

In term one students encounter theoretical and conceptual knowledge of service learning, social justice and the social, political and economic context of the city. In term two students complete their service with dedicated opportunities for reflection and consideration of the root causes of their service. There is a formative group presentation mid-way through term two, which partners are invited to attend and feed back to students. There are two summative academic assessments, a group poster (30 per cent) and an individual reflective report (70 per cent). The final work is an agreed output for the partner. This must be submitted but no academic credit is attached.

Interrogating our critical service learning claims: are we dreaming of critical service learning rather than living it?

In response to Butin's (2015) challenge that critical service learning often falls short of its social justice dreams we have reflected on the integrity of our social justice claims. We accept 'what educators dream of – a critical service learning able to ameliorate real-world inequalities may be a case of their dreaming being fulfilled, rather than their dreams' (Butin, 2015: 5). So, to help illustrate our critical service learning claims (and their failings) we have taken the three core orientations identified by Mitchell (2008), that distinguish traditional from critical service learning; a social change orientation, working to redistribute power and developing authentic relationships. Set against each of these orientations are three service learning projects to illustrate and to interrogate our claims.

A social change orientation

This is understood as an emphasis on change in both the student and the community. Students work with partners on social justice projects, understand and reflect on why the service exists in the first place and, in doing so, deepen their critical consciousness. The case study below highlights some key moments of change.

Hollaback Chalk Walk

Reported incidents of hate crime have been on the increase in our city for a number of years. Since 2014 our students have engaged in a number of initiatives with local organisations and universities to research and work in solidarity against hate crime. The Chalk Walk project, part of a bigger campaign with Nottingham Citizens, resulted in Nottingham being the first police authority to record misogyny as a hate crime (Wood ,2018). Students were tasked with organising an action on the university campus where passers-by were invited to write, in chalk, reactions, comments relating to their experiences of street harassment. It was a powerful and participatory way to engage the public in outing their experiences bringing opportunity for changed awareness and solidarity. The student group were enormously energised and transformed by this action; we might suggest a new critical consciousness emerged from these experiences.

The Chalk Walk action allowed for the issue of sexual and street harassment to be understood in a wider political and social context. Did this campaign ignite our student's critical consciousness? Absolutely it did, they were part of the community experiencing the issue they were exploring, key to developing critical consciousness. Is this how we experience service learning generally? No, unfortunately, as we tend to work on multiple but discreet projects across the sector. It is, however, a great example of a social justice orientation resulting in both social change and student transformation. We can be encouraged by this but need to replicate the success.

Working to redistribute power

Mitchell (2008) argues little attention is given to issues of power in the traditional service learning relationship and, at times may replicate power imbalances present in the wider society. It may be in asking the community to work to the university academic year, the university curriculum and the university learning goals. Add to this a view that academic knowledge can 'fix' the community and you have a deficit model that may ultimately reproduce power and inequalities (Kahn and Westheimer, 1996; Pompa, 2002; Mitchell, 2008). Importantly power within all aspects of 'service' needs to be outed, understood and challenged. One project where we felt this shift in the balance of power is the Stand By Me initiative developed by Communities Inc. a social enterprise dedicated to tackling inequalities and building stronger communities.

Stand By Me. Communities Inc.

Stand By Me, developed by Communities Inc. works to inform bystanders on interventions that can be applied by anyone without putting themselves at risk as 'a practical way of disrupting and countering hate incidents, and supporting victims'. (Communities Inc, 2009). They recruited 35 intervention ambassadors who are now sharing their knowledge and expertise to raise awareness in the community. This cascade model creates opportunity to inform and empower but, importantly, is led by expertise in the community not the university. The service learning project is wholly dedicated to working to their agenda, their activities and their knowledge and expertise. Students have been tasked with introducing the Stand By Me initiative to the university, supporting the National Bystanders Awareness Week and we hope will continue beyond the academic year, something Butin (2015) suggests is evidence of critical service learning practice.

Admitting that our critical service learning may reinforce power differentials is tough and absolutely counter to all our hopes. On reflection, we acknowledge that the label and values underpinning 'service' are more troublesome than first imagined. It risks replicating the 'have-have not' paradigm that underlies many social problems' (Pompa, 2002: 68). This can be disrupted and we argue working with Communities Inc. achieved this on a number of levels. Firstly, they were the experts, this was their community-led initiative and we were invited to share it with our university. Opportunities for learning outside the academy, notably the National Bystanders Awareness Day on 13 March did what Pompa (2002: 75) suggests service learning can, 'cultivate a passion for social justice concerns' and our students got that from their partner not the university. This is not about the university dreaming but the community enacting their social justice dream.

Developing authentic relationships

The third orientation rests on the development of authentic relationships and for us the work of Freire is central. In taking his commitment to social change, based on a 'profound love for humanity' (Freire, 2000: 89) we do not diminish the place of love in the work we do. For some this may lack a certain academic robustness, but partnerships between the university and the community need to mirror the values and practices of a social justice agenda. This requires more than a commitment to learning goals, student experience and academic credentials. A long-term commitment to social justice built on Freirean notions of radical love whereby love is essential to dialogue and becomes radical when attached to a political project (Liambas, A. and Kaskaris, I., 2012) We suggest radical love is vital for building authentic relationships and it is this secular, Freirean notion of love that guides our authentic relationships (Cloke et al, 2010).

New Rose Associates and the real living wage for third sector workers

Sonia Long, CEO of New Rose Associates is exploring a city wide endeavour to begin discussions and actions on the pay of third sector workers. Our city has the lowest levels of annual disposable income in the UK, £12,232 compared to £19,432 (Office for National Statistics, 2018). Sonia is committed to initiating a dialogue here. The project seeks to establish a broad coalition of community members to build a shared commitment to action the real living wage across the sector. Students have built a working and respectful relationship with Sonia. It is wonderful to witness their respect and desire for social change emerge because of their trust and relationship with Sonia – they see her authenticity.

Butin (2015) places relationships at the heart of critical service learning. Without authentic relationships the consequences on the community, students and the issue can be disastrous, resulting in the loss of community partner, disengaged and apathetic students. Where we have built authentic relationships, we can plot the beginning, the ongoing journey, mutual respect and love, their mobile numbers are in our personal phones as Butin suggests they should be. But we need time to extend these conversations and build relationships beyond and outside the university. Authentic relationships like social justice cannot be achieved in one term but require resource and value commitments that need to be firmly agreed before undertaking such work. The risks of service learning becoming instrumental are very high without this.

Building sustainable critical service learning

Having established critical service learning as an ongoing value-based process for social justice and public sociology we offer a series of discussion points, insights and critical questions to challenge. They are simply openers for dialogue, not the definitive guide. If we could go back to the pilot we would not, under any circumstances, scale up service learning without agreement from the department to resource and commit to it. We are genuinely exhausted, and this means at times service learning has become instrumental, pragmatic and we have become social justice dreamers. But, we hope these reflections can reinvigorate, help present clear arguments for rethinking our practices and give occasion to reconnect with our early love for this work. In doing so bring 'Joy As An Act of Resistance' (Idles, 2018) back to our work creating genuine opportunity for critical service learning.

Service learning needs to be adequately resourced to support a social justice approach

The success of our pilot in 2013–2014 led to the immediate scaling up our service learning provision and this was done without any corresponding increase in staff and resources. Hamilton (2013: 27) rightly challenges Burawoy's vision of public sociology suggesting he ignores the 'material conditions of work in a university' and service learning with its heavy workloads and 'drag on professional careers' and does not make it an attractive route for colleagues. Ensure resources are committed to and then enact the dream. We are still dreaming of this.

Tackle issues of power

In claiming a social justice orientation, we must reaffirm the underpinning value of mutual benefit. Universities are keen to utilise the community for experiential opportunities, but it is important that they are not used as a 'cultural commodity' to simply enhance the student experience. Here the usefulness of taking a post-colonial lens helps acknowledge the questions of power and privilege that may exist between the community and the university (Sandmann et al, 2012). On a practical level, recognise the expertise held in the community, invite them into the university or, better still, take students to learn in places outside the university as an opportunity to challenge the banking concept of education.

Build opportunities for solidarity

Some of our colleagues are organic public sociologists and have existing relationships in the community. Make use of these links to support and develop opportunities for service learning. Find ways to build more authentic relationships outside the university, for example becoming trustees with community groups, advocates or activists within grassroots organisations. This sense of solidarity also needs to be extended to students, and we are reminded of the place of unconditional positive regard, and the essential attitudes for facilitating learning, in the work of Carl Rogers (Rogers, 2002).

Establish a steering group

We set up a steering group early on and we believe this is core to critical service learning endeavours, but it has not flourished. We would suggest this is a result of our partners and colleagues simply being too busy and a lack of institutional structures to support. Success here may address the 'cultural commodity' issue and imbalances of power as community knowledge and expertise could be brought to the table. We need a concerted effort here to make partnership work genuine. If we could work towards explicit agreement as to the purpose of the service learning with our partners this could bring the dream closer. At the moment, we do not have the time for the extended dialogue to identify the most pressing issues across the city but we accept this is necessary for a more sustainable social justice approach.

Use networks and alliances within the university

Find support within the department, school and wider university. Recent moves towards a public sociology orientation in our team has created a place for discussion at least. The team support and cherish service learning but it needs more concrete outcomes. A recent commitment by colleagues to mentor students on their service learning projects has been agreed and work loaded accordingly: a small move but one to build on. Beyond the sociology team we have shared our service learning dreams with senior managers, standards and quality teams, employment and placement teams. We have had some success here in so far as our university-wide volunteering team has recently committed to taking a critical service learning approach to their work. This gives us allies and a possible momentum for critical service learning in key strategic arenas.

Consider the risk involved in institutionalising service learning?

An extension of the ideas above relates to institutionalising service learning. Should we work towards this? We acknowledge that service learning has gained interest within the university but, having fought hard to maintain the integrity of a social justice approach, we might risk losing the right to direct it. This may prove challenging as we will need to work towards ensuring the community is not perceived as a 'cultural safari' or a 'highly innovative textbook' for students (Mitchell, 2008: 54; Petray and Herbert, 2013: 441).

Create opportunities to develop critical consciousness

If we want critical service learning to be understood by our students it needs, as Barrera et al (2017) state, to be built in to the curriculum. Our sociology students are generally good critical thinkers, but we hope their service learning experiences will further develop their critical consciousness. Working in the community may do this but we know students can successfully complete assessments even with limited engagement in their service and this is deeply troublesome. Some students see the world differently because of their service learning experiences but how far this challenges/raises their critical consciousness is debatable. Here the constraints of a marketised HE are deeply felt. How do we reconcile the lack of integrity in their service learning relationship but the success of their academic endeavours? We do not – we get very unsettled and frustrated by it. We could look to engage the community partners in the assessment process, but this brings a host of new problems and demands for our already stretched partners. We suggest some students develop a sense of 'empathy' if not yet critical consciousness, but this may be the first step towards a sense of social justice, so for now we will take that.

Build academic credibility and communities of practice for service learning

Service learning is sometimes perceived as lacking academic rigour. Those critical of service learning suggests it is due to an orientation to action rather than scholarly pursuits and a general resistance to theorising (Eby, 1998; Butin 2010). Of course, those of us living the service learning dream would argue otherwise, theory is essential to critical service learning and very present in our teaching and reflections. Butin (2010) suggests service learning needs its own disciplinary home in order to fulfil its social justice potential. We argue public sociology fits that requirement beautifully. One action we would like to progress is to develop a UK-wide critical service learning community of practice to encourage debate and collaborations.

A service learning city?

Could we work better with our community and consider a service learning city approach? Currently we work with many organisations on many discreet projects. This piecemeal approach to social justice, whilst commendable on some levels, reflects the dangers Ledwith brings to our attention from a community development perspective:

> Community development is about radical, transformative change for social justice and sustainability, and this calls for us to situate our practice in its political context. Otherwise, we are easily distracted by the symptoms, rather than focusing on the root causes of discrimination. We drift along the surface of life, patting people on the head, making life a little bit better around the edges, but not lifting the lid off and going deep enough to find the root causes of what's creating an unjust reality. Practices become placatory, ameliorative rather than transformative, and we stand accused of being duplicitous. (Ledwith, 2015: 157)

We do not want to be 'part of the problem'. Plans to work on one city-wide issue, agreed and understood by a range of partners, may help minimise the dangers identified above.

Final thoughts

When we began service learning in 2013, we were full of optimism but at times it would be true to say we lost some of the energy and, we might add, some of the joy for this endeavour. The demands and constraints of working towards a social justice agenda with limited resources in the current HE landscape has left us at times feeling depleted and, quite frankly, at times too tired to do public sociology. Since we introduced service learning, we have had to fight for its place, in effect becoming activists for our disciplinary endeavours. By reflecting on how 'critical' our service learning is we have been challenged and find ourselves agreeing with Butin (2015: 6) that, 'the analysis has been more successful than the enactment' This potential for damage to the community is brought clearly into focus again by Ledwith:

> [C]ommunity development is a contested occupation that sits at the interface of reactionary practice and revolutionary practice; the first reacts to the symptoms of oppression; the second transforms structural discrimination that embeds inequalities in the fabric of society. If we fail to stay critical, constantly re-examining our practice in political times, we are likely to err on the side of domination rather than liberation. (Ledwith, 2015: 9)

To this end we reaffirm social justice as the non-negotiable aspect of service learning. We acknowledge at times it is less critical than we would like, but remain clear that it is not just an experiential pedagogy, a teaching and learning technique, rather it is a set of values underpinning critical practices moving towards social justice. The last word goes to Paulo Freire. He sums up beautifully both the possibility of our dreams and just how critical it is to enact them:

> If I am not in the world simply to adapt to it, but rather transform it, and if it is not possible to change the world without a certain dream or vision for it, I must make use of every possibility there is not only to speak about my utopia, but also to engage in practices consistent with it. (Freire, 2005: 7)

References

Asghar, M. and Rowe, N. (2016) 'Reciprocity and critical reflection as the key to social justice in service learning: a case study', *Innovations in Education and Teaching International*, 54(2): 117–125.

Barrera, D., Willner, L.N. and Kukahiko, K. (2017) 'Assessing the development of an emerging critical consciousness through service learning', *Journal of Critical Thought and Praxis*, 6(3).

Burawoy, M. (2005) 'For public sociology', *American Sociological Review*, 70: 4–28.

Butin, D.W. (2010) *Service-Learning in Theory and Practice: The Future of Community Engagement in Higher Education*, Basingstoke: Palgrave Macmillan.

Butin, D.W. (2015) 'Dreaming of justice: critical service-learning and the need to wake up', *Theory Into Practice*, 54: 5–10.

Cloke, P.J., May, J. and Johnsen, S. (2010) *Swept Up Lives? Re-envisioning the Homeless City*, Chichester: Wiley-Blackwell.

Concannon, K. and Finley, L. (2015) *Peace and Social Justice Education on Campus: Faculty and Student Perspectives*, Newcastle upon Tyne: Cambridge Scholars Publishing.

Department for Communities and Local Government (2015) *The English Indices of Deprivation 2015: Statistical Release*, https://assets.publishing.service.gov.uk/government/uploads/system/uploads/attachment_data/file/465791/English_Indices_of_Deprivation_2015_-_Statistical_Release.pdf

Eby, J.W. (1998) *Why Service-Learning is Bad*, www1.villanova.edu/content/dam/villanova/artsci/servicelearning/WhyServiceLearningIsBad.pdf

Freire, P. (2000) *Pedagogy of the Oppressed* (30th anniversary edn), New York: Continuum.

Freire, P. (2004) *Pedagogy of Indignation*, Boulder, CO: Paradigm.
Furco, A. (1996) *Service-Learning: A Balanced Approach to Experiential Education. Expanding Boundaries: Service and Learning*, Washington DC: Corporation for National Service: 2–6.
Giroux, H. (2002) 'The corporate war against HE', *Workplace*, 9: 103–117.
Hamilton, C. (2013) 'Towards a pedagogy of public criminology', *Enhancing Learning in the Social Sciences*, 5(2): 20–31.
Idles (2018) *Joy as an Act of Resistance*, recorded by Partisan Records, www.roughtrade.com/gb/music/idles-joy-as-an-act-of-resistance
Jacoby, B. and Mutascio, P. (eds) (2010) *Looking In, Reaching Out: A Reflective Guide for Community Service Learning Professionals*, Boston, MA: Campus Compact.
Ledwith, M. (2015) *Community Development in Action*, Bristol: Policy Press.
Liambas, A., and Kaskaris, I. (2012) ' "Dialog" and "love" in the work of Paulo Freire', *Journal for Critical Education Policy Studies*, 10(1): 185–196.
Martin F. and Pirbhai-Illich, F. (2015) 'Service learning as post-colonial discourse', in Reynolds, R. et al (eds) *Contesting and Constructing International Perspectives in Global Education*, Rotterdam: Sense Publishers.
Marullo, S. (1999) 'Sociology's essential role: promoting critical analysis in service-learning', in Ostrow, J., Hesser, G. and Enos, S. (eds) *Cultivating the Sociological Imagination: Concepts and Models for Service-Learning in Sociology*, Washington DC: American Association of Higher Education.
Mitchell, T.D. (2008) 'Traditional vs. critical service-learning: engaging the literature to differentiate two models', *Michigan Journal of Community Service Learning*, Spring, 50–65.
Mooney, L.A. and Edwards, B. (2001) 'Experiential learning in sociology: service learning and other community-based learning initiatives', *Teaching Sociology*, 29(2):181–194.
Morton, K. (1995) 'The irony of service: charity, projects and social change in service learning', *Michigan Journal of Community Service Learning*, 2: 19–32.
Nyden, P. Hossfeld, L. and Nyden, G. (eds) (2012) *Public Sociology: Research, Action, and Change*, Thousand Oaks, CA: Sage.
Office for National Statistics (2018) *Regional Gross Disposable Household Income, UK: 1997 to 2016*, www.ons.gov.uk/economy/regionalaccounts/grossdisposablehouseholdincome/bulletins/regionalgrossdisposablehouseholdincomegdhi/1997to2016

Petray, T. and Halbert, K. (2013) 'Teaching engagement: reflections on sociological praxis', *Journal of Sociology*, 49(4): 441–455.

Pompa, L. (2002) 'Service-learning as crucible: reflections on immersion, context, power, and transformation', *Michigan Journal of Community Service Learning*, 9(1): 67–76.

Rogers, C. (2002) 'The interpersonal relationship in the facilitation of learning', in Clarke, J., Hanson, A., Harrison, R., Reeve, F. (eds) *Supporting Lifelong Learning*, vol 1, London: Routledge Falmer and Open University, 25–39.

Sandmann, L.R., Moore, T.L. and Quinn, J. (2012) 'Center and periphery in service-learning and community engagement: a postcolonial approach', in Hatcher, J.A. and Bringle, R.G. (eds) *Understanding Service-Learning and Community Engagement: Crossing Boundaries Through Research*, Charlotte, NC: Information Age Publishing, 25–46.

Wood, J. (2018) *Still No Place For Hate: Analysis of the Findings of the Nottingham Citizens Hate Crime Survey Including Recommendations*, Nottingham: Citizens UK.

CASE III.6

Trade Unionism as Collective Education

Lena Wånggren

When you're telling me to be resilient you are really telling me that I am failing the system, when really it is the system that is failing me.
So fuck you.
Fuck you for sending me invitations to stress reduction courses
While you make me teach larger classes for less money.
Fuck you for sending me booklets with breathing exercises
While my workload grows higher and higher …
Don't think for a second that they will make me forget
The better world that I deserve.
The better world I can imagine.
The world I have seen on picket lines
And community halls
In whispered conversations
And shouted in slogans
Scrawled all over sidewalks
And written on the internet.
Because fuck you and your individualising bullshit.

> Grace Krause, 'Resilience or Fuck You Neoliberalism – a strike poem' (Permission to reproduce this poem has been granted by Krause.)

The marketisation of higher education in the UK has brought not only job insecurity, increased workloads, and an increase in tuition fees alongside a student-as-consumer or 'customer service approach' to education, but a number of individualised performativity measures that monitor the productivity (in a narrow sense of the word) of individual staff members (Brown and Carasso, 2013). While trade unions primarily aim to improve representation and gain fairer working conditions for its members, trade union work can simultaneously be considered as part of public sociology education. As Scandrett (2017) notes, education not only concerns the production of knowledge but it is also a social relation: 'knowledge continues to be created *both* in collectively challenging ... social relations *and* in experimenting with alternatives' (Scandrett, 2017: 81). Trade union work becomes an educational project first and foremost through students or union members learning about their rights as workers through training and campaigns, in which a kind of 'learning by doing' or embodied knowledge spur members to analyse the social and political power dynamics of work: making clear the relation between 'personal troubles' and 'public issues' (Mills, 2000), such work shifts the understanding of workplace struggles from one of individual failure to one bound up in structural contexts. However, trade union work becomes an educational project also through a fostering of collective action and a sense of community; a way of being and doing that counteracts the individualising culture of marketised academia. As the above-quoted 'strike poem' asserts, trade union work allows us to imagine a better world, the world of collective agency 'seen on picket lines' (Krause, 2018b). This chapter explores some ways in which organising collectively becomes a necessary way of doing public sociology education, not only through a 'learning by doing' about one's role within wider social and political structures but also as a way of fostering new selfhoods. Building on personal experiences of organising and working in UK higher education institutions, the chapter uses blogs, social media and other discussions and discourses around trade union activism as primary material, and the 2017–2018 pensions strike as case study, to explore trade unionism as collective education.

Responsibilisation and marketised subjectivities

The conditions of the neoliberal university mean not only degraded working conditions and pay, but the fabrication of 'new professional subjectivities, requiring us to add certain kinds of value to our professional selves' (Walker and Nixon, 2004: 2). If the main characteristic of neoliberalism is the extension of 'the rationality of the market, the schemas of analysis it offers and the decision-making criteria it suggests, to domains which are not exclusively or not primarily economic' (Foucault, 2008: 323), neoliberalism is not merely a political theory, but even more so it is a governmental practice that is constitutive of a particular type of subject. As economic rationality is extended to formerly non-economic domains and institution, 'neoliberalism normatively constructs and interpolates individuals as entrepreneurial actors in every sphere of life' (Brown, 2003). Thus, all human actions and policies are considered only in terms of profitability, instrumentality, utility.

Indeed, the commodification of education changes the roles of both staff and students; the ways we are governed to think and act. While many colleagues work against the market logics imposed on us, other colleagues are complicit or even embrace this change. A monetarised view of education is adopted by certain university staff, as seen in the actions of Guy Halsall, professor of history at the University of York, who when students did not show up for his lecture told them they were failing to make the most out of the 'obscene amounts of money' that 'mummy and daddy' were paying for their education. For that money, he said,

> you get the chance to hear (probably) the most significant historian of early medieval Europe under the age of 60 anywhere in the world give 16 lectures on his current research. ... [P]eople pay said lecturer large sums of money and fly him around the world to talk to their students, or to give keynote lectures at conferences. (Jump, 2013)

In this way, university staff themselves can reinforce a model of the student-as-consumer who should get their money's worth by attending lectures, encouraging students to perceive their education as a commodity exchange.

The marketisation of higher education thus does not simply get in the way of the academic work many of us want to do, both in terms of teaching and research, but indeed 'fundamentally changes what academic life is' (Ball, 2000: 17). The workplace is marked by a culture of constant performativity (Ball, 2000); it becomes a space of 'hyper-competition', surveillance, and performative productivity (Fochler et al, 2016; Morley, 2016). In the neoliberal workplace, everything one does must be measured and counted, as '[t]rust in professional integrity and peer regulation has been replaced with performance indicators' (Lynch, 2006: 7). These metrics do not simply add another dimension to working life, but rather 'materialise new ways of doing and being in the academy' (Gill, 2017: 9): they produce 'new structures of feeling in the academy, and contribute to our own self-surveillance and monitoring and commodification' (Gill, 2017: 10). While students are forced into roles as 'consumers' of knowledge, teachers are made to occupy the roles of 'knowledge providers' in an education marketplace, with both parties under constant pressure to 'perform' as walking CVs. While the marketisation of higher education extends across the Americas, Australia and Europe, metricisation of academic work in the UK is shaped specifically through the use of two 'frameworks': with the Research Excellence Framework (REF) constantly looming, early-career researchers are advised by senior colleagues to neglect 'un-REFable' but academically important works such as edited collections and collaborative work, while the Teaching Excellence Framework (TEF) ignores decades of pedagogical research and projects a flawed 'customer satisfaction' approach, which puts increased pressures on staff.

Key to understanding changing relations in the marketised workplace is the governing technique of responsibilisation, or as Gill (2017: 11) describes it: the ways in which everyday experiences are lived 'through a toxic individualising discourse'. Gill explains this discourse as the 'dominance of an individualistic register – a tendency to account for ordinary experiences in the academy through discourses of excoriating self blame, privatised guilt, intense anxiety and shame':

> Whether it is paralysing job insecurity which made it impossible to make any kinds of plans for the future, or 100 hour working weeks, academics are more likely to respond in a way that suggested that *they* are failing, than to express legitimate anger at being placed in such a situation. (Gill, 2017: 11)

A key technology of neoliberal governmentality, responsibilisation shifts responsibility from the structural to the individual. Through this mechanism the neoliberal subject is an 'entrepreneur of himself', and is seen as solely responsible for a number of problems that might otherwise be considered as structural, social or political (Foucault, 2008; McLeod, 2017). Responsibilisation has thus become 'one of the most successful tactics' of neoliberal capitalism, as each individual is made to feel that 'their poverty, lack of opportunities, or unemployment, is their fault and their fault alone' (Fisher, 2014), which leads them to blame themselves rather than social structures.

Stress and ill health due to unmanageable workloads and insecure work are on the rise in the UK: scholars and trade union research have noted in recent years increasing levels of ill health, fear and anxiety among university staff, tied to constant monitoring and individualisation (Gill, 2010; UCU, 2013, 2015; Gill and Donaghue, 2016). Despite the fact that neoliberal universities themselves cause 'immense personal suffering to their staff and students' (Krause, 2018a), in a marketised workplace ill health, stress, overwork, or unemployment are framed as individual problems of self-management to be countered by courses in stress control, resilience, mindfulness, or time management (Gill and Donaghue, 2016), rather than spurring action by employers to deal with the structural causes of stress and overwork. Completely reasonable difficulties at 'dealing with hundreds of emails per day on top of "regular" work' are seen as signs of failure, while '[i]llness signifies an inability to cope and probable confirmation that one is not good enough or tough enough to be there' (Gill, 2017: 11). This mechanism of placing individuals' actions as the cause and solution to structural problems increasingly seeps into every aspect of university staffs' working lives. However, both trade unionism and public sociology education work in the opposite direction of such forces; they deindividualise experiences of exploitation through collective action and dialogue with sociological theories.

Trade unionism as collective education

Considering the hegemonic ideology and structures of neoliberal marketisation in contemporary universities, is resistance at all possible? While marketised workplaces frame colleagues as competitive neoliberal entrepreneurial subjects solely responsible for a number of problems that might otherwise be considered structural or political (including their own 'resilience' to stress and their own well-being), trade union work opens up possibilities to resist this trend and can be considered an educational project. Indeed, the collective nature of trade union organising can be used to counteract the individualising impulse or responsibilisation of neoliberal governmentality.

In the marketised university, academics become walking CVs or entrepreneurs of themselves, working double or triple shifts as even one's social media presence and non-work hours are co-opted (Gill and Donaghue, 2016), and every publication and public speaking engagement are entered into a digital system and showcased on the university website or on one's personal CV. As pointed out in this section's provocation, one's own academic work, however radical and counter-institutional – including public sociology education – is 'vulnerable to co-option ... with appeal to fee-paying students and the potential for income-generating, commercialised knowledge exchange' (np). Presenting at a research conference recently on health and the marketised university, however, I was struck by a comment from a colleague. The paper, which delineated the gendered and racialised effects of stress caused by unmanageable workloads and insecure contracts, prompted a colleague to highlight that in the entrepreneurial university, everything one does is included in one's CV – except, the colleague (who had been a union representative) noted, trade union work. While almost everything can be and often is co-opted by neoliberal university structures and sucked up by the always-performing self, trade union work is different: it cannot be subsumed as easily, and indeed its workings and values – which are based on collectivity, solidarity, and a shared purpose – go against the neoliberal individualism of contemporary higher education, opening up an alternative selfhood and community.

While the trade union work considered in this chapter takes place in and is connected to higher education institutions, carried out by all sorts of university workers, the work in itself is not *of* higher education. It is a different form of public sociology, then, than the sociological research and teaching taking place in academic departments. As noted in the provocation, the *where* of public sociology is important: the institutional locations of potential public sociology education are ambivalent. Falling outside definitions of sociological knowledge such as research reports, articles, books or other 'REF-able' items, trade union work in higher education can become a form of knowledge. Through representing other members or organising collective actions, another kind of professional self can be fostered than that neoliberal self-serving 'entrepreneurial subject' working to erase others and neglecting collaborative work (Walker and Nixon, 2004). 'If subjectivity is the key site of neoliberal government', it makes sense that 'it is here also, in "our relation to ourselves", that we might begin to struggle to think about ourselves differently' (Ball, 2016: 1134).

While much trade union work takes the form of 'winning small concessions through negotiation and tactics', the ongoing struggle to gain fair working conditions 'takes a strongly pedagogical form' as members understand the contradictions of their situation at work (Scandrett, 2017: 93). Trade unionism encourages staff who might see themselves as separate from other workers to consider themselves as workers engaged in labour struggles alongside others. Through trade union work, university staff become not only researchers or educators but organisers, colleagues, and members of a community that collectively envisages alternatives to the status quo. Indeed, hooks notes that education is at heart about community, as it 'enables us to confront feelings of loss and restore our sense of connection'; education in its true sense 'teaches us how to create community' (2003: xv). Trade unionism can thus be considered as a pedagogical project not primarily concerning students – although working alongside students is important – but also through members' learning about their rights as workers. This happens both on an individual level, as representatives helping colleagues often have to research policy and law, and on a collective level through campaigns and actions. These practices of public sociology education 'emerge as a prefigurative politics, as alternative possibilities to neoliberal business as usual' (Provocation III). Organising collectively, union members not only learn about employment rights and industrial relations, but they also produce new knowledge: through counteracting neoliberal narratives or managerial 'knowledges' one comes to enact or *do* knowledge while learning.

The next section demonstrates how one instance of trade union work can create such a collective thinking and being that goes against the individualising culture of performativity in contemporary universities, opening up to new ways of being and doing public sociology education. Moving from a neoliberal framing of responsibility to a collective one that emphasises care, interdependence and relational responsibility (McLeod, 2017), trade union work emphasises responsibility towards others, not only the self.

Learning by doing: the 2018 pensions strike

Writing on trade union work as a teacher, researcher, and union representative, requires a degree of 'uncomfortable reflexivity' for the author of this chapter (Pillow, 2003). One's own experiences and observations from years of organising and representing colleagues are moulded to produce new forms of knowledge that attempt to formulate practice as theory, or theorise practice. Indeed, the period in between this chapter being accepted for this collection, and the writing of the chapter, was filled with the largest industrial action in the author's trade union's history: the 2017–2018 pensions dispute in UK higher education. As part of this dispute, 65 branches of the University and College Union (UCU), the trade union representing academic and academic-related staff, engaged in 14 days of strike action across four weeks, and an extending period of action short of a strike, which included working to contract (Bergfeld 2018; UCU 2017–2018). This dispute, which involved the longest strike action the UK higher education system has ever seen, both intensified and highlighted the crucial role of trade unionism as collective education.

Throughout the UK, union branches and individual members shared their experiences – online and in person – of being engaged in industrial action. Colleagues got together on picket lines, at rallies, teach-outs, and union meetings, and in Scotland even a snow storm could not stop the action. One of the revelations for members on strike has been a 'rekindling of the spirit of the collective out on the picket lines' (Morrish, 2018) and an 'intense feeling of solidarity' (Krause, 2018a) borne out of the collective action. This 'really exhilarating solidarity' or 'new spirit' of collegiality has also accompanied a 'boldness and fearlessness among the staff' which – according to one member – is 'about to transform relationships in UK universities' (Morrish, 2018). Morrish (2018) shares tweets and letters from UCU members, one indicating that 'It has been on the picket lines and in meetings and in teach-outs that I have (re)discovered the "community" and "collegiality" of which [university management] so often speak', while another member found the strike period 'strangely liberating': 'The friendship and collegiality I have felt from colleagues across the university and sector, and the sense that these are shared challenges we all face, has been a massively positive experience' (Morrish, 2018). At the author's own institution, one member emailed the branch committee describing their experience of being on strike as 'an energising, celebratory and meaningful experience':

> I've often found myself thinking, 'This is how university should be ALL the time.' A lot of the typical boundaries are down, and the uni has become what it's supposed to be – a space where people are sharing knowledge and experiences in an enthusiastic way. (Permission to reproduce this email anonymously has been granted by the member)

Other colleagues remarked on the way in which the strike had affected them positively in different aspects of their life, both professionally and personally. Some colleagues said that they had not had such fun together in years. Seen in these quotes is a sense of awakening, a learning of a new way of being and interacting in the workplace, as workers. As one article notes, through the collective action the strike turned from a focus on pensions to wider discussions about job security, marketisation and workload, and into a 'sounding board about the big questions, the biggest of them being: what kind of university do we want?' (Hoene and Wånggren, 2018: 24–25). The collective sense of purpose in industrial relations shared by seasoned trade unionists became available also to lay members as many of them joined a picket line for the first time.

Not just the picket lines – more about them later – but also the teach-outs that took place at many institutions opened up new forms of collective learning. The space of the teach-out, whether a pub, a community centre, or a bookshop,

> blossomed into everything current universities are not, but *should* be ... a space where meaningful relationships have flourished in the space of days; a setting where staff and students have come together and learned more about and from each other, and (re)discovered how to empathise with each other. (Costas Batlle and Mondon, 2018)

These informal workshops and lectures, often on radical subjects (such as class struggle throughout history, political art, land rights, feminism, social justice, and pensions ('Teach Outs During the UCU Strike', 2018)), offered a different view of education itself, reminding staff and students that education is 'not just about passing exams and churning out employees' but rather about 'encouraging individuals to take learning into their own hands and to shape their learning environment as agent rather than passive recipients', and about 'sharing, challenging and exploring ideas in a creative and democratic setting which allows human beings to feel both vulnerable and empowered' (Costas Batlle and Mondon, 2018). Indeed, one member noted that the strike gave members 'an opportunity to really talk about how badly we have been hurt' (Krause, 2018a) by the working conditions of the marketised university.

Student–staff solidarity and collectivity were placed at the centre of the industrial action to defend pensions, with branches making sure to communicate with student unions and invite students to events and rallies. The industrial action received support from wide groups of students (including the National Union of Students), with 22 student occupations springing up across campuses not only in support of staff's actions but 'also in protest at fees and excessive marketisation' (Morrish, 2018). At the University of Edinburgh, the occupation lasted for six weeks, longer than the strike itself, and became a way to not only show solidarity with staff on strike but also to open some cracks in the neoliberal university and envisage alternatives. In a brilliant move, the occupants named themselves the Edinburgh Futures Institute, after the title of a criticised new multi-million institute to be set up at

Edinburgh. Highlighting the university's investment in buildings rather than in staff and students, they created their own institute for how the future of universities should function – complete with teach-outs, seminars, and political meetings (Edinburgh Futures Institute, 2018). The feeling shared by many union members, that of a new and shared sense of collectivity, purpose, and energy, through the students' actions transformed into political plans and imaginings.

The picket lines, where members braced the winter cold to ask colleagues and students to not go into work, provided a particular place to produce and enact new forms of knowledge and new ways of being. Sharing stories, experiences, and knowledge on the picket lines and during teach-outs, Krause (2018a) experienced an 'intense feeling of solidarity':

> I don't think I ever really understood what solidarity meant before this, which is ironic since I've taught what feels like a thousand undergraduate seminars on the topic. ... The picket lines, the rallies, the Teach Outs and meetings, all made me feel I was part of something bigger, part of a community. ... [S]ociology allows us to connect 'private problems to public issues'. By recognising that our own personal experience is connected to those of others we are able to better understand the social structures around us. Listening to all these stories most certainly did that.

Krause's description of the experience of being on strike signals that public sociology knowledge cannot be validated exclusively by the institutions and epistemologies of professional sociology. Rather the validity – and usefulness – of public sociology is established in dialogue with publics, and often through a form of incidental learning taking place in non-educational spaces or informal contexts (Foley, 1999); spaces such as on a picket line. Comparing the picket lines to the various kinds of knowledges produced at academic conferences, Henderson (2018) describes the transformative experience of being on strike alongside colleagues as a 'learning by doing':

> [T]here is no doubt that, by coming out to picket alongside my colleagues, I observed and emulated a knowhow that cannot be underestimated. It is a knowhow that takes many forms ... a knowhow that is about engaging differently with the spaces that we normally work-work-work in and the people that we normally unquestioningly trust or stare

blankly through; a knowhow that involves doing what academics say we do all the time, and should definitely do more of at conferences – enacting thinking.

Trade union work thus, as demonstrated by the case of the recent pensions dispute, can work against the belief in self-sufficient neoliberal individualism proposed by marketised universities. Indeed, Krause (2018a) notes, during the pensions strike '[t]he idea that we, a group of people, could stand with one another and refuse to compete is a tremendous threat' to that belief and governmentality. Discovering this solidarity, Krause writes, 'is like opening Pandora's Box; it's unleashing forces that according to neoliberal ideology shouldn't even exist' (Krause, 2018a). Krause goes as far as to suggest that, with the intense 'feeling of collective agency' enabled by industrial action, the strike showed university workers 'glimpses of a utopia': 'It has shown us ways of being together and working together that are built on cooperation and solidarity. It has allowed us to think about what higher education could and, arguably, should be like' (Krause, 2018a).

Rather than reading theories and histories of labour rights and struggles, public sociology education took place as union members simultaneously enacted such struggles. Through collective trade union action, solidarity becomes an 'embodied knowledge' that one is not alone in one's struggles, 'that there are many on my side and that together we can change things that alone I could never manage' (Krause, 2018a):

> Because while I refuse to take
> Responsibility for my own suffering
> I will gladly accept
> Responsibility for our collective wellbeing.
> We are the university.
>
> (Krause, 2018b)

Rather than conforming to the neoliberal definition of responsibility that blames the individual for structural faults, the strike made possible a collective responsibility and a new way of thinking, doing, being. It should also be noted that, while the action over pensions has not been fully concluded at the time of writing, the dispute was at least partly won. Union members voted in 2019 to take further action to defend pensions, and simultaneously – this time including all branches of UCU, including those not involved in the Universities Superannuation Scheme (USS) pension strike – taking action on pay and equality (importantly, the claim and action include addressing casualisation, gender and ethnicity pay gaps, and workload). The 2018 USS pensions strikes were thus accompanied by a 'second round' of strikes in November and December 2019, accompanied by the same levels of enthusiasm and determination as the 2018 strikes. At the time of writing, the pay and equality dispute, and continued pensions dispute, are still ongoing. With more members joining UCU every month, and many branches growing stronger, members continue to transform their union through action.

Conclusion

Trade union organising is not always as empowering or transformative as sketched out above. Often it takes the form of rather dull and sometimes emotionally draining meetings with management, taking minutes at committee meetings, sorting papers, or assisting members through stressful grievances. The fact that trade union work can add stress to an already speeded-up and fractured workplace due to mounting workloads and precarious contracts also needs to be mentioned. Speaking out against unfair working conditions can furthermore prove risky for marginalised and precariously employed staff:

> We may be in a position where we would not feel safe, physically or emotionally, to call out the injustices we observe. We may be employed so precariously that 'rocking the boat' is too costly. We may be unwell or too tired to fight. It is not the job of one person to solve the problems of the world: this is what makes the strength of the collective so important. (Res-Sisters, 2016: 281)

When crushed by ever-increasing workloads, or stressed due to not knowing how to pay the rent or if one's immigration status will change for the worse, it might be difficult to find time and energy to be active in one's union. Doing trade union work in a country with some of the most restrictive industrial relations laws in Europe is hard; during the 2018 pensions strike, and the continued 2019 strikes over pensions and pay and equality, non-striking branches of the union could only do so much as secondary picketing and solidarity action are prohibited, and the significance of the UCU pensions ballot overcoming the restrictions of the Trade Union Act 2016 should not be underestimated (Gall, 2017). Maintaining facility time, that is to say paid time off for representatives to carry out trade union duties, is a priority in the light of recent anti-union legislation in the UK, alongside campaigning for the rights of precariously employed and international staff.

In light of recent trade union action in the UK, we ask: is resistance to the marketisation of universities possible? What can university workers do with our complicity and implication in the structures we seek to resist and rework? Despite the difficulties in organising collectively in one's workplace, there is no alternative to continuing the work. During the 2010 student protests in the UK, one poster plastered on the author's university campus declared that 'the more you crush us, the more we resist'. This statement has been verified in increased union activity on behalf of precarious workers (such as the Scottish Trade Union Congress-supported BetterThanZero campaign) and in the 2017–2018 pensions dispute. As demonstrated in this chapter, while trade union work cannot be measured via the neoliberal metrics of the REF, cited in terms of a research 'output', or included on one's academic CV, it opens up new ways of challenging, enacting, and producing knowledge by formulating new collective ways of being and working. Questioning neoliberal narratives of responsibilisation and entrepreneurial subjectivity, the embodied and collective nature of trade union work upsets ways of thinking and doing public sociology education in universities and beyond.

References

Ball, S. (2000) 'Performativities and fabrications in the education economy: towards the performative society?', *The Australian Educational Researcher*, 27(2): 1–24.

Ball, S. (2016) 'Subjectivity as a site of struggle: refusing neoliberalism?', *British Journal of Sociology of Education*, 37(8): 1129–1146.

Bergfeld, M. (2018) '"Do you believe in life after work?" The university and college union strike in Britain', *Transfer*, 24(2): 233–236.

Brown, R. and Carasso, H. (2013) *Everything for Sale? The Marketisation of UK Higher Education*, London: Society for Research into Higher Education.

Brown, W. (2003) 'Neo-liberalism and the end of liberal democracy', *Theory & Event*, 7(1) Project MUSE, doi:10.1353/tae.2003.0020.

Costas Batlle, I, and Mondon, A. (2018) 'University strikes: reclaiming a space for emancipatory education', *Discover Society*, 6 March, https://discoversociety.org/2018/03/06/university-strikes-reclaiming-a-space-for-emancipatory-education/

Edinburgh Futures Institute (2018) 'Our Declaration', *Edinburgh Futures Institute: Occupying for a Democratic University*, https://edinburghfuturesinstitute.wordpress.com/declaration

Fisher, M. (2014) 'Good for nothing', *The Occupied Times*, 19 March, http://theoccupiedtimes.org/?p=12841

Fochler, M., Felt, U. and Müller, R. (2016) 'Unsustainable growth, hyper-competition, and worth in life science research: narrowing evaluative repertoires in doctoral and postdoctoral scientists' work and lives', *Minerva*, 54(2): 175–200.

Foley, G. (1999) *Learning in Social Action: A Contribution to Understanding Informal Education*, London: Zed Books.

Foucault, M. (2008 [1979]) *The Birth of Biopolitics. Lectures at the College de France 1978–1979*, Basingstoke: Palgrave.

Gall, G. (2017) 'The Trade Union Act 2016: what has its impact been so far?', *The Jimmy Reid Foundation*, http://reidfoundation.org/jrftradeunionacteffectsfinal18062107/

Gill, R. (2010) 'Breaking the silence: the hidden injuries of the neoliberal university', in Ryan-Flood, R. and Gill, R. (eds) *Secrecy and Silence in the Research Process: Feminist Reflections*, London: Routledge: pp 228–244.

Gill, R. (2017) 'Beyond individualism: the psychosocial life of the neoliberal University', in Spooner, M. (ed) *A Critical Guide to Higher Education and the Politics of Evidence: Resisting Colonialism, Neoliberalism, & Audit Culture*, Regina, RI: University of Regina Press: pp 1–21, http://openaccess.city.ac.uk/15647 [pre-print].

Gill, R. and Donaghue, N. (2016) 'Resilience, apps and reluctant individualism: technologies of self in the neoliberal academy', *Women's Studies International Forum*, 54: 91–99.

Henderson, E. (2018) 'Gathering at the picket line – UCU Strike 2018', *Conference Inference*, 6 March, https://conferenceinference.wordpress.com/2018/03/06/gathering-at-the-picket-line-ucu-strike-2018

Hoene, C. and Wånggren, L. (2018) '"In order to be utopian, you have to feel utopian": two perspectives on the recent strike at UK universities', *Hard Times*, 101(1): 24–30.

hooks, b. (2003) *Teaching Community: A Pedagogy of Hope*, London: Routledge.

Jump, P. (2013) 'Don't you kids know who I am?', *Times Higher Education*, 3 January, www.timeshighereducation.co.uk/story.asp?storycode=422246

Krause, G. (2018a) 'Sadness and solidarity – the strike as utopia', *Thinking in the Open*, 12 March, http://blogs.cardiff.ac.uk/rsrc/2018/03/12/sadness-and-solidarity-the-strike-as-utopia

Krause, G. (2018b) 'Resilience or fuck you neoliberalism – a strike poem', *Thinking in the Open*, 1 May, http://blogs.cardiff.ac.uk/rsrc/2018/04/29/resilience-or-fuck-you-neoliberalism-a-strike-poem

Lynch, K. (2006) 'Neo-liberalism and marketisation: the implications for higher education', *European Educational Research Journal*, 5(1): 1–17.

McLeod, J. (2017) 'Reframing responsibility in an era of responsibilisation', *Discourse: Studies in the Cultural Politics of Education*, 38(1): 43–56.

Morley, L. (2016) 'Troubling intra-actions: gender, neo-liberalism and research in the global academy', *Journal of Education Policy*, 31(1): 28–45.

Morrish, L. (2018) 'Embracing the dinosaur of solidarity', *Academic Irregularities: Critical University Studies, Discourse and Managerialism*, 19 March, https://academicirregularities.wordpress.com/2018/03/19/embracing-the-dinosaur-of-solidarity

Pillow, W. (2003) 'Confession, catharsis, or cure? Rethinking the uses of reflexivity as methodological power in qualitative research', *International Journal of Qualitative Studies in Education*, 16(2): 175–196.

Res-Sisters (2016) '"I'm an early-career feminist academic: get me out of here?" Encountering and resisting the neoliberal academy', in Thwaites, R. and Pressland, A. (eds) *Being an Early-Career Feminist Academic: Global Perspectives, Experiences, and Challenges*, London: Palgrave Macmillan: pp 267–84.

Scandrett, E. (2017) 'Still spaces in the academy? The dialectic of university social movement pedagogy', in Hall, R. and Winn, J. (eds) *Mass Intellectuality and Democratic Leadership in Higher Education*. London: Bloomsbury: pp 81–95.

'Teach Outs During the UCU Strike' (2018) *Teach Outs: Edinburgh*, https://edinburghteachout.wordpress.com

University and College Union (2013) *Higher Stress: A Survey of Stress and Well-Being Among Staff in Higher Education*, London: UCU, www.ucu.org.uk/media/5911/Higher-stress-a-survey-of-stress-and-well-being-among-staff-in-higher-education-Jul13/pdf/HE_stress_report_July_2013.pdf

University and College Union (2015) *Making Ends Meet: The Human Cost of Casualisation in Post-Secondary Education*, London: UCU, www.ucu.org.uk/media/7279/Making-ends-meet---the-human-cost-of-casualisation-in-post-secondary-education-May-15/pdf/ucu_makingendsmeet_may15.pdf

University and College Union (2017–2018) *Strike for USS*, www.ucu.org.uk/strikeforuss

Walker, M. and Nixon, J. (2004) *Reclaiming Universities from a Runaway World*, Maidenhead: Open University Press.

Wright Mills, C. (2000 [1959]) *The Sociological Imagination*, Oxford: Oxford University Press.

DIALOGUE III

Public Sociology Practices, Privatising Universities

Eurig Scandrett, Jim Crowther, Sharon Hutchings, Karl Johnson, Mae Shaw and Lena Wänggren

As a dialogue, this section engaged a wider range of participants than previous attempts. The email invitation to respond to the provocation and cases generated responses from contributors to four of the six cases, interestingly reflecting the contexts of England and Scotland; early career and recently retired academics, on more or less precarious contracts; and in ancient and modern universities. To what extent is public sociology as educational practice sustainable, even possible, within the neoliberal university? The challenges of engaging with integrity in educational practice within the neoliberal university, however that is mediated and experienced, has prompted an engaging and impassioned debate which will undoubtedly continue. Moreover, the personal cost of public sociology as educational practice has also been articulated. The context of the neoliberal university makes public sociology, and indeed educational practice with any integrity, a constant battle: exhausting, upsetting and demoralising. The medium of email exchange has mediated the emotional content, but the experience of rage, and tears, and indignation, is clearly shared by the dialogical participants.

The focus of this section is on the university, the institution in which many public sociologists are located, at least partially. To what extent does the neoliberal university provide spaces for public sociology education, for the generation of really useful knowledge with subaltern counterpublics? Elsewhere Scandrett argued that 'The current crisis potentially makes universities privileged places for the realisation of mass intellectuality, because they are educational spaces in which the structural contradictions of neoliberal capital are so explicitly being played out' (Scandrett, 2017: 83). Can this be argued for public sociology education? Should we understand these spaces, such as those documented in this section, to be *because of* (as opposed to *despite*) the structural contradictions of neoliberal capitalism? This assertion proved to be controversial in dialogue with the contributors.

Lena Wånggren, for example, questioned the assertion that the neoliberal university provides spaces for public sociology education, and 'mass intellectuality'. Because (as the collection asks elsewhere) of who gets to enter this educational space of knowledge production? Who gets to be considered as knowledge producer? Many do not even have a chance to enter the university space because of institutional racism, sexism, border controls, and capitalism: tuition fees still apply in Scottish higher education institutions (HEIs) – it is only Scottish and (for now) EU students who do not pay them, and only undergraduate studies are free. Students from the rest of UK and international students (which make up the majority in certain Scottish universities) and postgraduate studies have fees. International fees are absolutely monstrous at Scottish universities.

So, Lena asks, if there is an opportunity for 'mass intellectuality' – whose intellect are we talking about? Who gets to – or wants to – be part of this mass intellectuality? As we know, many HEIs are built on slave labour and imperialist exploitation, and these patterns are continuing, for example in international student fees, and the use of universities as border control agents facilitating visa fees and checks. While institutional racism and whiteness (which, of course, is inextricably linked with capitalist processes) shut out Black, Asian and Minority Ethnic students and staff, neocolonial patterns shut out international students, for example from the Global South. Lena drew attention to examples from Scotland such as disabled student Bamidele Chika Agbakuribe at Dundee University, who suffered both from the neoliberal university's structural ableism and UK border control regimes; and a recent conference in Edinburgh where a large number of invited speakers, including keynote speakers – researchers and activists, many engaging in public sociology – were stopped by UK border controls (https://transgender-intersectional-international.com).

There remains a dialectical contradiction between, on the one hand, the undoubted exclusionary role of neoliberal universities that reproduce structures of exploitation and, on the other, the pedagogical spaces that can expose, analyse and forge counterpublic spaces. The capacity for public sociologists therefore to work 'in and against' the neoliberal university continues to be under scrutiny and contingent on the struggles with which many public sociologists are engaged, including through our collective organisation in trade unions.

In 1979, a group of radical intellectuals published *In and Against the State* (London Edinburgh Weekend Return Group, 1987), which addressed the contradictions of the welfare state as employer and service provider, whilst at the same time agent of capitalist reproduction, remote from the working people who relied on it. The state in late 1970s Britain was facing a crisis borne of the achievements and limitations of social democracy, which, the authors argued, could lead to a democratic socialist resolution with a more thorough socialisation of the state itself. Instead, it led to the election of the Thatcher Government and the process of dismantling the achievements of the welfare state in favour of a state that created the conditions for private acquisition of resources, by force if necessary, and abandoned responsibility for welfare.

The title of their pamphlet *In and Against the State* has been regularly adopted in the face of other crises, not least our analysis of public sociology and education in and against the university. Most of our contributors are employed by, are recent students of, or in some way are attached to universities. In the crisis generated by the current development of the neoliberal university, public sociologists find themselves operating in, against (and at the margins of) the university.

During the dialogue, Eurig had proposed to contributors that the idea of the university is something that they wish to defend, despite its complex historical manifestations of elite, liberal, mass and neoliberal forms. This proposal was contested. Lena argued that she wants

> to defend free, accessible and critical education for all, but the idea of the university – not really that bothered. There is so much institutional racism, sexism, capitalist processes in the current system – other alternatives are probably more practical for moving society. I'd also like to add sexist, racist, ableist, imperialist and colonial in addition to your adjectives 'elite, liberal, mass and neoliberal' forms. A complication to your claim that most contributors are employed by or attached to universities can be made by the fact of precarity: a lot of researchers, academic workers, etc are not just attached to universities but actually have very few ties to the institution: working in between four or five workplaces, the university might only be the classroom where one goes to deliver a few tutorials per week and

then leaves, with no interaction in university processes or collegial relations, before eg working in hospitality or healthcare (i.e. completely different sectors) – that's the nature of academic work/university association for many precariously employed researchers and teachers.

Jim Crowther and Mae Shaw also addressed the connection between the university as an institution – moulded today by neoliberal forces of marketisation that have exacerbated inequality – and the need for 'really useful knowledge', that is critical knowledges that enable people to think both about the world that shapes their experience, and how to change that world. Historically, such spaces in the university have always been limited, but there were, nonetheless, legitimate spaces for exploring social and political alternatives. An essential component of action, therefore, was the capacity to develop or reflect on theoretical frameworks that would expose vested interests, challenge dominant assumptions reinforcing the status quo, and highlight counter-possibilities. As neoliberalism 'rolls out', penetrating ever further into institutions, these once-legitimate spaces for critical thought are being further reduced or eliminated, as attacks on professional sociology make clear.

In one sense, Jim and Mae argued, we need to go beyond the position advocated by the radical intellectuals involved in publishing *In and Against the State*, in that public sociology is not only positioned 'in and against' the university, but also 'for' the university as a public good. Whilst such concerns are anathema to the neoliberal university, there are a wide range of potential alliances in diverse communities – inside and outside the institution – who are drawn to the wider purposes of the university that go beyond the cash nexus.

Concurring with Lena's argument, Jim and Mae suggested that the original 'in and against the state' argument may not pay sufficient attention to the material realities of the current context, and their existential impact. The disciplinary power of precarious working conditions in the neoliberal university (as well as elsewhere) should not be underestimated. It is becoming clear that such conditions, and the surveillance systems that sustain them, have psychological and material consequences for individuals and for how they assess and exercise their relative autonomy. Survival strategies may therefore need to be developed in ways that differ from, or extend, those associated with 'working in and against' the institution.

Perhaps a more realistic way of sustaining a counter-identity in such precarious times is to see oneself as being in the academy, but not of it; of creating some necessary distance. This may require a re-evaluation of available strategies for expressing opposition and contradiction: developing individual and collective survival plans; stretching dominant discourses; subverting or circumventing damaging developments; avoiding, ignoring, or mitigating the effects of, managerial systems; exploiting potential gaps between rhetoric and reality; operating under the radar where necessary. Above all, a candid assessment of the contemporary conjuncture in these terms can help to limit the danger, always present, of making radical claims whilst settling for acquiescent practices.

In the various contributions to this section, the university is understood from multiple angles: its political economy, its ecology, and its social function. The dynamics of subalternity are reflected in the student body, both as the widening access agenda focuses on working class students (Karl Johnson's Case III.2), and as students are proletarianised (or precariatised) by working in the precarious economy whilst studying – and, as others have pointed out, by a kind of racialised, neo-colonial capitalism through the extraction of particularly high tuition fees from international students. Phil Mignot and Ricky Gee's Case III.1 demonstrate that Paul Willis' 1977 critique of class reproduction in education, *Learning to Labour*, has deepened in the twenty-first century neoliberal university, where students are also 'labouring to learn'. At the same time, in Case III.6, Lena Wånggren draws attention to the role of academics and other university employees as increasingly proletarianised workers, engaged in collective industrial action to defend pensions. The 2018 University and College Union strike in defence of the Universities Superannuation Scheme was a significant (if incomplete) victory in preventing the marketisation of deferred salaries, but the picket line debates, teach-outs and student occupations covered the wide range of issues facing the neoliberalisation of higher education. Arguably, in the neoliberal university, its workers are subaltern and experience new forms of exploitation (although this claim is challenged by some contributors), and trade union collective action is a significant counterpublic sphere. Whilst an overt crisis in the form of a threat to pensions or job cuts is a particularly fruitful source of public sociology education, the question arises of how to sustain that level of analysis and critique during 'normal' periods where contradictions and conflicts are more hidden. Is provoking a crisis – or making the crisis more explicit – part of the educational method? Certainly this constitutes an important contribution from non-violence theory, in which the hidden violations are made public and confronted with the impacts of exploitation. At the same time, does the 'enemy' also learn?

Karl Johnson noted that if it does learn, then it simultaneously learns to ignore and press ahead as far as possible. He was struck by another thread that runs through the chapters in this section to varying degrees: the impact of neoliberalism on mental health. We see the support and opportunity that the university, albeit via direct interventions from individual workers, can provide publics living with forms of mental health condition (for example, Docherty-Hughes et al). However, several references are made in this section to the harm to mental health caused by institutional policies – particularly those policies directly impacting upon the workforce – with seemingly little or no managerial self-awareness.

Notwithstanding her emphasis on the precarity of university workers, Lena questioned my application of the term 'subaltern' to academics – firstly given the theoretical political history of the term (thinking specifically of Spivak's adoption of it), and also because many university staff are in an extremely privileged position. She questions whether a grade 10 white male upper class professor is in any way 'subaltern' and argued that the term might be used more carefully. The point is well made that the term needs to be used carefully and public sociology practice benefits from a close reading of subalternity as used in the Gramscian tradition. Indeed, arguably, this is precisely the kind of specifically sociological work which public sociology brings to other forms of activism, and which requires constant attention in changing times. This issue was raised in Provocation I and it is valuable to return to it here. Certainly the use of 'subaltern' by Spivak (1988) and the Subaltern Studies group differs from its use here to refer to the precariatisation of university academics. However, Glenn (2007) uses the term in the context of public sociology to refer to Black Studies and Women's Studies, and the scholars of these subdisciplines. Moreover, Valentine (2019) refers to subaltern workers in universities as

> those academic workers who adopt a more positive and supportive approach to those neo-liberal policies adopted by [Senior Management Teams] and the political processes devised to implement them in order to position themselves advantageously in relation to the hierarchy of power through which they are secured. (88)

Whilst this is not the interpretation used here, this is a salutary reminder of the complexity of Gramsci's term, as well as the contradictory roles that university workers play.

The issue here is not so much a quest for the definition most true to Gramsci's notoriously multi-interpretable *Prison Notebooks*, but rather an exercise in interpreting different modes of exploitation, oppression and injustice. This task somewhat correlates with the work of intersectionality scholars, albeit not without contestation (for example, McNally, 2017). Moreover, subalternity is contingent, and it is part of the job of public sociologists to interpret the axes of subalternity in any particular context. University employed academics hold a position of privilege, undoubtedly, and that position has been, and continues to be, used to legitimise social hierarchies and forms of oppression and exploitation. However, my argument here, which is clearly not shared by all contributors, is that the increasing proletarianisation of academics (including 'the professoriate') through precarious employment, the commercialisation of knowledge, privatisation of pensions, intensification of workload etc, has revealed axes of subalternity around which a counterpublic has mobilised.

Focusing beyond 'the neoliberal university', these cases demonstrate that the university is taking on a distinctive role in the wider neoliberal political economy: students as precarious workers; academics as precarious workers; workers as precarious students and precarious knowledge workers. Neoliberalism makes its components (universities, identities, practices) work in the interests of class realignment. It also, as has been highlighted through dialogue, works in the interests of neocolonial structures (for example, the Research Excellence Framework (REF) forces academics to publish in Eurocentric and US-centric journals, otherwise they do not count). The precise relationship between class and race in the context of neocolonialism (and how this plays out in the experiences of university workers) is a subject of critical debate in the sociological literature, and public sociology has a role, here, to recognise and expose the influence of neoliberal interests – interest of capital – in sociological practices, both in and in the edges of the university.

A crucial part of the ecology of the neoliberal university is its relationship with communities outside the campus. As indicated in the provocation, this has always been a preoccupation with some academics concerned with social relevance, and in different historical contexts has generated such activities as specialist institutions (Andersonian, Birkbeck), university extension, university settlements, the Workers' Educational Association (WEA), workers' colleges, science shops, university departments of adult, continuing and community education, community-based research, service-based learning. Three chapters in this section provide case studies of different aspects of these practices in current times: community-based sociology education (Docherty-Hughes et al); university-based community education (Crowther and Shaw) and university service learning (Hutchings and Lewis). All these three cases present the real struggles of university–community relations within contradictory social contexts. The practice of public sociology and of education in these contexts is not about getting the practice 'right' but responding adequately to the inevitable contradictions.

Karl Johnson points out the significant contradiction of the role of higher education in the political agenda of social mobility (in place of equalling opportunity and challenging entitlement and inequality perpetuated by vested interest). In Scotland, for example, the widening access and participation drive has not translated into a democratisation of education and forms of capital across the demographics and regions of the country. Rather, social mobility is target-driven and efforts are generally directed at spreading middle-class norms and values rather than meeting subaltern (typically working-class) publics on their own terms.

Universities still have a privileged, but not unique, position in the practice of sociology, and many public sociologists have sought to democratise that privilege through public sociology. At the same time, this privilege is being lost through marketisation, not through democratisation. The Augar (2019) review's assertion that sociology is one of the academic subjects that is not 'value for money' is part of the threat to public sociology practice in the neoliberal university. Although this claim is based on a rather dubious extrapolation from the English business model of student fees with state-underwritten loans that are repaid only when graduates achieve high enough salaries, the market assumptions of 'value for money' are influencing Scottish higher education where the state pays fees for at least some undergraduate students[1] even that perverse logic does not apply to the same extent.

University sociology departments have been a resource and a somewhat protected space for public sociology, at the same time as downplaying public sociology practice by privileging professional sociology and social policy. Ironically, as sociology departments are threatened and closed, it is professional sociology that may suffer more than public sociology. Public sociology, as the cases in this collection have shown, occurs in diverse academic and extra-academic contexts. In dialogue, Eurig argued that, *contra* Burawoy (2005), it is public sociology that is the core discipline, and not professional sociology, although other contributors remain unconvinced. Sharon Hutchings pointed out that many of the contributors to this section (such as Chapters III.3, III.5 and III.6) see public sociology as risky and exhausting whereas there is a certainty and tidiness to professional sociology. Professional sociology conforms to accepted ways of doing things in universities: there are few risks, academic credibility is a given and there are clear rewards. For those public sociologists that work in 'diverse academic and extra-curricula contexts' there is often a huge cost. For example, for Docherty-Hughes et al (Chapter III.3) 'This was far from a linear, harmonious process; it was unpredictable and sometimes involved difficult discussions. ... This process was often perilous; practising public sociology in this way is not for the faint-hearted.' This concurs with experiences elsewhere:

> We may be in a position where we would not feel safe, physically or emotionally, to call out the injustices we observe. We may be employed so precariously that 'rocking the boat' is too costly. We may be unwell or too tired to fight. It is not the job of one person to solve the problems of the world: this is what makes the strength of the collective so important. (Res-Sisters, 2016: 281)

Nonetheless, public sociology emerges wherever there are attempts by subaltern groups to understand their social context, and then make demands on professional sociology – and others – to provide analytical resources. Social movements from below – whether in the proto-organisational stage of the movement process (local rationality, militant particularism) or as mobilised movements (Cox and Nilsen, 2014) – have historically asked questions of society, have demanded a social understanding of their situation and the causes of their oppression, exploitation and injustice, and generated new understandings of society. (And, it must be remembered, that social movements from above – the proponents and beneficiaries of neoliberalism and the groups and classes seeking to exploit the crisis in their own privileged interests – are also learning and generating their own analyses and strategies to reproduce the conditions of oppression.)

As people in subaltern groups meet together and recognise that their exploitation is socially produced, and can be countered, they collectively seek answers through social analysis. The development of this social analysis has often tended to be the work of sociologists – sociologists understood as Gramsci understands intellectuals:

> All men are intellectuals, one could therefore say: but not all men have in society the function of intellectuals. Thus, because it can happen that everyone at some time fries a couple of eggs or sews up a tear in a jacket, we do not necessarily say that everyone is a cook or a tailor. (Gramsci, 1971: 9)

Public sociologists therefore are all those who draw on a systematic analysis of the social world in pursuance of a subaltern counterpublic project of emancipation, much of which is not published in refereed journals or established publishers, but in zines, blogs or oral narratives. As Lena puts this 'if we're talking about public sociology, is there a specific demarcation of where sociology starts and everyday work ends (or vice versa)'.

The neoliberal crisis of universities, and the impact on sociology – whether using and distorting the discipline to reproduce the interests of capital through managerialism, marketisation and precarity, or else by closing down departments as not 'value for money' – potentially could increase the practice of public sociology as subaltern groups seek to interpret their struggles socially. This always takes educational forms, as these interpretations require a constant and dialectical process of learning and acting. In Gelpi's words, 'in every society there is some degree of autonomy for educational action, some possibility of political confrontation, and at the same time an interrelation between the two' (Gelpi, 1979: 11).

Note

[1] At the time of publication of the Augar review, undergraduate fees for Scottish domiciled and EU citizens from outwith the UK were paid for by the Scottish Government up to a capped number of places.

References

Augar, P. (2019) *Independent Panel Report to the Review of Post-18 Education and Funding*, London: HMSO.

Burawoy, M. (2005) 'For public sociology', *American Sociological Review*, 70: 4–28.

Cox, L. and Nilsen, A.G. (2014) *We Make Our Own History: Marxism and Social Movements in the Twilight of Neoliberalism*, London: Pluto Press.

Gelpi, E. (1979) *The Future of Lifelong Education*, Manchester: University of Manchester Press.

Glenn, E.N. (2007) 'Whose public sociology? The subaltern speaks, but who is listening?', in Clawson, D., Zussman, R., Misra, J., Gerstel, N., Stokes, R., Anderton, D.L. and Burawoy, M. (eds) *Public Sociology: Fifteen Eminent Sociologists Debate Politics & the Profession in the Twenty-First Century*, Berkeley, Los Angeles: University of California Press, pp 213–230.

Gramsci, A. (1971) *Selections from Prison Notebooks* (ed and trans, Q. Hoare and G. Nowell Smith), London: Lawrence and Wishart.

London Edinburgh Weekend Return Group (1987) *In and Against the State: Discussion Notes for Socialists* (2nd edn), London: Pluto Press.

McNally, D. (2017) 'Intersections and dialectics: critical reconstructions in social reproduction theory', in Bhattacharya, T. (ed) *Social Reproduction Theory: Remapping Class, Recentring Oppression*. London: Pluto Press: pp 94–111.

Res-Sisters (2016) '"I'm an early career feminist academic: get me out of here?"' Encountering and resisting the neoliberal academy', in Thwaites, R. and Godoy-Pressland, A. (eds) *Being an Early Career Feminist Academic: Global Perspectives, Experiences and Challenges*, London: Palgrave Macmillan: pp 267–284.

Scandrett, E. (2017) 'Still spaces in the academy? The dialectic of university social movement pedagogy', in Winn, J. and Hall. R. (eds) *Mass Intellectuality and Democratic Leadership in Higher Education*, London: Bloomsbury Academic, pp 81–95.

Spivak, G.C. (1988) 'Can the subaltern speak?', in Nelson, C. and Grossberg, L. (eds) *Marxism and the Interpretation of Culture*, London: Macmillan.

Valentine, J. (2019) 'Neo-liberalism and the new institutional politics of universities', Jimmy Reid Foundation, http://reidfoundation.org/2019/05/neo-liberalism-and-the-new-institutional-politics-of-universities-paper-now-available/jrfnewinstitutionalpoliticsofuniversities/

Conclusion

Eurig Scandrett

This collection makes an argument for understanding public sociology more dialectically. The focus of our practice is on dialogue, and the dynamics of knowledge production involves dialectical relations: between teachers and students; researchers and publics; practice and theory; between different practices of sociology reflected in Burawoy's 'quadrants'; between the parochial and the universal; the local and global; and between the neoliberal university and the spaces that public sociologists find to engage in dialogue with subaltern counterpublics.

Through a process resonant with Burawoy's extended case method aiming to stimulate a dialectical process through provocation, case studies and dialogue, this book has foregrounded questions about the publics with which public sociologists engage. Nancy Fraser's concept of the subaltern counterpublic is used as a heuristic device for understanding the counterpublic spheres that public sociology as educational practice helps to create. It has also encouraged interrogation of the subalternity of the publics with which we engage. Through a series of dialogues, it has attempted to explore the extent to which public sociology as educational practice contributes to social processes in which mechanisms of exploitation and oppression can be challenged. This has helped to clarify that the 'subaltern counterpublic' device has heuristic, rather than definitional value for the practice of public sociology. It has helped to shape how we interpret the tasks of public sociologists as well as how publics interact with the social world and its negotiations over power, meaning and practices. This is a dynamic process. The subaltern counterpublic is not a fixed category of the social world, but rather always contingent, relational and subject to realignment.

These insights suggest that there is important work to be done by public sociologists at the interfaces of social change, and in the strains of social disruption that emerge. Such future work for public sociologists requires educational practice: in a strict pedagogical sense of formal, non-formal or informal education; but also in research, student support, community engagement, industrial relations and social movement activism. This would address the shifting dimensions of subalternity that may, in different contexts, be declining, emergent, contested, contradictory, contextual or incorporated.

Analysing subalternity in this way recognises the dynamic nature of relations of oppression and exploitation in historical development, and is intrinsic to Gramsci's use of the term subaltern. Groups may be subaltern at particular periods of time and may increase their relative position through building alliances with or achieving concessions from hegemonic groups through counterpublic action, or may challenge hegemony through 'discursive encounters' (Baviskar, 2005) and alliances with other subaltern groups to undermine the sources of their collective oppression or exploitation. They may emerge as new categories of subalternity, potentially from the fragmentation of other subaltern groups. Alternatively, groups may decline in relative position, which in some cases may result in exclusion, oppression or even exploitation by other groups, thereby increasing their subalternity. Raymond Williams' concepts of 'residual and emergent cultures' (Williams, 1973: 10) may be understood as those cultures that resonate with the experiences of subaltern class formations and other 'sources of real human practice' (Williams, 1973: 13) that are neglected or excluded by the dominant culture, some of which have been more dominant or resonant in previous social relations, and others are emerging in current relations of production and reproduction. In Williams' formulation, both emergent and residual cultures may exist alongside and as alternatives to the dominant 'corporate' culture, or may be oppositional to it, challenging its role in reproducing hegemony. The corporate culture will also incorporate aspects of emergent and residual cultures that can be accommodated without detriment to the hegemonic status of classes and groups whose dominance such culture legitimises. Both the material base of subaltern groups, and cultural superstructure of the subaltern human practices, determine the axes of exploitation and oppression in complex ways, which are constantly subject to renegotiation and struggle including the construction of counterpublic spaces and educational practices.

Thus, for example, it is possible to understand the achievements of feminism in incorporating into public policy practices that seek to tackle violence against women, as the Scottish Government has demonstrated. Through counterpublic action, the subalternity of women has declined in this context, although continues to be a significant aspect of social life, with varying intersections with other oppressions and exploitations. Both Orr and Whiting, and Young, in this volume, have demonstrated the ongoing counterpublic action of public sociology through dialogical pedagogy and participatory research. The movement associated with Mad identity is, moreover, an emergent counterpublic in which aspects of subalternity are being challenged. Very much in its early stages of development, the trajectory of a Mad counterpublic in relation to corporate culture and hegemonic struggle is still in the process of discernment and, as Ballantyne accounts, public sociology education is providing a crucial contribution to this process. The working class in post-industrial societies, however, is in a very different position. The axis of subalterntiy of the working class, the nature of its exploitation and exclusion, and its cultural expression, is in a constant process of renegotiation. The development of class consciousness is not linear, but multidimensional and intersectional. The roles that public sociology can play in making this process visible, developing the self-understanding of specific working class publics, interpreting the changing nature of its subalternity and discerning the opportunities for counterpublic action, are distinctly educational practices.

As the contributors to this book have demonstrated, praxis is also occurring in relation to the changing subalternity and potentialities for counterpublic action with children, teenagers, students, communities, refugees and workers, all in changing social contexts driven both by the increasing penetration of neoliberal economic logics and ideologies into areas of the social world, and by the collective agency of such groups challenging their subalternty. Such public sociology praxis is also contingent, and includes such diverse activities as dialogical pedagogy, informal learning, participatory action research, community development, service learning, policy work, art and multilingual practices.

This suggests that an important future for public sociology, both as research programme and as educational practice, is at the interfaces of the changing nature of subalternity, where counterpublic action is being considered, cultural meanings of identity forged, alliances being constructed and agency being discerned. This includes areas at the interaction between subaltern publics, where subalternity may be contested, counterpublic action may be conflicting and social contradictions may be exposed. Three examples can be given where I have had some engagement and where there are opportunities for public sociology as educational practice: the Just Transition, the trans/feminist conflict and the relationship between antisemitism and international solidarity with the Palestinian anti-colonial struggle.

The Just Transition (JT) is a concept that emerged from the trade union movement to describe a process by which the jobs, skills and livelihoods of the workers currently employed in ecologically unsustainable sectors of the economy, in particular the fossil fuel industries, can be protected during a transition to a sustainable, decarbonised economy (Morena, Krause and Stevis, 2020). This developed as a means of overcoming the 'jobs versus environment' discourse, and has roots in other trade union proposals for worker-led transitions including defence diversification and the alternative plans associated with Lucas Aerospace Shop Stewards' Combine in Britain in the 1970s (Cooley, 1980, Wainwright and Elliot, 1982). Having spent many years in the margins of trade union action and social policy, JT has recently become a more mainstream concept and, as a result, is being interpreted in a wide range of ways. Resistance to JT has come from many angles: from some in the trade union movement itself in sectors seeing it as a Trojan Horse, threatening jobs and industries with strong trade union membership and organisation; from some environmentalists who regarded JT as a distraction from the necessary task of a rapid transition to avoid ecological catastrophe; from some businesses who regarded JT as a threat to profit from interference by trade unions and/or environmentalists; and from policy makers who have regarded trade union involvement as a negative and unnecessary complication in addressing environmental concerns (Rosemberg, 2020). The recent mainstreaming of JT exemplified by the inclusion of the term in the preamble to the Paris Agreement of the UN Framework Convention on Climate Change is a result of considerable lobbying effort by trade union bodies and some environmental non-governmenal organisations (NGOs), combined with other areas of social movement activities that have put the climate emergency higher up the agenda of policy makers and in the public sphere, and insisted on a social justice agenda to be incorporated into actions on climate change (Jafry, 2018). It has also resulted in a considerable variation in meaning (Stevis, Morena and Krause, 2020), some of which actually exclude trade unions from the process, others that barely constitute a transition from the status quo, and still others that equate JT with a means of implementing radical socialism. As Snell (2020) points out, there are distinctly different approaches being taken in practice, in social democratic and liberal market economies.

Whilst there has been some growing academic interest in JT, there appears to have been no significant use of public sociology educational practice of a kind which has been documented in other reflections of working class interests in climate discourse (for example Scandrett, Crowther and McGregor, 2012). The opportunities to draw on sociologies of work and production alongside social analysis of environmental change is an important area of academic work, with potential for educational action.

A second area where there is significant potential for public sociology as educational practice is the issue of the conflict around feminism, trans-activism and sex-based rights, currently generating a great deal of hostility in academia, including around this book. In this case, both 'sides' in the argument engage with different subaltern counterpublics and draw on distinct and contested sociologies – on the one hand that of structural / materialist feminism (radical and socialist) and the praxis of the women's movement, and on the other hand queer theory and the praxis of LGBTQ+ activism (in an acronym of what has become a contested alliance of increasing initials). *In extremis*, each side denies the existence of the subaltern of the other: trans-activists seeking to deconstruct biological sex and therefore the category 'woman' to the extent that a biological man may be considered a woman through self-identity; whereas some feminists, in advocating for the interests of women, deny the possibility of changing biological sex, such that people's biological sex at birth determines their sex throughout life, irrespective of self-identity, social practice or surgical intervention.

Whilst sociology clearly cannot adjudicate between these positions, or points in between, it does provide resources through which the debate can be conducted if allowed to do so, and the practice of dialogical education provides a valuable potential praxis through which this may be done. Challenging the sources of oppression of both women and trans-sexual people, identifying, clarifying and seeking to overcome where these contradict, is an obvious area of potential activity for public sociology educational practice. Nancy Fraser's own analysis provides a useful framework (although certainly not the last word) in distinguishing between different and sometimes contradictory claims for social justice in terms of redistribution, recognition and representation (which, in turn, has been critiqued from a Queer perspective by Judith Butler and countered by Fraser: Butler, 2008, Fraser, 2008) and where these contradictions might be transcended. There is an analytical debate in the sociological literature (Connell, 2012; Murray and Hunter Blackburn, 2019). Sociological research has been conducted into the risks faced by trans-sexual individuals, and risks to women from some of the demands of trans-activists. Much sociological work has been conducted by feminists in understanding gender as a contingent social structure within the reproduction of a patriarchal order, in which biological men and women negotiate their social location, and which historically constructed and malleable gender relations are thereby subject to collective political action. Such analysis, and political project, is threatened when gender becomes confused with sex and, and both are individuated and relativised to 'identity' (arguably, also to the detriment of trans-sexual individuals). Moreover, the popular debate has served to privilege individualised 'identity' over any form of sociological analysis, so that the social is deemed irrelevant as individuals pick and choose amongst a marketplace of reified 'genders' and other identities, divorced from social and historical processes of their construction.

Whilst it is perhaps inevitable that such debates generate considerable emotional engagement, it is of particular concern that there is, in some areas of higher education in particular, the refusal of trans-activists to engage in such dialogue, and in many cases to seek to 'no platform' feminists who have attempted to do so, including through bullying, seeking to destroy reputations and careers, threats and physical violence. The production of this book encountered some difficulties in engaging in the debate, which led to the withdrawal of an editor, and it is a source of regret that it has not been possible to provide a space for dialogue between sociologically informed activists on both sides of the conflict in the pages of a book on public sociology and educational practice.

A further area of contested politics between groups with claims to subaltern counterpublics constitutes the confusion of antisemitism and anti-Zionism, in particular in relation to the international Palestine anti-colonial solidarity movement. It is, of course, certainly true that Jews are subaltern in many parts of the world, and in the Nazi Holocaust have suffered the worst scale of genocide in modern history. Campaigns against antisemitism constitute counterpublic action, and are ever more necessary in the context of the growth of neo-fascism and other forms of far right populism worldwide. An argument could even be made that some early strands of Zionism constituted a counterpublic sphere in response to European antisemitism in the nineteenth and early twentieth centuries (Greenstein, 2014). However, at least since 1948, Zionism is equated with defence of the Israeli state and justifying Jewish control over Palestinian land and resources. Some Zionist Jews go so far as to claim that Zionism is an intrinsic part of their Jewish identity, so that any critique of Zionism or the Israeli state constitutes antisemitism. For the international Zionist movement, equating a critique of Zionism and Israel with antisemitism has been used as a political tool to silence any analysis of the settler colonisation of Palestine.

It is also certainly true that the Palestinian population and its resistance to the Zionist settler colonisation project is a subaltern counterpublic. In the West Bank, Palestinians live under military occupation; in Gaza under siege; in Israel under a Jewish state with a discriminatory constitution, nationality status and law; in the refugee diaspora as forced exiles whose rights are denied; in Israeli gaols as political prisoners; and in all locations subject to the violence of the Israeli state. Those outwith Palestine/Israel who act in solidarity with the Palestinians are being deliberately targeted by the apologists for that colonial project in order to silence counterpublic activity. Whilst, again, sociology does not adjudicate absolutely in this conflict – there are Zionist sociologists for example – there are strong sociological justifications for rejecting Zionism and identifying it as an ideological justification of a settler colonial project – as indeed the ideological justification of other colonial projects have been exposed and critiqued through sociological analysis. Thus, the conflict here is not between contested subaltern counterpublics, but rather Zionism as a tool of exploitation of the Palestinians, and antisemitism being used as a means of closing down solidarity action with the Palestinian subaltern counterpublic (ironically, to the detriment of the subaltern counterpublic struggle against antisemitism). It is therefore a legitimate activity for public sociology education to engage with the Palestinian counterpublic and challenge Zionism in solidarity with the Palestinian people (al Butmeh, al Shalalfeh and Zwahre, 2019), which could include challenging antisemitism where it occurs. It is also legitimate public sociology education to engage with Jewish counterpublic action against antisemitism outwith Israel, which could also include challenging Zionism and distinguishing between antisemitism and anti-Zionism.

These are areas where public sociology as educational practice can have more of a role than it currently does. This is partially due to the difficulties of, but necessity of, genuine dialogue, rather than argument between entrenched positions, and the requirement of a sociological analysis in the terms of the dialogue (there is no dialogue, for example, when sociological analysis is denied in the debate, as would be the case of settler-colonisation deniers). It is also made more difficult by the paucity, or even denial, of sociological analysis in the public sphere generally. In the UK, this is often traced to Margaret Thatcher's neoliberal revolution and her widely quoted assertion that 'there is no such thing as society' (there are only individuals and families). Such a denial of the meta-level of analysis beyond the interactions of individual choices leads to the absence of sociological discourse in the public sphere and allows Zionists, militant trans-activists, and their ideologically-driven colonial apologists and anti-feminist allies, to silence counterpublic spheres against oppression.

The public sphere is increasingly devoid of sociological literacy, which creates a vacuum for ideological warfare. Not that sociology provides answers; but it does provide a domain of analysis in which struggles between subalterns take place. The public sphere is increasingly devoid of sociological literacy, let alone sociological imagination – public affairs are interpreted in individualistic, colonial- and consumer-ideological narratives in which the social is denied. Thus, although not addressed through this book, there is potentially a 'public education' role for 'traditional' public sociology, even if the risk of this is incorporation.

The desociologising trend raises the question of the future of sociology, let alone public sociology, in an increasingly neoliberal higher education. The institutions entrusted with knowledge are in the process of selling it off. How can subaltern publics ever trust universities? Where now can we find knowledge? Posing the question whether universities provide distinctive opportunities for public sociology education, because they provide 'educational spaces in which the structural contradictions of neoliberal capital are so explicitly being played out' (Scandrett, 2017: 83) provoked controversy amongst contributors to Dialogue III. As with any crisis, we look for the educational opportunities afforded by the crisis, the struggle of the subaltern to make sense of their situation. Ettore Gelpi's hopeful refrain is pertinent, that 'in every society there is some degree of autonomy for educational action, some possibility of political confrontation, and at the same time an interrelation between the two' (Gelpi, 1979: 11)

All the contributors to this volume are operating at the margins of sociology. Some are sociologists for whom their public sociology work needs to be justified and defended; others are academics in different disciplines who have drawn on social analysis in making their work relevant to publics; a few are operating from NGOs and making use of academic sociology in their public action. Whilst university sociology is relevant to all and provides welcome spaces for the practices of dialogical knowledge co-production with subaltern counterpublics, nonetheless the relentless logic of the neoliberal university is a constant presence, a spectre that haunts public sociology education, closing down, incorporating and seeking to commodify these spaces as practitioners open them up. As Harney and Moten (2013) in the North American context put it:

> [I]t cannot be denied that the university is a place of refuge, and it cannot be accepted that the university is a place of enlightenment. In the face of these conditions one can only sneak into the university and steal what one can. To abuse its hospitality, to spite its mission, to join its refugee colony, its gypsy encampment, to be in but not of – this is the path of the subversive intellectual in the modern university. (Harney and Moten, 2013: 26)

The university is in crisis. The von Humboldt / Newman ideal of an institution entrusted with Enlightenment knowledge, with all the liberal elitism that implies, was only ever an ideal type myth, but one that could be drawn on to provide some ballast against commercialisation. On the other hand, the neoliberal university exists for the commodification of knowledge, and for the surveillance of knowledge workers. That most of the contributors to this book are employed by or operating out of universities, and draw on public sociology in their pedagogical practice irrespective of their discipline or profession, demonstrates that the crisis is fertile with possibilities – as most crises are. However, the situations explored in the book are unstable and unsustainable. They are not models for the future of academic sociology – or indeed higher education practice – but reflections on action in the midst of struggle.

In recent years, university campuses have (again) become battlegrounds. In Greece, South Africa, Hong Kong, India, Egypt, Chile, battles over surveillance and repression by state security forces, over control of ideological reproduction, over the role of education in political economy and neocolonial sovereignty, over the centrality of the social in the production of knowledge. Proposals for ways forward for universities have been emerging, whether intersectional feminist (Taylor and Lahad, 2018; Breeze, Taylor and Costa, 2019), democratising the production of knowledge (Neary and Winn, 2019; Neary 2020), engendering mass intellectuality (Hall and Winn, 2017) or celebrating subversion from the undercommons (Harney and Moten, 2013). The way out of the crisis will only come from the diverse struggles within it, and in the dialectical contradictions between Enlightenment knowledge and commodified knowledge; between university workers' labour and students as workers (Mignot and Gee, Case III.1 and Wånggren, Case III.6); between sociology as discipline and as a resource for praxis.

The Augar review of post-18 education in England (Augar, 2019) determined that sociology, along with all kinds of social sciences and humanities, constitute 'low value' degrees, on the basis that higher education provision has perversely expanded beyond the demands of the UK economy, and tuition fees have increased beyond escalation in costs. The report argued that universities in England were expanding income from provision of education in social sciences and humanities in order to subsidise expensive education in Science, Technology, Engineering and Mathematics, for which the economy requires graduates: 'It is difficult to explain why spend on ... Social Studies should have increased at more than twice the rate of Physics and Engineering, for any other reason than that the additional income became available attached to these subjects' (Augar, 2019: 73). The result of this:

> has personal consequences for those whose expectations have been disappointed [because they are 'left stranded with poor earnings and mounting "debt"'] and economic consequences for the state that foots the bill [because these debts for student fees are repayable only by graduates with incomes over a certain level]. (Augar, 2019: 65)

This of course is a consequence of universities behaving as economically rational actors in a quasi-market constructed by the UK government in England (with different but knock-on effects for Scotland, Wales and Northern Ireland). Similar logics will apply in other political economies of higher education that drive university governing bodies (often willingly) into behaving as economically rational actors in quasi-markets. Nonetheless, the lesson is clear, that educational practices must be disciplined by the economic demands of the neoliberal economy and that much sociology is not value for money for either the student (as a consumer of educational products) or the taxpayer (as a consumer of the economic benefits of education).

In its essence antagonistic to neoliberalism, public sociology is not value for money. As the practices in the case studies of this book attest, it has survived – even thrived – in the margins of the neoliberal university: claiming legitimacy opportunistically under the cover of respectable liberal demands of social policy (against violence against women, for refugee integration); service learning; peer-reviewed publications; training students for (the victims of) the demands of the economy despite the economy not wanting to pay for this. Public sociology, through its dual accountability to academic rigour and the political demands of subaltern counterpublics, refuses to be commodified – where it succeeds in a market economy, it fails in its dual accountability and, therefore, ceases to exist.

The future of public sociology as educational practice is therefore likely to remain in the margins. Contrary to Burawoy's appeal for the discipline of sociology to welcome public sociology (in North America), 'into the framework of our discipline ... [to] make public sociology a visible and legitimate enterprise, and, thereby, invigorate the discipline as a whole' (Burawoy, 2005: 4), such an endeavour is only feasible, indeed desirable, in conditions where sociology can survive as a non-commodifiable space in a university political economy intent on commodifying all spaces. This may be the case in the University of California, Berkeley, that employs Burawoy, or indeed in the institutions that employ the members of the American Sociological Association (ASA). For the universities of Scotland and England, especially the smaller, newer institutions largely represented here (Queen Margaret University, Nottingham Trent University), more exposed to the winds of neoliberalism, the future of public sociology as educational practice is likely to be from the margins, emerging as surely as counterpublics emerge wherever subaltern groups stand up and demand dignity, and seek solidarity in their attempts to analyse the society that oppresses and exploits them. It is such emergent groups in their militant particularism that legitimise the educational practices of public sociology.

Michael Burawoy introduced his 'For public sociology' address to the ASA with an allusion to Walter Benjamin's angel of history, who, in the face of the storm blowing from Paradise, 'can no longer close [his wings]'. This storm irresistibly propels him into the future to which his back is turned, while the pile of debris before him grows skyward. There is perhaps a more appropriate metaphor for the analysis developed in this book. Remaining with the metaphysical, I wondered if it is a spectre, haunting the neoliberal university? However, I prefer a more organic allegory. Is it, rather than an angel of history, a worm of history, ubiquitously burrowing underground, emerging wherever there is some disturbance, regenerating itself from the fragments wherever attempts are made to package it, destroy or distort it, disappearing again into the shadows, becoming semi-dormant until the next time?

References

al Butmeh, A., al Shalalfeh, Z. and Zwahre, M. with Scandrett, E. (2019) 'The environment as a site of struggle against settler-colonisation in Palestine', in Harley, A. and Scandrett, E. (eds) *Environmental Justice, Popular Struggle and Community Development*, Bristol: Policy Press, pp 153–171.

Augar, P. (2019) *Independent Panel Report to the Review of Post-18 Education and Funding*, Department of Education, HM Government. London: HMSO.

Baviskar, A. (2005) 'Red in tooth and claw? Looking for class in struggles over nature', in Ray, R. and Katzenstein, M.F. (eds) *Social Movements in India*, New Delhi: Oxford, pp 161–178.

Breeze, M., Taylor, Y. and Costa, C. (2019) (eds) *Time and Space in the Neoliberal University: Futures and Fractures in Higher Education*, London: Palgrave Macmillan.

Burawoy, M. (2005) 'For public sociology', *American Sociological Review*, 70: 4–28.

Butler, J. (2008) 'Merely cultural', in Olson, K. (ed) *Adding Insult to Injury: Nancy Fraser Debates Her Critics*, London: Verso: pp 42–56.

Connell, R. (2012) 'Transsexual women and feminist thought: toward new understanding and new politics', *Signs*, 37(4), Sex: A Thematic Issue: 857–881.

Cooley, M. (1980) *Architect or Bee? The Human Price of Technology*, London: Hogarth Press.

Fraser, N. (2008) 'Heterosexism, misrecognition, and capitalism: a response to Judith Butler', in Olson, K. (ed) *Adding Insult to Injury: Nancy Fraser Debates Her Critics*, London: Verso: pp 57–68.

Gelpi, E. (1979) *The Future of Lifelong Education*, Manchester: Manchester University Press.

Greenstein, R. (2014) *Zionism and its Discontents: A Century of Radical Dissent in Israel/Palestine*, London: Pluto Press.

Harney, S. and Moten, F. (2013) *The Undercommons: Fugitive Planning and Black Study*, Wivenhoe / New York / Port Watson, NY: Minor Compositions.

Hall, R. and Winn, J. (eds) (2017) *Mass Intellectuality and Democratic Leadership in Higher Education*, London: Bloomsbury.

Jafry, T. (ed) (2018) *Routledge Handbook of Climate Justice*, London: Routledge.

Morena, E, Krause, D. and Stevis, D. (eds) (2020) *Just Transitions: Social Justice in the Shift Towards a Low-Carbon World*, London: Pluto Press.

Murray, K. and Hunter Blackburn, L. (2019) 'Losing sight of women's rights: the unregulated introduction of gender self-identification as a case study of policy capture in Scotland', *Scottish Affairs*, 28.3: 262–289.

Neary, M. (2020) *Student as Producer: How do Revolutionary Teachers Teach?*, Alresford: Zero Books.

Neary, M. and Winn, J. (2019) 'Making a co-operative university: a new form of knowing – not public but social', *FORUM*, 61(2): 271–279.

Rosemberg, A. (2020) ;"No jobs on a dead planet": the international trade union movement and just transition', in Morena, E., Krause, D. and Stevis, D. (eds) *Just Transitions: Social Justice in the Shift Towards a Low-Carbon World*, London: Pluto Press: pp 32–55.

Scandrett, E. (2017) 'Still spaces in the academy? The dialectic of university social movement pedagogy', in Winn, J. and Hall, R. (eds) *Mass Intellectuality and Democratic Leadership in Higher Education*, London: Bloomsbury Academic.

Scandrett, E., Crowther, J. and McGregor, C. (2012) 'Poverty, protest and popular education: class interests in discourses of climate change', in Carvalho, A. and Rai Peterson, T. (eds) *Climate Change Politics: Communication and Public Engagement*, Amherst, NY: Cambia Press: pp 207–366.

Snell, D. (2020) 'Just transition solutions and challenges in a neoliberal and carbon-intensive economy', in Morena, E., Krause, D. and Stevis, D. (eds) *Just Transitions: Social Justice in the Shift Towards a Low-Carbon World*, London: Pluto Press: pp 198–218.

Stevis, D., Morena, E. and Krause, D. (2020) 'Introduction: the genealogy and contemporary politics of just transitions', in Morena, E., Krause, D. and Stevis, D. (eds) *Just Transitions: Social Justice in the Shift Towards a Low-Carbon World*, London: Pluto Press: pp 1–31.

Taylor, Y. and Lahad, K. (2018) (eds) *Feeling Academic in the Neoliberal University: Feminist Flights, Fights and Failures*, London: Palgrave Macmillan.

Wainwright, H. and Elliot, D. (1982) *The Lucas Plan: A new Trade Unionism in the Making?*, London: Alison and Busby.

Williams, R. (1973) 'Base and Superstructure in Marxist Cultural Theory', *New Left Review*, 1/82.

Index

Note: page numbers in *italic* type refer to figures; those in **bold** type refer to tables.

A
ableism 332
academic credibility, and critical service learning 310
academics 95
 engaged 32
 precarity of 336–337
 proletarianisation of 88, 89, 337
 sociology 260–261
 subalternity of 336–337
accumulation by dispossession 86, 87
Act of Union, 1707 229
action 179
 and children's participation 172, 176
active citizenship:
 and children 171, 172, 173, 176, 178, 180
Addington, Elaine 267–285
adult education 231
 Scotland 229
 see also Experts by Experience arts and sociology project; WEA (Workers Educational Association)
adult-child relationships 171, 173, 175
 in participative research enquiry 178–180
advertising, regulation of 106
Advertising Standards Authority Ltd. 106
Afghanistan, refugees and asylum-seekers from 137
African Americans 102
Agbakuribe, Bamidele Chika 332
agency 179, 220
Ahmed, Sara 185, 234
Albania, refugees and asylum-seekers from 137
Alcohol Focus Scotland 153–154
alcohol use, by young people *see* young people and alcohol use

AlcoLOLs project *see* young people, and alcohol use
'Alec' (research participant), WEA Fife 80, 98–101, 104–106
Alexander Report on Adult Education: The Challenge of Change (Scottish Education Department) 287, 295
Alston, Philip 204–205
American Sociological Association:
 Buroway's Presidential Address 1, 3, 13, 113, 230, 253, 260, 353
 hegemony of 6
Andersonian Institution 111, 229, 230, 337–338
angel of history 353
Anglo-normativity 186, 193, 195
anti-psychiatry 95
antisemitism and the Palestine anti-colonial struggle 346, 348–349
Arendt, Hannah 171, 172, 175, 176, 179
Argyll Commission report, 1868 229
arts-based approaches 345, 183–197
 Experts by Experience arts and sociology project 267–283
 and mental health 269
 photographic exhibition and performance piece, 'Same Hell, Different Devils' study 59–61
 value of 62
Asylum Aid 141
Asylum and Immigration Act 1996 136
Asylum and Immigration Appeals Act 1993 136
asylum-seeking women in Scotland *see* refugee and asylum-seeking women in Scotland
Athena SWAN 233–234
Athens 138
Audit Scotland 208

Augar review (*Independent Panel Report to the Review of Post-18 Education and Funding*) 338, 351–352
Augé, Marc 75
austerity 94–95, 204–205, 290, 295
Australian Aborigines 115
Australian Sociological Association 2017 conference 183–184
authentic relationships, and critical service learning 306–307

B

Back, L. 253
Ball, S. 317, 320
Ballantyne, Elaine 20–21, 25–35, 220, 345
BAME (Black, Asian and Minority Ethnic) communities:
 exclusion from universities 332
 Scotland 103
banking model of education 158
Barrera, D. 310
Bartky, S.L. 58
Bauman, Z. 75
BBC 85
Benjamin, Walter 353
Beresford, P. 25, 30–31, 31–32
Besbris, M. 257
BetterThanZero campaign 327
Bhattacharya, T. 18, 20, 80, 84
Birkbeck 337–338
Birmingham City University 231
Black feminist theory 116–117, 221, 233
Black Studies 336
Blackledge, A. 191
Blind Leading the Blind, The (Shawa) 274–276, *275*
Bohm, D. 155
Boliver, V. 258
Bonatti, M. 212
Booth, Charles 123
border control, HEIs as agents of 229, 332
Bourdieu, Pierre 76, 85, 255, 260
Bouverne De-Bie, M. 177
Bradley, David 267–285
Brady, David 125–126
brave space 153, 155, 161
Brexit 103, 296
British Empire, Scotland's role in 115, 230
British Sign Language 192
British Sociological Association 231
Broadcast Committee of Advertising Practice Ltd 106
Brookhouse, Linda 267–285
Brougham, Lord Henry 111
Brown, Eleanor L. 142

Brown, J. 291
Brown, W. 316–317
Brownell, K.D. 277
Bryson, E. 141–142
Buber, M. 164
Bunting, Jenny 267–285
Burke, Gregory 75
Buroway, Michael 5, 47, 65, 77, 85, 93, 96, 97, 101–102, 131, 132, 256, 257, 268, 273, 276, 282, 302–303, 308, 338
 American Sociological Association Presidential Address 1, 3, 13, 113, 230, 253, 260, 353
 and class 18
 and extended case methodology 1, 2–3
 policy sociology 121, 124–126, **125**
 sociological quadrant 122, 217, 218, 343
Burris, M.A. 55
Bute Mansions, Gibson Street, Glasgow (Hay) 278, *279*
Butin, D.W. 302, 304, 306, 307, 310, 311
Butler, Judith 347
bystanders, and interventions 306

C

Caledonian antisyzygy 76
Callaghan, James 244
Cameron, Deborah 192
Canaan, Joyce 81–82
Canada:
 Mad Studies 26, 30
capitalism:
 appropriation of the 'commons' by 245
 nature of 19, 20
 neo-Marxist analysis of 245
CAPS Independent Advocacy 27, 30
Casey Review, The: A Review Into Opportunity and Integration (UK Government) 191–192
Castelrione, P. 154, 156, 1598
Chartists 112
childcare issues, refugees and asylum-seeking women 143, 145
childhood, constructions of 174–175
children:
 and active citizenship 171, 172, 173, 176, 178, 180
 agency of 171, 174, 176, 178
 children's rights movement 172
 critique of 174–176
 developmental psychology 174, 176, 219
 research with 172
 rights of 171, 172–174
 surveillance of 176

INDEX

see also young children, and participative research enquiry
Children and Young People's Commissioner Scotland 47
Chile 351
Chomsky, N. 274
Chow, Rey 221
Christie Commission 207
Church, Kathryn 30
citizen sourcing 290
citizen's jury stage, young people and alcohol use 164–167, *166*
citizenship:
  and children 171, 172, 173, 176, 177, 178, 180
  feminist perspective on 138–139
civic republicanism 139
civil society 291
Clark, C.D. 176, 180
class 94
  as basis for analysis 14–15, 18–19
  changing nature of 21
  decline in identification with subaltern classes 96
  GBCS ('Great British Class Survey') 85, 86
  HEIs and exclusion 229, 233
  and intersectionality 20
  invisibility of 21, 79, 80, 96, 98, 106–107
  Marxist analysis of 18, 19, 83, 84, 85, 86, 96
  problems with 79–82
  and professional sociologists 83–84
  sociological approaches to 84–87
  soundings on 82–84, 96
  subaltern counterpublics of 87–89
class analysis 82–83, 88, 89
class consciousness 82
class identity 82, 88
client capture in policy sociology 129–131
climate change, and the JT (Just Transition) movement 97, 345, 346–347
closed social problems 294
coercive controlling behaviour 39
cognitive decolonialisation 115–116
Collie, Shirley-anne 25–35
colonial languages 190, 220
colonialism 114–115
  and knowledge 114
  and Scotland 115–116
'colonisation', of the subaltern 94, 98
Comic Relief 141
Commissioner for Fair Access 233
Committee of Advertising Practice Ltd 106

common sense knowledge 16
'commons', appropriation of by capitalism 245
Communist Party of Britain (CPB) 83
Communist Party of Great Britain (CPGB) 83
Communities Inc. 305–306
communities of practice, and critical service learning 310
community 290–291, 292
  and the *Experts by Experience* arts and sociology project 268, 269
community education 1, 231, 289, 338
  Scotland 287, 295
Community Empowerment (Scotland) Act 2015 200, 208, 209
community engagement 200, 345
  background and context 287–289
  critical curriculum for 289–292
  cultivating critical awareness 296–297
  education for citizenship 295–296
  framing problems and formulating solutions 292–294
  learning for democracy 295, 296
  and universities in Scotland 213
Community Engagement: A Critical Guide for Practitioners (Shaw and Crowther) 287
community planning partnerships (CPPs), Scotland 200, 201, 204, 211–213, 218
community workers, and WEA Fife 66–67, 70–71, 73–74
Comte, A. 231
Concannon, K. 302
Connell, Raewyn 7, 45, 115, 220, 231, 280
conscientisation 2, 55, 301
  young people and alcohol use 158, 161–164
consciousness raising 116
Conservative governments:
  marginalisation of sociology from public policy 124
  neoliberal economic policies 81
  see also Thatcher, Margaret
consumer protection law, and HEIs (higher education institutions) 241
consumers, HE students as 228, 316, 317, 318
contract research:
  'confessional' narratives of 127–128
  experiences of in policy sociology 122, 127–129
Convention of Scottish Local Authorities (COSLA) 136, 141
Convention of the Rights of the Child (United Nations) 173, 175, 177

Convention Relating to the Status of Refugees, 1951 (United Nations) 136, 137
Cooke, A. 229
Cornwall, A. 177–178
corporate culture 344
Cosh, Lorna 267–285
COSLA (Convention of Scottish Local Authorities) 136, 141
Costa, Beverley 193
Costa, L. 30
Costas Batlle, I. 323
counter-hegemony 6, 33, 296
countering 14, 94
counter-narratives 55
counterpublic action 345–346
Cox, L. 89
CPB (Communist Party of Britain) 83
CPGB (Communist Party of Great Britain) 83
CPPs (community planning partnerships), Scotland 200, 201, 204, 211–213, 218
  as a place-based response to inequality 205–211
  social, economic and policy context 204–205
Creese, A. 191
Crehan, Kate 15–16, 113
Crenshaw, K. 45
Cresswell, M. 32
critical consciousness, and critical service learning 310
critical feminist theory 55
critical pedagogy 1
  MPHI (Mad People's History and Identity) course, Queen Margaret University, Edinburgh 26
critical service learning 299, 301–302
  authentic relationships 306–307
  and critical consciousness 310
  Hollaback Chalk Walk 305
  rationale for 302–303
  redistribution of power 305–306
  social change orientation 304–305
  Stand By Me initiative, Communities Inc. 305–306
  sustainability in 307–310
  see also service learning
Crowther, Jim 200, 235, 287–298, 331–341
Cultural Action for Freedom (Freire) 181
cultural capital 85
  of students 255
cultural hegemony of HE (higher education) 279
cultural rationality 201–202
culture circles 162
curriculum 111, 112, 113
  critical curriculum for community engagement 289–292
  and critical service learning 310
  decolonisation of 115
  relevance of 244
  school 219

D

Dane, John 267–285
decoding 163–164
decolonialisation 114–115, 231
Decolonising the Mind (Ngugi wa) 196
Deeming, Liz 25–35
deindustrialisation, in Scotland 69
democracy 291
  democratic deficit of women in Scotland 41
  democratic education 1
  'democratic engagement' 200
  'Democratic Intellect' 230
deschooling 112
developmental psychology 174, 176, 219
Dewaele, Jean Marc 192
dialogue 1, 343
  dialogical method, with young people and alcohol use 18–159, 153, 155, 161–164
  dialogical pedagogy 1–2, 112–113, 113–114, 117, 345
  and knowledge production 218–219
  in research with children 173–174
difference paradigm of justice 18, 19
disability:
  and ableism 333
  and class 20
disciplinary power 118, 190
  of precarity in universities 334
diversity 185
  class-based analysis of 15
  and HEIs (higher education institutions) 233–234
Dobash, Rebecca 40–41, 45
Dobash, Russell 40–41, 45
Docherty-Hughes, John R. 235, 267–285, 338
domestic abuse 38, 40–41
  and coercive controlling behaviour 39
  SWA's education for gender justice work 43–44
  see also GJV (Gender Justice and Violence: Feminist Approaches) course, SWA (Scottish Women's Aid) and QMU (Queen Margaret University); VAW (violence against women)

domestic abuse survivors; 'Same Hell,
  Different Devils' study 53–54, 61–62
  background and context 54–55
  educational life of study beyond research
    setting 59–61
  research outline 55
  risk to survivors of speaking out 56–59
domination, and children's
  participation 172
Dorling, D. 207
drama students, and the 'Same Hell,
  Different Devils' study 60–61
drinking culture in Scotland 156–157,
  159–160
drinks industry 155–156, 157–158, 160
du Bois, W.E.B. 122
Dundee University 332
Durkheim, E. 18, 116, 231

E

economic capital 85
economic crash, 2008 82
Edgell, S. 246–247
Edinburgh Association for the University
  Education of Women 230
Edinburgh City Council 208–209
Edinburgh Futures Institute 323–324
Edinburgh Voluntary Organization
  Council (EVOC) 201, 210
education:
  banking model of 158
  emancipatory 14–15
  problem-posing 55
  refugees and asylum-seeking
    women 142–144
  see also adult education; community
    education; pedagogy of the oppressed
Egypt 351
Eikeland, O. 58
Elias, N. 260
Elliott, K. 280
Ellison, Marion 199–216, 217–223
emancipatory education 14–15
emancipatory struggles 17
emergent cultures 344
emotional reactions 269–270, 283
employment:
  refugees and asylum-seeking
    women 142–144
  see also precarity
engaged academics 32
Engels, F. 111
England:
  immigration policy 137
  language policies 192
  see also UK
English language:
  Anglo-normativity 186, 193, 195
  domination in Zimbabwe 194
  domination of in research 187, 190,
    193, 196, 220, 223
  and integration 191–192
  in Scotland 75–76, 77
  Standard English speech 255–256
Enlightenment knowledge 111, 112,
  116, 125
Enlightenment, Scottish 7, 76, 230
environment:
  HEIs as agents of environmental
    destruction 229
  and the JT (Just Transition)
    movement 97, 345, 346–347
environmental justice 17, 97
Eritrea, refugees and asylum-seekers
  from 137
Escrigas, C. 213
ethnic nationalism 96
Evans, G. 98
EVOC (Edinburgh Voluntary
  Organization Council) 201, 210
Ewe language 188
exclusion:
  class-based analysis of 15
  and HEIs 229, 233, 332
  from public sphere 96
Exiled (Spence) 276, 276–278
Experts by Experience arts and sociology
  project 267–271
  reflections on 282–283
  students' experiences 271–282
exploitation 17, 344
  and capitalism 19
extended case methodology 1,
  2–3, 4, 343

F

Fairbairn, J. 257
Falk, R.F. 281–282
Fanon, F. 114–115
Fanti language 187
far Right movements 96
feminism 16–17, 21, 94, 221
  Black feminist theory 116–117,
    221, 233
  critical feminist theory 55
  and dialogue with students 257
  feminist knowledge
    production 232–233
  FPAR (feminist participatory action
    research) 21, 53, 55
  and participatory action research 114,
    116–117
  and refugee and asylum-seeking women
    in Scotland 135

second-wave 38–39
structural 18
as a subaltern counterpublic 95–96
third world feminists 221
trans/feminist conflict 97, 345–346, 347–348
and VAW (violence against women) 38–39, 344–345
Ferguson, S. 18–19
Fife:
  WEA Fife 65–67, 68–75, 77, 79, 94, 98
Finely, L. 302
First Nations 115
Fleming, P. 245
Foskett, N. 244
fossil fuel industries, and the JT (Just Transition) movement 97, 345, 346–347
Foucault, M. 18, 172, 175, 190, 278, 316–317
  and participatory action research 114, 117
'founding fathers' narratives of sociology 231
FPAR (feminist participatory action research) 21, 53, 55
  see also domestic abuse survivors; 'Same Hell, Different Devils' study
Frankfurt School 114
Fraser, Esther 25–35
Fraser, Nancy 4, 17, 18, 45, 54, 93, 95, 96, 97, 102, 104, 107, 254, 258–259, 347
Freedom Programme 56
Freire, Paulo 1–2, 3, 16, 55, 96, 113, 185, 187, 191, 194, 195, 219, 260, 297, 301
  and active citizenship 172, 173, 176, 180
  Cultural Action for Freedom 181
  culture circles 162
  on decoding 163–164
  definition of praxis 31
  humanisation 164
  liberating action 165
  and participatory action research 114, 117
  pedagogy of the oppressed 1–2, 157–158, 159
  and the *Experts by Experience* arts and sociology project 269, 282
  problematisation stage 159
  and radical love 306–307, 312
  and sub oppression 160–161
French language 190
French Revolution 138
Friedman, S. 254

Furco, A. 300–301
Further and Higher Education Act 1992 230

G

Gaelic language 192
GAMH (Glasgow Association for Mental Health):
  Experts by Experience arts and sociology project 267–283
Gaza 349
GBCS ('Great British Class Survey') 85, 86
Gee, Ricky 89, 235, 335
Geertz, C. 76
Gelpi, Ettore 112, 219, 340, 350
gender:
  and class 20
  HEIs and exclusion 229, 233
  and labour market precarity 247
  stereotyping 106, 140
  structural and cultural aspects of 96
  structural feminist understandings of 18
gender justice:
  educational programme 21
  see also GJV (Gender Justice and Violence: Feminist Approaches) course, SWA (Scottish Women's Aid) and QMU (Queen Margaret University)
gender politics 21
gender violence see GJV (Gender Justice and Violence: Feminist Approaches) course, SWA (Scottish Women's Aid) and QMU (Queen Margaret University); VAW (violence against women)
gendered shame 58
'generative themes' 2
German language 190
Giatsi Clausen, Maria 118, 171–182, 219
Giddens, A. 281
Gilfillan, Paul 19, 21, 65–78, 79–80, 83, 93–108
Gill, R. 318, 319
Giroux, H. 302, 303
GJV (Gender Justice and Violence: Feminist Approaches) course, SWA (Scottish Women's Aid) and QMU (Queen Margaret University) 21, 37–38, 41, 44–46, 97
  Scottish context 38–42
  Scottish Women's Aid and education for gender justice 43–44
  students' reflections on course impact 47–49
Glasgow Association for Mental Health (GAMH):

INDEX

Experts by Experience arts and sociology project 267–283
Glasgow City Council 146
Glasgow English as a Second Language (ESOL) Forum 141
Glasgow Museums Resource Centre (GMRC):
  Experts by Experience arts and sociology project 268–283
Glasgow Open Museum (OM):
  Experts by Experience arts and sociology project 267–283
Glasgow Violence Against Women Partnership 141
Glenn, E.N. 336
Glenn, Evelyn Nakano 102, 262
Global South, centrality of public sociology 231
globalisation 114–115
glossophobia 192
GMRC (Glasgow Museums Resource Centre):
  Experts by Experience arts and sociology project 268–283
Goffman, E. 272
'good work' 248
Gouldner, A.W. 256
Gramling, David 186, 190
Gramsci, Antonio 5–6, 14, 15, 16, 45, 93, 102, 113, 260, 268, 283, 296, 337, 339–340, 344
'Great British Class Survey' (GBCS) 85, 86
Greece 351
Greig, David 75, 76
Grenfell fire tragedy, London 294
Griffon, C. 112
Gutberlet, J. 212
Guy, Alexander 280, *281*

H

Habermas, J. 17, 102
habitus clivé 76
habitus, of students 255
Halsall, Guy 317
Halsey, A.H. 124
Hamilton, C. 308
Haraway, D. 116, 221
Hardt, M. 245, 246
Harney, S. 350–351
Harper, S.R. 260
Hartmann, D. 256
Harvey, David 19, 84, 86–87
hate crime 305
Hawkesworth, Mary 139–140
Hay, Andrew 278, *279*
HE (higher education):

cultural hegemony of 279
marketisation of 228, 246, 288, 315–316
massification of 246
political economies of 352
Scotland 230
students' experiences 235
tension between 'academic' and 'vocational' aspects 244–245
hegemonic masculinity 280–281
hegemony 5–6, 14
decline of 296
HEIs (higher education institutions)/ universities:
and ableism 333
access and participation issues 231, 233–234, 235, 257, 288
Scotland's WP (widening participation) agenda 253, 254, 257, 261
as agents of border control 229, 332
as agents of environmental destruction 229
and class 229, 233
and colonialism 333
commodification of education 288
community relationships 213, 337–338
and consumer protection law 241
crisis in 351–352
and diversity 233–234
employability issues 301–302
postgraduate employment and earnings metrics 241–242
England 229–230, 353
and exclusion 229, 233, 332
expansion following Robbins report 229–230
and imperialism 333
and inequality and oppression 229, 233, 254
international students 335
and mass intellectuality 332, 351
neoliberal 4, 228, 231, 234, 316–319, 331–341, 351
pensions strike, 2017-2018 321–326, 335–336
performance measurement 317–318
as places of conflict 351
and precarity 333, 334
provider-consumer relationship with students 241, 316, 317, 318
and public sociology practice 227–237, 331
and racism 332, 333
responsibilisation and marketisation 316–319
role as co-generators of public knowledge 212

363

Scotland 6, 7, 229–230, 353
  and sexism 333
  as social factories 245
  stress and ill-health among
    staff 318–319
  survival strategies 334–335
  trade unions 235, 316, 319–327,
    335–336
  tuition fees 332, 335
  whiteness of 332
Henderson, E. 324–325
Herman, A. 274
heteronormativity 101
Hill Collins, Patricia 128, 221, 233
Himmah 303
Hirsu, L. 141–142
Hoare, Q. 14
Hoene, C. 322
Holtby, A. 56
Home Office, and immigration
  policy 147
Home Secretary:
  Call to End Violence against Women
    and Girls 145
homophobia 96, 101
Hong Kong 351
hooks, bell 194
Horkheimer, T. 114
Hoschchild, Arlie 269–270
humanisation 164
humanities, as 'low value' degrees 351–352
Hume, David 76
Hutchings, Sharon 31–341, 235, 299–314

I

identitarianism 96
identity:
  and the *Experts by Experience* arts and
    sociology project 268, 269
  nature of, and class 81
Idles 308
Illich, I. 112
immigration policy:
  border control, HEIs as agents
    of 229, 332
  England 137
  Scotland 137
  UK 136–137, 142
imperial colonialism 115
In and Against the State (London Edinburgh
    Weekend Return Group) 333, 334
*Independent Panel Report to the Review of
    Post-18 Education and Funding* (Augar
    review) 338, 351–352
India 351
indigenous languages 187–189
  see also multilingualism

indigenous practice 186
induction projects with students 258
industrial action 88
inequalities:
  at local level 199
infantilisation of students 241, 242
institutional ethnography 127
intercultural listening and
    speaking 191, 192
International Social Science
    Council 199–200
intersectionality 18
  and citizenship 139–140
  and class 19–20
interventions, by bystanders 306
Invention of Monolingualism, The
  (Gramling) 190
invisibility of class 21, 79, 80, 96, 98,
    106–107
Iran, refugees and asylum-seekers from 137
Iraq, refugees and asylum-seekers from 137
Israel:
  antisemitism and the Palestine anti-
    colonial struggle 346, 348–349
Italian language 190

J

Jackson, M.C. 157
Janowitz, Morris 124
Jenkins, C. 81
Jews, subalternity of 348
  see also antisemitism and the Palestine
    anti-colonial struggle
Johnson, Karl 31–341, 89, 235
Johnson, R. 45, 112
'Joy As An Act of Resistance' (Idles) 308
JT (Just Transition) 97, 345, 346–347
Judicial Institute for Scotland 43
Jump, P. 317
Just Transition (JT) 97, 345, 346–347

K

Kane, L. 1–2, 14, 112–113, 257, 259
Kelly, Liz 41
Khaldun, Ibn 231
Khan, S. 257
Kimmel, M. 280
Kinsella, E.A. 26
Klaehn, J. 274
Kleidman, R. 32
knappin' (Shetland dialect) 255–256
knowledge:
  colonial 114
  common sense 16
  decolonialisation 114–115
  Enlightenment knowledge 111, 112,
    116, 125

and feminism 116
political economy of 223
validation of 113
women's 116
see also public knowledge; really useful knowledge
knowledge production 343
  dialectical approach to 118
  dialogical 222
  feminist 232–233
  by mad people 32
  participatory 222
  by subaltern groups 16
Knowledges theme 3–4
Krasteva, Anna 142
Krause, Grace 315, 316, 319, 322, 323, 324, 325

L

Labour Party 98, 123
language 220
  colonial 190, 220
  metaphoricity of 190–191
  and psychotherapy 193
  see also multilingualism
Laube, H. 228–229
Law, Jan 117–118, 121–134, 217, 218
Law, John 125
LeFrançois, B.A. 26
Learning to Labour (Willis) 335
Leblanc, S. 26
Ledwith, M. 311
Leff, E. 201–202
Left parties 83
Left-wing political parties 98
LEO (Longitudinal Educational Outcomes) dataset 241–242
LGBTQ+ activism 347
liberating action 165
Lifelong Education 112, 219, 288
Lindsay, Robert 267–285
linguaphobia 192
linguistics, as a barrier in HE 255–256
liquid modernity 75
localism 290
London Edinburgh Weekend Return Group 333, 334
Longitudinal Educational Outcomes (LEO) dataset 241–242
Lothian, Scotland, mental health service user movement 29–30
Loveday, V. 261
Lovin, C. Laura 118, 135–151, 217–223
Lozano, A.A. 282
LSE (London School of Economics) 123
Lucas Aerospace Shop Stewards' Combine 346

Lynch, K. 317
Lyons Lewis, Andrea 235, 299–314, 338

M

MacArthur, Peigi 156
Macaskill, A. 240
MacAulay, Lord 76
MacDairmid, Hugh 74, 75, 76, 77
Maclean, Kirsten 25–35
mad identity 20, 95, 345
Mad People's History and Identity (MPHI) course, Queen Margaret University, Edinburgh 25–26, 27, *28*, 29, 32, 33, 94
Mad Studies 20–21, 26, 30–33, 94, 95
Madame X (Guy) 280, *281*
'Maesie' (community development manager), WEA Fife 65–67, 68, 69–71, 73–74, 75
Malawi 167
Manufacturing Consent (Herman and Chomsky) 274
Maori 115
marketisation 118, 290, 316–317, 317–318, 334
Martin, I. 18
Marx, K./Marxism 18, 21, 84, 85, 86, 96, 231, 248
  and class 18, 19, 83, 84, 85, 86, 96
Mary Queen of Scots 74
masculinity, hegemonic 280–281
mass intellectuality 332, 351
Massey, Douglas 126, 127, 129
materialist feminism 127
Mayall, B. 175
McGimpsey, I. 290
McLean, John 229
McNally, D. 18–19
Meade, E. 290
Mechanics Institutes 111, 229
media, the, and victim-blaming 57–58
men:
  hegemonic masculinity 280–281
  VAW (violence against women) *see* GJV (Gender Justice and Violence: Feminist Approaches) course, SWA (Scottish Women's Aid) and QMU (Queen Margaret University); VAW (violence against women)
  see also gender
mental health 25
  and arts-based approaches 269
  bio-medical model of 26, 27
  impact of neoliberalism on 336
  people with lived experience of as a subaltern counterpublic 26–27
  of students 240–241, 242–243

see also Experts by Experience arts and sociology project; Mad Studies; MPHI (Mad People's History and Identity) course, Queen Margaret University, Edinburgh
Menzies, R. 26, 31, 33
Messerschmidt, J.W. 280
#MeToo movement 58
Mignot, Philip 89, 235, 335
Miller, N.B. 281–282
Mills, C. Wright 122
Ministry of Reconstruction 229
misogyny 96, 305
Mitchell, Juliet 16–17
Mitchell, T.D. 301, 304, 305
Mohandy, Chandra Talpade 221
Mojatu 303
Mondon, A. 323
monolingualism 190, 220
'moral Darwinism' 81
Morrish, L. 322
Moten, F. 350–351
MPHI (Mad People's History and Identity) course, Queen Margaret University, Edinburgh 25–26, 27, 28, 29, 32, 33, 94
Muir, A. 74, 75–76, 77
Mullen, A. 274
multilingualism 185–186, 220, 345
researching multilingually 186–196
museums see Experts by Experience arts and sociology project
mutual benefit, in service learning 300–301

N

Narayan, Umma 221
National Asylum Stakeholder Forum 147
National Bystanders Awareness Week 306
National Student Survey (NSS) 228, 241
National Training Strategy (NTS), Scotland 42, 43
National Union of Students 323
Native Americans 115
native dialects 255–256
Nazi Holocaust 348
Negri, A. 245
neoliberal globalisation 114–115
neoliberalism 17, 124
impact on mental health 336
neoliberal economic policies, Conservative Governments 81 UK 289–290
New Labour:
marginalisation of sociology from public policy 124
New Left 69, 104

New Rose Associates 307
New Scotland discourse 71, 94, 97
New Scots refugee integration strategy, Scottish Government 118, 136, 148, 192, 218
Ngugi wa, T. o. 196
NHS Lothian Mental Health and Wellbeing Programme 27
Nilsen, A.G. 89
Nixon, J. 316
No (Sutcliffe) 271–274, *272*
'no platforming' 348
Noble, Andrew 74, 75, 77
non-traditional students 235, 254, 257, 289
'North British Whig' thesis 76, 77
Nottingham:
social and economic environment 302
see also NTU (Nottingham Trent University)
Nottingham Citizens 303, 305
Nottingham Trent University see NTU (Nottingham Trent University)
Nottinghamshire Sexual Assault Centre 303
Noy, D. 274
NSS (National Student Survey) 228, 241
NTS (National Training Strategy), Scotland 42, 43
NTU (Nottingham Trent University) 7, 231, 353
critical service learning 299, 302–312
Nyden, P. 260, 303

O

O'Brien, M. 130
occupational therapy 172
O'Donnell, A. 95
O'Hare, P. 291
Old Left 21, 67, 69
OM (Glasgow Open Museum):
Experts by Experience arts and sociology project 267–283
OMH (Oor Mad History) 29–30
One Step Closer: Confidence Building and Employability Schemes for Refugee and Asylum-Seeking Women (OSC) 141, 144–145
open social problems 294
oppression 17, 19, 344
oral history, and mental health 30
organic public sociology 13, 53–54, 113, 308
and class 18
and the *Experts by Experience* arts and sociology project 268, 283
Orr, Lesley 21, 37–51, 96, 97, 345

OSC *(One Step Closer: Confidence Building and Employability Schemes for Refugee and Asylum-Seeking Women)* 141, 144–145
O'Sullivan, K. 258
Owenites 112

P

PALAR (participatory action learning and action research) 213
Palestine anti-colonial struggle 346, 348–349
Palma coefficient 205
PALS (peer assisted learning support) 259
PAR (participant action research) 213
parenting, of students 241
Paris Agreement, UN Framework Convention on Climate Change 346
Park, Robert 122
participant action research (PAR) 213
participation *see* WP (widening participation) agenda
participative research enquiry:
  and young children 118, 171–172, 180–181
  child-adult interaction 178–180
  critique of the children's rights movement 174–176
  participation as a children's right 172–174
  right to participation 176–178
participatory action learning and action research (PALAR) 213
participatory action research 114, 345
partnerships:
  and place-making in Scotland 203, 206
  see also CPPs (community planning partnerships), Scotland
Pateman, Carole 139
pedagogy of the oppressed 1–2, 157–158, 159, 269, 282
peer assisted learning support (PALS) 259
Penta, L.J. 179–180
Pereira, Maria do Mar 117
periphery, sociologies of resistance from 7
Peru, working children's movement 178
Phipps, Alison 183–197, 220
photographic exhibition and performance piece, 'Same Hell, Different Devils' study 59–61
photovoice 27, 53, 55
  see also domestic abuse survivors; 'Same Hell, Different Devils' study
Physics degrees 352
Pieczka, M. 154, 156, 158
place-based approaches 200, 201, 206–207

place-making theory, role of public knowledge in 201–204
Platt, Edward 83
policy sociology, and public sociology 118, 121–126, **125**, 131–132, 217–218, 222, 345, 352
  client capture 129–131, 220
  false dichotomy between 125–126
  methodological reflexivity 127–129
political decolonialisation 114
political economy of knowledge 223
Pols, J. 177
Pompa, L. 306
popular education 1, 14–15, 18, 231
populism 96, 97, 296
pornography, conflicts over 97
Portobello High School, Edinburgh 155
Portuguese language 190
post-colonial theory 231
post-structuralism 18
poverty:
  pejorative images of poor people 293
  Scotland 205, 207
Poverty Alliance 141
power 179–180
  and adult-child relationships 171, 173, 175
  and children's participation 172
  and community involvement 204
  and public knowledge 212
  redistribution of and critical service learning 305–306
  see also disciplinary power
Practices theme 3–4
praxis, Freire's definition of 31
precarity 85, 86–87, 333
  of academics 336–337
  as an existential phenomenon 239, 243
  collective experience of, and solidarity 239–240, 248–249
  disciplinary power of in universities 334
  paradox of 246–248
  precarious workers 246–247
  of students 89, 239, 240
  productive anxiety at work 243–246
  productive anxiety during education 240–243
  survival strategies 334–335
Prison Notebooks (Gramsci) 337
'private troubles' 294
problem-posing education 55
problems, framing of 292–294
proletarianisation, of academics 88, 89, 337
proletariat 15
Propaganda Model 274
prostitution/sex work, conflicts over 97

Protestant Reformation, 1560 75
Protocol Relating to the Status of Refugees, 1967 (United Nations) 136, 137
psychiatric survivor movement 32
psychotherapy, and language 193
Public Health Department 278
public knowledge 199–200, 201
  conceptualising the construction and role of 201–202
  role in place-making theory 201–204
  role of universities in 212
  sources of 212
  as a 'special knowledge' 218
  transformative forms of 211–213
public service job cuts 88
public sociology 1–5, 6–8, 13, 15, 19
  ambivalent relationship to HE 232, 233
  Buroway's Presidential Address to the American Sociological Association 1, 3, 13, 113, 230, 253, 260, 353
  centrality of Global South in 231
  challenge of 259
  future of 345–346, 353
  increasing significance of in UK sociology 230–231
  institutional barriers to 228–229
  opportunities for 349
  and policy sociology 118, 121–126, **125**, 131–132, 217–218, 222, 345, 352
    client capture 129–131, 220
    false dichotomy between 125–126
    methodological reflexivity 127–129
  practices of 227–237
  and social change 343–344
  traditional 85
  see also organic public sociology
public sphere 17, 95, 102
  exclusion from 96
  lack of sociology literacy in 350
publics:
  definitions of 13–14
  identification of 87
Publics theme 3–4
Puhl, R. 277

Q

QMU (Queen Margaret University), Edinburgh 6–7, 230, 231, 353
  and the AlcoLOLs project 155, 158–167, *166*
  CA (contextualised admissions) policy 261
  Engaged Sociology programme 260
  Experts by Experience arts and sociology project 267–283
  and GJV (Gender Justice and Violence: Feminist Approaches) course 21, 37–38, 41, 44–46
  Identity, Community & Society module 267
  MPHI (Mad People's History and Identity) course 25–26, 27, *28*, 29, 32, 33
  RRWV *(Raising Refugee Women's Voices: Exploring the Impact of Scottish Refugee Council Work with the Refugee Women's Strategic Group)* 141
  WP (widening access) agenda 254, 257, 258–259, 261
Quaye, S.J. 260
Queen Margaret University, Edinburgh *see* QMU (Queen Margaret University), Edinburgh
queer theory 347

R

'race':
  anti-colonial understandings of 18
  and class 20
  HEIs and exclusion 229, 233
  stereotyping 140
racism 96, 97, 101
radical adult education theory 111
radical education practice 1
radio advertising, regulation of 106
Raffaelli, Christine 267–285
Raising Refugee Women's Voices: Exploring the Impact of Scottish Refugee Council Work with the Refugee Women's Strategic Group (RRWV) 141, 145
really useful knowledge 4, 111–118
  dialogue 217–223
  and the VAW movement 38, 40
Reay, D. 254
recognition 18, 19
redistribution 18, 19
REF (Research Excellence Framework) 228, 260, 318, 327, 337
reflective science 3
reflexivity:
  in contract research 128
  'reflexive project of the self' 281–282
Refugee Women's Strategic Group *see* RWSG (Refugee Women's Strategic Group)
refugees and asylum-seekers:
  definitions 136–137
  international protection of 136
  and language 186–187, 190, 191–192
  refugee and asylum-seeking women in Scotland 118, 135–136, 147–148, 217–218

INDEX

context and conceptual
  frameworks 136–140
participatory knowledge production
  and 'strong voice' to influence
  policy 140–147
UK policies 136, 218
relationality 179
  and children's participation 172
'relational citizenship' 177
Relph, E. 202–203
Renewal trust 303
research ethics 58–59
Research Excellence Framework
  (REF) 228, 260, 318, 327, 337
research funding issues 223
Researching Multilingually at the
  Borders of Language, the Body, Law
  and the State (AHRC Large Grant
  study) 186–187, 192, 193–196
residual cultures 344
resilience 290
  weakening of among students 241
'Resilience or Fuck You Neoliberalism – a
  strike poem' (Krause) 315
responsibilisation 318, 327
Res-Sisters 326, 339
Reville, David 30
'Rhodes must fall' movement 115
rights, of children 171, 172–174
risk taking 163
Robbins report 229–230
Rogers, Carl 308
Roman Empire 138
Roose, R. 177
RRWV (Raising Refugee Women's Voices:
  Exploring the Impact of Scottish Refugee
  Council Work with the Refugee Women's
  Strategic Group) 141, 145
Rule, P.N. 203
Ruskin College speech, James
  Callaghan 244
Russo, J. 31–32
RWSG (Refugee Women's Strategic
  Group) 118, 135, 136, 140, 141, 142,
  144–145, 146, 147–148
participants' experiences of 146–147
Ryerson University, Toronto, Canada 30

S

'Same Hell, Different Devils' study see
  domestic abuse survivors; 'Same Hell,
  Different Devils' study
Sanchez, J.G. 213
Sandoval, Chandra 221
Sapouna, L. 95
Sartre, J.P. 207, 212
Savage, Mike 84, 85, 86, 87

Scandrett, Eurig 1–9, 13–23, 32, 44–45,
  93–108, 111–119, 217–223, 316,
  331–341, 343–355
Science, Technology, Engineering and
  Mathematics degrees 352
scientific methodology, in social
  sciences 125
Scotland:
  BAME (Black, Asian and Minority
    Ethnic) communities 103
  Brexit referendum 103
  and colonialism 115–116
  community empowerment 200
  constitutional issues 70–71, 94
  as context 6–7
  deindustrialisation/postindustrial
    context 69, 75
  drinking culture 156–157, 159–160
  ethnic minority population 230
  immigration policy 137
  impact of austerity policies and welfare
    reforms 205
  independence referendum 2014 275
  Just Transition 97
  Labour Party 98
  language policies 192
  nationalism 19, 74
  New Scotland discourse 71, 94, 97
  New Scots refugee integration
    strategy 118, 136, 148, 192, 218
  political context 41
  refugee and asylum-seeking women 118
  representational deficit 41, 74–75
  role in expansion of British Empire 230
  subaltern counterpublics 101, 102–105
  trade unions 97
  VAW (violence against women) 38–44,
    54–55, 344–345 (see also domestic
    abuse survivors; GJV (Gender Justice
    and Violence: Feminist Approaches)
    course, SWA (Scottish Women's
    Aid) and QMU (Queen Margaret
    University); 'Same Hell, Different
    Devils' study)
  women's democratic deficit 41
  women's movement 41–42
  working class culture 79–80, 104
    (see also WEA (Workers Educational
    Association))
  WP (widening participation)
    agenda 253, 254, 257, 261, 338
    QMU (Queen Margaret University),
      Edinburgh 254, 257, 258–259, 261
  see also UK; WEA (Workers Educational
    Association)
Scots language 75–76, 77, 103
Scott, J. 259

Scottish Credit and Qualification
    Framework (SCQF) 270
Scottish culture 71, 73–74, 75–77, 103
Scottish Enlightenment 7, 76, 230
Scottish Executive:
    'National Strategy to Address Domestic
        Abuse in Scotland' 42
    refugee and asylum-seeker policies 136
Scottish Government 205–206, 209–211
    New Scots refugee integration
        strategy 118, 136, 148, 192, 218
    OSC *(One Step Closer: Confidence
        Building and Employability Schemes
        for Refugee and Asylum-Seeking
        Women)* 141
    SFY *(Speak for Yourself: Report from
        Our Engagement with 100 Refugee and
        Asylum-Seeking Women between June and
        November 2013)* 141
    'Solidarity Purpose' 206, 207
Scottish Index of Multiple Deprivation
    (SIMD) 69, 205
Scottish Parliament 77
Scottish Police College 43
Scottish Prosecution College 43
Scottish Refugee Council 118, 146
Scottish Refugee Council (SRC) 135–
    136, 140–141, 142, 144–145, 146, 148
Scottish Refugee Policy Forum 142
Scottish Social Attitudes Survey 156
Scottish Trade Union Congress 327
Scottish Women's Aid *see* SWA (Scottish
    Women's Aid)
SCQF (Scottish Credit and Qualification
    Framework) 270
SDUK (Society for the Diffusion of
    Useful Knowledge) 111, 112
Sen, A. 208
service learning 235, 299, 311–312,
    338, 352
    critical 299, 301–302
    authentic relationships 306–307
    rationale for 302–303
    redistribution of power 305–306
    social change orientation 304–305
    sustainability in 307–310
    definition and scope 300–301
    practice of 303–304
    service learning city 310–311
    traditional 301
settler colonialism 115
sex-based rights:
    trans/feminist conflict 345–346,
        347–348
sexual harassment 305
sexual health research 117–118, 122–123,
    127, 129, 218

client capture in 129–131
sexual violence:
    continuum of 41
    see also domestic abuse; VAW (violence
        against women)
sexuality, and class 20
SFY *(Speak for Yourself: Report from Our
    Engagement with 100 Refugee and
    Asylum-Seeking Women between June and
    November 2013)* 141
*Sharing Lives, Sharing Languages: A
    Pilot Peer Education Project for New
    Scots' Social and Language Integration*
    (SLSL) 141–142, 145
Shaw, Mae 200, 235, 287–298, 331–341
Shawa, Laila 274–276, *275*
Shetland dialect 255–256
silencing:
    'Same Hell, Different Devils'
        study 57–58
SIMD (Scottish Index of Multiple
    Deprivation) 69, 205
Simmel, G. 256
Sitholé, Tawona 183–197, 220
SLSL *(Sharing Lives, Sharing Languages:
    A Pilot Peer Education Project for
    New Scots' Social and Language
    Integration)* 141–142, 145
Smith, Adam 76
Smith, Barbara 221
Smith, Dorothy 127
Smith, G.N. 14
Smith, Gregory 76
Snell, D. 346
social capital 85
    of students 255
social change orientation, in critical
    service learning 304–305
social democracy 103, 333
social factories, universities as 245
social justice 18–19
    and service learning 299, 301, 302
    and subaltern groups 16
social movement process approach 6, 18,
    26, 31, 32, 33, 45, 89, 113, 124, 339,
    344, 346
social movements:
    from above 339
    from below 339
    and counter-hegemonic narratives 33
social problems:
    framing of 292–294
    open and closed 294
'social purpose' education 66
social reproduction theory 20
social sciences, as 'low value'
    degrees 351–352

INDEX

Socialist Workers Party (SWP) 83
society, and the *Experts by Experience* arts and sociology project 268, 269
Society for the Diffusion of Useful Knowledge (SDUK) 111, 112
socioconstructivism 201
sociological imagination 72, 76, 81, 96, 221, 235, 270, 273, 277, 292, 350
sociological knowledge 221
sociological quadrant 122, 217, 218, 343
sociology 121
  British 123
  'founding fathers' narratives of 231
  and government policy 124
  lack of sociology literacy in the public sphere 350
  'not value for money' (Augar review) 338
solidarity:
  and critical social learning 308
  and the HE pensions strike, 2017–2018 322, 323–324, 325, 335–336
  and precarity 239–240, 248–249
Somalia, refugees and asylum-seekers from 137
South Africa 351
Southern theory 231
Spandler, H. 32
Spanish language 190
Speak for Yourself: Report from Our Engagement with 100 Refugee and Asylum-Seeking Women between June and November 2013 (SFY) 141
speech acts 191
Spence, Jo 276, 276–278
Spivak, G.C. 101, 102, 185, 196, 249, 336
Sprague, J. 228–229
Springburn Tenement (Andrew Hay) 278
SRC (Scottish Refugee Council) 135–136, 140–141, 142, 144–145, 146, 148
Stand By Me initiative, Communities Inc. 305–306
Standing, G. 85
Stark, Evan 41, 45
STC *(The Struggle to Contribute: A Report Identifying the Barriers Encountered by Refugee Women on Their Journey to Employment in Scotland)* 140–141, 143
Stephenson, C. 277
stereotyping:
  in advertisements 106
  racialised and gendered 140
Stirling, J. 277
Stirling University 40, 41
storytelling approach, young people and alcohol use 161–164

stratification sociology 86
Streeck, W. 296
street harassment 305
structural feminism 18
structural paradigm of justice 18
structuralism 117
structure 18, 19
Struggle to Contribute, The: A Report Identifying the Barriers Encountered by Refugee Women on Their Journey to Employment in Scotland (STC) 140–141, 143
students:
  dialogue with academic staff 256–258
  dialogue with publics beyond the university 259–260
  induction projects 258
  infantilisation of 241
  mental health of 240–241, 242–243
  non-traditional 235, 254, 257, 289
  PALS (peer assisted learning support) 259
  peer interaction 258–259
  precarity of 89, 239, 240, 335
  productive anxiety at work 243–246
  productive anxiety during education 240–243
  provider-consumer relationship with HEIs (higher education institutions) 241, 316, 317, 318
  as public sociology's first public 253, 255–260
student protests 2010 327
and subalternity 335
Sturgeon, Nicola 100
subaltern counterpublics 4, 17, 343
  and class 87–89
  and definitions of publics 13–14
  dialogue with 1, 5
  feminism as a 95–96
  and HEI widening access agendas 254
  and intersectionality 20
  Scandrett/Gilfillan dialogue on 93–108
  Scotland 101, 102–105
Subaltern Studies group 336
subalternity 14, 15–16, 54, 94, 113, 219–220, 344
  of academics 336–337
  'colonisation,' of the subaltern 94, 98
  conflicts between groups 97
  and counter-hegemony 6
  knowledge production 16
  public sociology analysis of 17
  and social justice 16, 18–19
  and students 335
super-structural analyses 18
support workers, 'Same Hell, Different Devils' study 56–57

Sutcliffe, Stephen 271–274, *272*
SWA (Scottish Women's Aid) 38, 42, 47
  education for gender justice 43–44
  and GJV (Gender Justice and Violence: Feminist Approaches) course 21, 37–38, 41, 44–46
  origins and context 39, 40
SWP (Socialist Workers Party) 83
Syria, refugees and asylum-seekers from 137
'systematic integralism' 105

T

Taft, Jessica K. 174, 178
Tate, Allen 75
Taylor, M. 248
Teaching Excellence and Student Outcomes Framework 241
Teaching to Transgress (hooks) 194
TEF (Teaching Excellence Framework) 228, 260, 318
Thatcher, Margaret 41, 81, 124, 333, 349
  see also Conservative governments
theorising practice 288–289
third world feminists 221
Tilley, J. 98
Tordzro, Gameli 183–197, 220
Tordzro, Naa Densua 183–197, 220
Trade Union Act 2016 326
trade unions:
  as collective education 316, 319–321, 326–327
  pensions strike, 2017–2018 321–326, 335–336
  and the JT (Just Transition) movement 97, 345, 346–347
  Scotland 97
traditional public sociology 85
trans-activism, conflict with feminism 97, 345–346, 347–348
translanguaging 191
translingual practice 191
Tremblay, C. 212
Trump, D. 296
TV advertising, regulation of 106

U

UCU (University and Colleges Union), pensions strike, 2017–2018 321–326, 335–336
UK:
  austerity policies 204–205
  refugees and asylum-seeker policies 136, 218
  widening HE access agenda 254
UK Visas and Immigration Scotland and Northern Ireland 141

UN High Commissioner for Refugees 136–137
UNESCO 231
Union of Crowns, 1603 75
United Nations:
  Convention of the Rights of the Child 173, 175, 177
  Convention Relating to the Status of Refugees, 1951 136, 137
  Paris Agreement, UN Framework Convention on Climate Change 346
  Protocol Relating to the Status of Refugees, 1967 136, 137
universities/HEIs (higher education institutions):
  and ableism 333
  access and participation issues 231, 233–234, 235, 257, 288
    Scotland's WP (widening participation) agenda 253, 254, 257, 261
  as agents of border control 229, 332
  as agents of environmental destruction 229
  and class 229, 233
  and colonialism 333
  commodification of education 288
  community relationships 213, 337–338
  and consumer protection law 241
  and diversity 233–234
  employability issues 301–302
    postgraduate employment and earnings metrics 241–242
  England 229–230, 353
  and exclusion 229, 233, 332
  expansion following Robbins report 229–230
  and imperialism 333
  and inequality and oppression 229, 233, 254
  international students 335
  and mass intellectuality 332, 351
  neoliberal 4, 228, 231, 234, 316–319, 331–341, 351
  pensions strike, 2017–2018 321–326, 335–336
  performance measurement 317–318
  as places of conflict 351
  and precarity 333, 334
  provider-consumer relationship with students 241, 316, 317, 318
  and public sociology practice 227–237, 331
  and racism 332, 333
  responsibilisation and marketisation 316–319
  role as co-generators of public knowledge 212

Scotland 6, 7, 229–230, 353
  and sexism 333
  as social factories 245
  stress and ill-health among
    staff 318–319
  survival strategies 334–335
  trade unions 235, 316, 319–327,
    335–336
  tuition fees 332, 335
  whiteness of 332
University and Colleges Union (UCU),
    pensions strike, 2017–2018 321–326,
    335–336
University of California, Berkley 6, 353
University of Edinburgh 230
University of Glasgow 230
University of Strathclyde 230
University of York 317
USS (Universities Superannuation
    Scheme) 325, 335
  see also UCU (University and
    Colleges Union)

V

Valentine, J. 336
VAW (violence against women) 37, 38,
    94, 96, 344–345
  continuum of 41
  Scottish context 38–42
  SWA's education for gender justice
    work 43–44
  and victim-blaming 57–58
  see also domestic abuse; GJV (Gender
    Justice and Violence: Feminist
    Approaches) course, SWA (Scottish
    Women's Aid) and QMU (Queen
    Margaret University)
voice 53
  risk to domestic abuse survivors in
    speaking out 56–59
vulnerability:
  of students 241, 242
  see also precarity

W

WA (Women's Aid) 38, 41, 47, 55, 56
  origins and development of 39–40
  see also GJV (Gender Justice and
    Violence: Feminist Approaches)
    course, SWA (Scottish Women's
    Aid) and QMU (Queen Margaret
    University); SWA (Scottish Women's
    Aid); VAW (violence against women)
Wacquant, L. 260
Wales:
  language policies 192
  see also UK

Walker, M. 316
Wallace, William 74
Walliasper, J. 202
Wang, C. 55
Wånggren, Lena 88, 95, 235, 315–329,
    331–341
WEA (Workers Educational
    Association) 21, 65, 96, 231, 337–338
  WEA Fife 65–67, 68–75, 77,
    79–80, 83, 94
    'Alec' (research participant) 80,
      98–101, 104–106
    'Maesie' (community development
      manager) 65–67, 68, 69–71,
      73–74, 75
  WEA Scotland 67–68
Weber, M. 18, 231, 276
  and class analysis 84, 86, 88, 96
WEIE (Women's Employment
    Information Event) 140–141
welfare reforms, impact of 204–205
welfare state, contradictions within 333
West Bank 349
WFGS (women's, feminist, and gender
    studies) 232
Whiting, Nel 21, 37–51, 96, 97, 345
'why is my curriculum white?'
    movement 115
widening participation agenda see WP
    (widening participation) agenda
'wife battering' 40
  see also domestic abuse; VAW (violence
    against women)
Williams, J. 241
Williams, R. 184, 344
Willis, Paul 335
women:
  and labour market precarity 247
  misogyny, as a hate crime 305
  in the USA 102
  see also feminism; VAW (violence against
    women); WA (Women's Aid)
Women's Employment Information Event
    (WEIE) 140–141
women's, feminist, and gender studies
    (WFGS) 232
Women's Liberation Movement, 1970s
    (second-wave feminism) 17, 38–39
women's movement 16–17
  Scotland 41–42
Women's Studies 232, 336
Women's Support Project 141
Women's Voluntary Sector Network 141
Wood, Emma 118, 153–170, 219
workers' education 231
  see also WEA (Workers Educational
    Association)

Workers Educational Association *see* WEA (Workers Educational Association)
working class 19, 94, 107
  access to HE in Scotland 229
  adult education 111, 112 (*see also* WEA (Workers Educational Association))
  and counter-hegemony 6
  radical movements 112
  'revisualisation' of 80
  Scotland 79–80, 104
  subalternity of 345
  university students 81–82
  white male 79–80
world café method 159–161
World Science report 199–200
WP (widening participation) agenda 288
  Scotland 253, 254, 257, 261, 338
  QMU (Queen Margaret University), Edinburgh 254, 257, 258–259, 261
  see also Experts by Experience arts and sociology project
Wright, Erik Olin 84, 85–96, 88, 96

X

xenophobia 96

Y

young children, and participative research enquiry 118, 171–172, 180–181, 219
  child-adult interaction 178–180
  critique of the children's rights movement 174–176
  participation as a children's right 172–174
  research methods 181
  right to participation 176–178
Young, Julie 21, 53–63, 96, 345
young people and alcohol use 118, 153–156, 219
  citizen's jury stage 164–167, *166*
  conscientisation stage 158, 161–164
  context 156–158
  decoding 163–164
  drinks industry 155–156, 157–158, 160
  health risks of 153, 165
  humanisation 164
  liberating action 165
  and oppression 155–156, 157–158, 162
  problematisation stage 159–161
  project content and analysis 158–167, *166*
  Scotland's drinking culture 156–157, 159–160
  and sub oppression 160–161
  young offenders 160, 165
Yuval-Davis, Nira 139

Z

Zimbabwe, English language domination in 194
Zionism and anti-Zionism 346, 348–349
ZT (Zero Tolerance) Campaign, Edinburgh Council 41–42